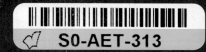

THIS IS THE LAST PAGE.

GOLDEN KAMUY has been printed in the original Japanese format in order to preserve the orientation of the original artwork.

Please turn it around and begin reading from right to left. Unlike English, Japanese is read right to left, so Japanese comics are read in reverse order from the way English comics are typically read. Have fun with it!

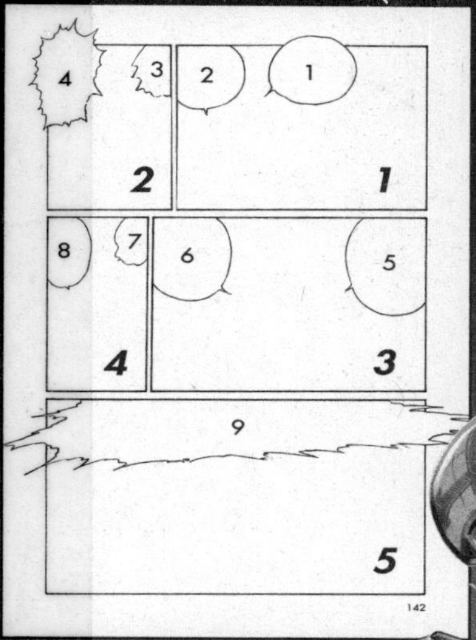
1
2
3
4
1
2
5
6
7
8
3
4
9
5
142

←Follow the action this way.

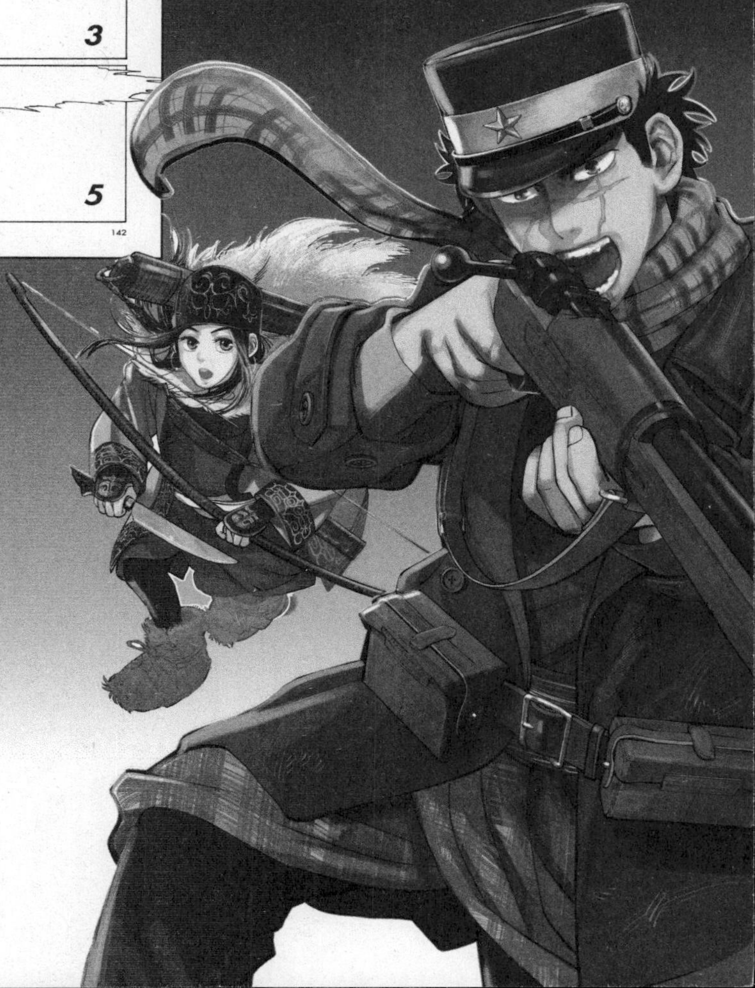

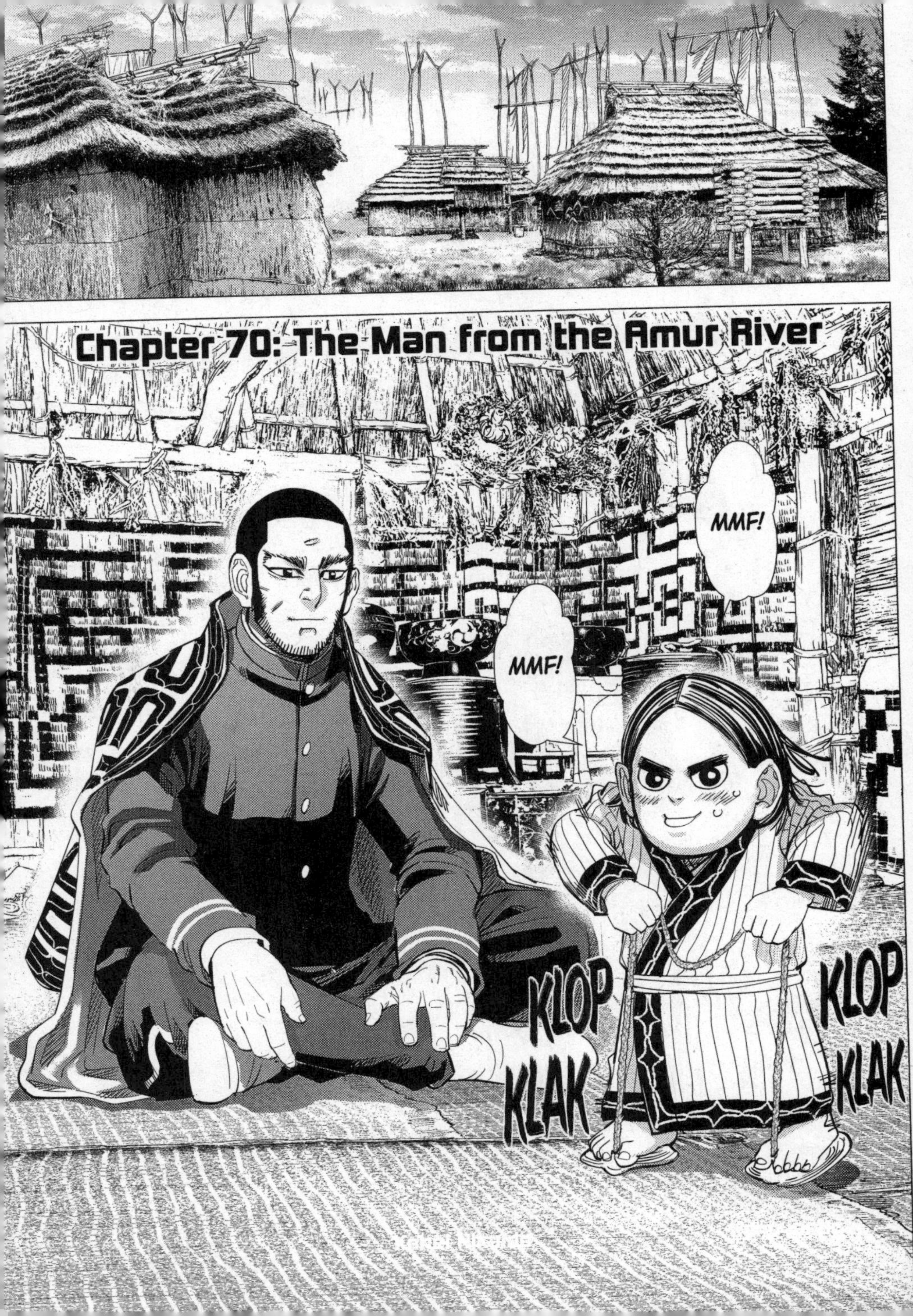
Chapter 70: The Man from the Amur River
MMF!
MMF!
KLOP KLAK
KLOP KLAK

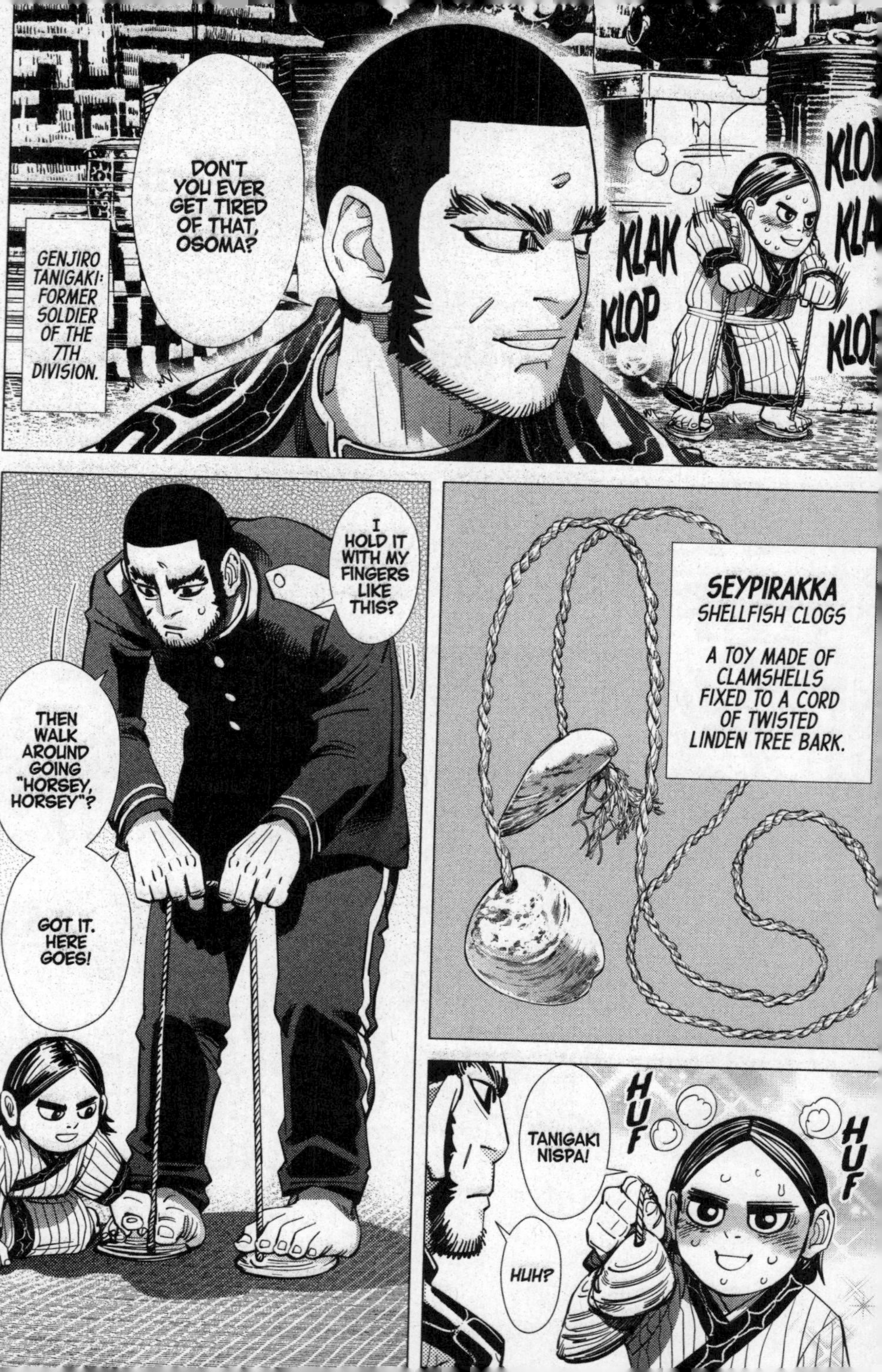

KLO
KLA
KLO
KLAK
KLOP
DON'T YOU EVER GET TIRED OF THAT, OSOMA?
GENJIRO TANIGAKI: FORMER SOLDIER OF THE 7TH DIVISION.
SEYPIRAKKA
SHELLFISH CLOGS
A TOY MADE OF CLAMSHELLS FIXED TO A CORD OF TWISTED LINDEN TREE BARK.
HUF
HUF
TANIGAKI NISPA!
HUF
HUH?
I HOLD IT WITH MY FINGERS LIKE THIS?
THEN WALK AROUND GOING "HORSEY, HORSEY"?
GOT IT. HERE GOES!

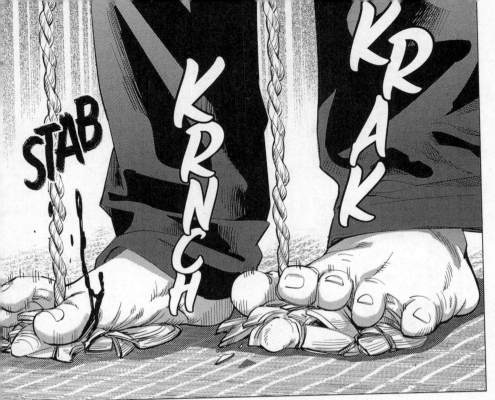

STAB

KRNCH

KRAK

GO CALL YOUR GRAND-MOTHER!

TANIGAKI'S STAY IN THE KOTAN GREW EVEN LONGER.

THUD

...

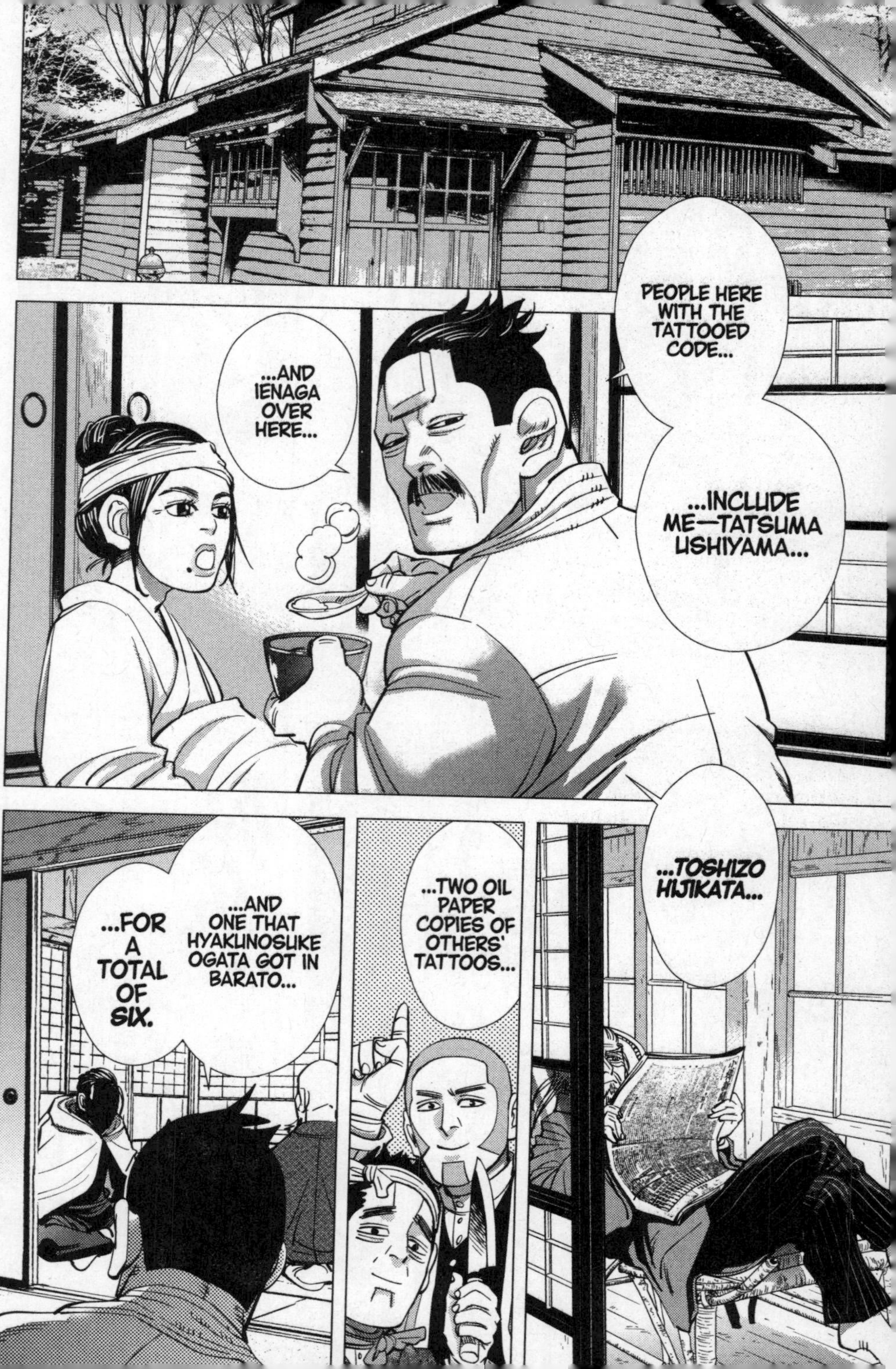
PEOPLE HERE WITH THE TATTOOED CODE...
...INCLUDE ME—TATSUMA USHIYAMA...
...AND IENAGA OVER HERE...
...TOSHIZO HIJIKATA...
...TWO OIL PAPER COPIES OF OTHERS' TATTOOS...
...AND ONE THAT HYAKUNOSUKE OGATA GOT IN BARATO...
...FOR A TOTAL OF SIX.

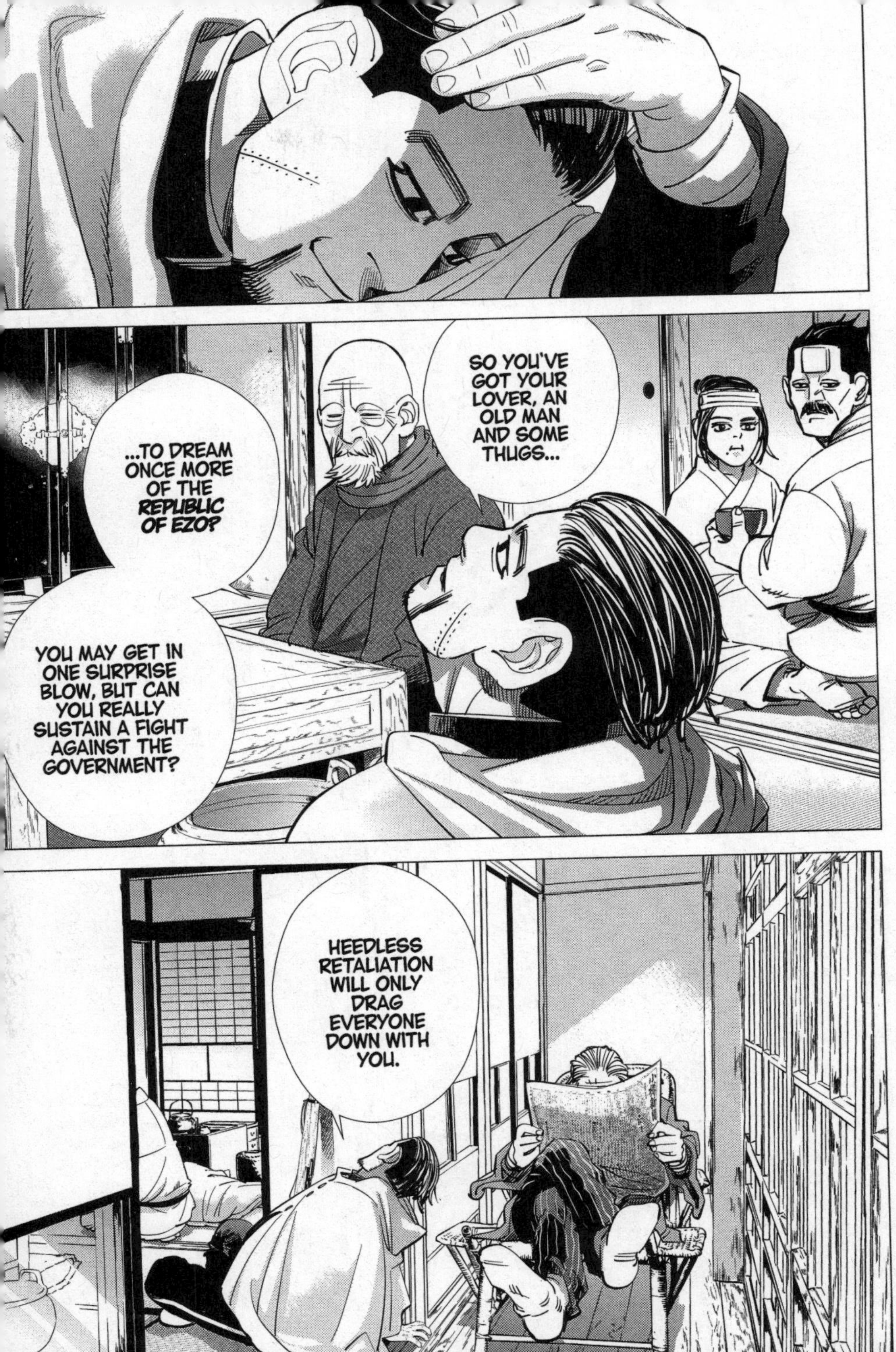
SO YOU'VE GOT YOUR LOVER, AN OLD MAN AND SOME THUGS...
...TO DREAM ONCE MORE OF THE REPUBLIC OF EZO?
YOU MAY GET IN ONE SURPRISE BLOW, BUT CAN YOU REALLY SUSTAIN A FIGHT AGAINST THE GOVERNMENT?
HEEDLESS RETALIATION WILL ONLY DRAG EVERYONE DOWN WITH YOU.

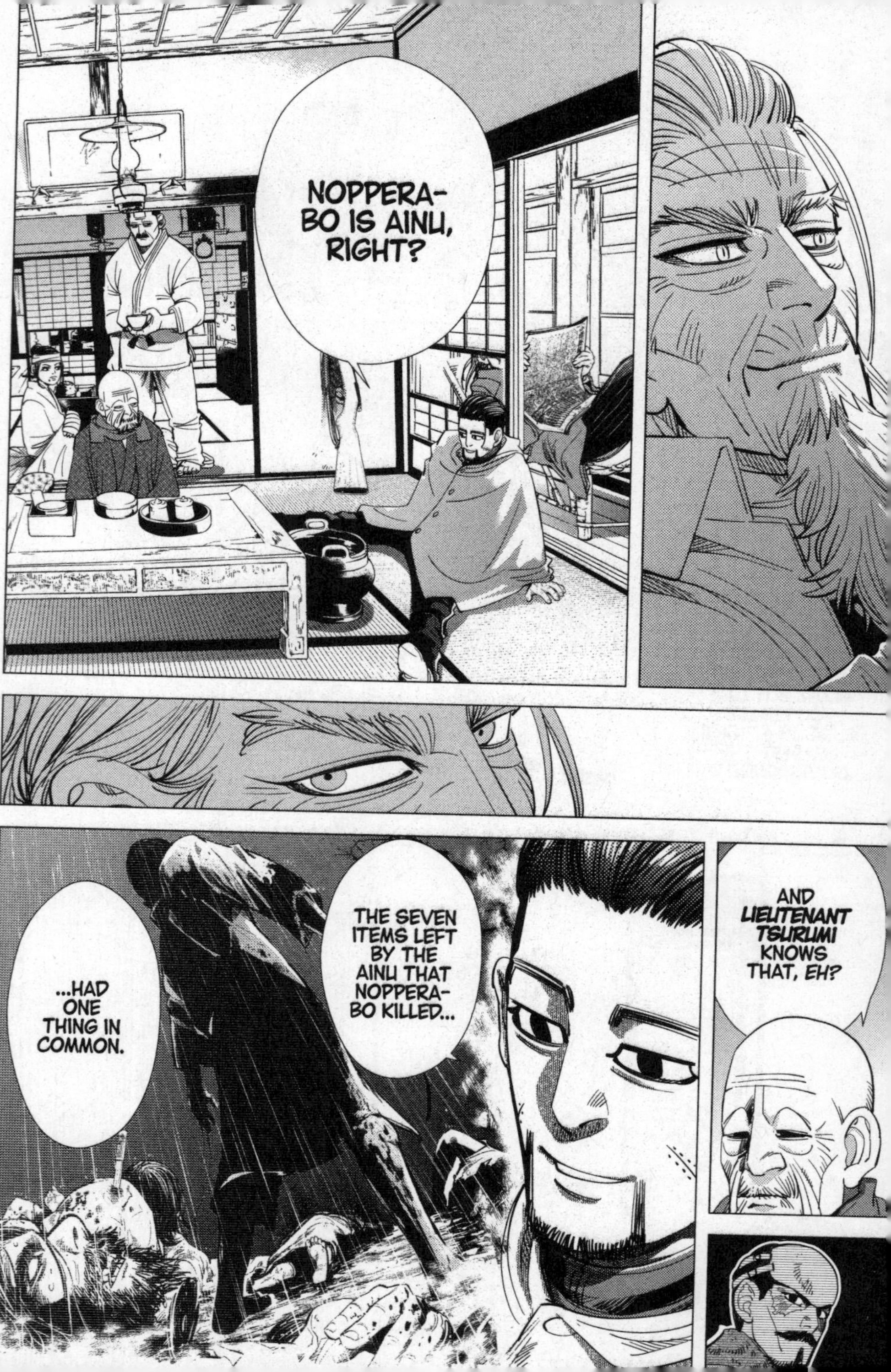
NOPPERA-BO IS AINU, RIGHT?
AND LIEUTENANT TSURUMI KNOWS THAT, EH?
THE SEVEN ITEMS LEFT BY THE AINU THAT NOPPERA-BO KILLED...
...HAD ONE THING IN COMMON.

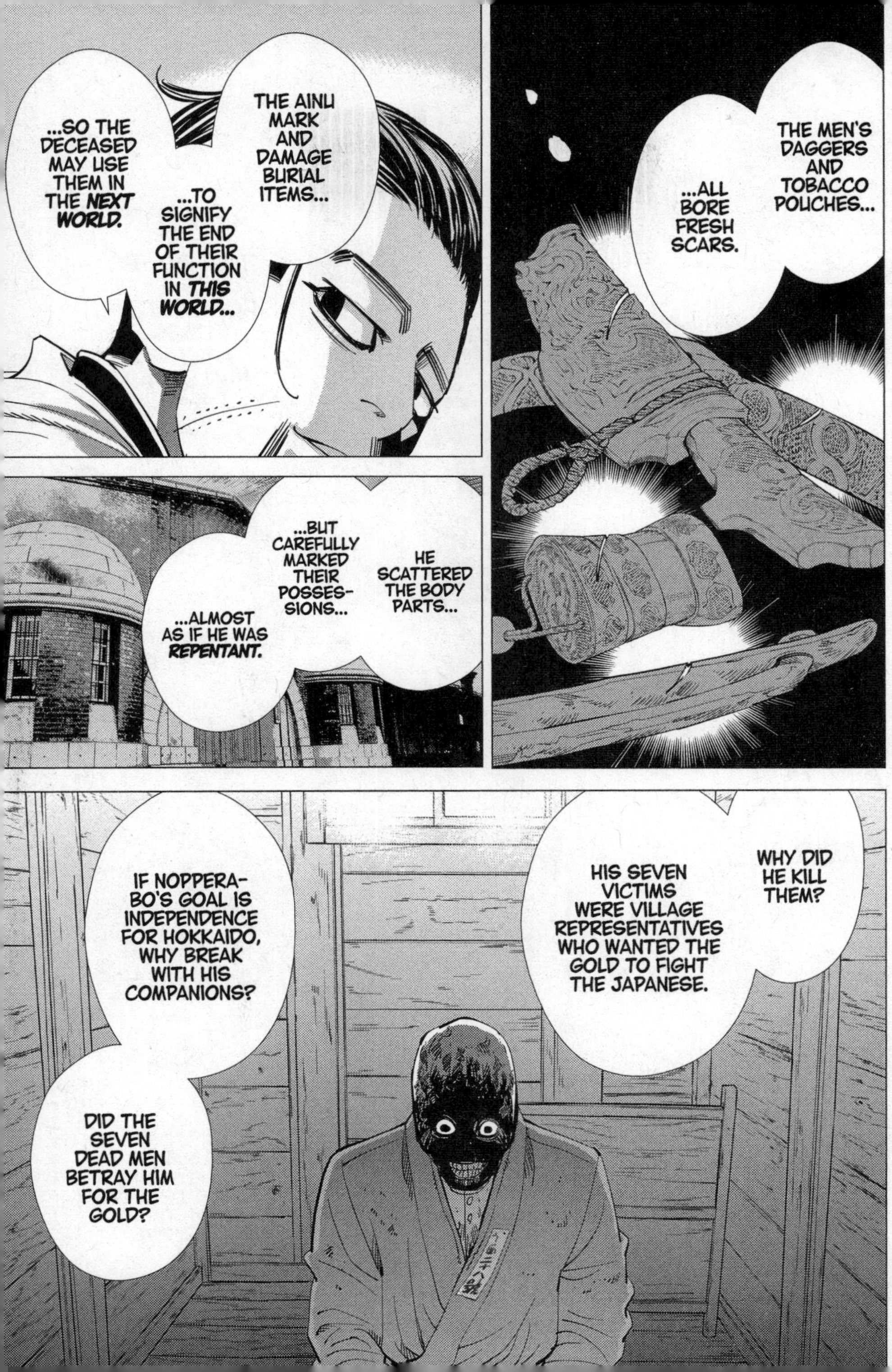
THE MEN'S DAGGERS AND TOBACCO POUCHES...
...ALL BORE FRESH SCARS.
THE AINU MARK AND DAMAGE BURIAL ITEMS...
...TO SIGNIFY THE END OF THEIR FUNCTION IN THIS WORLD...
...SO THE DECEASED MAY USE THEM IN THE NEXT WORLD.
HE SCATTERED THE BODY PARTS...
...BUT CAREFULLY MARKED THEIR POSSESSIONS...
...ALMOST AS IF HE WAS REPENTANT.
WHY DID HE KILL THEM?
HIS SEVEN VICTIMS WERE VILLAGE REPRESENTATIVES WHO WANTED THE GOLD TO FIGHT THE JAPANESE.
IF NOPPERA-BO'S GOAL IS INDEPENDENCE FOR HOKKAIDO, WHY BREAK WITH HIS COMPANIONS?
DID THE SEVEN DEAD MEN BETRAY HIM FOR THE GOLD?

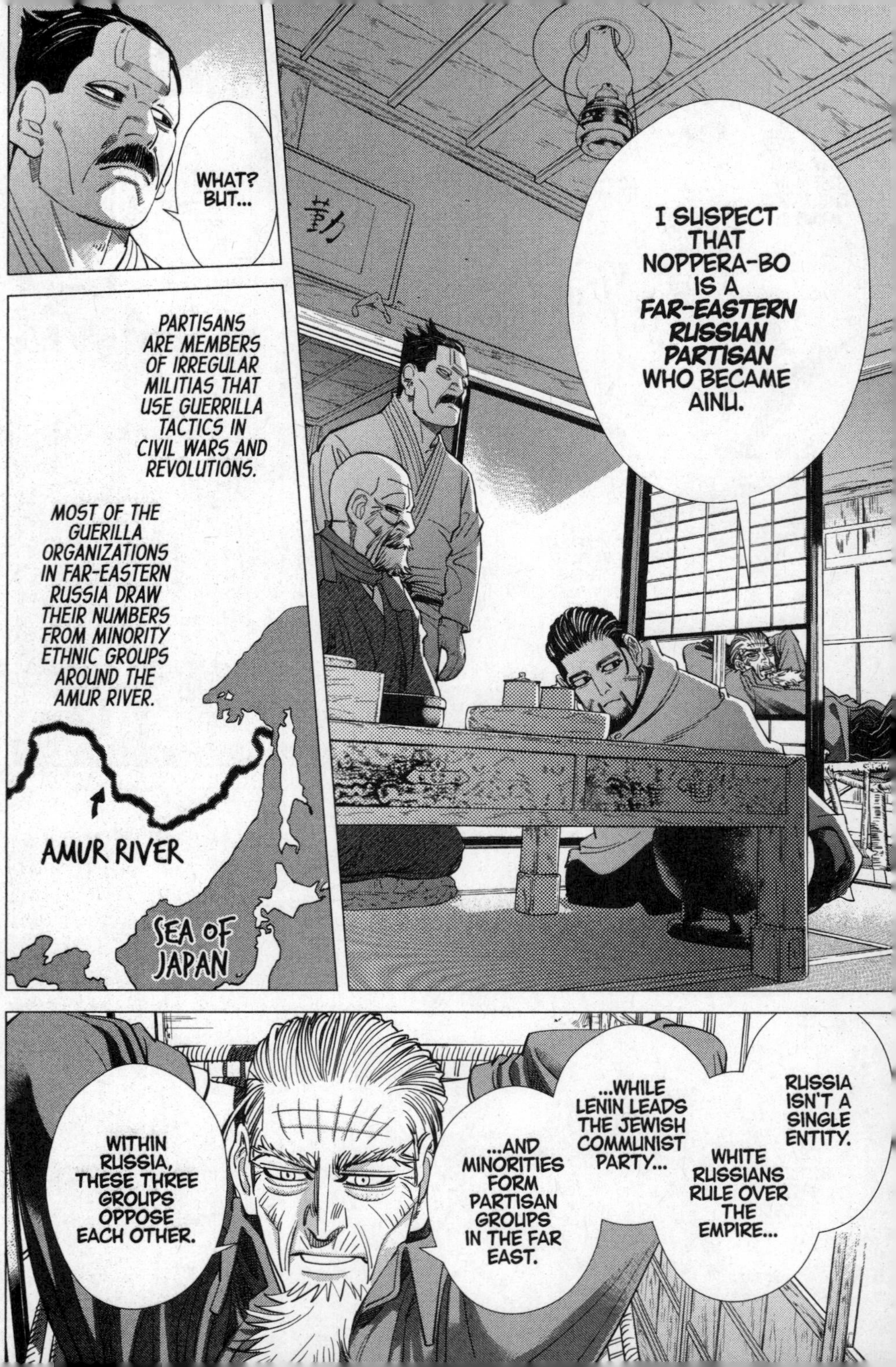
I SUSPECT THAT NOPPERA-BO IS A FAR-EASTERN RUSSIAN PARTISAN WHO BECAME AINU.
WHAT? BUT...
PARTISANS ARE MEMBERS OF IRREGULAR MILITIAS THAT USE GUERRILLA TACTICS IN CIVIL WARS AND REVOLUTIONS.
MOST OF THE GUERILLA ORGANIZATIONS IN FAR-EASTERN RUSSIA DRAW THEIR NUMBERS FROM MINORITY ETHNIC GROUPS AROUND THE AMUR RIVER.
AMUR RIVER
SEA OF JAPAN
RUSSIA ISN'T A SINGLE ENTITY.
WHITE RUSSIANS RULE OVER THE EMPIRE...
...WHILE LENIN LEADS THE JEWISH COMMUNIST PARTY...
...AND MINORITIES FORM PARTISAN GROUPS IN THE FAR EAST.
WITHIN RUSSIA, THESE THREE GROUPS OPPOSE EACH OTHER.

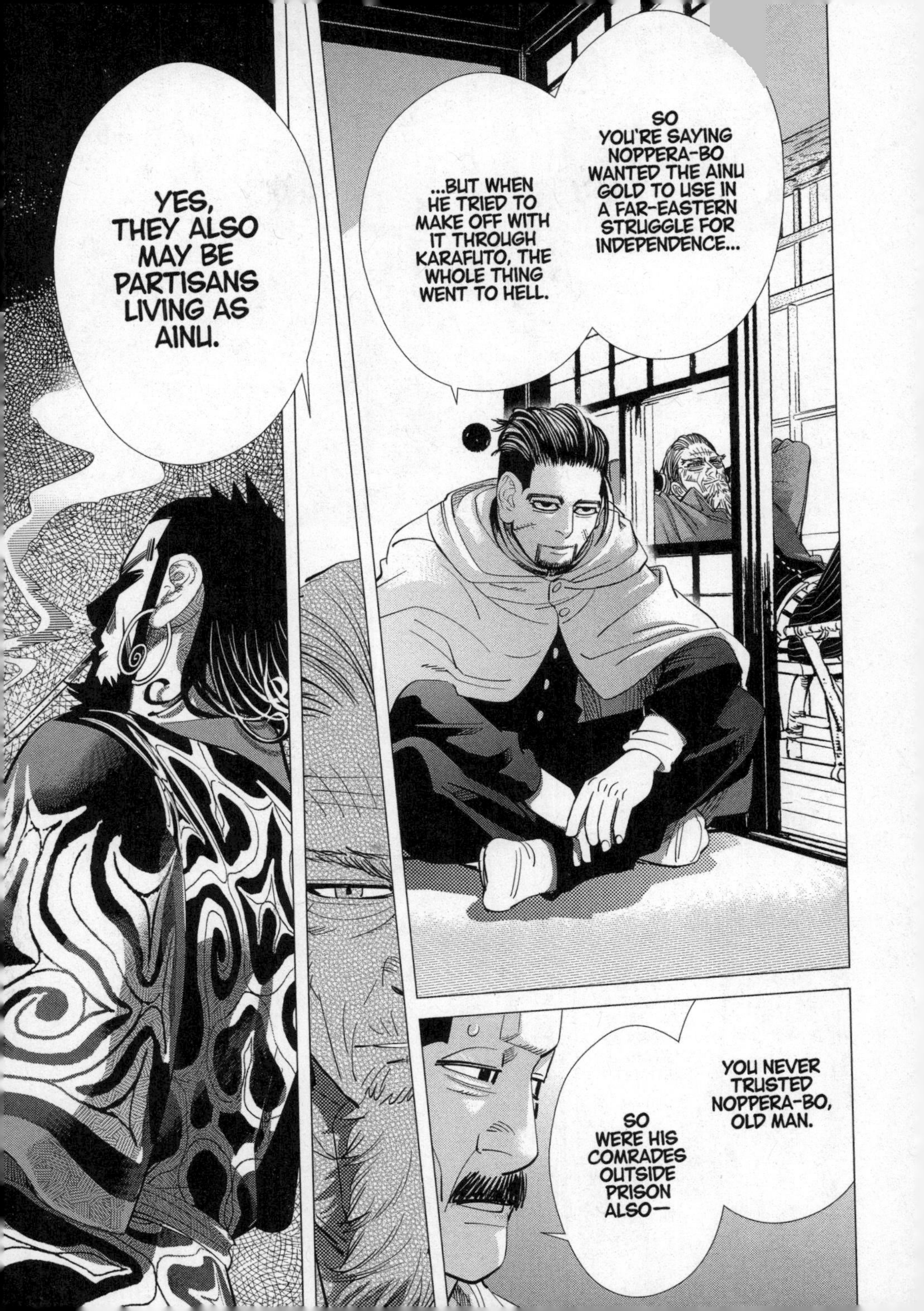
SO YOU'RE SAYING NOPPERA-BO WANTED THE AINU GOLD TO USE IN A FAR-EASTERN STRUGGLE FOR INDEPENDENCE...
...BUT WHEN HE TRIED TO MAKE OFF WITH IT THROUGH KARAFUTO, THE WHOLE THING WENT TO HELL.
YOU NEVER TRUSTED NOPPERA-BO, OLD MAN.
SO WERE HIS COMRADES OUTSIDE PRISON ALSO—
YES, THEY ALSO MAY BE PARTISANS LIVING AS AINU.

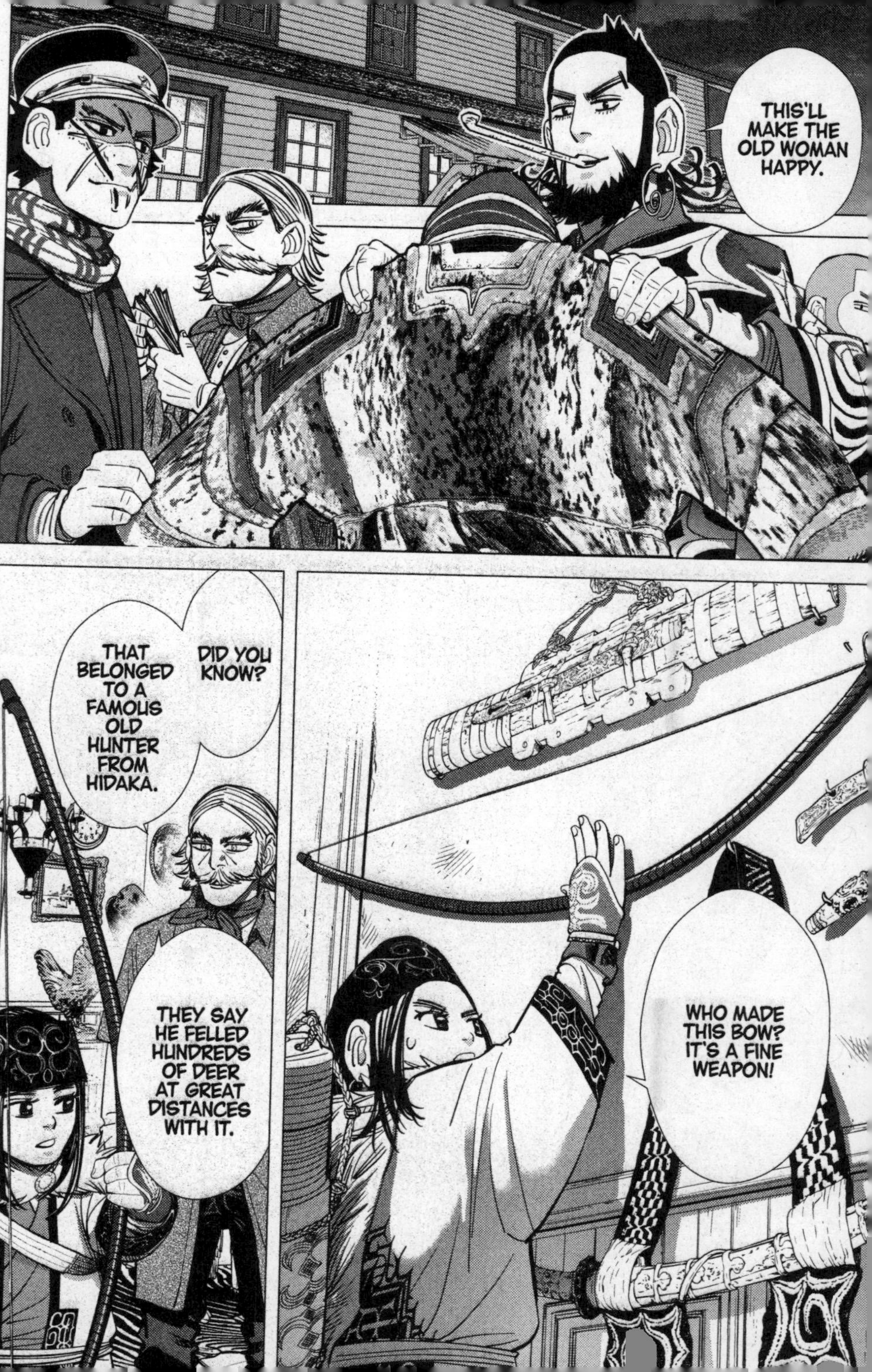
THIS'LL MAKE THE OLD WOMAN HAPPY.
WHO MADE THIS BOW? IT'S A FINE WEAPON!
DID YOU KNOW?
THAT BELONGED TO A FAMOUS OLD HUNTER FROM HIDAKA.
THEY SAY HE FELLED HUNDREDS OF DEER AT GREAT DISTANCES WITH IT.

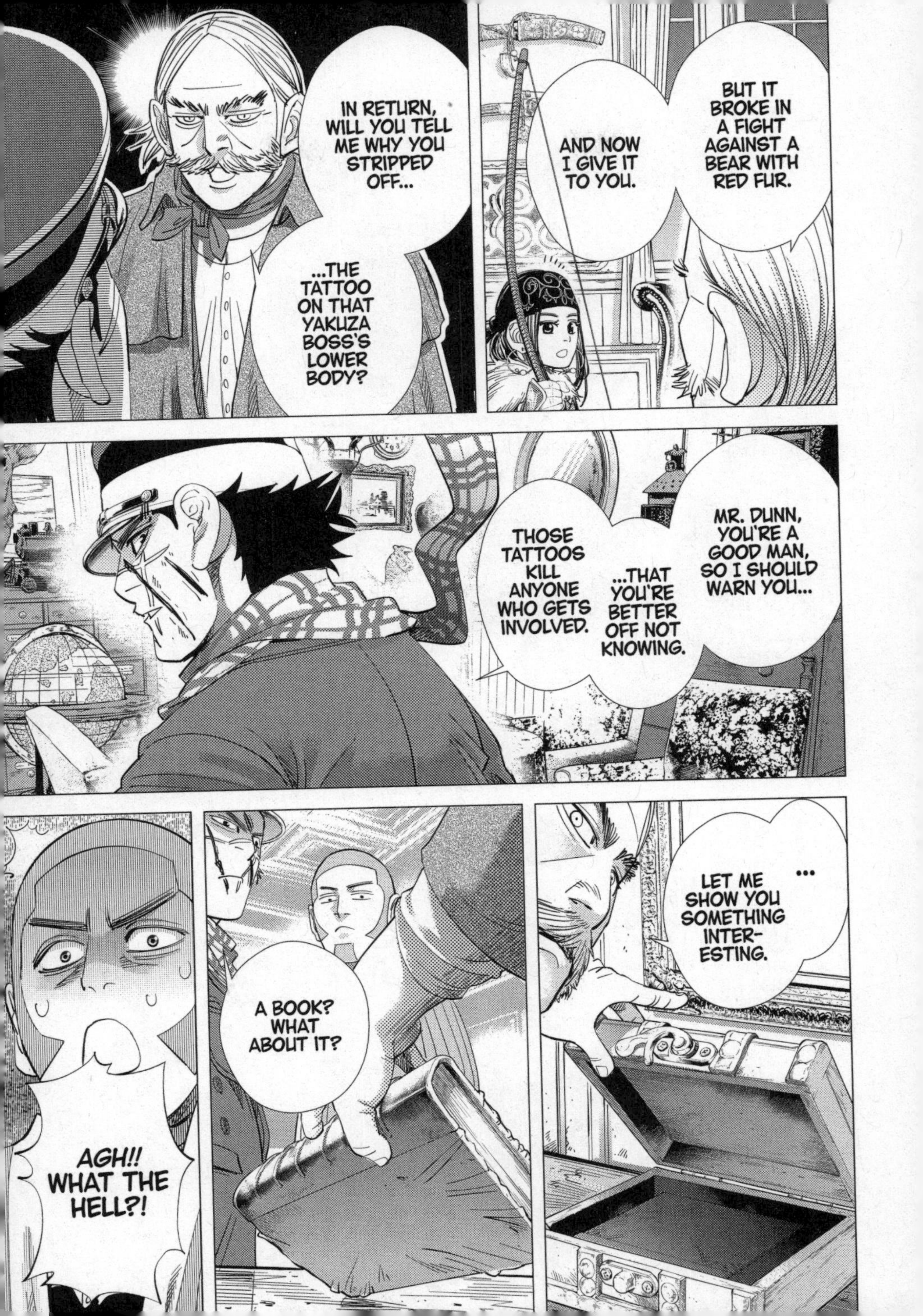
BUT IT BROKE IN A FIGHT AGAINST A BEAR WITH RED FUR.
AND NOW I GIVE IT TO YOU.
IN RETURN, WILL YOU TELL ME WHY YOU STRIPPED OFF...
...THE TATTOO ON THAT YAKUZA BOSS'S LOWER BODY?
MR. DUNN, YOU'RE A GOOD MAN, SO I SHOULD WARN YOU...
...THAT YOU'RE BETTER OFF NOT KNOWING.
THOSE TATTOOS KILL ANYONE WHO GETS INVOLVED.
...
LET ME SHOW YOU SOMETHING INTER-ESTING.
A BOOK? WHAT ABOUT IT?
AGH!! WHAT THE HELL?!

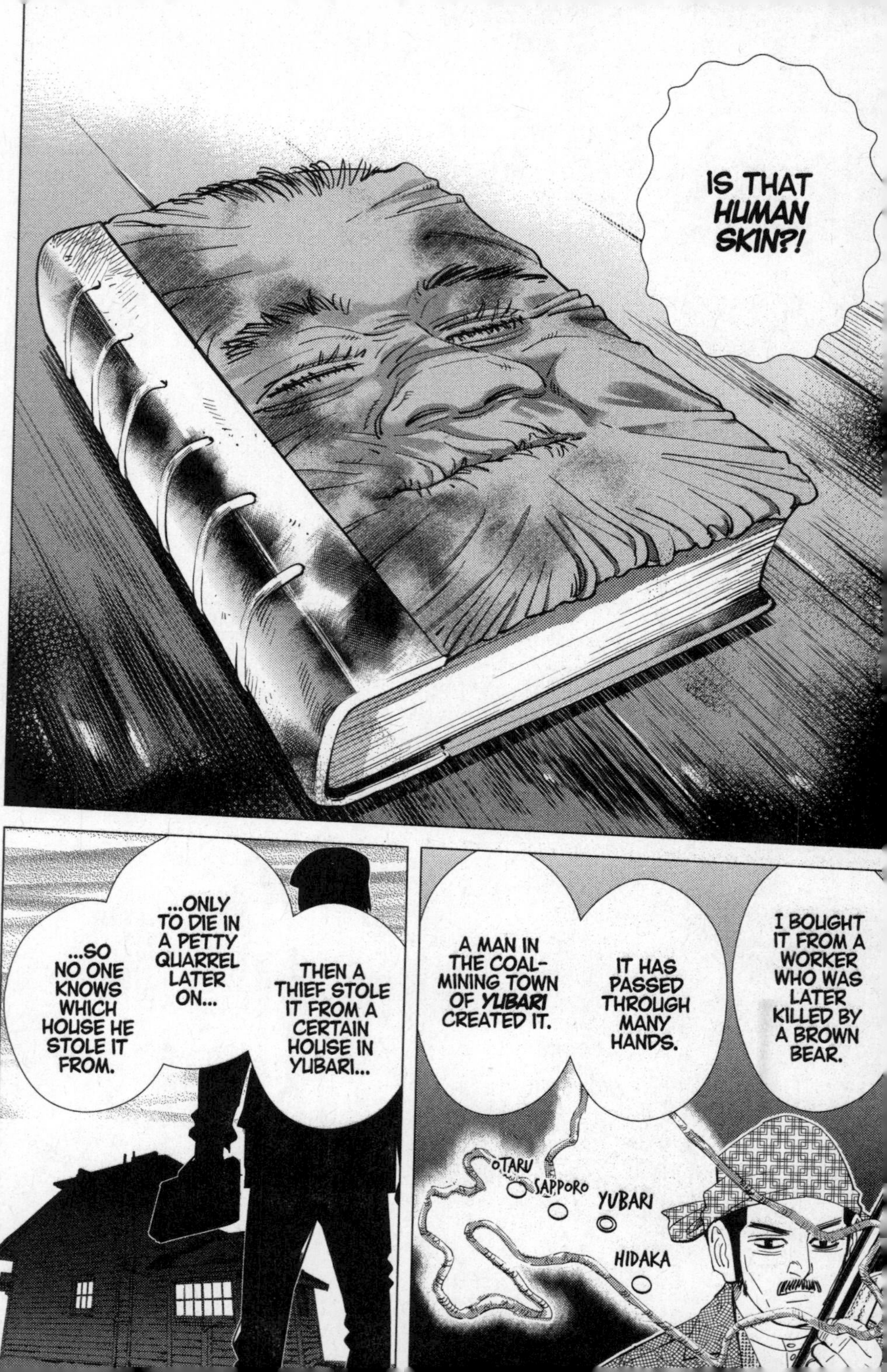
IS THAT HUMAN SKIN?!
I BOUGHT IT FROM A WORKER WHO WAS LATER KILLED BY A BROWN BEAR.
IT HAS PASSED THROUGH MANY HANDS.
A MAN IN THE COAL-MINING TOWN OF YUBARI CREATED IT.
OTARU
SAPPORO
YUBARI
HIDAKA
THEN A THIEF STOLE IT FROM A CERTAIN HOUSE IN YUBARI...
...ONLY TO DIE IN A PETTY QUARREL LATER ON...
...SO NO ONE KNOWS WHICH HOUSE HE STOLE IT FROM.

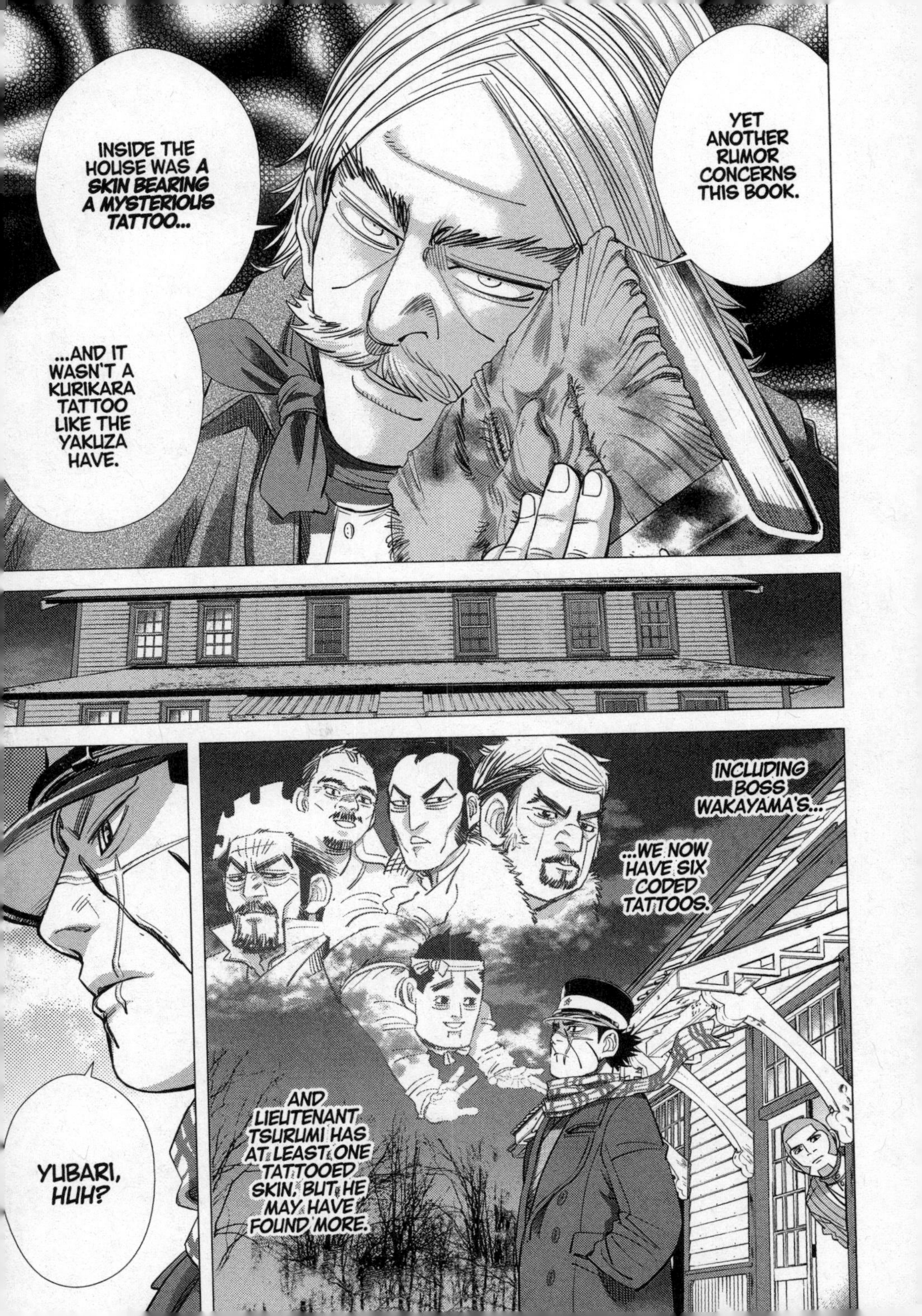
YET ANOTHER RUMOR CONCERNS THIS BOOK.
INSIDE THE HOUSE WAS A SKIN BEARING A MYSTERIOUS TATTOO...
...AND IT WASN'T A KURIKARA TATTOO LIKE THE YAKUZA HAVE.
INCLUDING BOSS WAKAYAMA'S...
...WE NOW HAVE SIX CODED TATTOOS.
AND LIEUTENANT TSURUMI HAS AT LEAST ONE TATTOOED SKIN, BUT HE MAY HAVE FOUND MORE.
YUBARI, HUH?

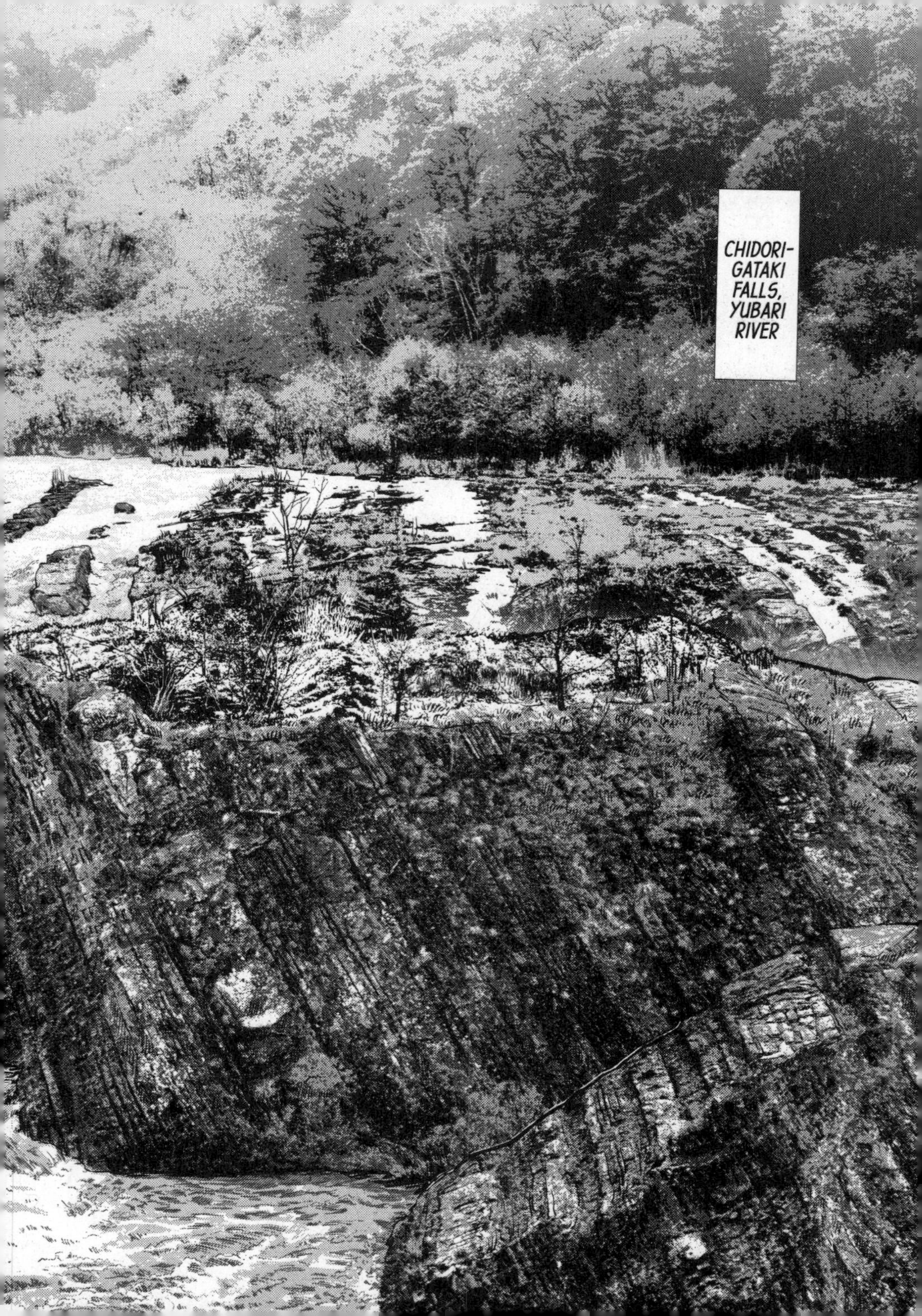
CHIDORI-GATAKI FALLS, YUBARI RIVER

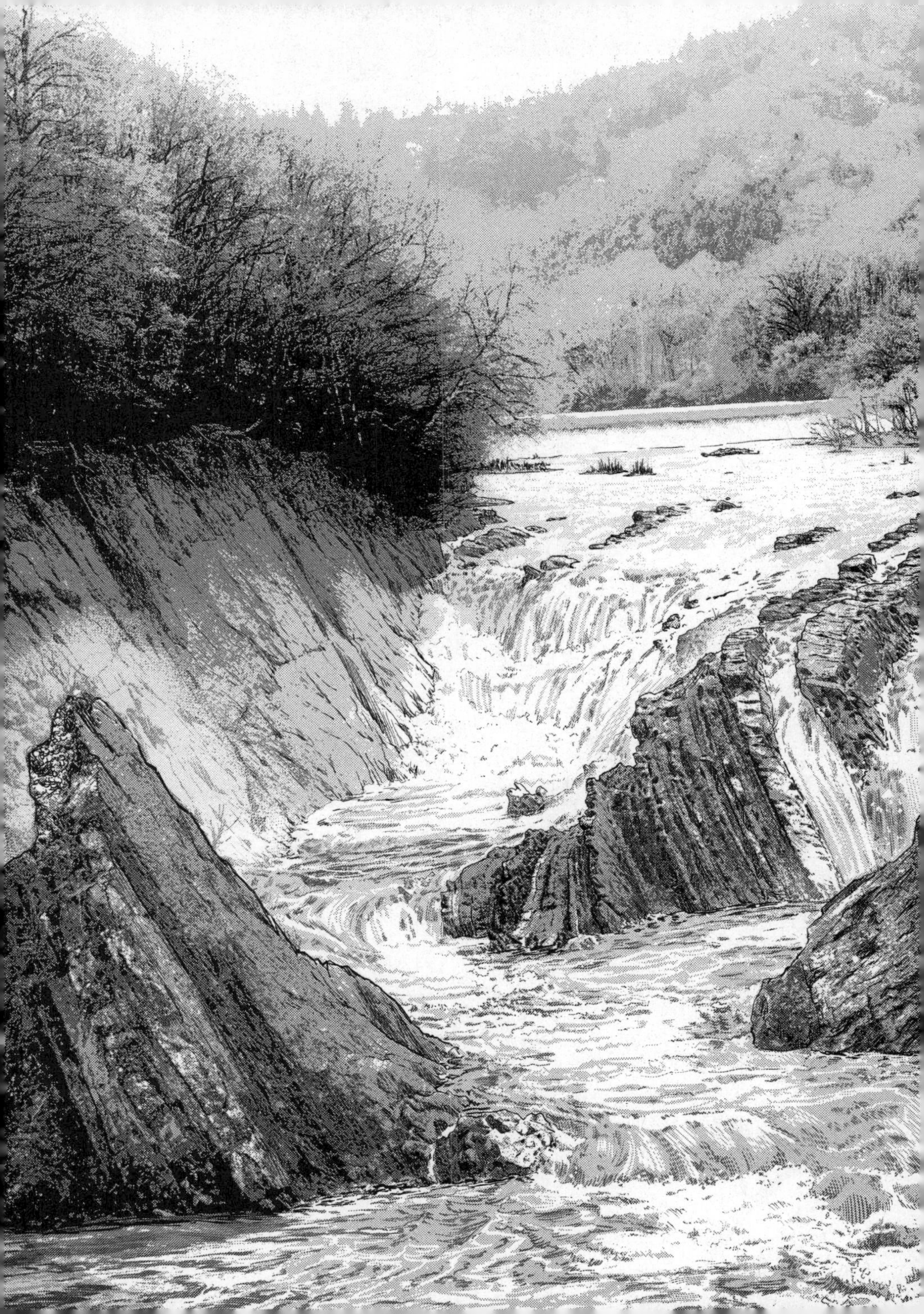

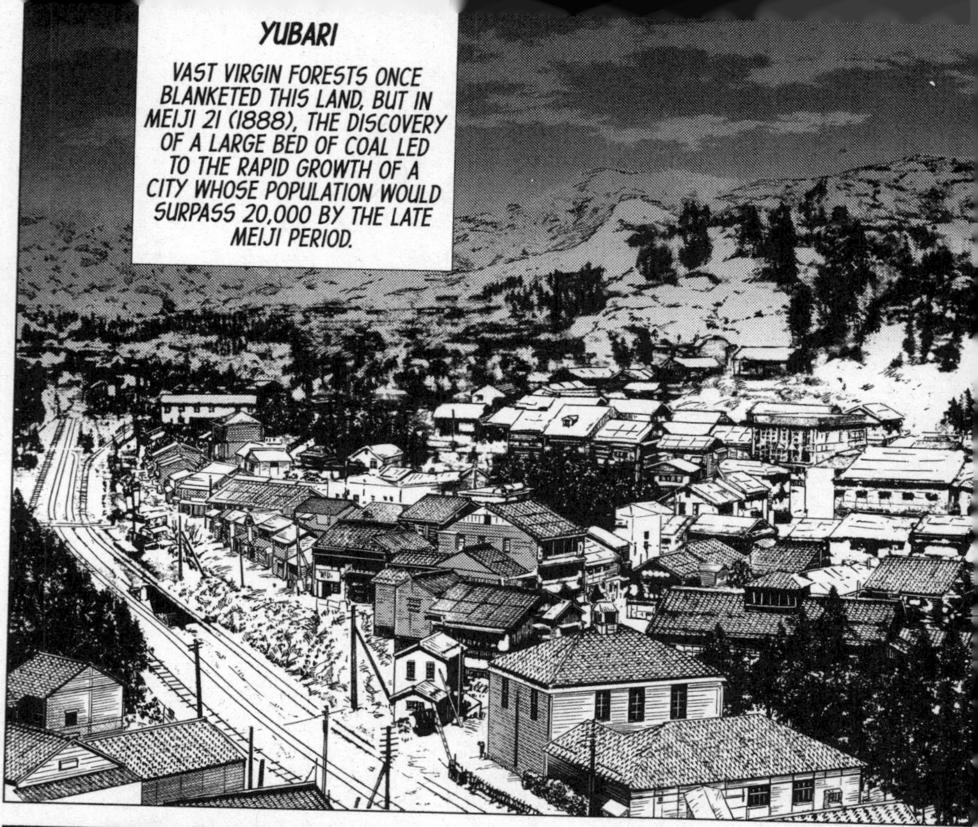
YUBARI
VAST VIRGIN FORESTS ONCE BLANKETED THIS LAND, BUT IN MEIJI 21 (1888), THE DISCOVERY OF A LARGE BED OF COAL LED TO THE RAPID GROWTH OF A CITY WHOSE POPULATION WOULD SURPASS 20,000 BY THE LATE MEIJI PERIOD.

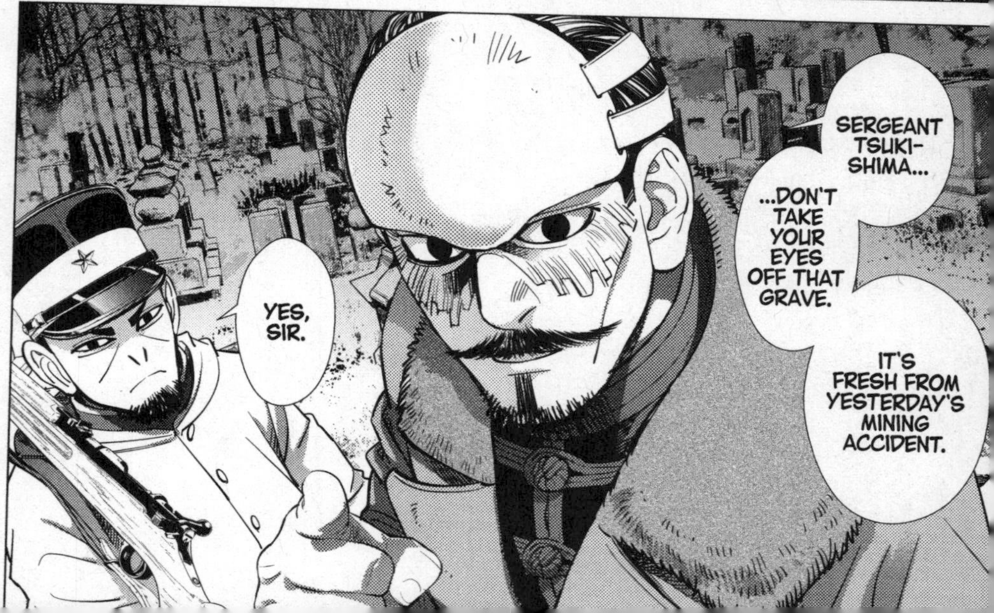
SERGEANT TSUKI-SHIMA...
...DON'T TAKE YOUR EYES OFF THAT GRAVE.
IT'S FRESH FROM YESTERDAY'S MINING ACCIDENT.
YES, SIR.

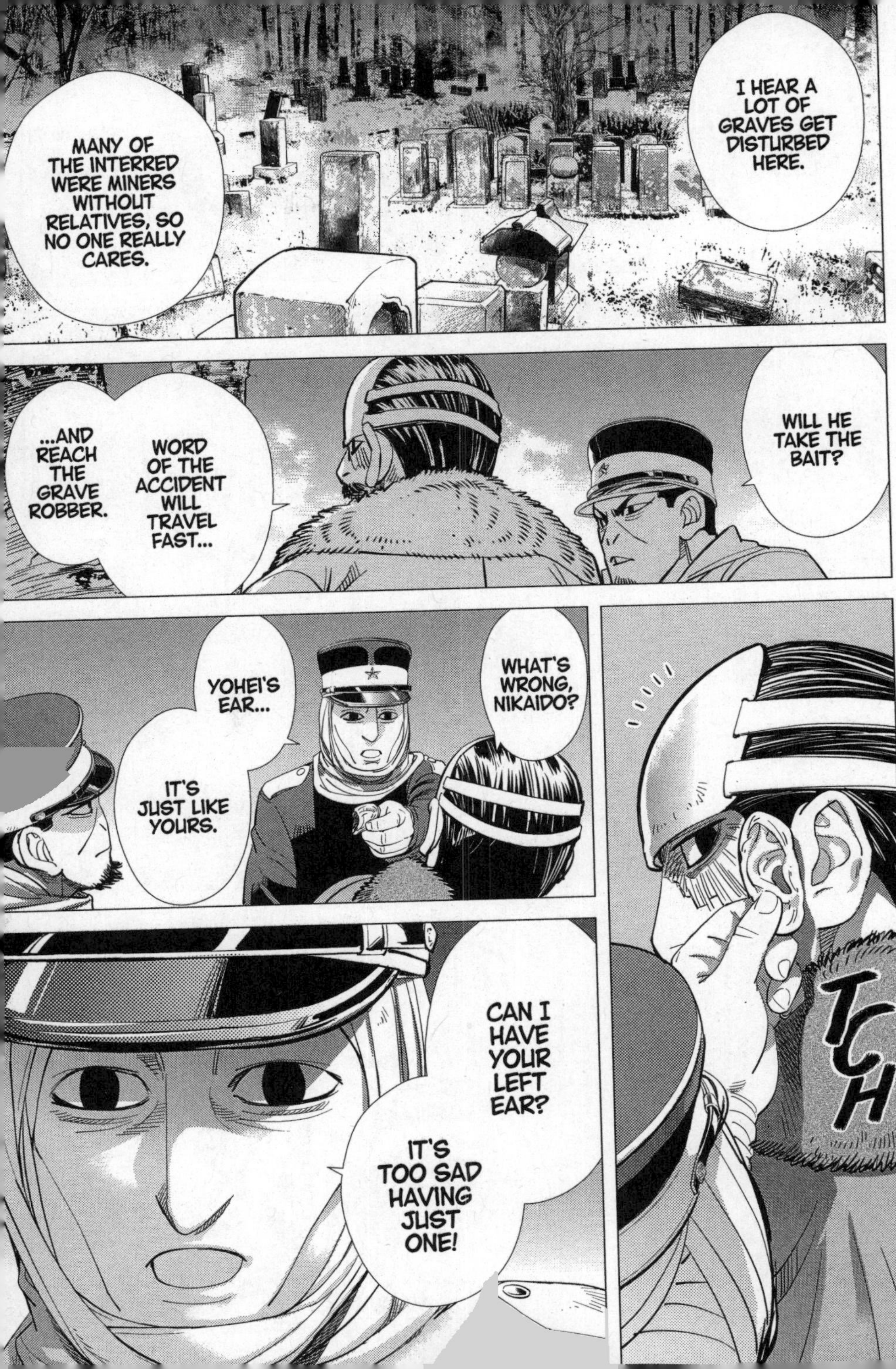
I HEAR A LOT OF GRAVES GET DISTURBED HERE.
MANY OF THE INTERRED WERE MINERS WITHOUT RELATIVES, SO NO ONE REALLY CARES.
WILL HE TAKE THE BAIT?
WORD OF THE ACCIDENT WILL TRAVEL FAST...
...AND REACH THE GRAVE ROBBER.
TCH
WHAT'S WRONG, NIKAIDO?
YOHEI'S EAR...
IT'S JUST LIKE YOURS.
CAN I HAVE YOUR LEFT EAR?
IT'S TOO SAD HAVING JUST ONE!

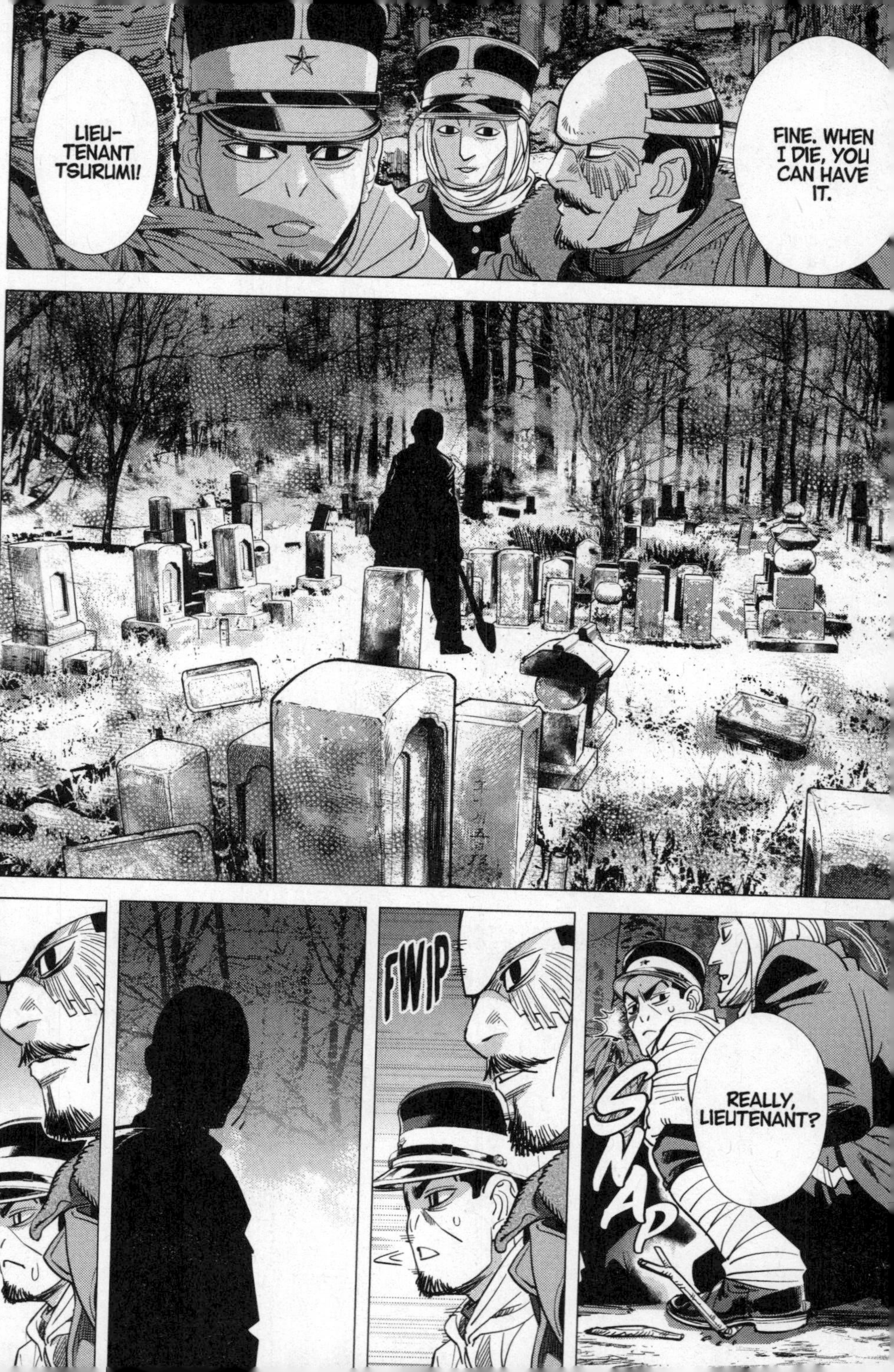
FINE. WHEN I DIE, YOU CAN HAVE IT.
LIEU-TENANT TSURUMI!
REALLY, LIEUTENANT?
SNAP
FWIP

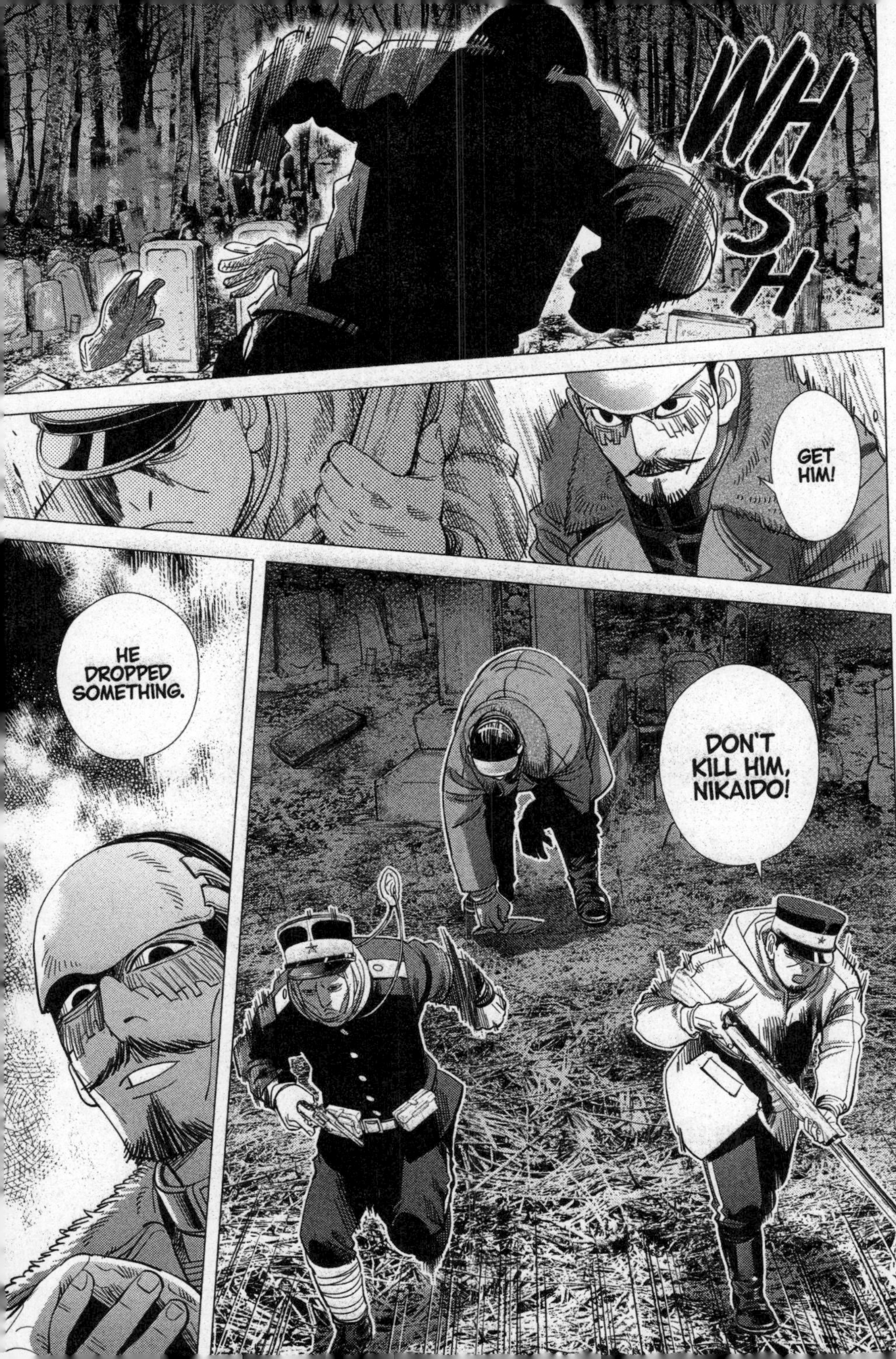
WHSH
GET HIM!
DON'T KILL HIM, NIKAIDO!
HE DROPPED SOMETHING.

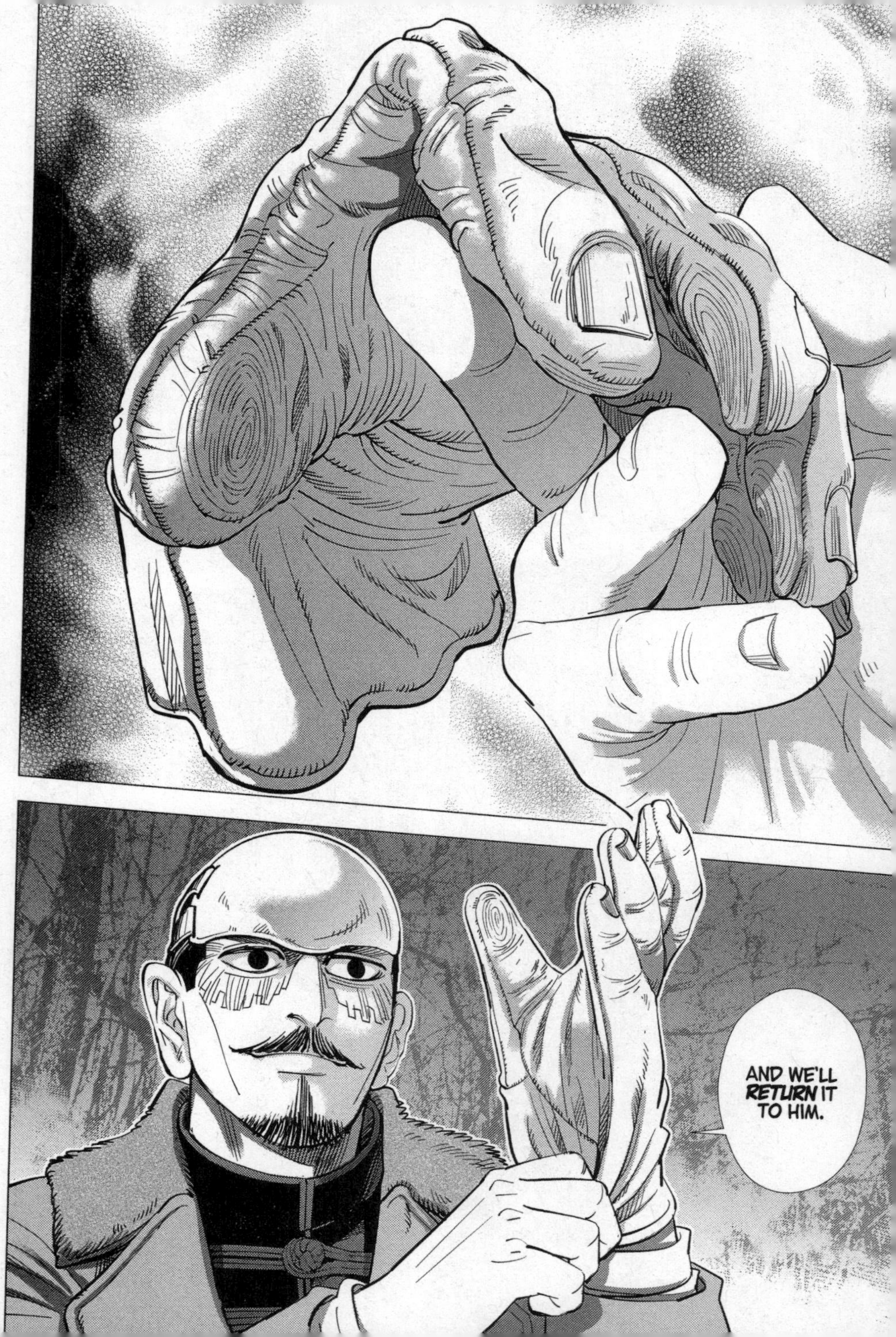
AND WE'LL RETURN IT TO HIM.

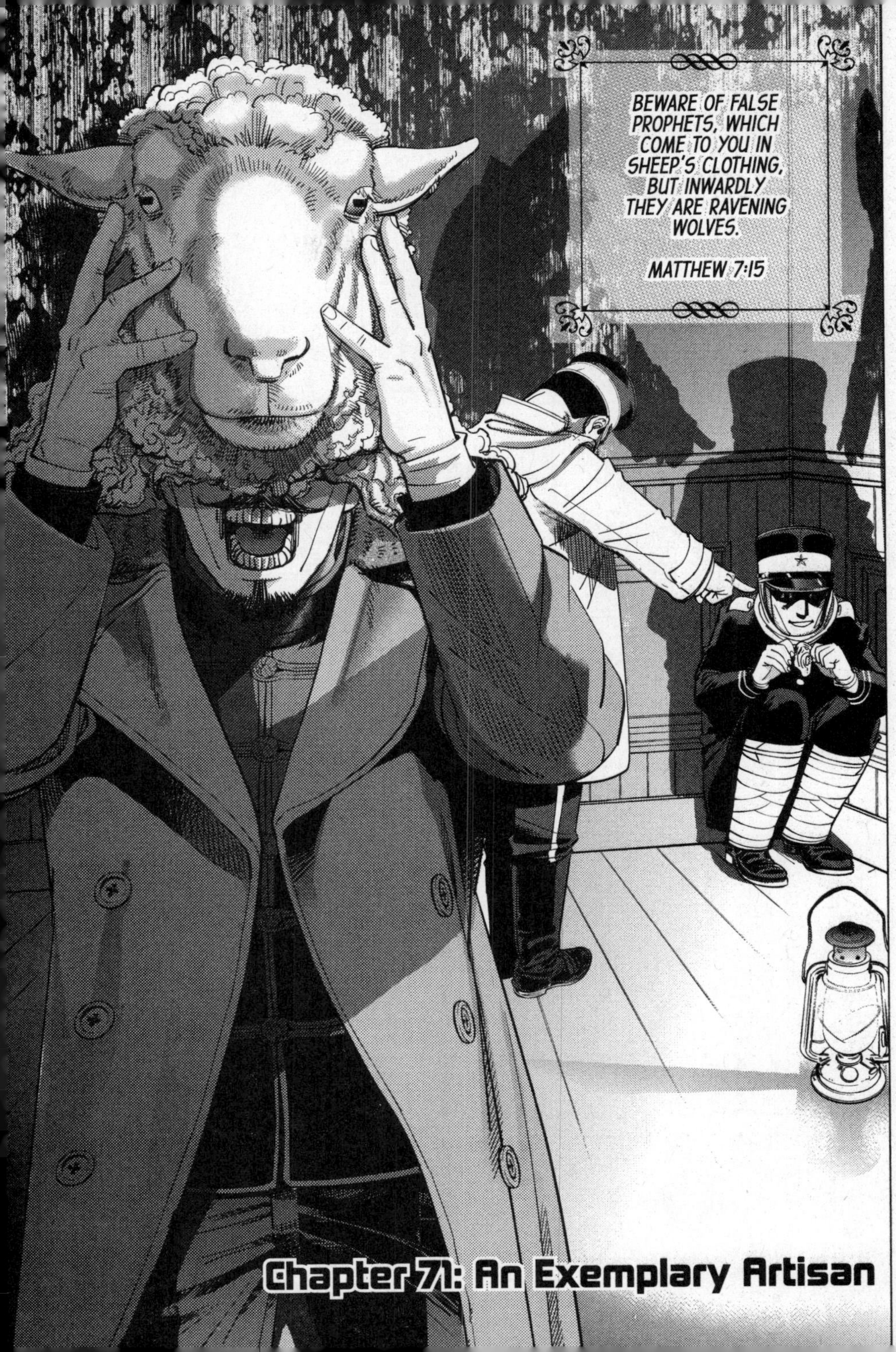
BEWARE OF FALSE PROPHETS, WHICH COME TO YOU IN SHEEP'S CLOTHING, BUT INWARDLY THEY ARE RAVENING WOLVES.
MATTHEW 7:15
Chapter 71: An Exemplary Artisan

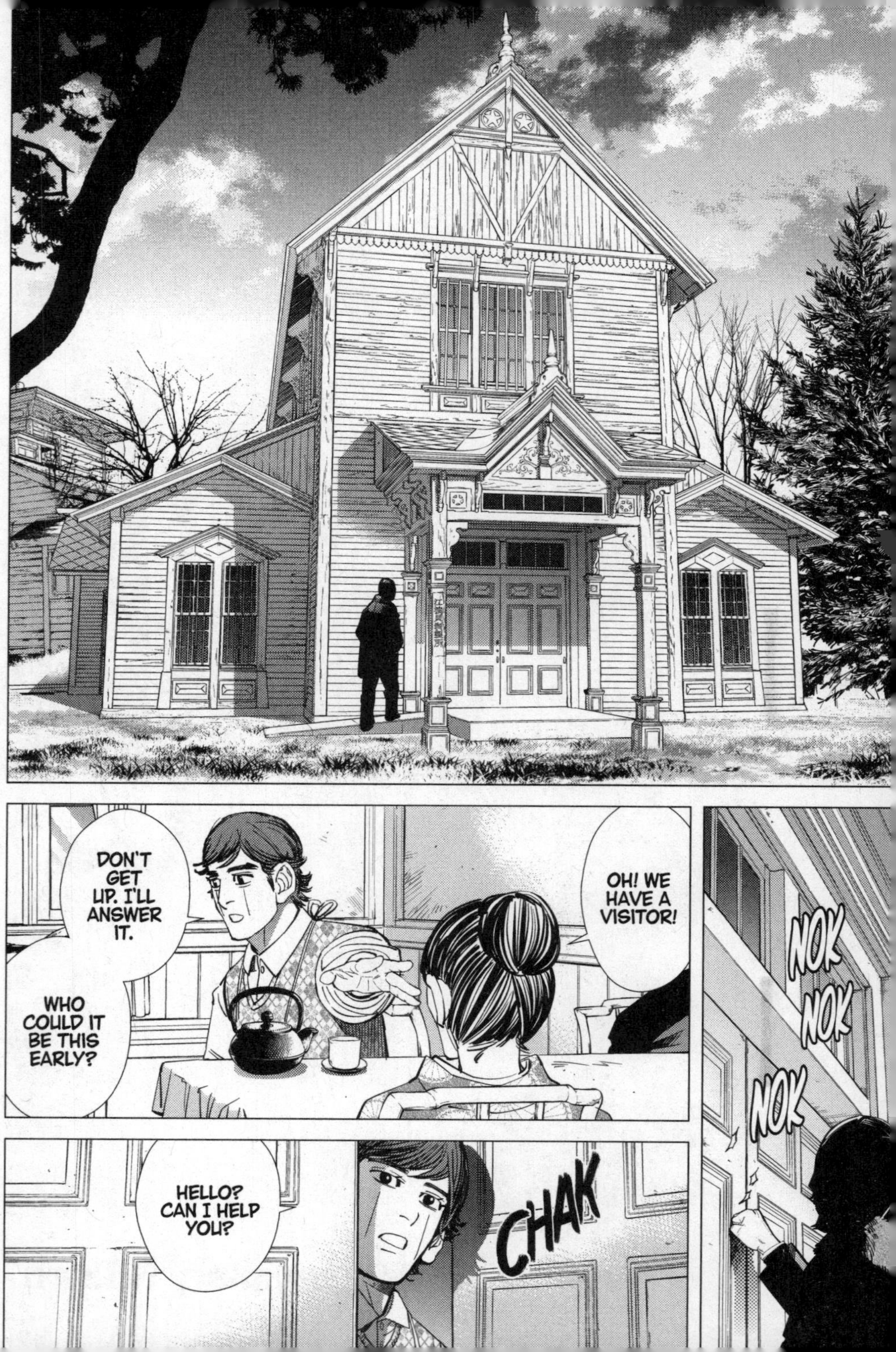
NOK
NOK
NOK
OH! WE HAVE A VISITOR!
DON'T GET UP. I'LL ANSWER IT.
WHO COULD IT BE THIS EARLY?
CHAK
HELLO? CAN I HELP YOU?

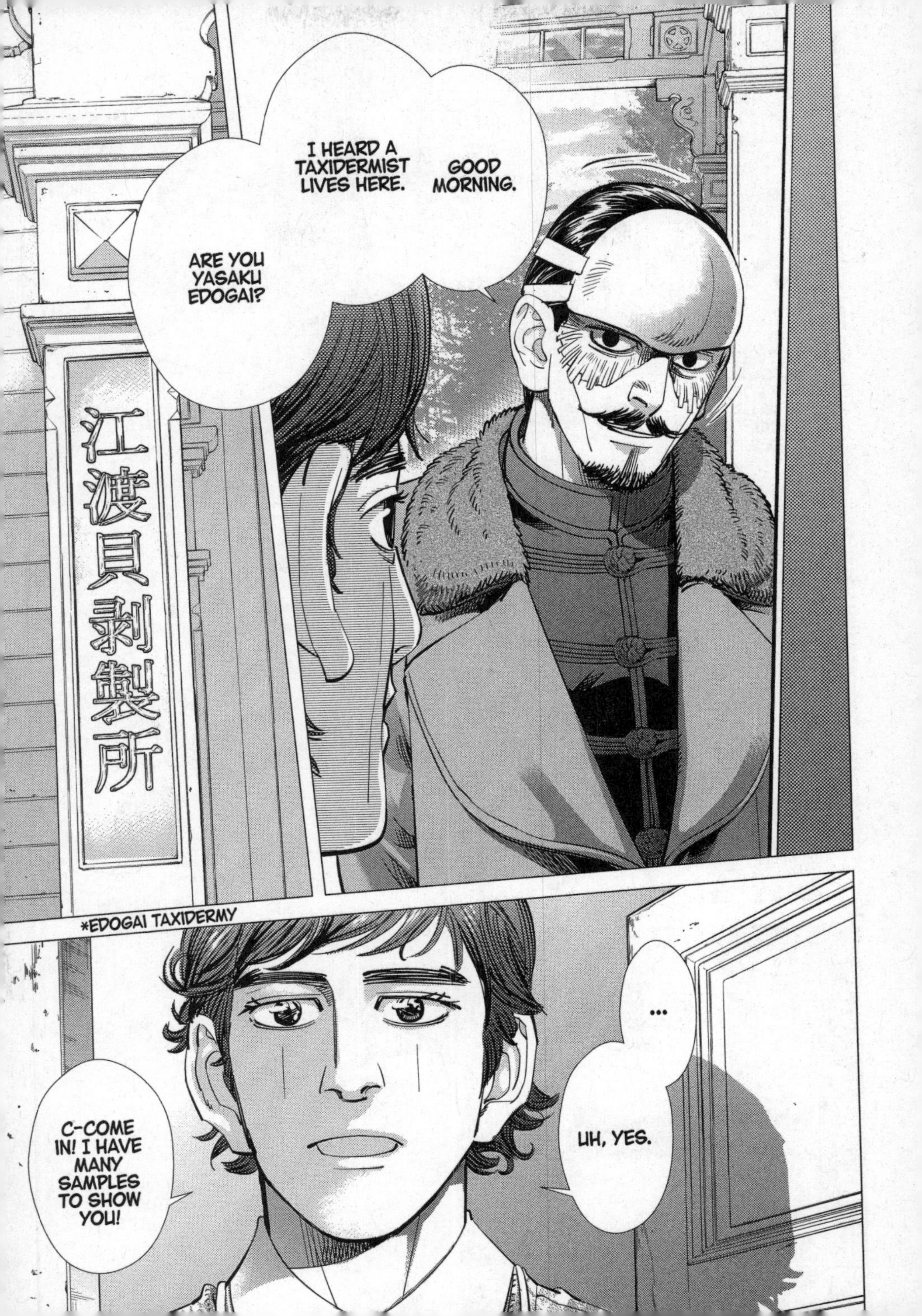
GOOD MORNING.
I HEARD A TAXIDERMIST LIVES HERE.
ARE YOU YASAKU EDOGAI?
江渡貝剥製所
*EDOGAI TAXIDERMY
...
UH, YES.
C-COME IN! I HAVE MANY SAMPLES TO SHOW YOU!

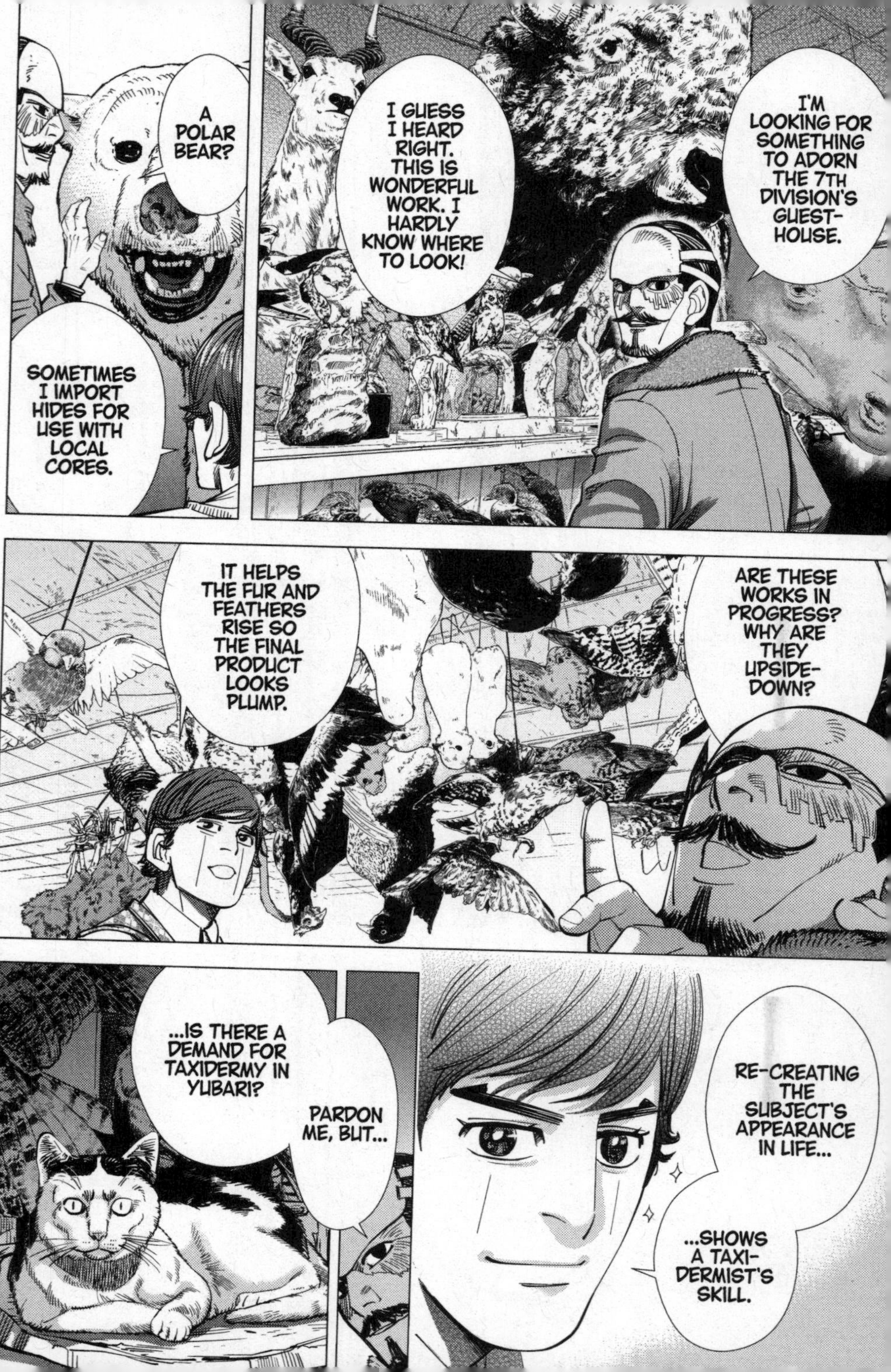
I'M LOOKING FOR SOMETHING TO ADORN THE 7TH DIVISION'S GUEST-HOUSE.
I GUESS I HEARD RIGHT. THIS IS WONDERFUL WORK. I HARDLY KNOW WHERE TO LOOK!
A POLAR BEAR?
SOMETIMES I IMPORT HIDES FOR USE WITH LOCAL CORES.
ARE THESE WORKS IN PROGRESS? WHY ARE THEY UPSIDE-DOWN?
IT HELPS THE FUR AND FEATHERS RISE SO THE FINAL PRODUCT LOOKS PLUMP.
RE-CREATING THE SUBJECT'S APPEARANCE IN LIFE...
...SHOWS A TAXIDERMIST'S SKILL.
PARDON ME, BUT...
...IS THERE A DEMAND FOR TAXIDERMY IN YUBARI?

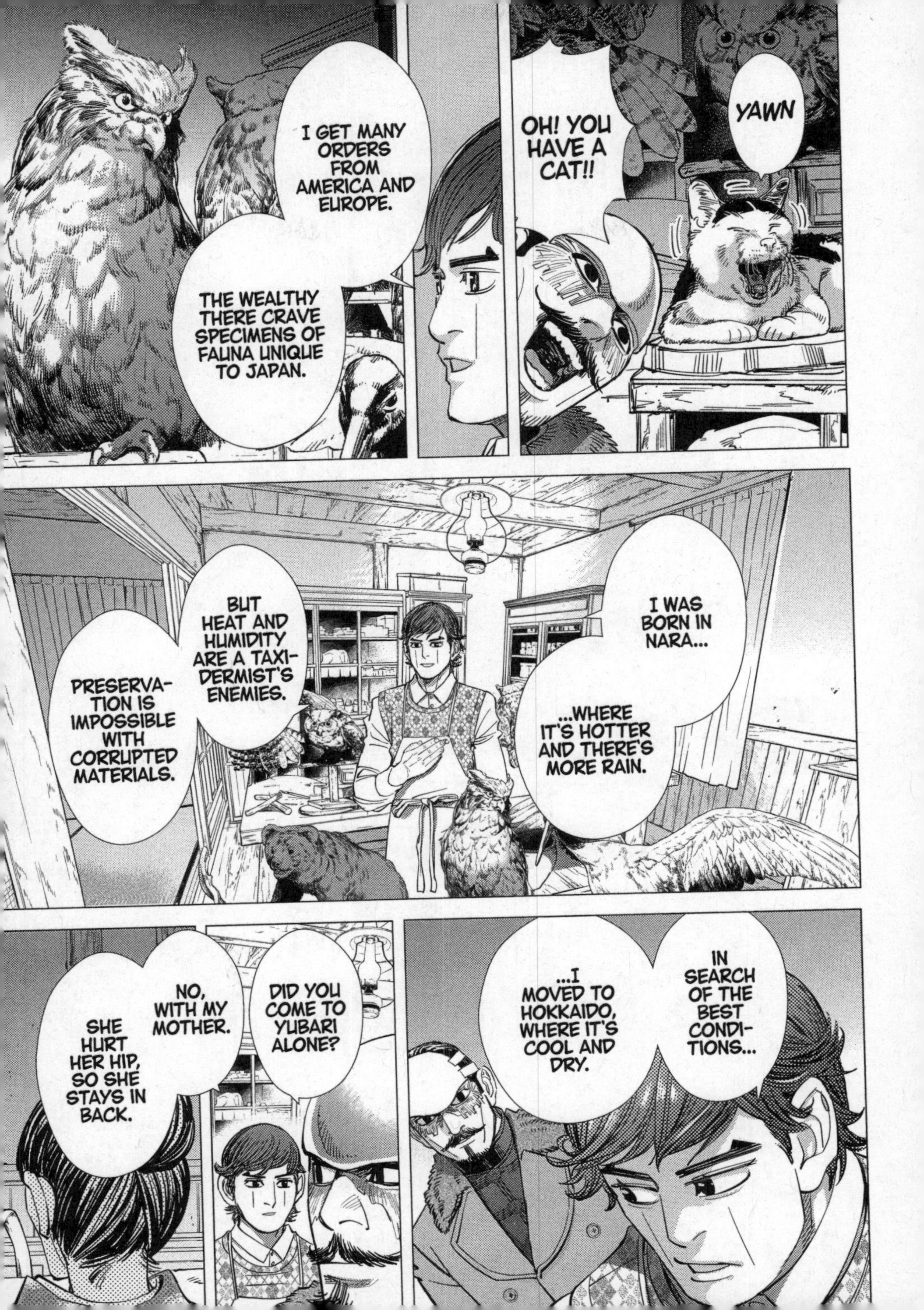
YAWN
OH! YOU HAVE A CAT!!
I GET MANY ORDERS FROM AMERICA AND EUROPE.
THE WEALTHY THERE CRAVE SPECIMENS OF FAUNA UNIQUE TO JAPAN.
I WAS BORN IN NARA...
...WHERE IT'S HOTTER AND THERE'S MORE RAIN.
BUT HEAT AND HUMIDITY ARE A TAXIDERMIST'S ENEMIES.
PRESERVATION IS IMPOSSIBLE WITH CORRUPTED MATERIALS.
IN SEARCH OF THE BEST CONDITIONS...
...I MOVED TO HOKKAIDO, WHERE IT'S COOL AND DRY.
DID YOU COME TO YUBARI ALONE?
NO, WITH MY MOTHER.
SHE HURT HER HIP, SO SHE STAYS IN BACK.

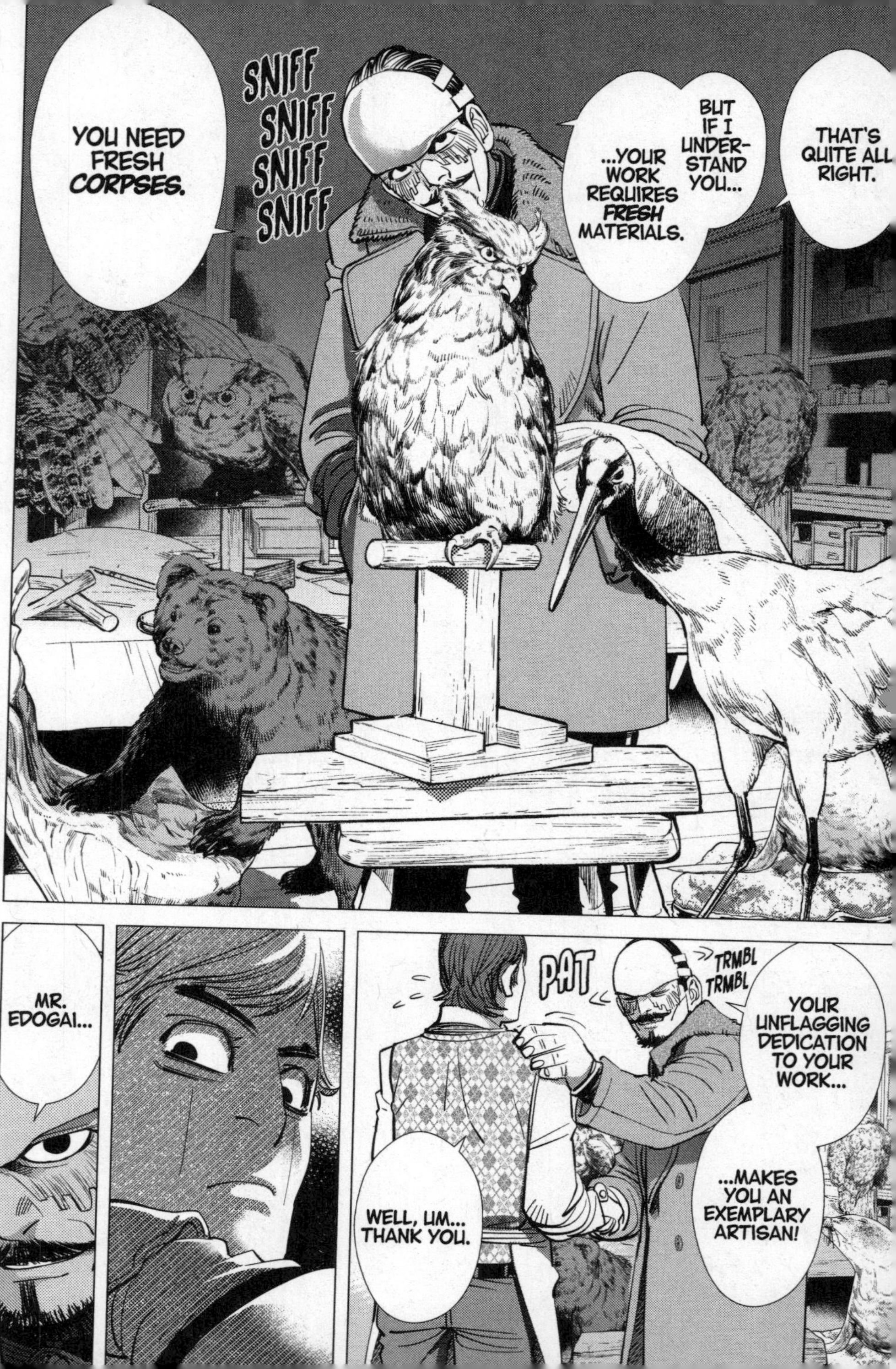
THAT'S QUITE ALL RIGHT.
BUT IF I UNDER-STAND YOU...
...YOUR WORK REQUIRES FRESH MATERIALS.
SNIFF SNIFF SNIFF SNIFF
YOU NEED FRESH CORPSES.
TRMBL TRMBL
YOUR UNFLAGGING DEDICATION TO YOUR WORK...
PAT
...MAKES YOU AN EXEMPLARY ARTISAN!
WELL, UM... THANK YOU.
MR. EDOGAI...

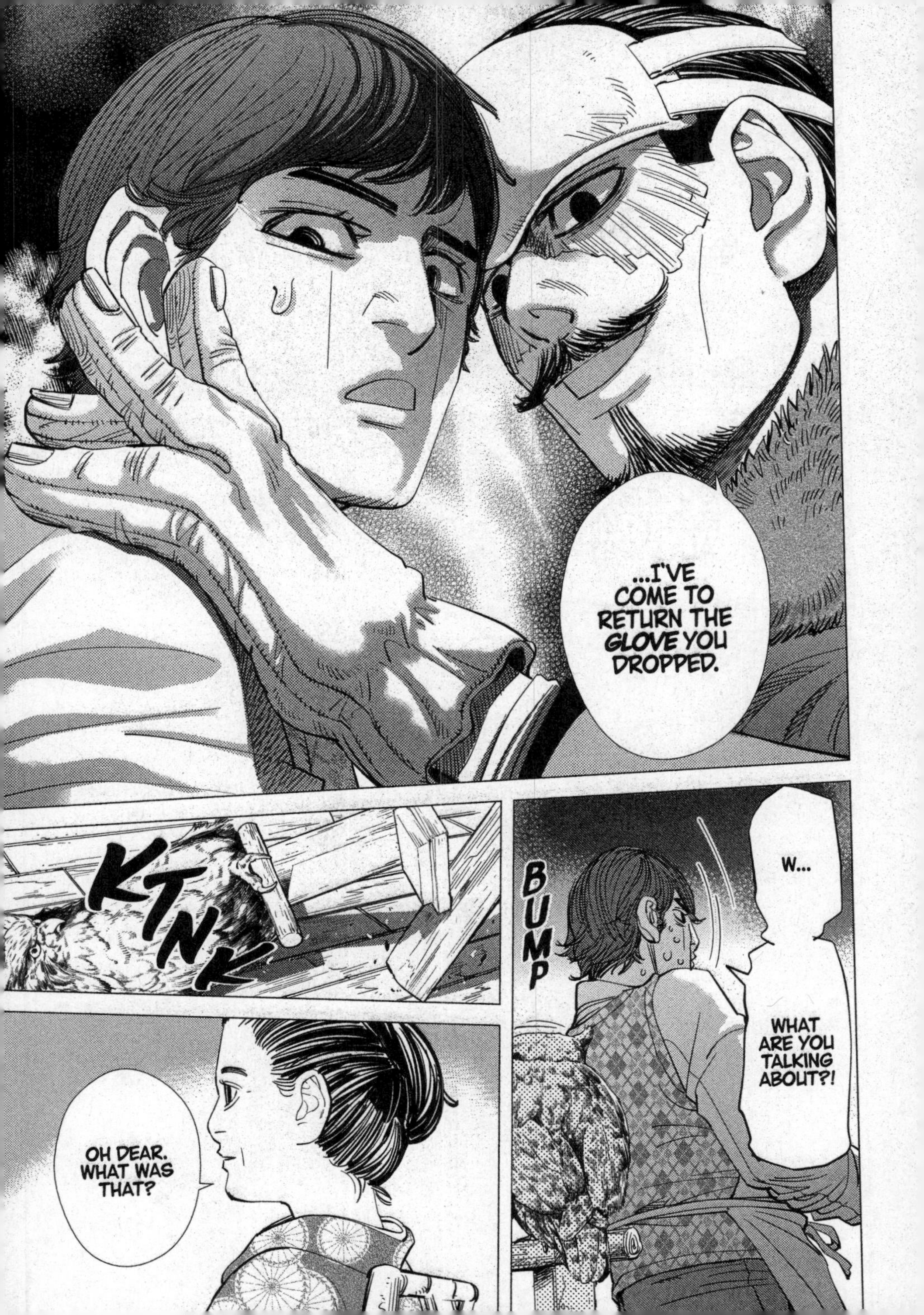
...I'VE COME TO RETURN THE GLOVE YOU DROPPED.
BUMP
W...
WHAT ARE YOU TALKING ABOUT?!
KTNK
OH DEAR. WHAT WAS THAT?

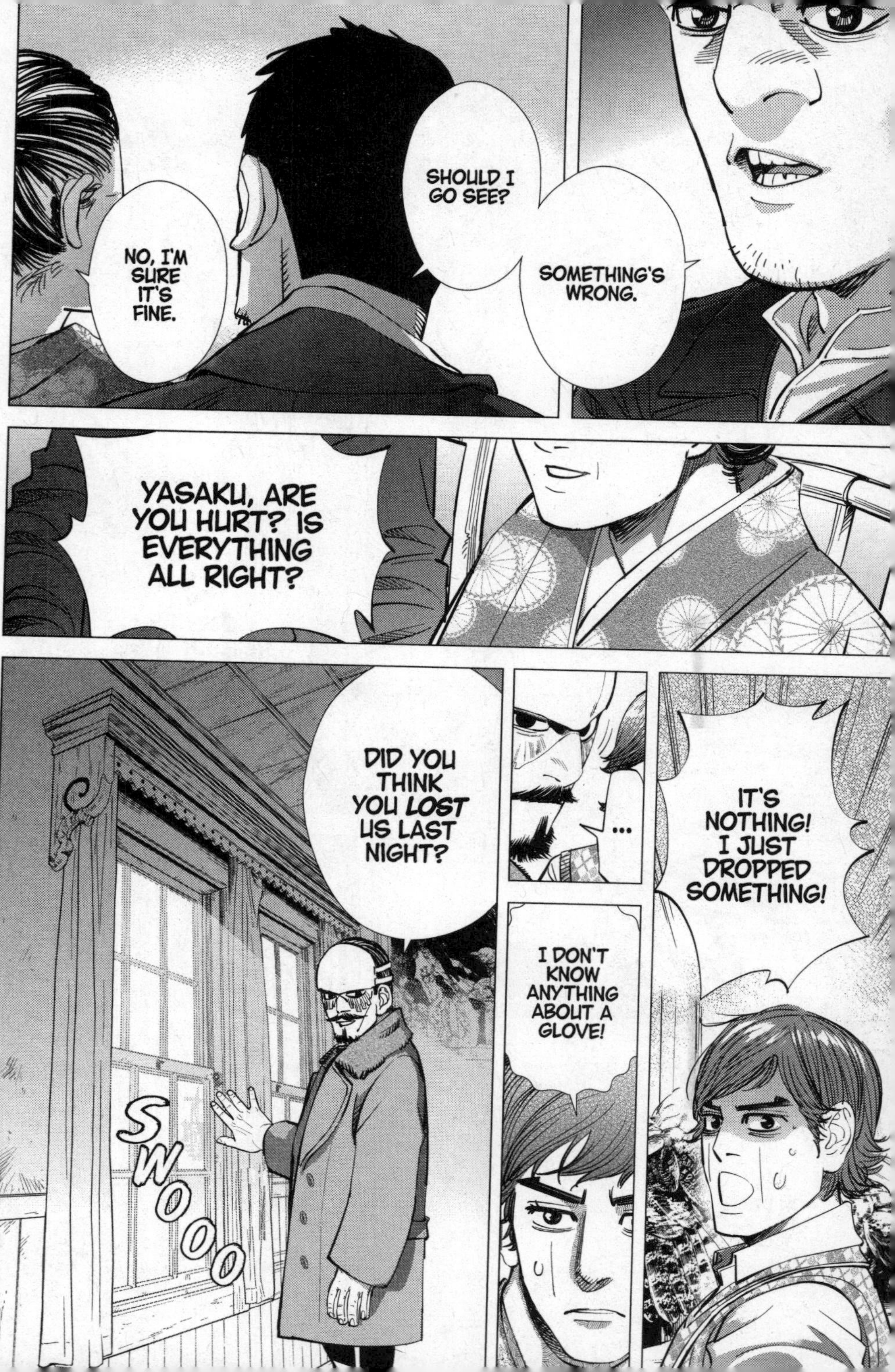
SOMETHING'S WRONG.
SHOULD I GO SEE?
NO, I'M SURE IT'S FINE.
YASAKU, ARE YOU HURT? IS EVERYTHING ALL RIGHT?
IT'S NOTHING! I JUST DROPPED SOMETHING!
...
I DON'T KNOW ANYTHING ABOUT A GLOVE!
DID YOU THINK YOU ***LOST*** US LAST NIGHT?
SWOOO

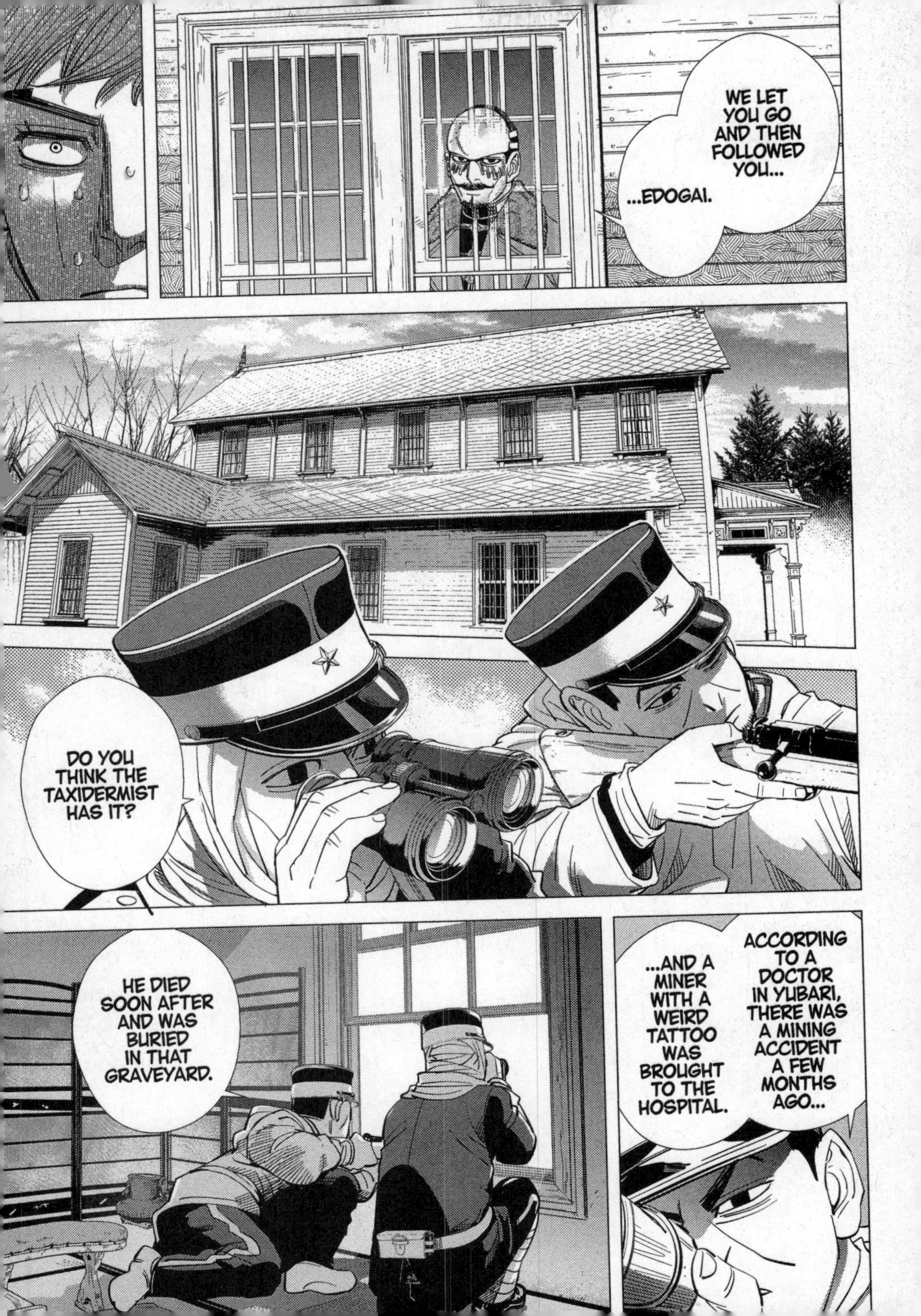
WE LET YOU GO AND THEN FOLLOWED YOU...
...EDOGAI.
DO YOU THINK THE TAXIDERMIST HAS IT?
ACCORDING TO A DOCTOR IN YUBARI, THERE WAS A MINING ACCIDENT A FEW MONTHS AGO...
...AND A MINER WITH A WEIRD TATTOO WAS BROUGHT TO THE HOSPITAL.
HE DIED SOON AFTER AND WAS BURIED IN THAT GRAVEYARD.

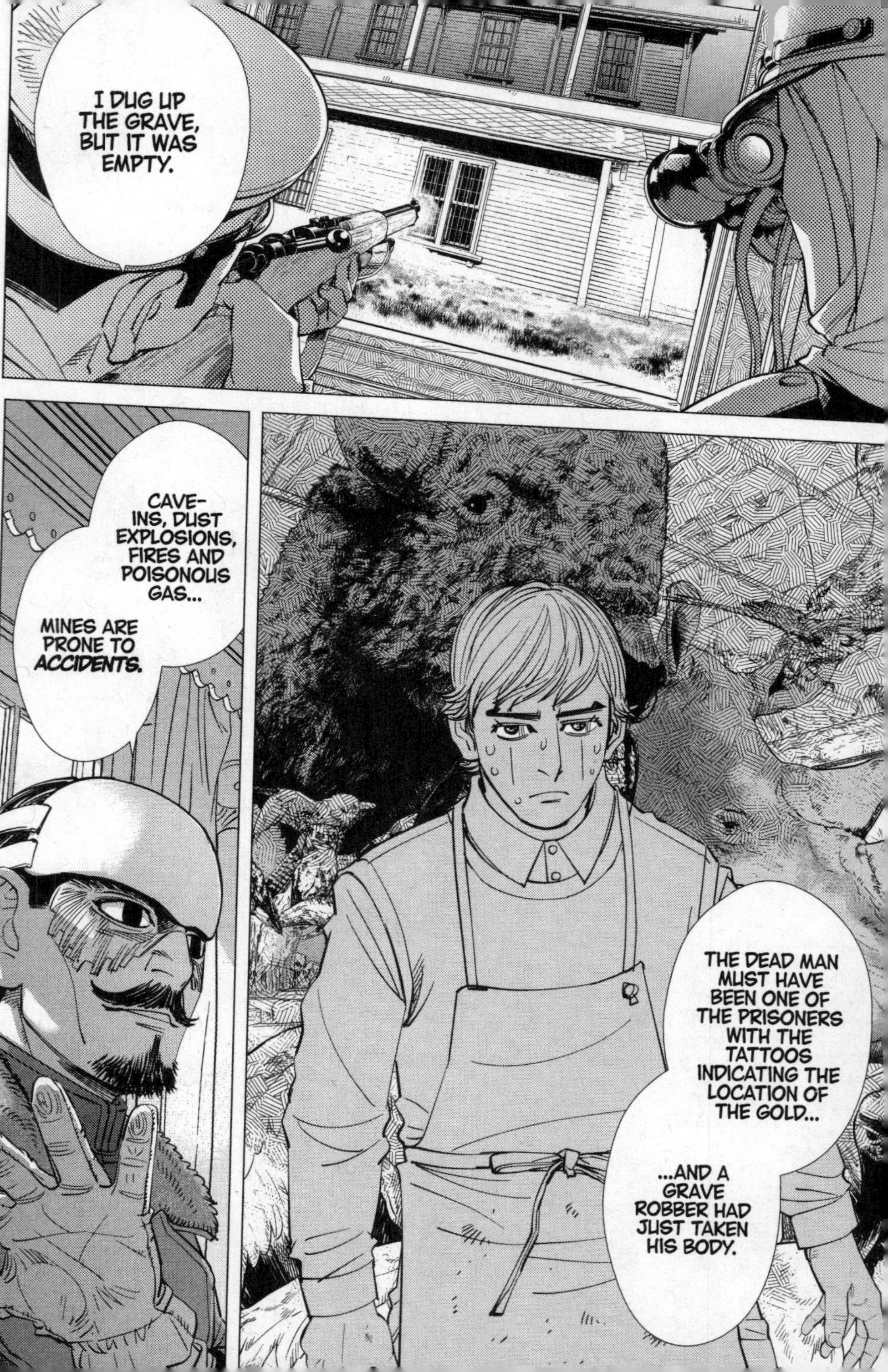
I DUG UP THE GRAVE, BUT IT WAS EMPTY.
THE DEAD MAN MUST HAVE BEEN ONE OF THE PRISONERS WITH THE TATTOOS INDICATING THE LOCATION OF THE GOLD...
...AND A GRAVE ROBBER HAD JUST TAKEN HIS BODY.
CAVE-INS, DUST EXPLOSIONS, FIRES AND POISONOUS GAS...
MINES ARE PRONE TO ACCIDENTS.

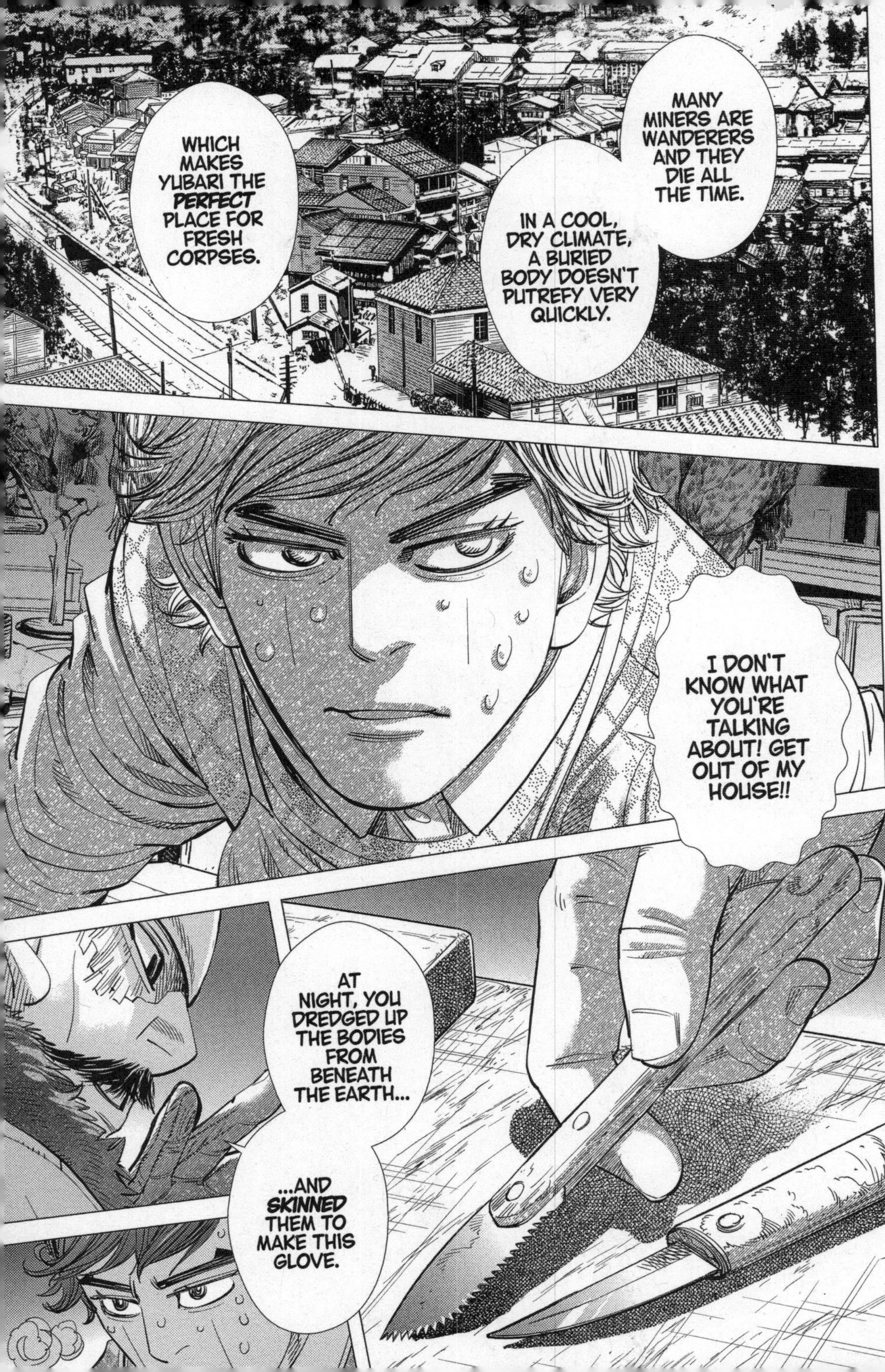
MANY MINERS ARE WANDERERS AND THEY DIE ALL THE TIME.
IN A COOL, DRY CLIMATE, A BURIED BODY DOESN'T PUTREFY VERY QUICKLY.
WHICH MAKES YUBARI THE **PERFECT** PLACE FOR FRESH CORPSES.
I DON'T KNOW WHAT YOU'RE TALKING ABOUT! GET OUT OF MY HOUSE!!
AT NIGHT, YOU DREDGED UP THE BODIES FROM BENEATH THE EARTH...
...AND **SKINNED** THEM TO MAKE THIS GLOVE.

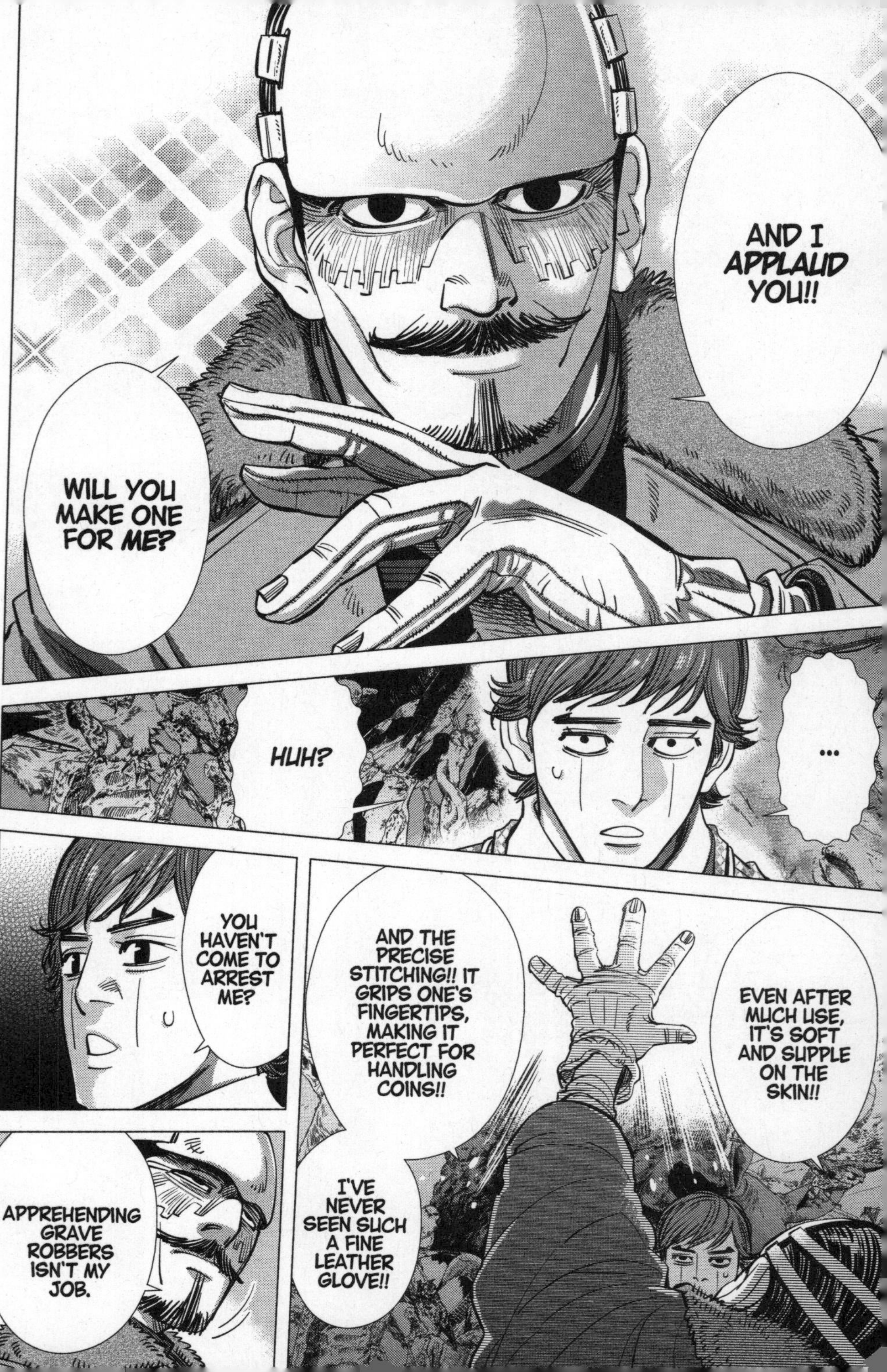
AND I APPLAUD YOU!!
WILL YOU MAKE ONE FOR ME?
...
HUH?
EVEN AFTER MUCH USE, IT'S SOFT AND SUPPLE ON THE SKIN!!
AND THE PRECISE STITCHING!! IT GRIPS ONE'S FINGERTIPS, MAKING IT PERFECT FOR HANDLING COINS!!
I'VE NEVER SEEN SUCH A FINE LEATHER GLOVE!!
YOU HAVEN'T COME TO ARREST ME?
APPREHENDING GRAVE ROBBERS ISN'T MY JOB.

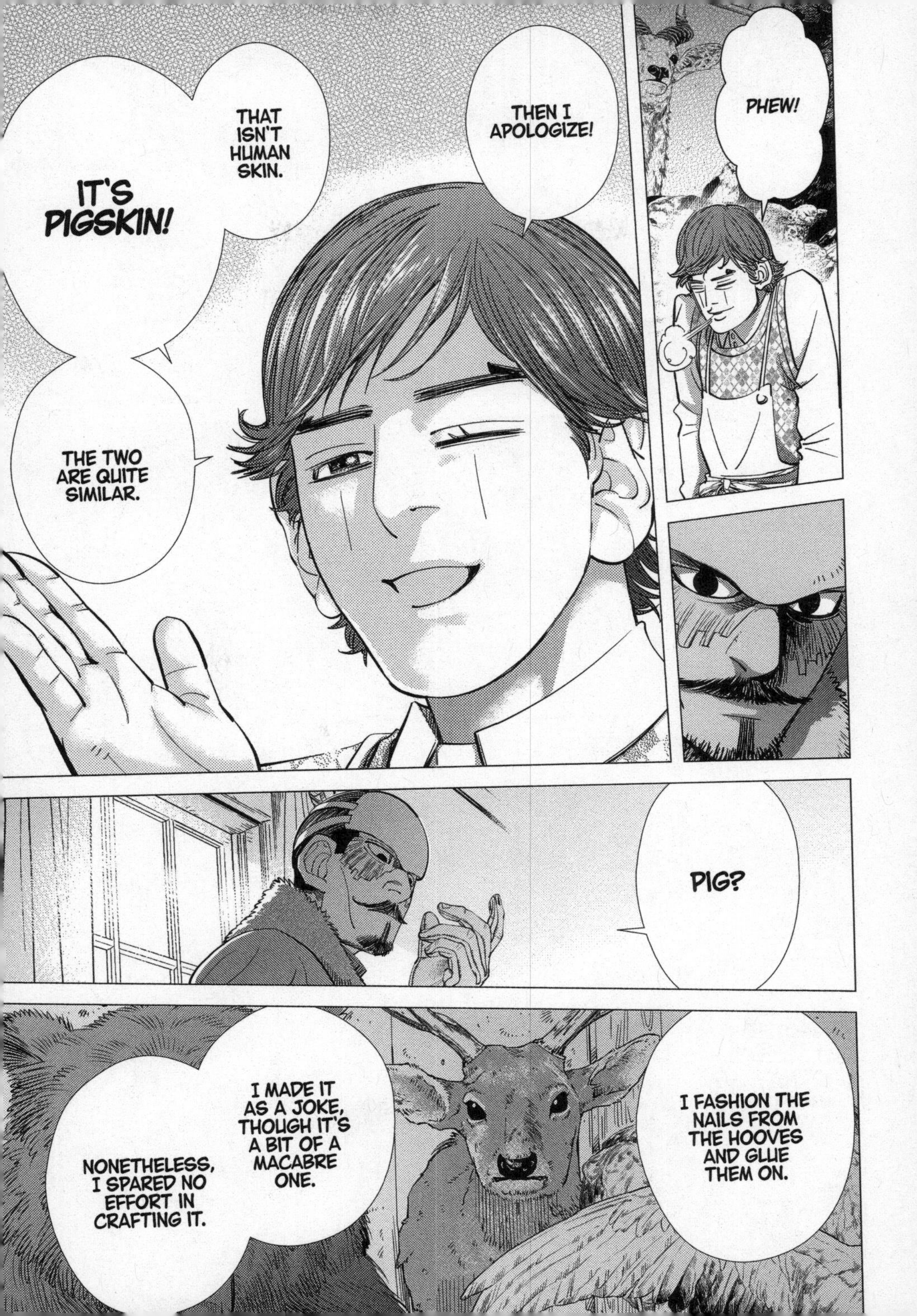
PHEW!
THEN I APOLOGIZE!
THAT ISN'T HUMAN SKIN.
IT'S PIGSKIN!
THE TWO ARE QUITE SIMILAR.
PIG?
I FASHION THE NAILS FROM THE HOOVES AND GLUE THEM ON.
I MADE IT AS A JOKE, THOUGH IT'S A BIT OF A MACABRE ONE.
NONETHELESS, I SPARED NO EFFORT IN CRAFTING IT.

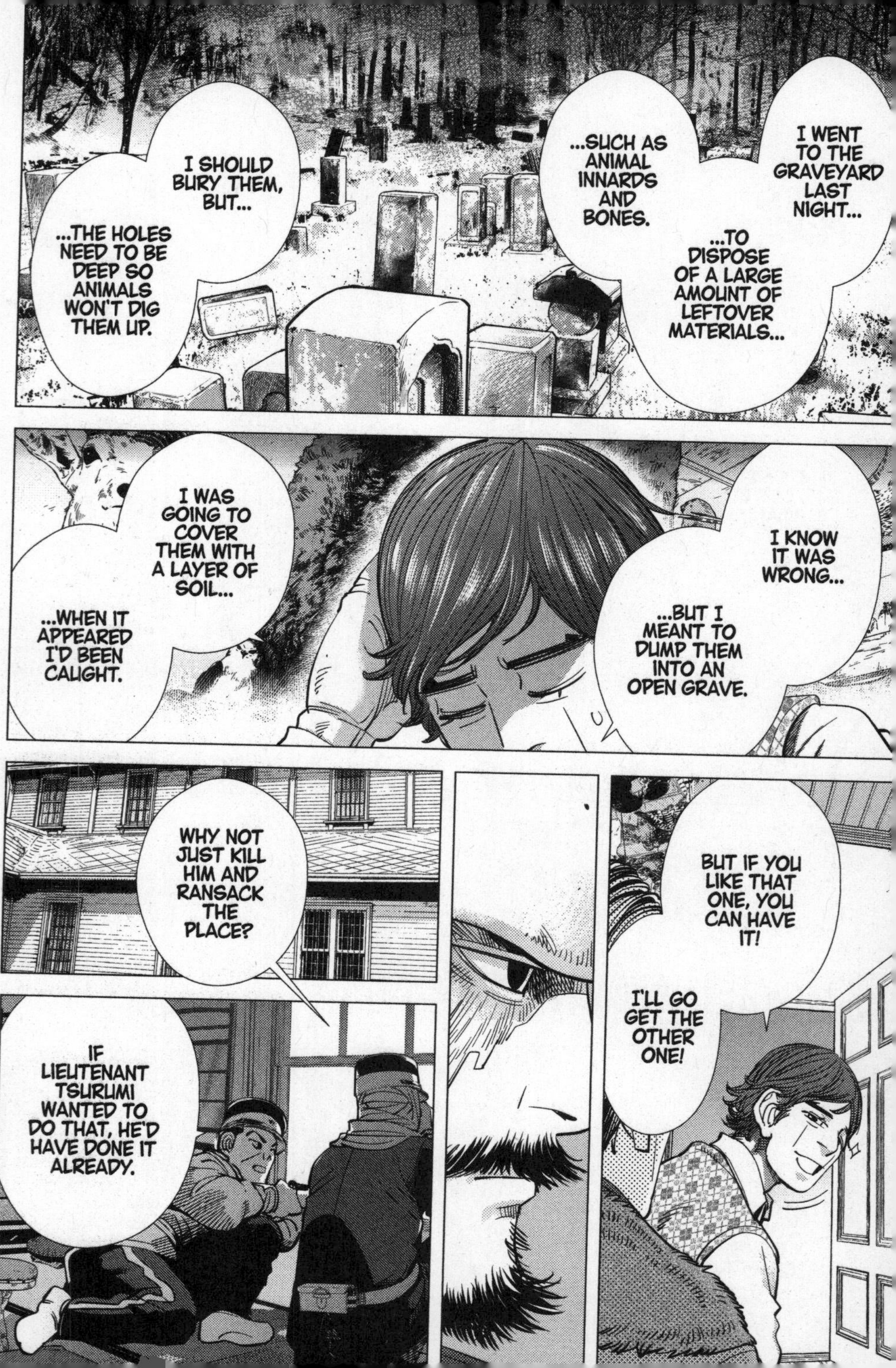
I WENT TO THE GRAVEYARD LAST NIGHT...
...TO DISPOSE OF A LARGE AMOUNT OF LEFTOVER MATERIALS...
...SUCH AS ANIMAL INNARDS AND BONES.
I SHOULD BURY THEM, BUT...
...THE HOLES NEED TO BE DEEP SO ANIMALS WON'T DIG THEM UP.
I KNOW IT WAS WRONG...
...BUT I MEANT TO DUMP THEM INTO AN OPEN GRAVE.
I WAS GOING TO COVER THEM WITH A LAYER OF SOIL...
...WHEN IT APPEARED I'D BEEN CAUGHT.
BUT IF YOU LIKE THAT ONE, YOU CAN HAVE IT!
I'LL GO GET THE OTHER ONE!
WHY NOT JUST KILL HIM AND RANSACK THE PLACE?
IF LIEUTENANT TSURUMI WANTED TO DO THAT, HE'D HAVE DONE IT ALREADY.

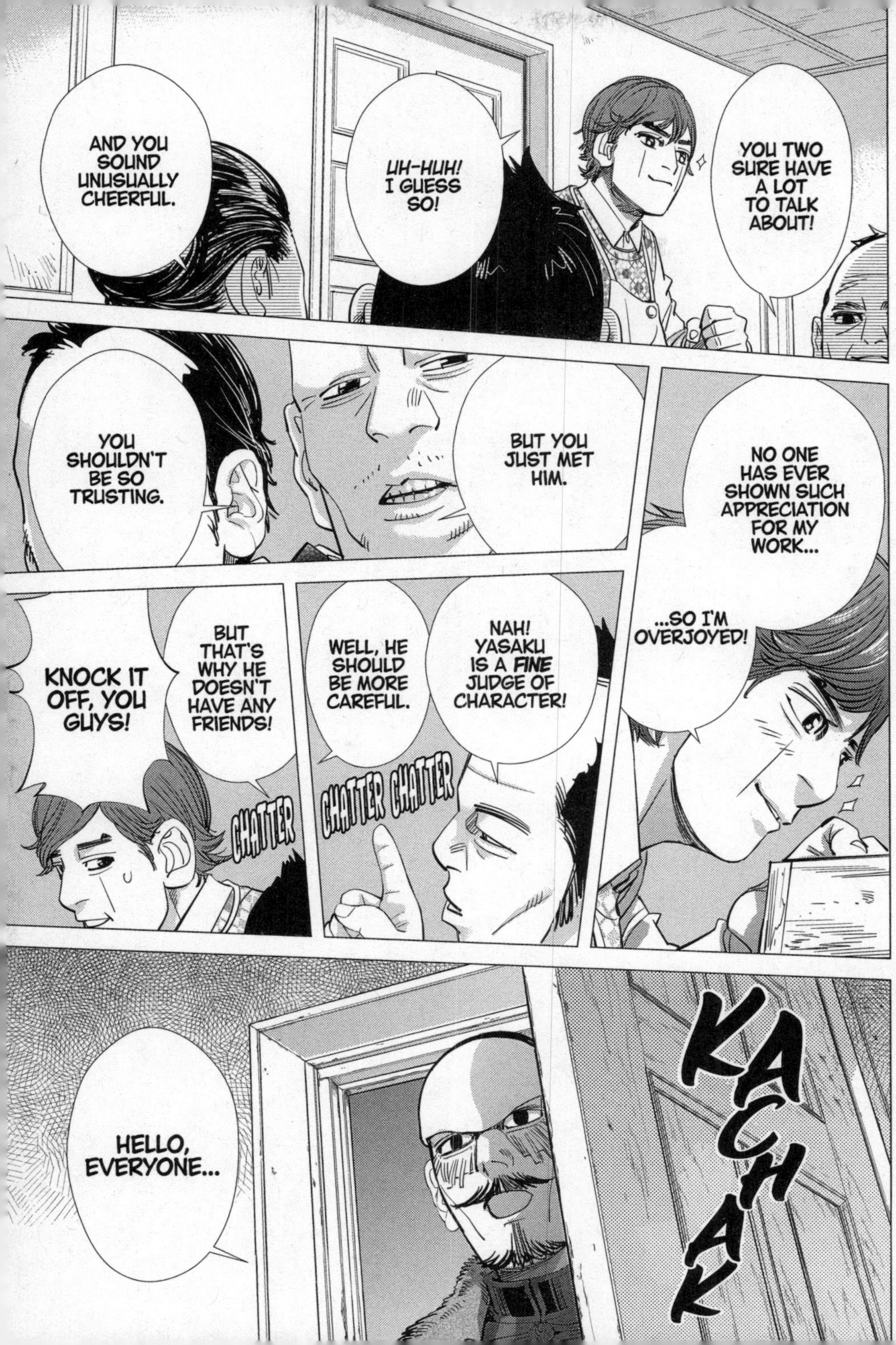
YOU TWO SURE HAVE A LOT TO TALK ABOUT!
UH-HUH! I GUESS SO!
AND YOU SOUND UNUSUALLY CHEERFUL.
NO ONE HAS EVER SHOWN SUCH APPRECIATION FOR MY WORK...
...SO I'M OVERJOYED!
BUT YOU JUST MET HIM.
YOU SHOULDN'T BE SO TRUSTING.
NAH! YASAKU IS A *FINE* JUDGE OF CHARACTER!
WELL, HE SHOULD BE MORE CAREFUL.
CHATTER CHATTER
BUT THAT'S WHY HE DOESN'T HAVE ANY FRIENDS!
KNOCK IT OFF, YOU GUYS!
CHATTER
KACHAK
HELLO, EVERYONE...

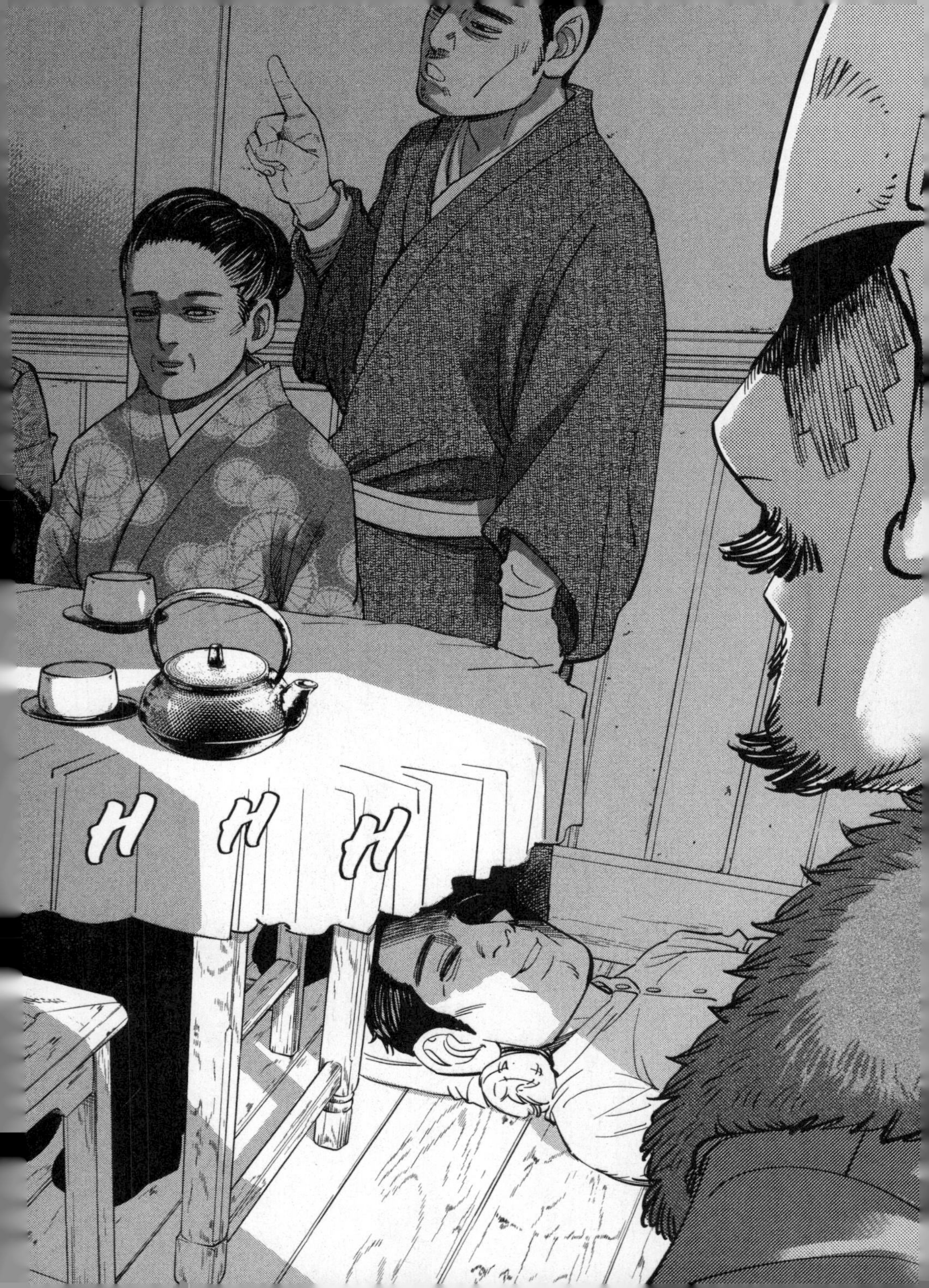
H
H
H

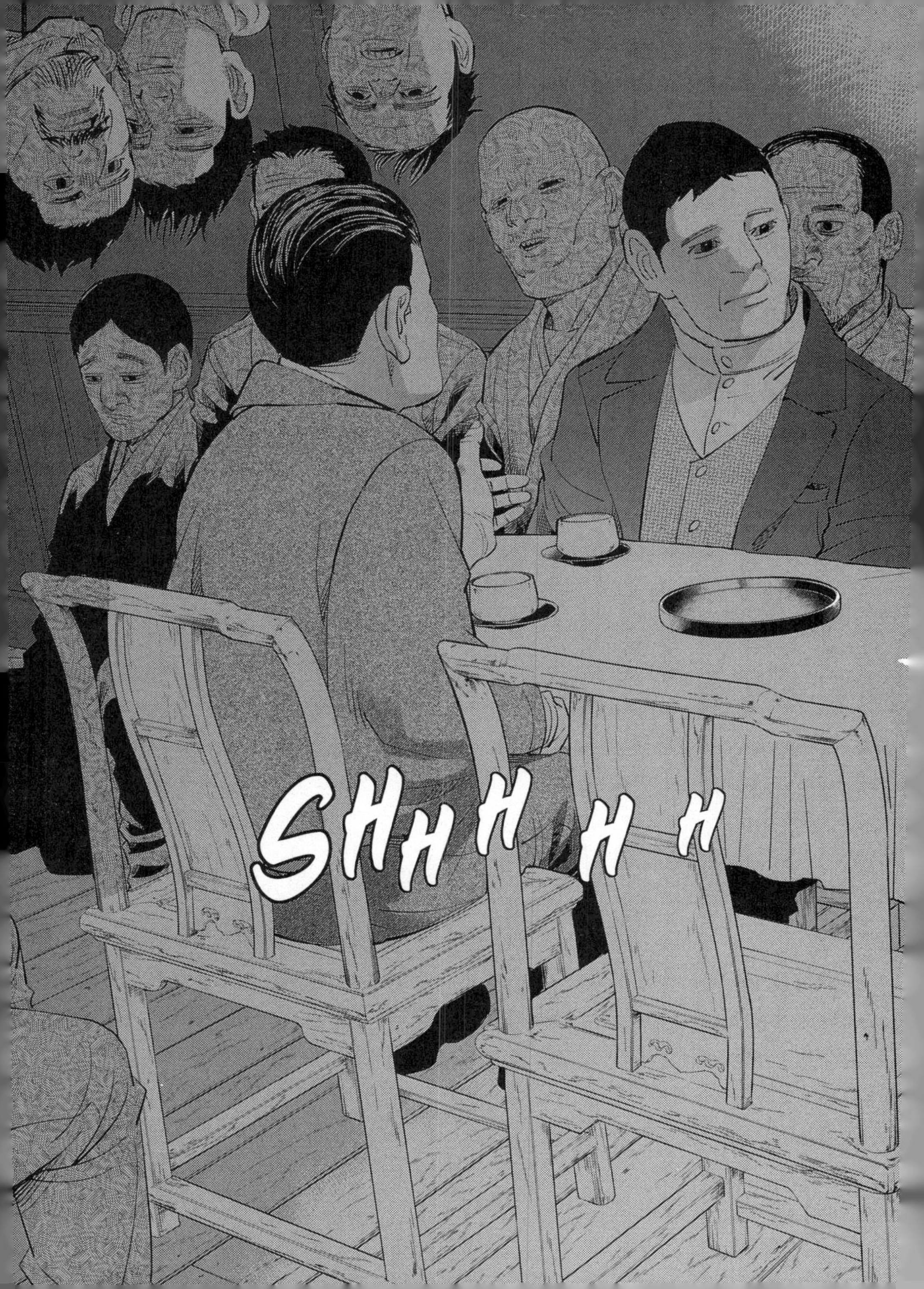
SHHHHH

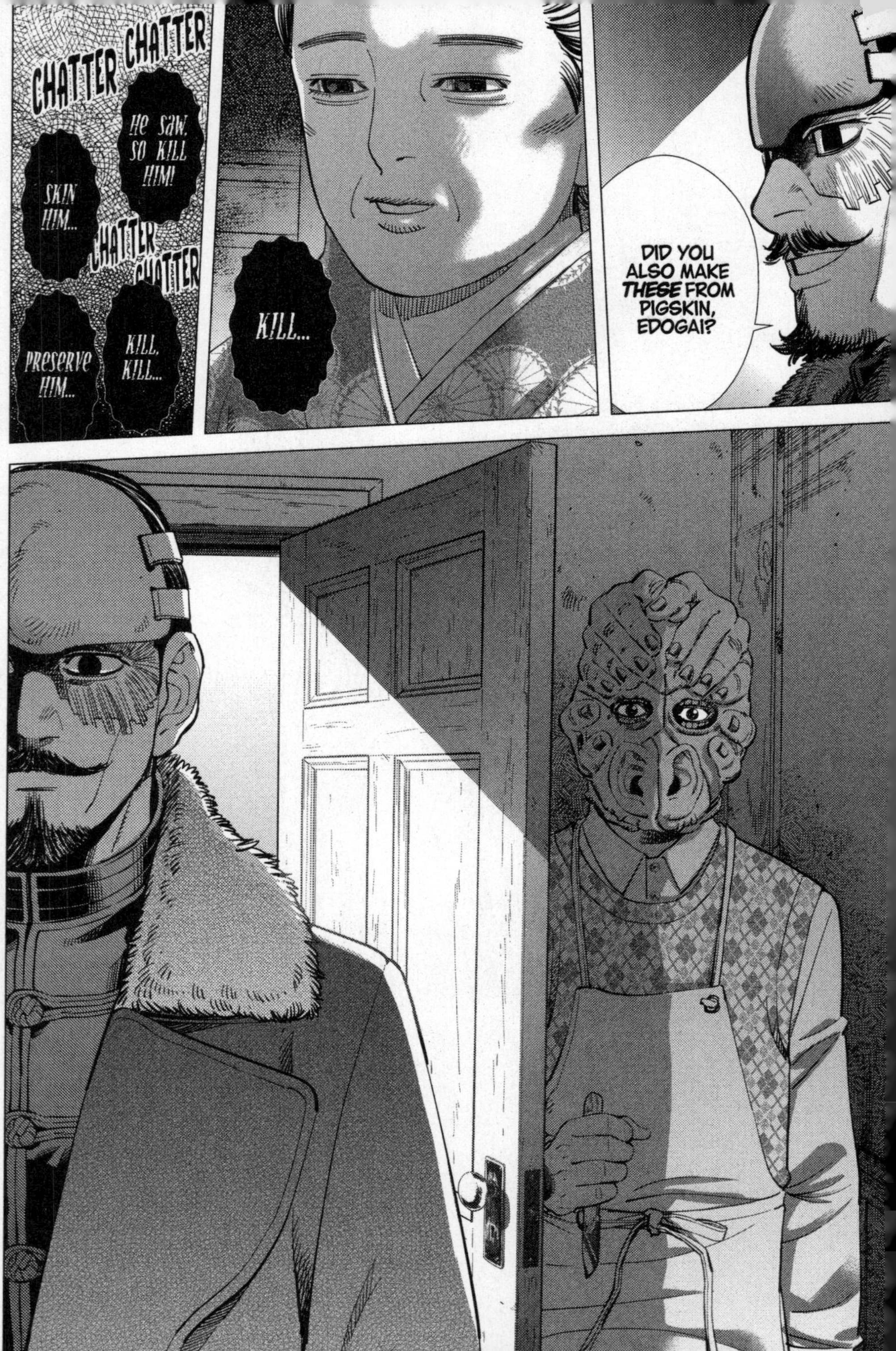
DID YOU ALSO MAKE THESE FROM PIGSKIN, EDOGAI?
KILL...
CHATTER CHATTER
He saw. So KILL HIM!
SKIN HIM...
CHATTER CHATTER
KILL. KILL...
Preserve HIM...

Chapter 72: Edogai

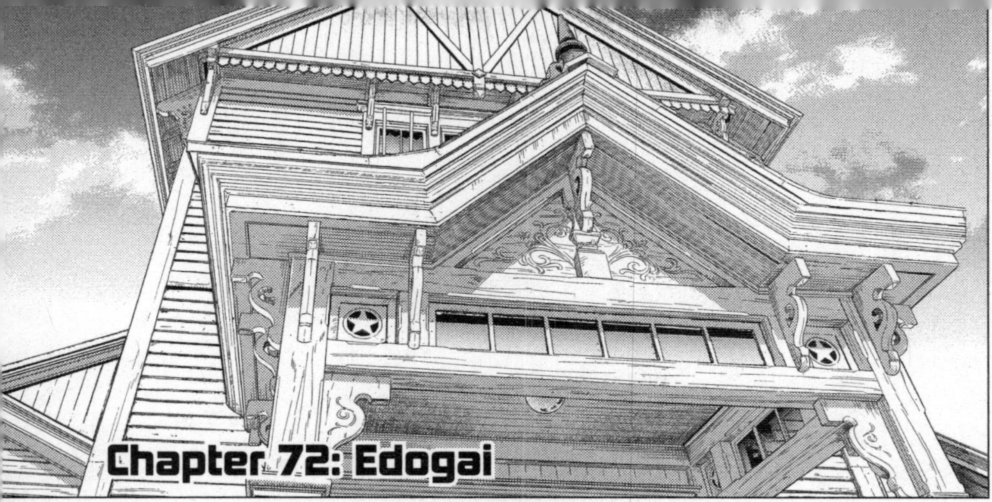

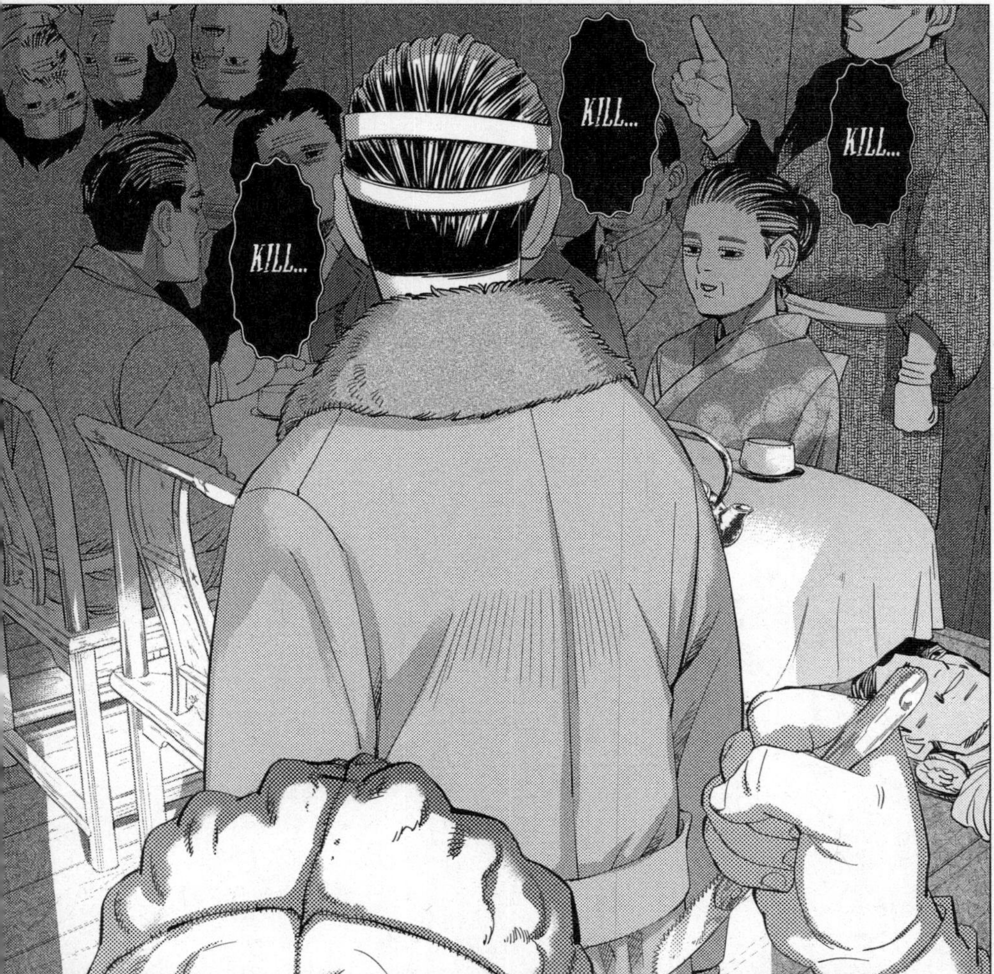
KILL...
KILL...
KILL...

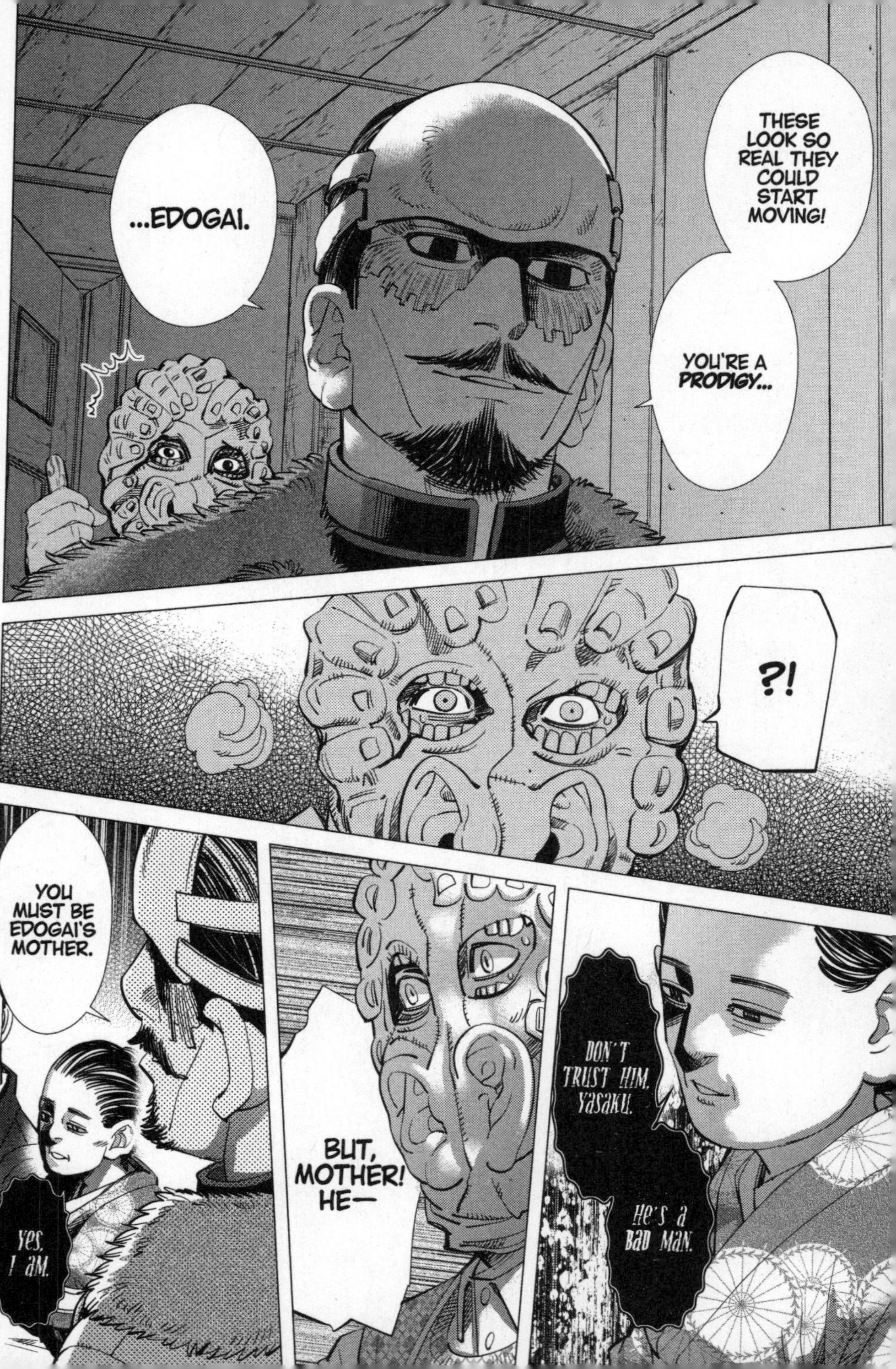
THESE LOOK SO REAL THEY COULD START MOVING!
YOU'RE A PRODIGY...
...EDOGAI.
?!
DON'T TRUST HIM, YASAKU.
HE'S A BAD MAN.
BUT, MOTHER! HE—
YOU MUST BE EDOGAI'S MOTHER.
YES, I AM.

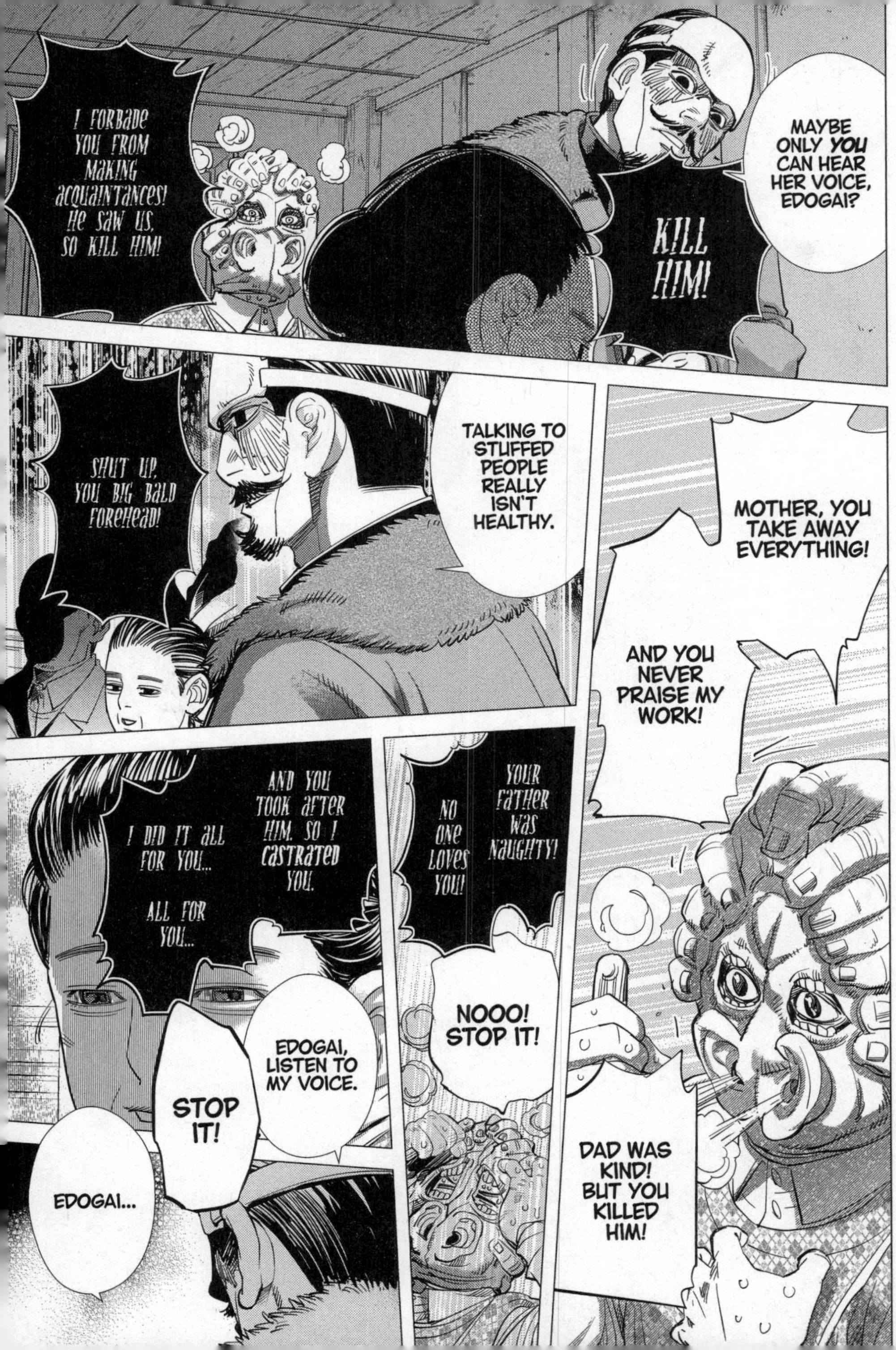
MAYBE ONLY YOU CAN HEAR HER VOICE, EDOGAI?
KILL HIM!
I FORBADE YOU FROM MAKING ACQUAINTANCES! HE SAW US, SO KILL HIM!
MOTHER, YOU TAKE AWAY EVERYTHING!
AND YOU NEVER PRAISE MY WORK!
DAD WAS KIND! BUT YOU KILLED HIM!
TALKING TO STUFFED PEOPLE REALLY ISN'T HEALTHY.
SHUT UP, YOU BIG BALD FOREHEAD!
YOUR FATHER WAS NAUGHTY!
NO ONE LOVES YOU!
NOOO! STOP IT!
AND YOU TOOK AFTER HIM, SO I CASTRATED YOU.
I DID IT ALL FOR YOU...
ALL FOR YOU...
EDOGAI, LISTEN TO MY VOICE.
STOP IT!
EDOGAI...

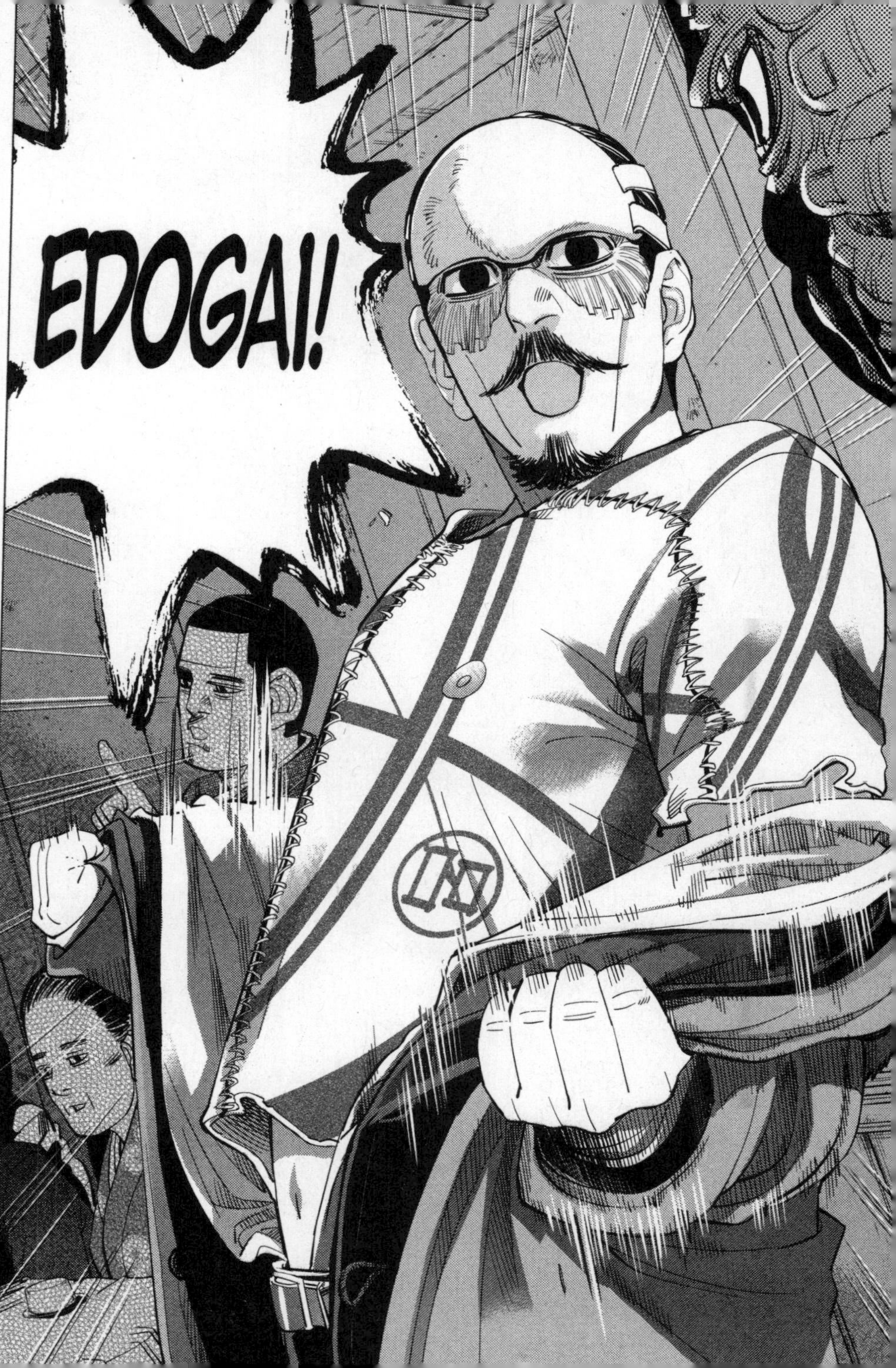
EDOGAI!

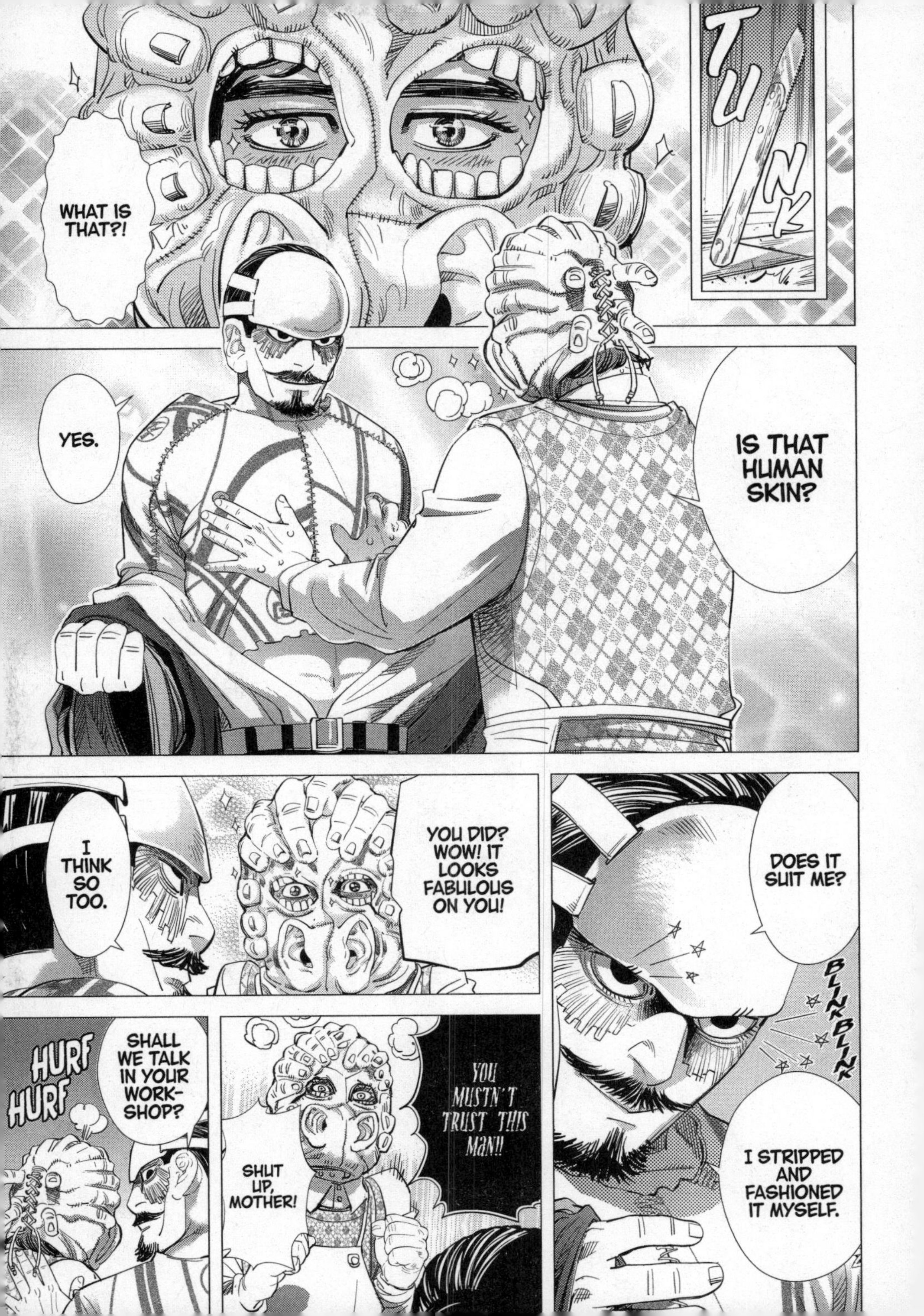
TUNK
WHAT IS THAT?!
IS THAT HUMAN SKIN?
YES.
DOES IT SUIT ME?
BLINK BLINK
I STRIPPED AND FASHIONED IT MYSELF.
YOU DID? WOW! IT LOOKS FABULOUS ON YOU!
I THINK SO TOO.
YOU MUSTN'T TRUST THIS MAN!!
SHUT UP, MOTHER!
SHALL WE TALK IN YOUR WORK-SHOP?
HURF HURF

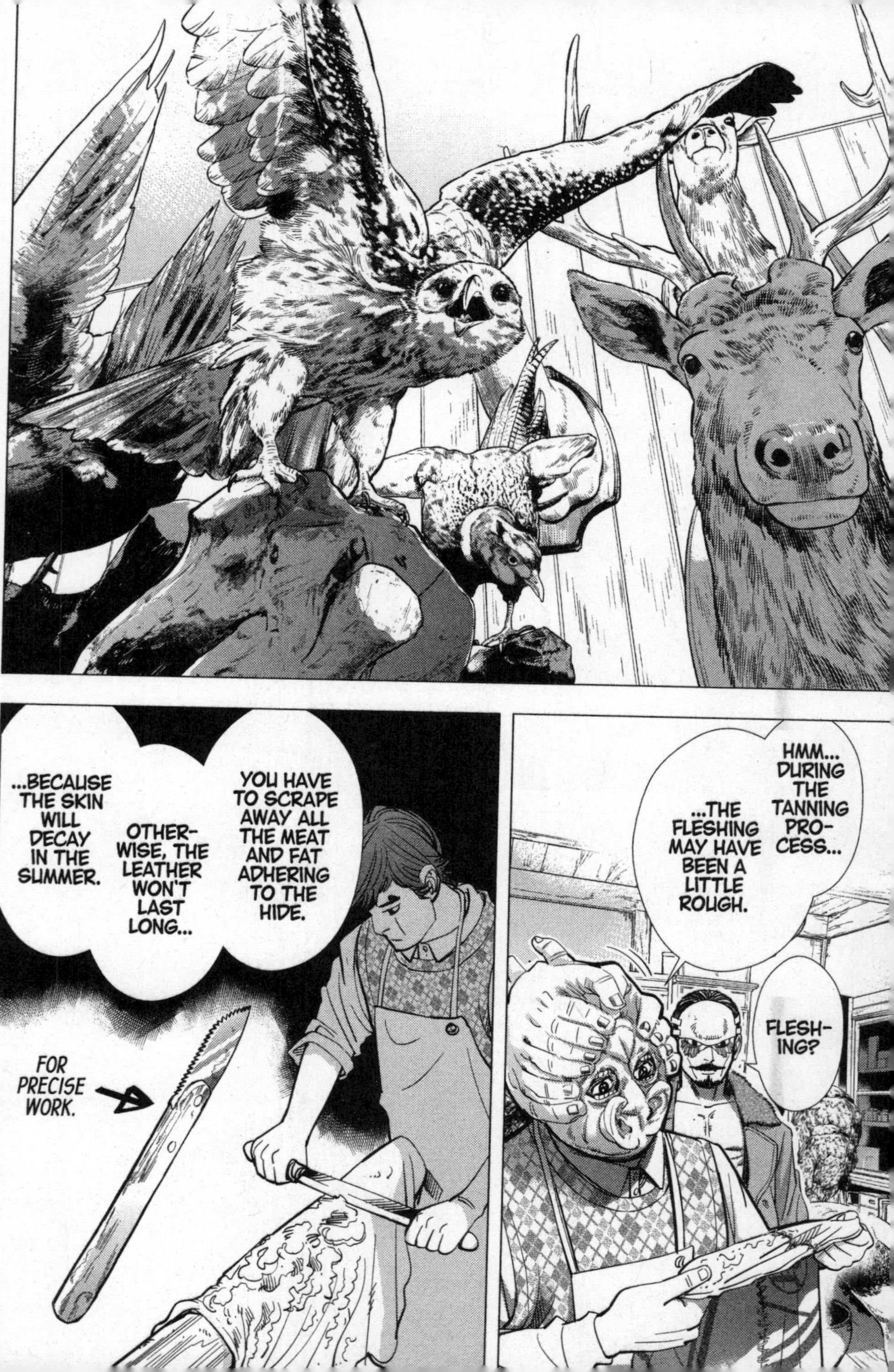
HMM... DURING THE TANNING PROCESS...
...THE FLESHING MAY HAVE BEEN A LITTLE ROUGH.
FLESHING?
YOU HAVE TO SCRAPE AWAY ALL THE MEAT AND FAT ADHERING TO THE HIDE.
OTHERWISE, THE LEATHER WON'T LAST LONG...
...BECAUSE THE SKIN WILL DECAY IN THE SUMMER.
FOR PRECISE WORK.

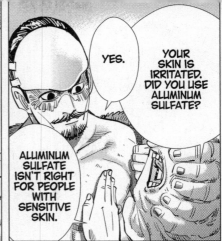

YOUR SKIN IS IRRITATED. DID YOU USE ALUMINUM SULFATE?
YES.
ALUMINUM SULFATE ISN'T RIGHT FOR PEOPLE WITH SENSITIVE SKIN.
ALUMINUM SULFATE TANNING IS AN EASY METHOD THAT MANY HUNTERS USE.
OTHER METHODS INCLUDE CHROME TANNING FROM GERMANY.
IT'S GOOD FOR MASS PRODUCTION BECAUSE IT'S CHEAP.
BUT THOSE PROCESSES ARE NO GOOD BECAUSE THEY USE CHEMICALS.
I RECOMMEND TANNIN TANNING...
...WHICH USES TANNIN FROM STACHYURUS PRAECOX FRUIT.
IT'S ORGANIC, SO IT WON'T IRRITATE YOUR SKIN.
THE INITIAL PRODUCT IS STIFF, BUT IT WILL SOFTEN WITH USE.
WITH CHROME, IT'S SOFT AT FIRST BUT GRADUALLY HARDENS.
BLAH BLAH
BLAH
EDOGAI...
...WOULD YOU SHOW ME YOUR OTHER DESIGNS?
OH, MAY I?!
ULP

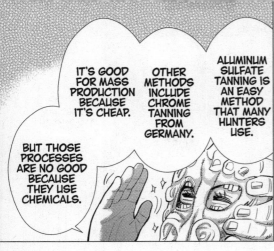

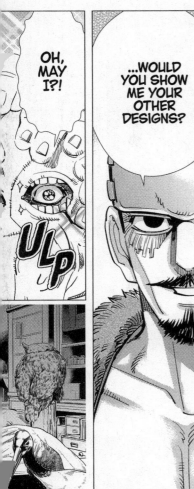

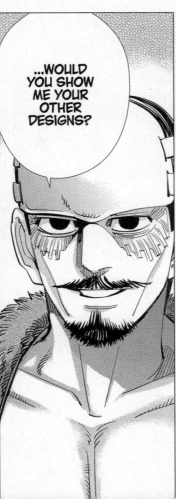

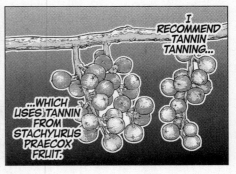

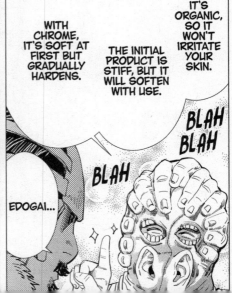

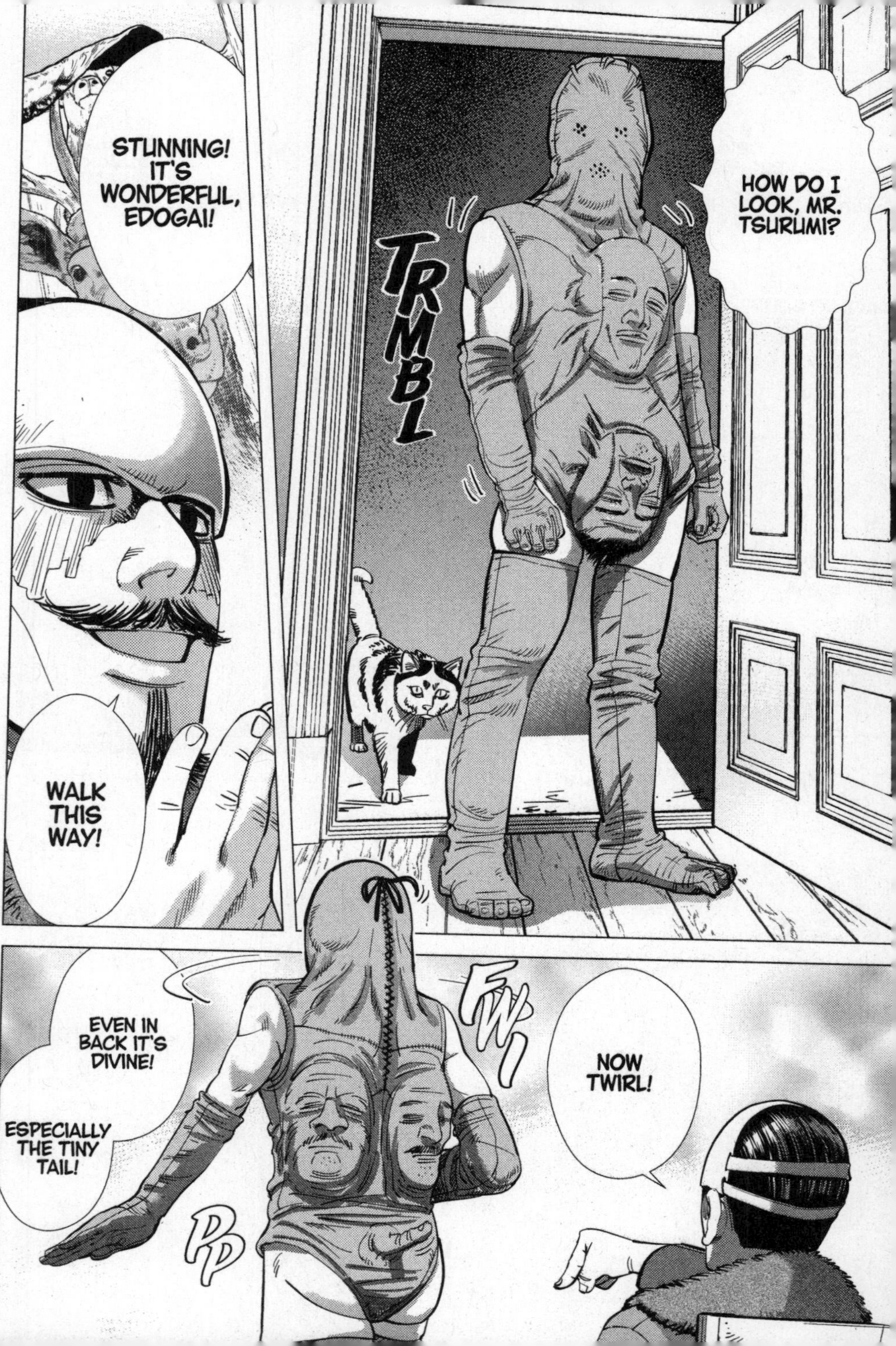
HOW DO I LOOK, MR. TSURUMI?
TRMBL
STUNNING! IT'S WONDERFUL, EDOGAI!
WALK THIS WAY!
NOW TWIRL!
FWI
EVEN IN BACK IT'S DIVINE!
ESPECIALLY THE TINY TAIL!
PP

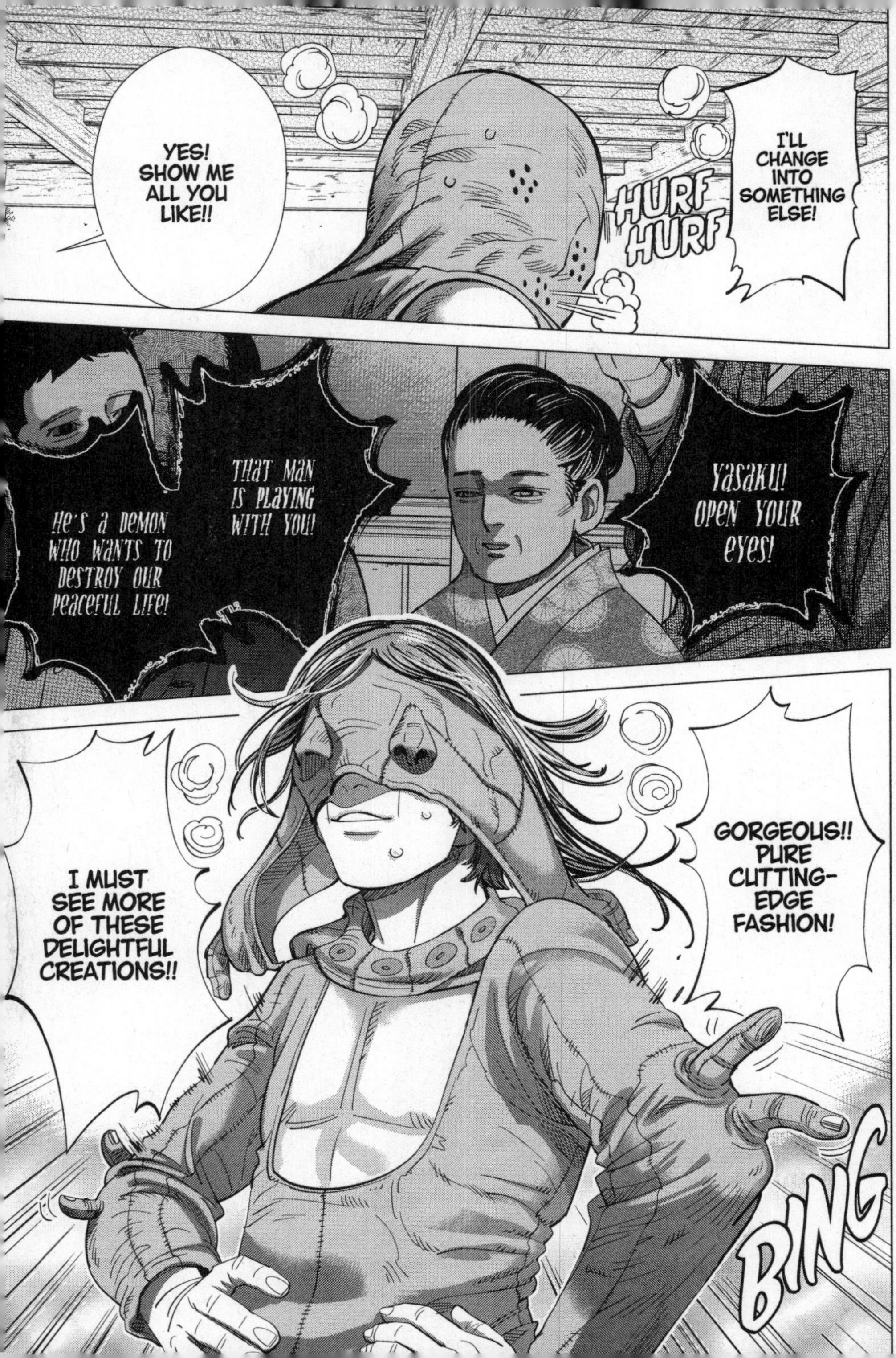
I'LL CHANGE INTO SOMETHING ELSE!
HURF HURF
YES! SHOW ME ALL YOU LIKE!!
YASAKU! OPEN YOUR EYES!
THAT MAN IS PLAYING WITH YOU!
HE'S A DEMON WHO WANTS TO DESTROY OUR PEACEFUL LIFE!
GORGEOUS!! PURE CUTTING-EDGE FASHION!
BING
I MUST SEE MORE OF THESE DELIGHTFUL CREATIONS!!

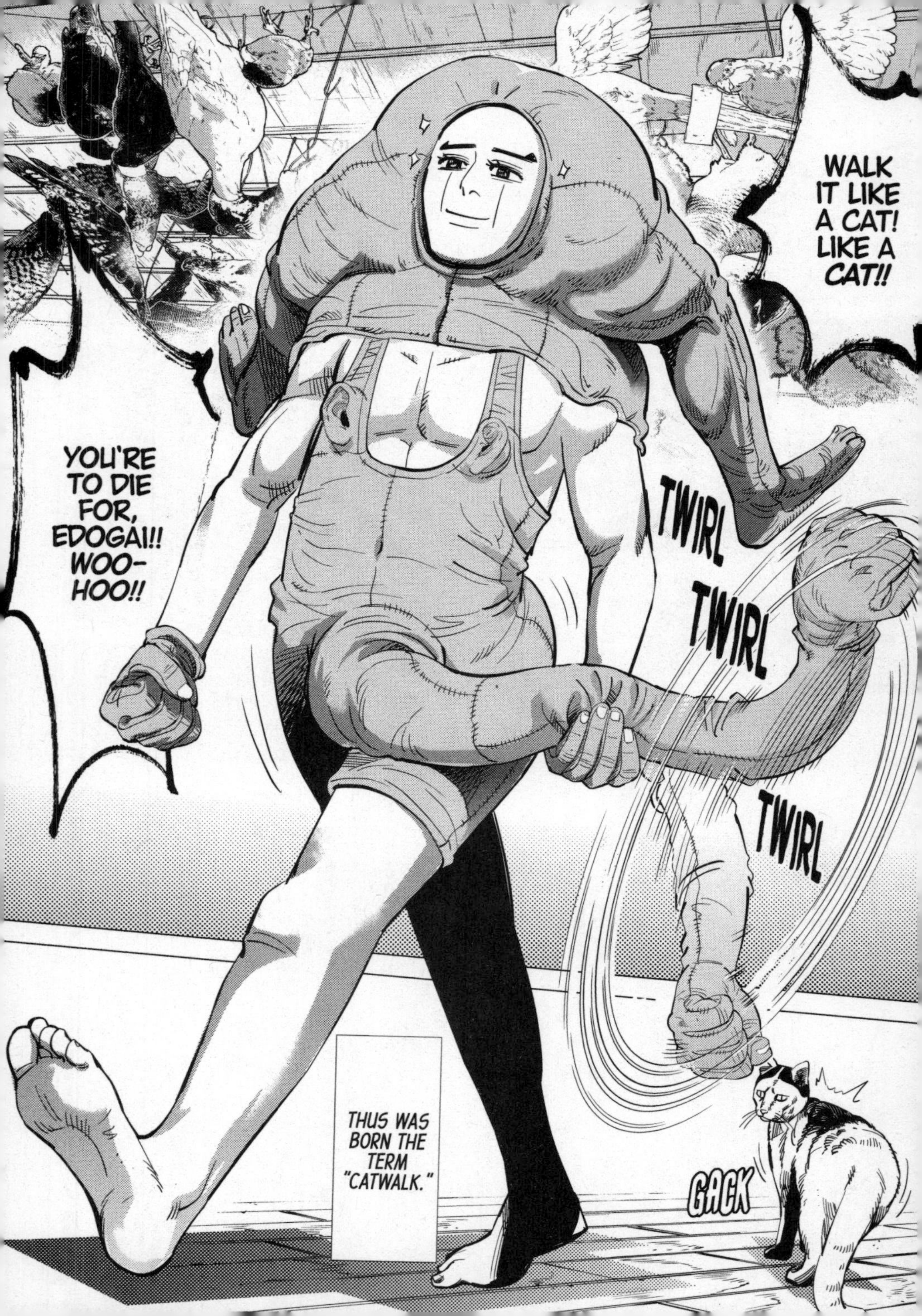
WALK IT LIKE A CAT! LIKE A CAT!!
YOU'RE TO DIE FOR, EDOGAI!! WOO-HOO!!
TWIRL
TWIRL
TWIRL
THUS WAS BORN THE TERM "CATWALK."
GACK

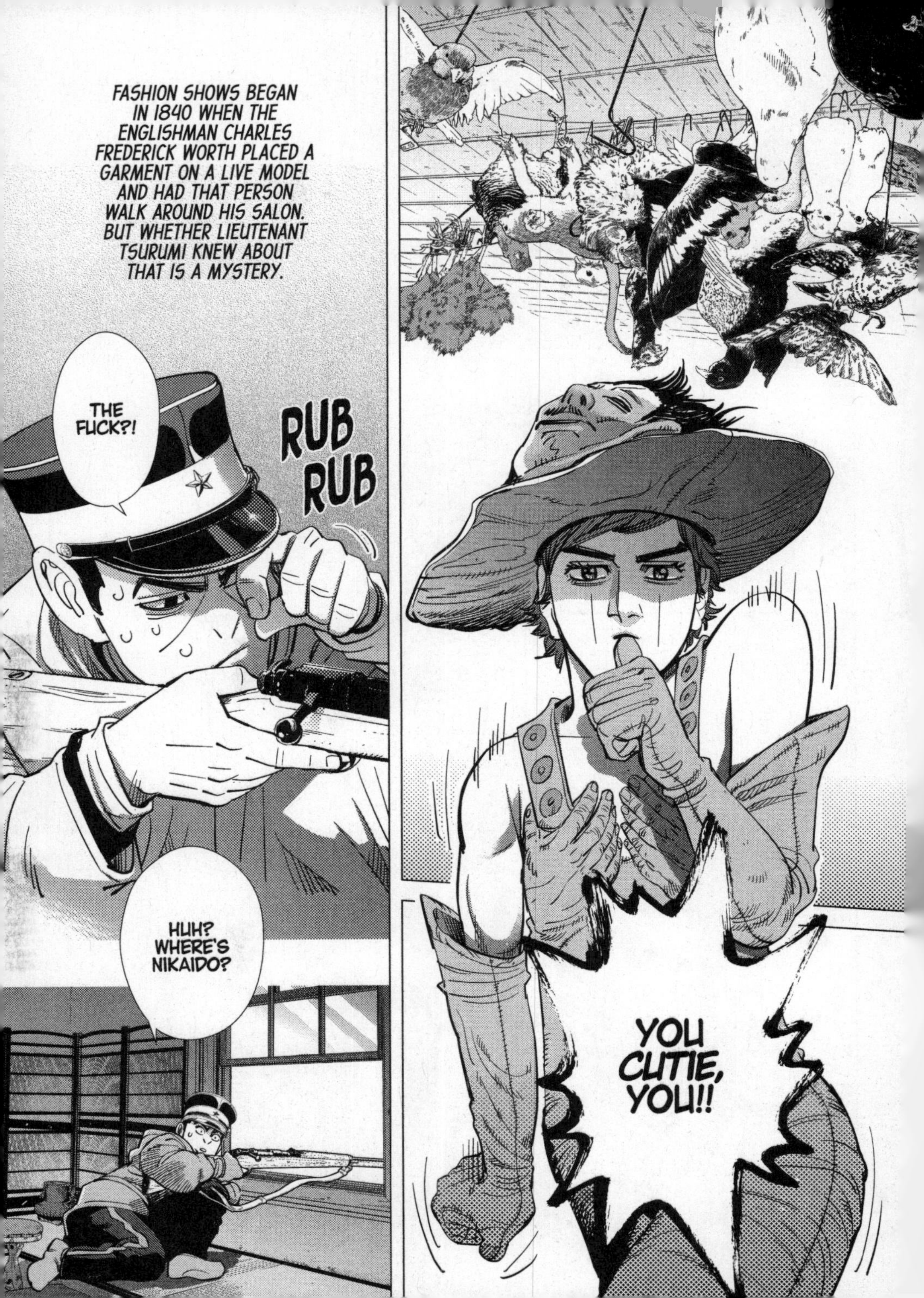
YOU CUTIE, YOU!!
FASHION SHOWS BEGAN IN 1840 WHEN THE ENGLISHMAN CHARLES FREDERICK WORTH PLACED A GARMENT ON A LIVE MODEL AND HAD THAT PERSON WALK AROUND HIS SALON. BUT WHETHER LIEUTENANT TSURUMI KNEW ABOUT THAT IS A MYSTERY.
THE FUCK?!
RUB RUB
HUH? WHERE'S NIKAIDO?

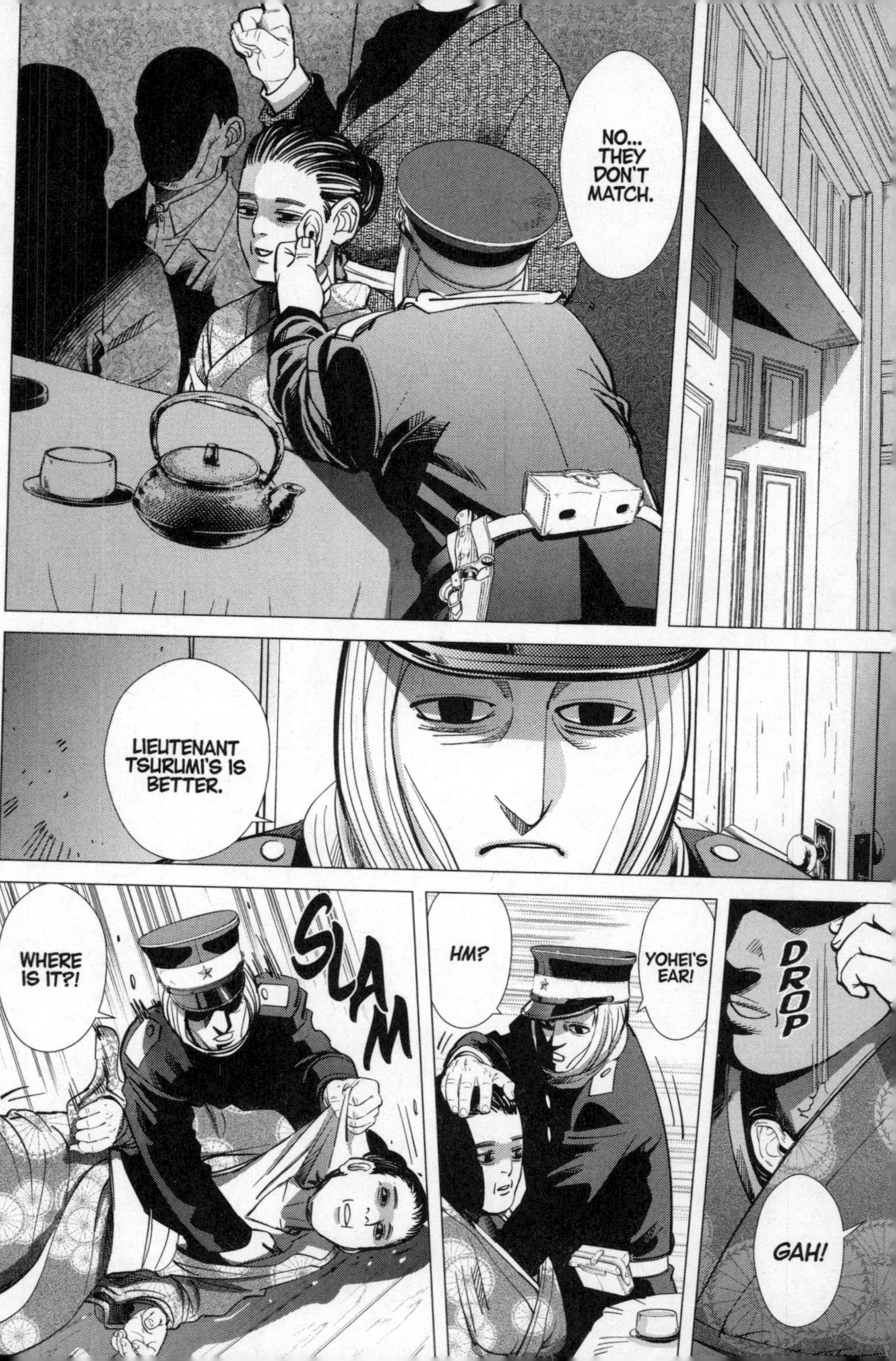
NO... THEY DON'T MATCH.
LIEUTENANT TSURUMI'S IS BETTER.
DROP
GAH!
YOHEI'S EAR!
HM?
SLAM
WHERE IS IT?!

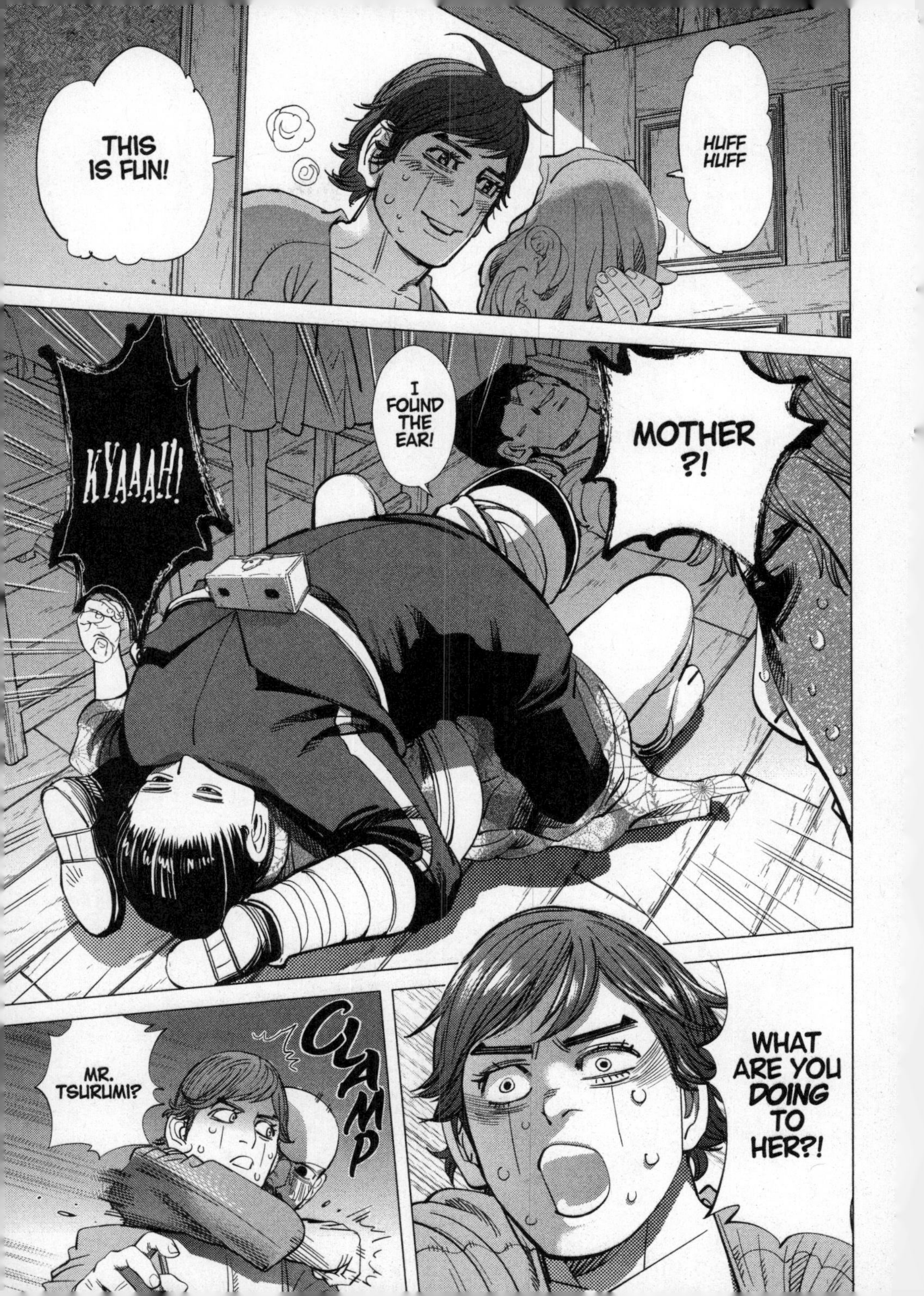
HUFF HUFF
THIS IS FUN!
MOTHER?!
I FOUND THE EAR!
KYAAAH!
WHAT ARE YOU DOING TO HER?!
CLAMP
MR. TSURUMI?

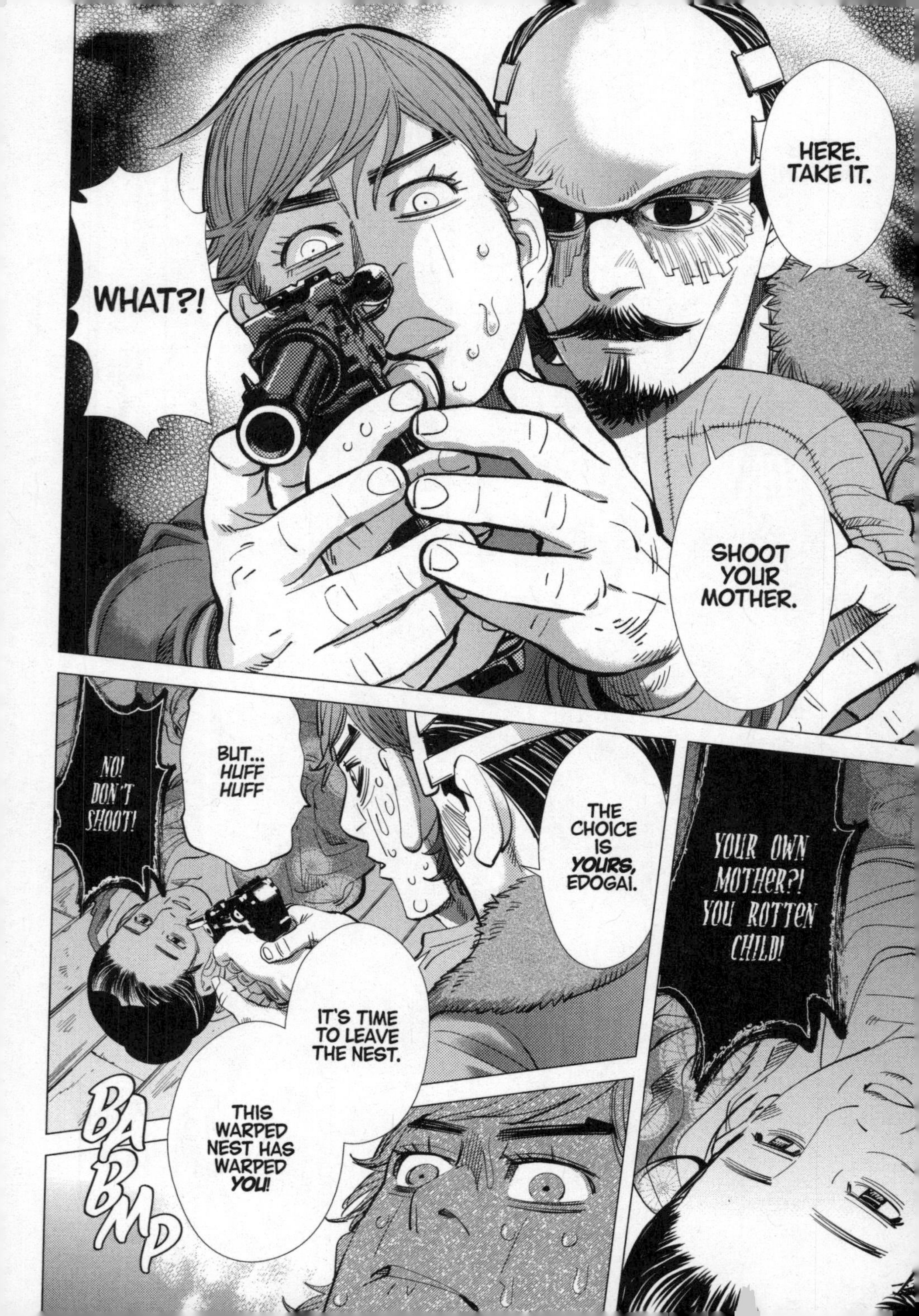
HERE. TAKE IT.
WHAT?!
SHOOT YOUR MOTHER.
YOUR OWN MOTHER?! YOU ROTTEN CHILD!
THE CHOICE IS *YOURS*, EDOGAI.
BUT... HUFF HUFF
NO! DON'T SHOOT!
IT'S TIME TO LEAVE THE NEST.
THIS WARPED NEST HAS WARPED *YOU*!
BABUMP

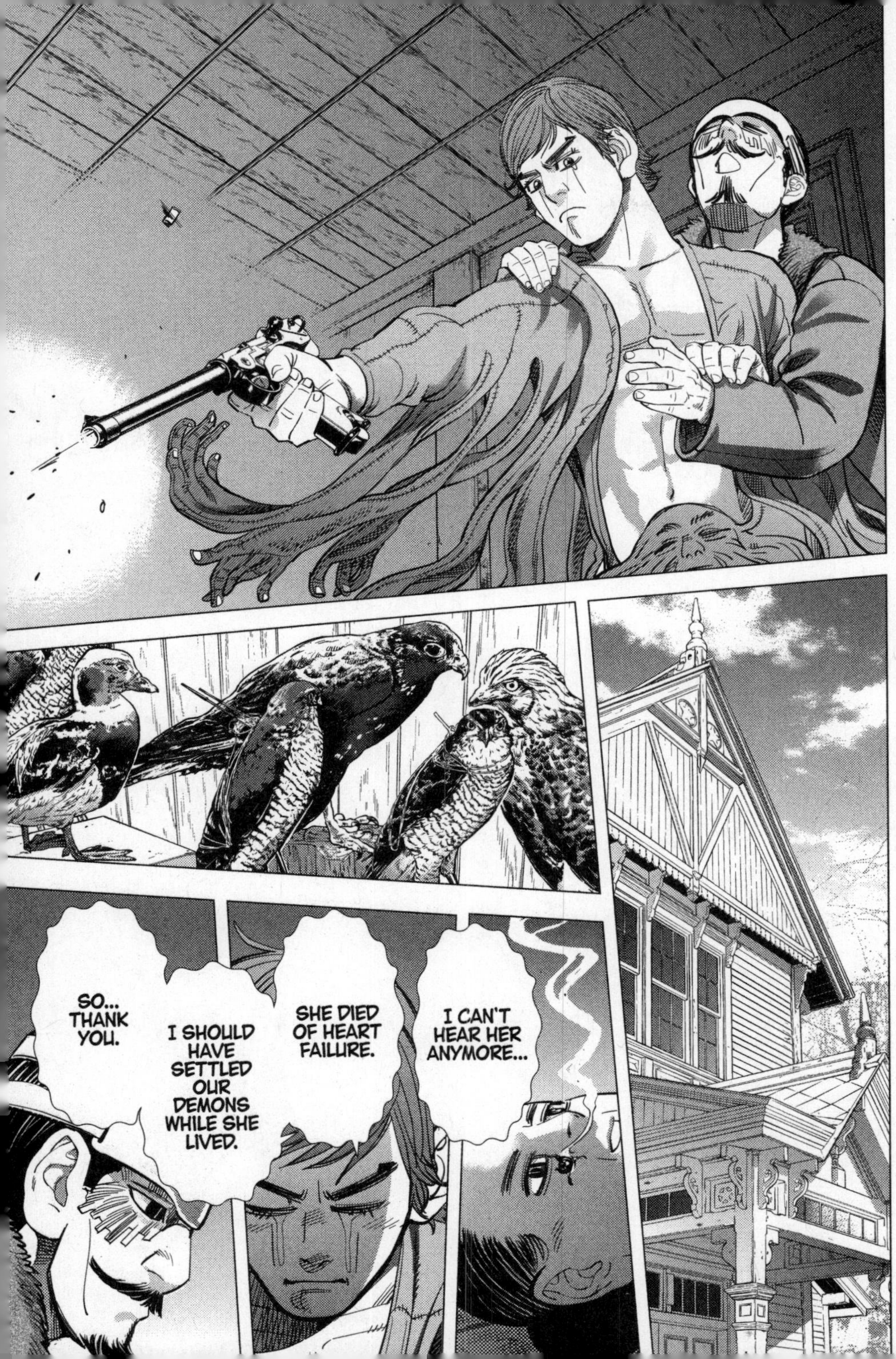
I CAN'T HEAR HER ANYMORE...
SHE DIED OF HEART FAILURE.
I SHOULD HAVE SETTLED OUR DEMONS WHILE SHE LIVED.
SO... THANK YOU.

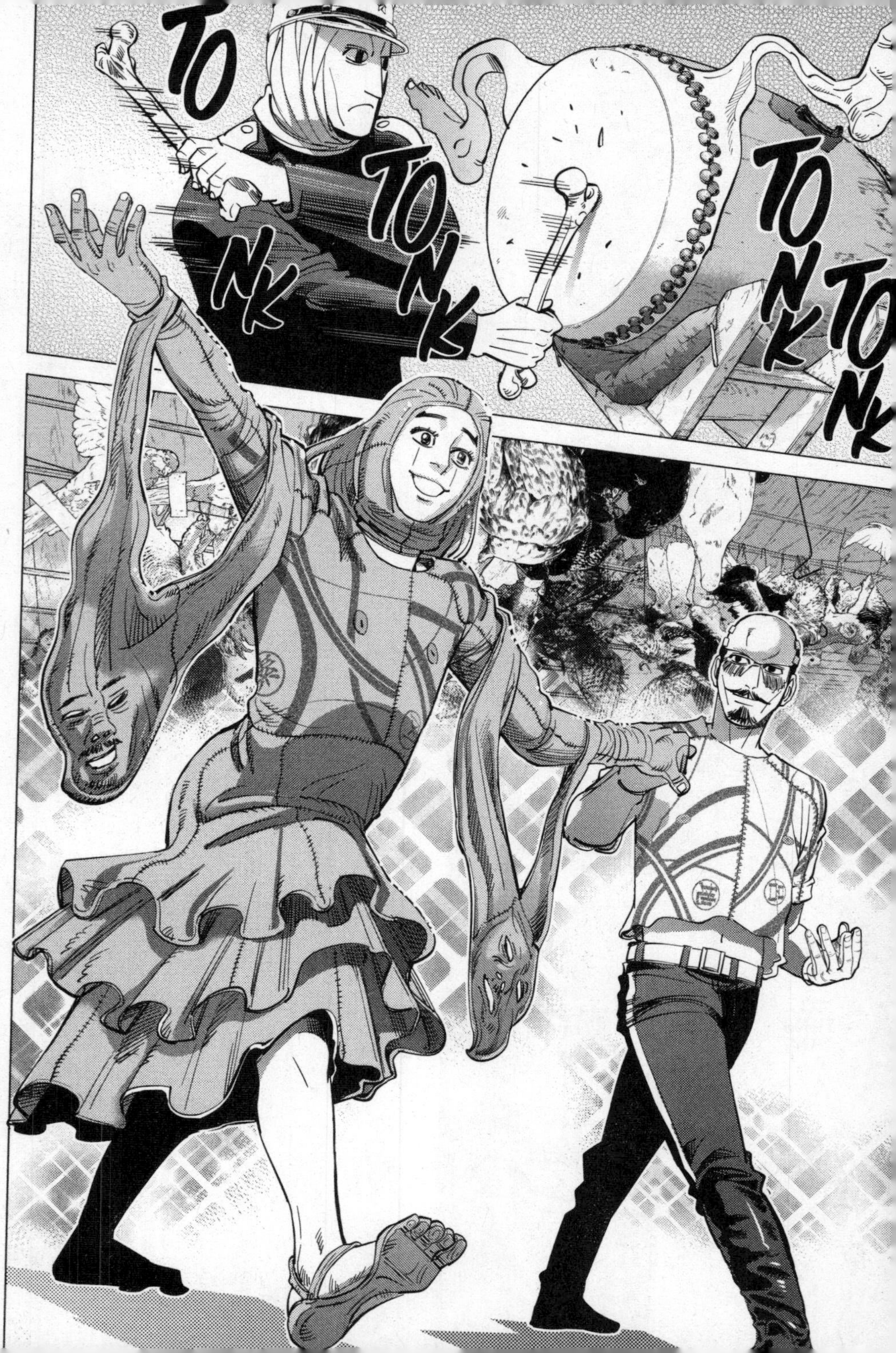
TONK
TONK
TONK
TONK

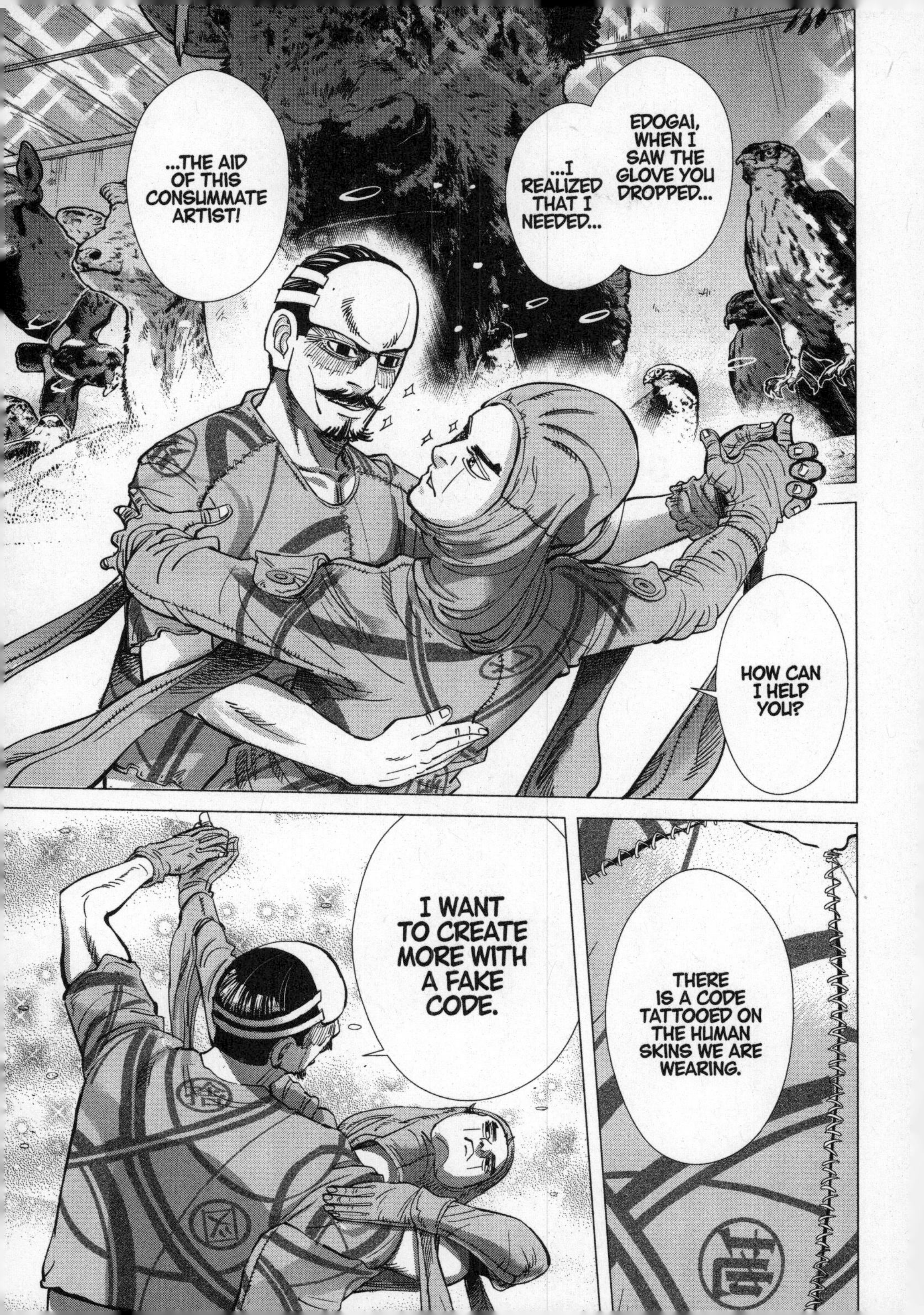
EDOGAI, WHEN I SAW THE GLOVE YOU DROPPED...
...I REALIZED THAT I NEEDED...
...THE AID OF THIS CONSUMMATE ARTIST!
HOW CAN I HELP YOU?
THERE IS A CODE TATTOOED ON THE HUMAN SKINS WE ARE WEARING.
I WANT TO CREATE MORE WITH A FAKE CODE.

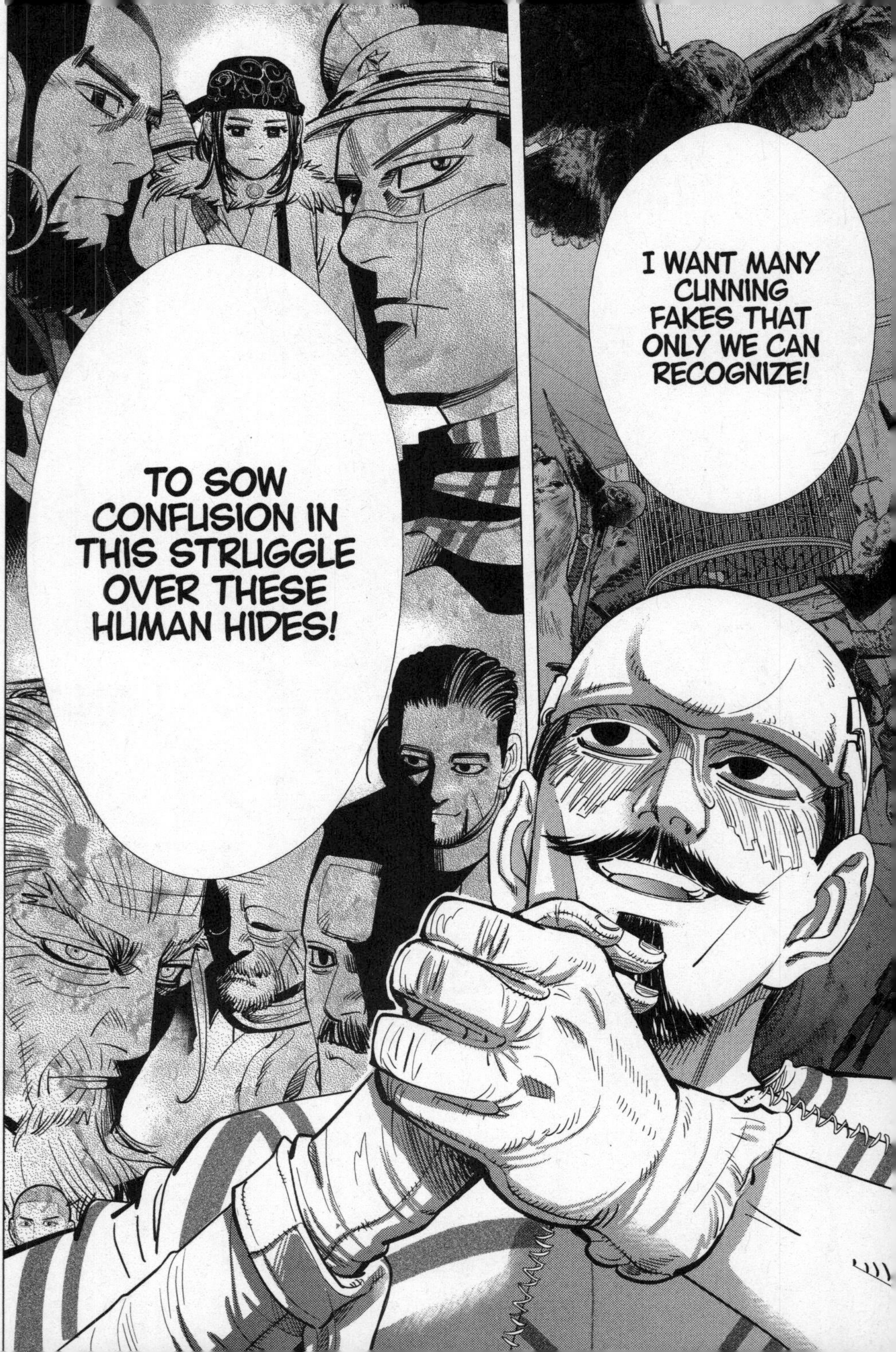
I WANT MANY CUNNING FAKES THAT ONLY WE CAN RECOGNIZE!
TO SOW CONFUSION IN THIS STRUGGLE OVER THESE HUMAN HIDES!

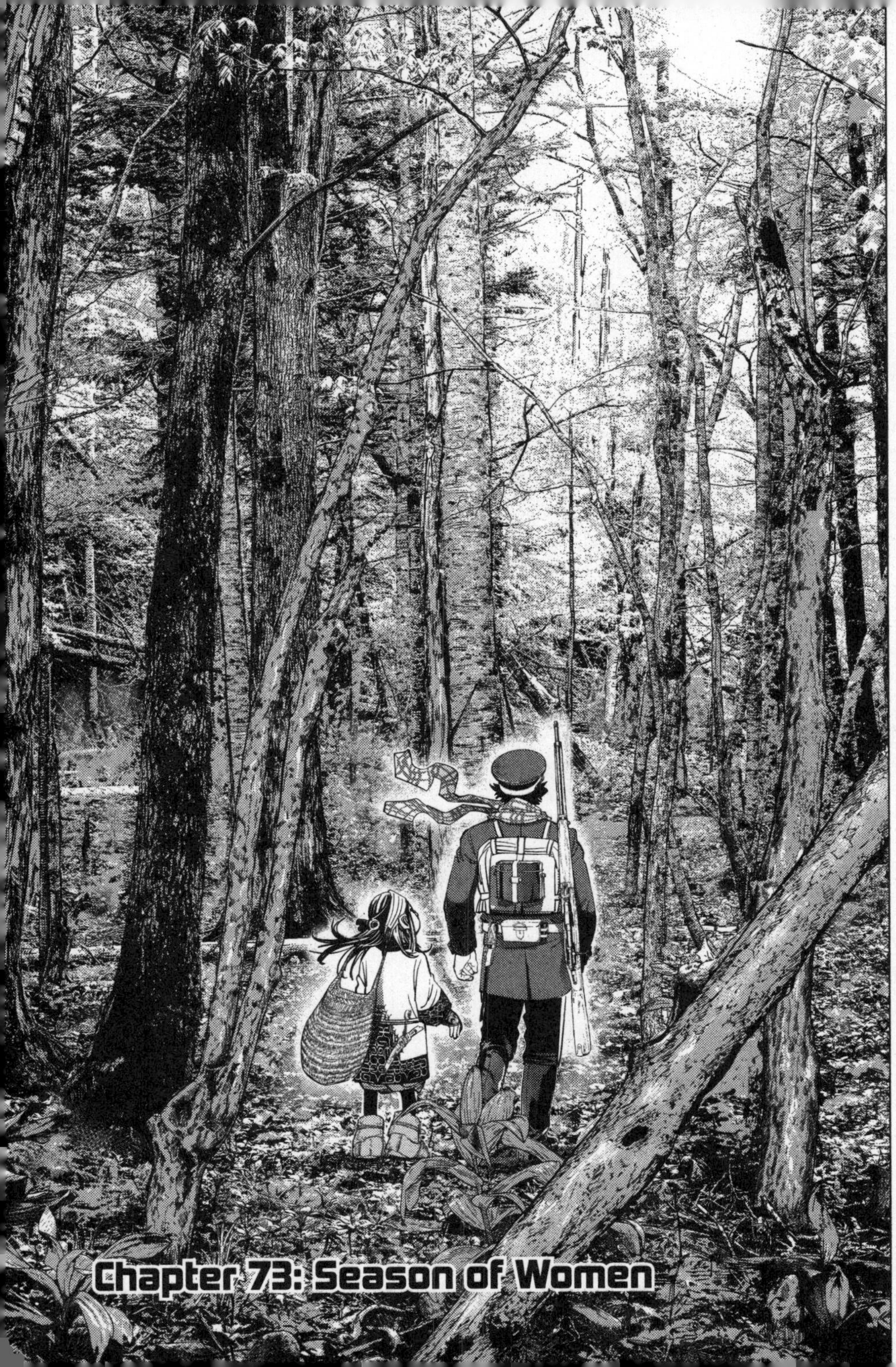
Chapter 73: Season of Women

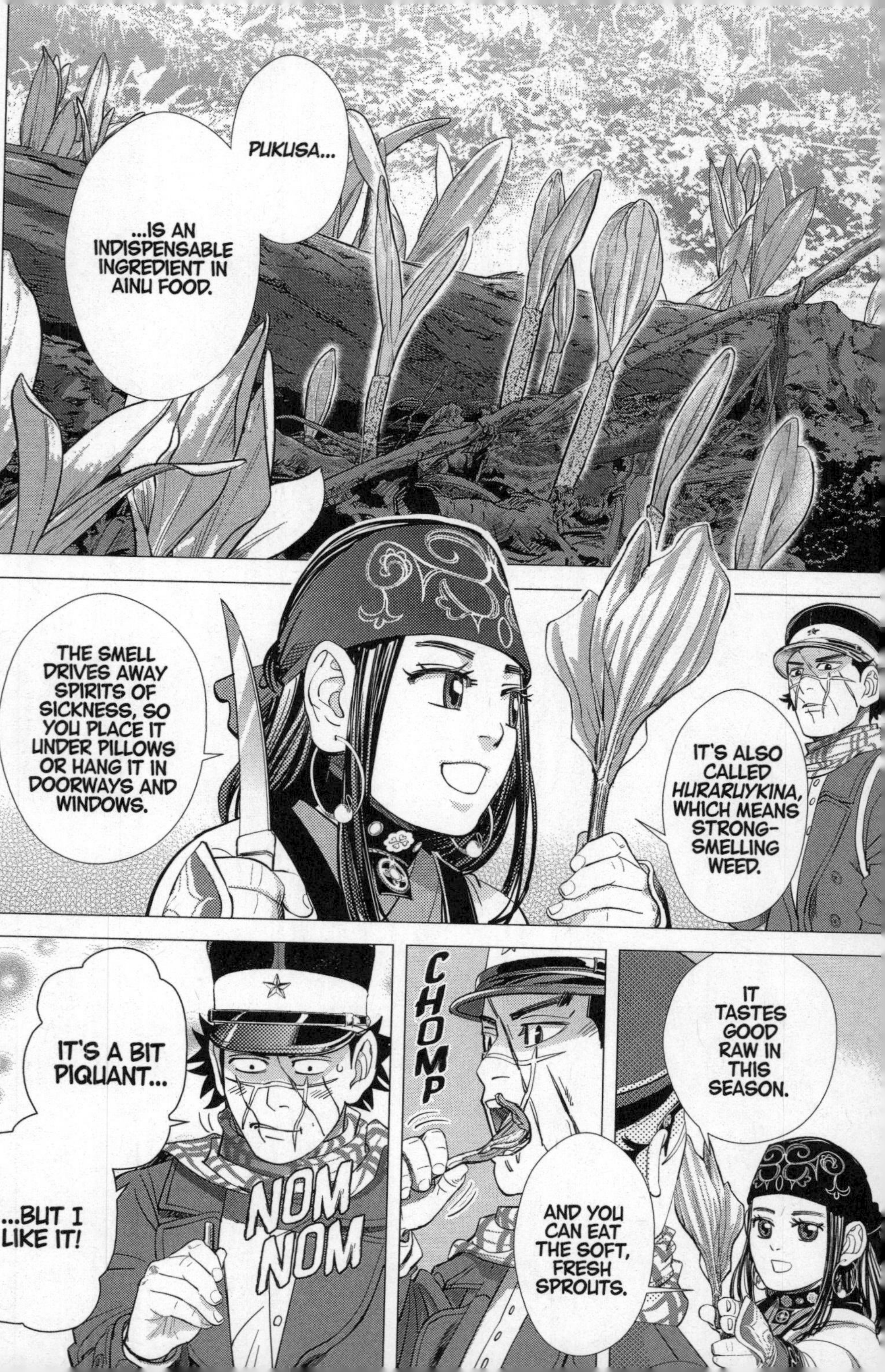
PUKUSA...
...IS AN INDISPENSABLE INGREDIENT IN AINU FOOD.
IT'S ALSO CALLED HURARUYKINA, WHICH MEANS STRONG-SMELLING WEED.
THE SMELL DRIVES AWAY SPIRITS OF SICKNESS, SO YOU PLACE IT UNDER PILLOWS OR HANG IT IN DOORWAYS AND WINDOWS.
IT TASTES GOOD RAW IN THIS SEASON.
AND YOU CAN EAT THE SOFT, FRESH SPROUTS.
CHOMP
IT'S A BIT PIQUANT...
NOM NOM
...BUT I LIKE IT!

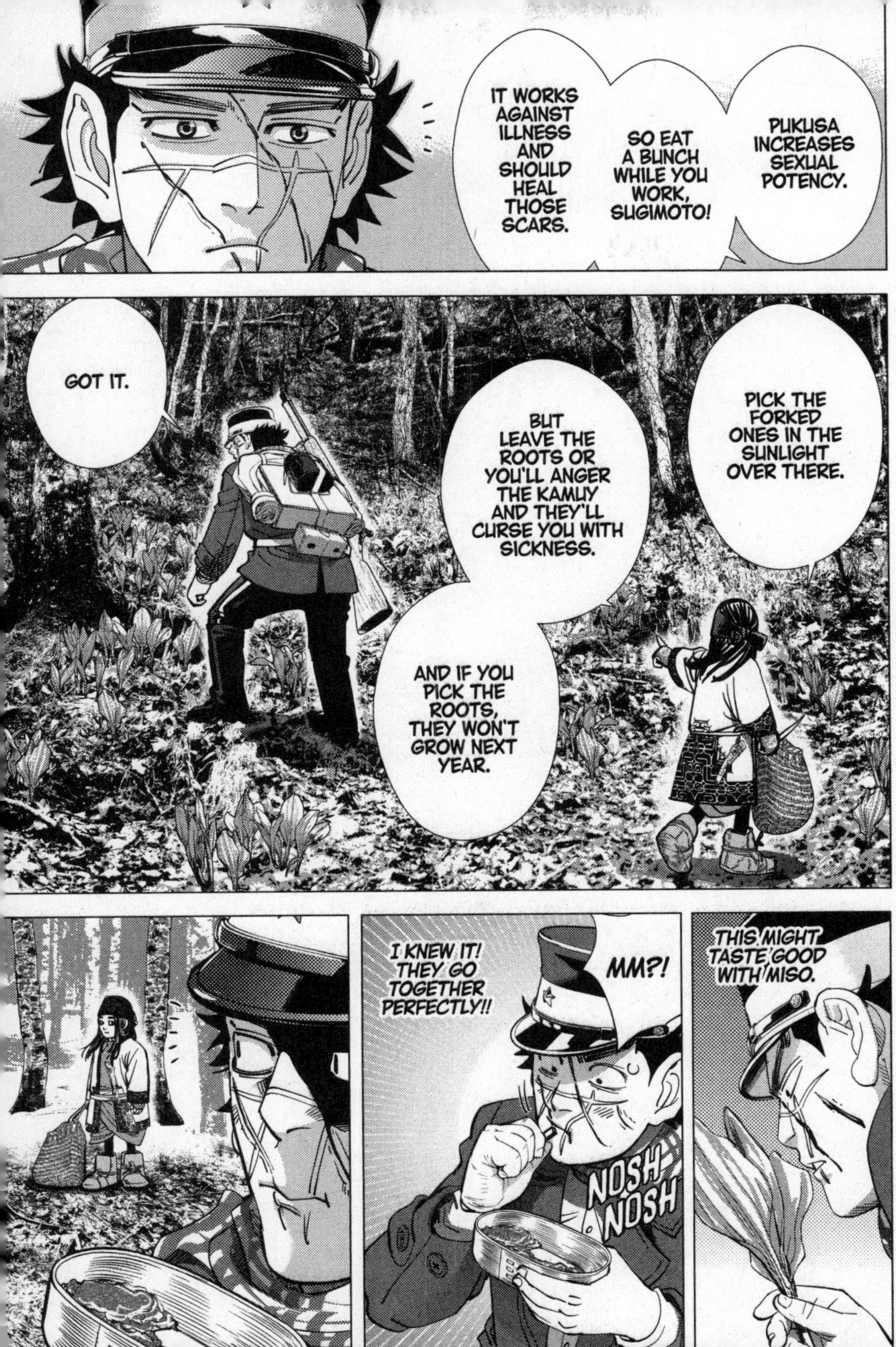
PUKUSA INCREASES SEXUAL POTENCY.
SO EAT A BUNCH WHILE YOU WORK, SUGIMOTO!
IT WORKS AGAINST ILLNESS AND SHOULD HEAL THOSE SCARS.
PICK THE FORKED ONES IN THE SUNLIGHT OVER THERE.
BUT LEAVE THE ROOTS OR YOU'LL ANGER THE KAMUY AND THEY'LL CURSE YOU WITH SICKNESS.
AND IF YOU PICK THE ROOTS, THEY WON'T GROW NEXT YEAR.
GOT IT.
THIS MIGHT TASTE GOOD WITH MISO.
MM?!
I KNEW IT! THEY GO TOGETHER PERFECTLY!!
NOSH NOSH

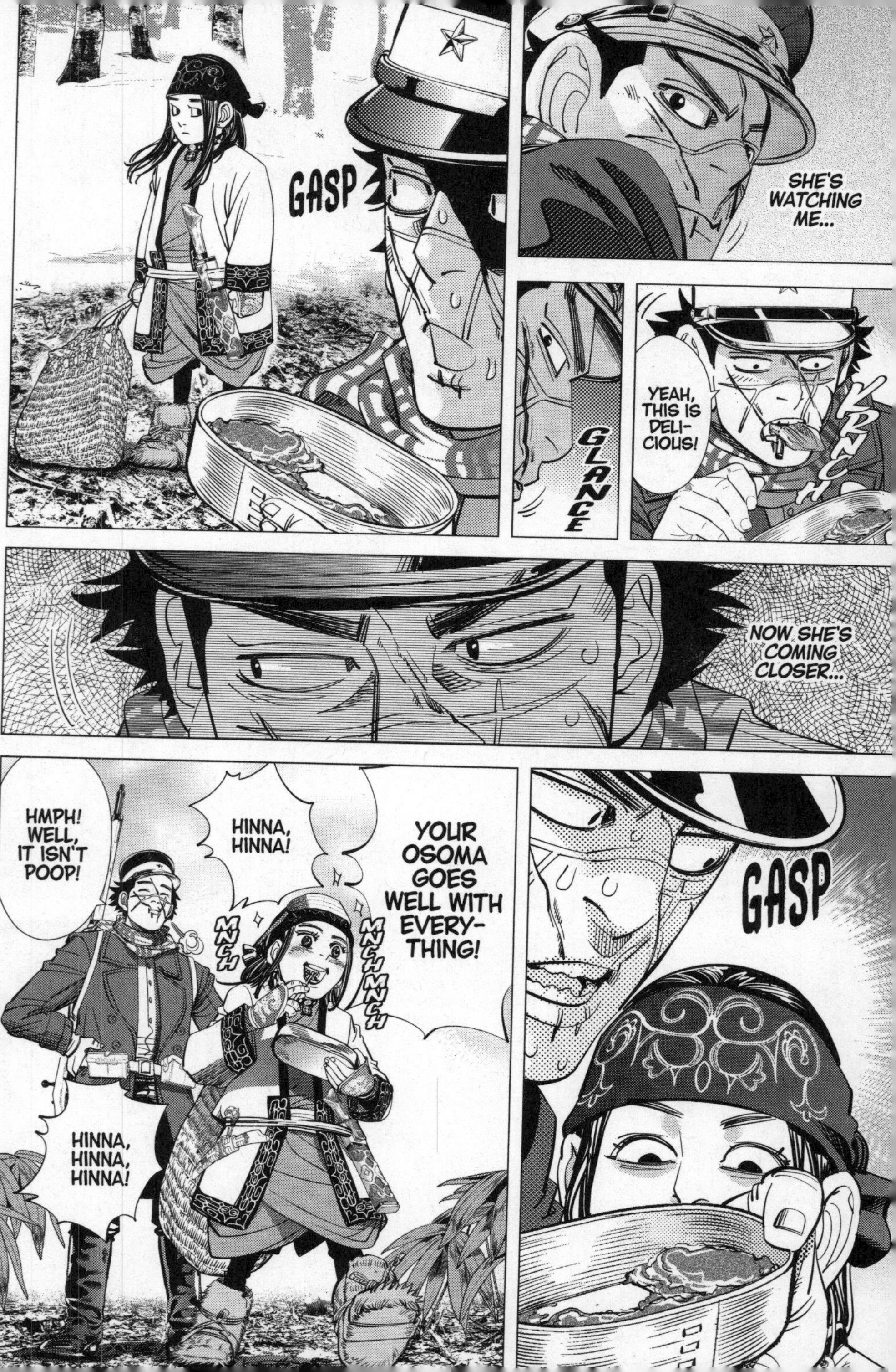

SHE'S WATCHING ME...
YEAH, THIS IS DELICIOUS!
KRNCH
GLANCE
GASP
NOW SHE'S COMING CLOSER...
GASP
YOUR OSOMA GOES WELL WITH EVERY-THING!
HINNA, HINNA!
MNCHMNCH
MNCH
HMPH! WELL, IT ISN'T POOP!
HINNA, HINNA, HINNA!

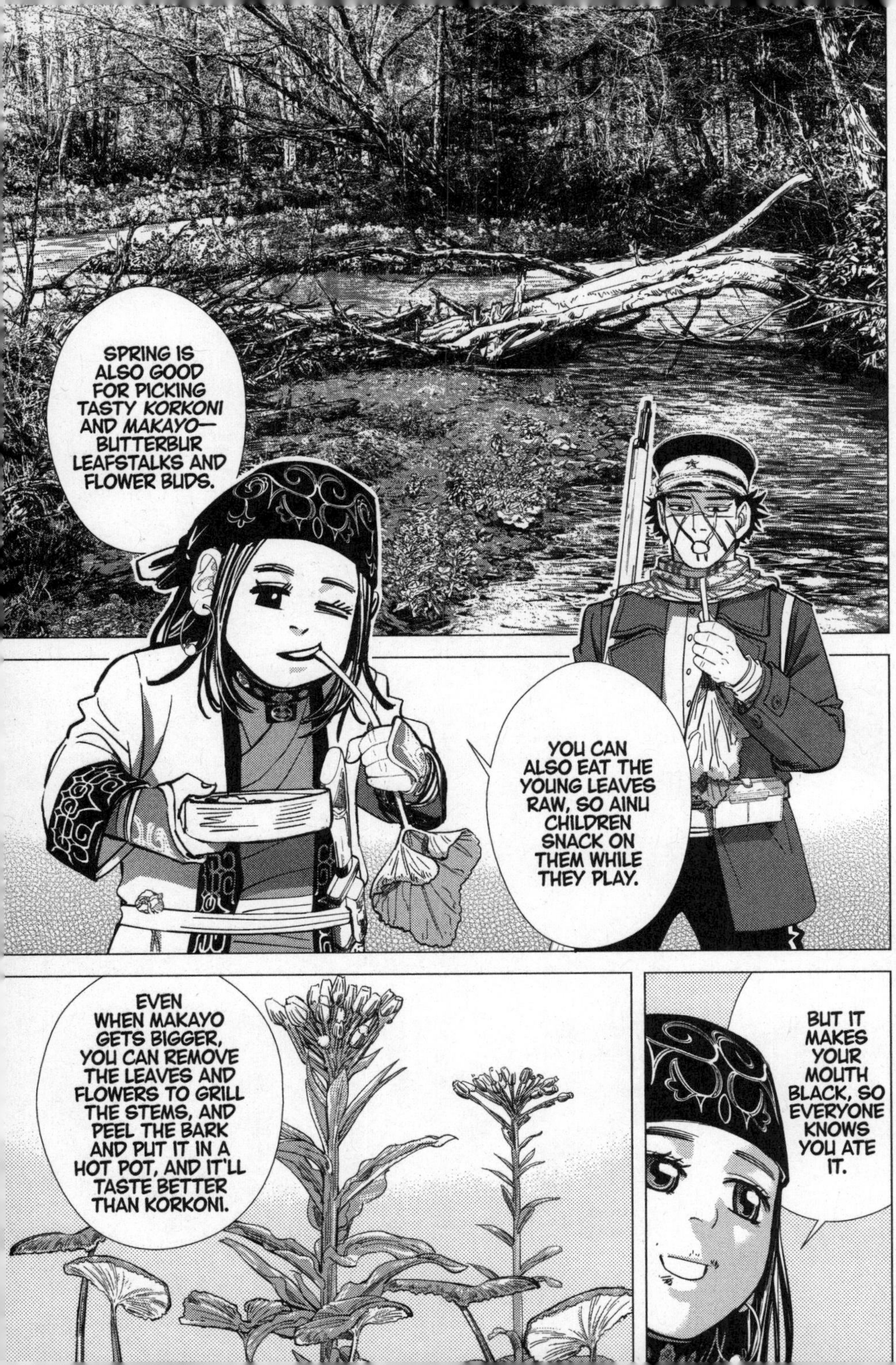
SPRING IS ALSO GOOD FOR PICKING TASTY *KORKONI* AND *MAKAYO*—BUTTERBUR LEAFSTALKS AND FLOWER BUDS.
YOU CAN ALSO EAT THE YOUNG LEAVES RAW, SO AINU CHILDREN SNACK ON THEM WHILE THEY PLAY.
BUT IT MAKES YOUR MOUTH BLACK, SO EVERYONE KNOWS YOU ATE IT.
EVEN WHEN MAKAYO GETS BIGGER, YOU CAN REMOVE THE LEAVES AND FLOWERS TO GRILL THE STEMS, AND PEEL THE BARK AND PUT IT IN A HOT POT, AND IT'LL TASTE BETTER THAN KORKONI.

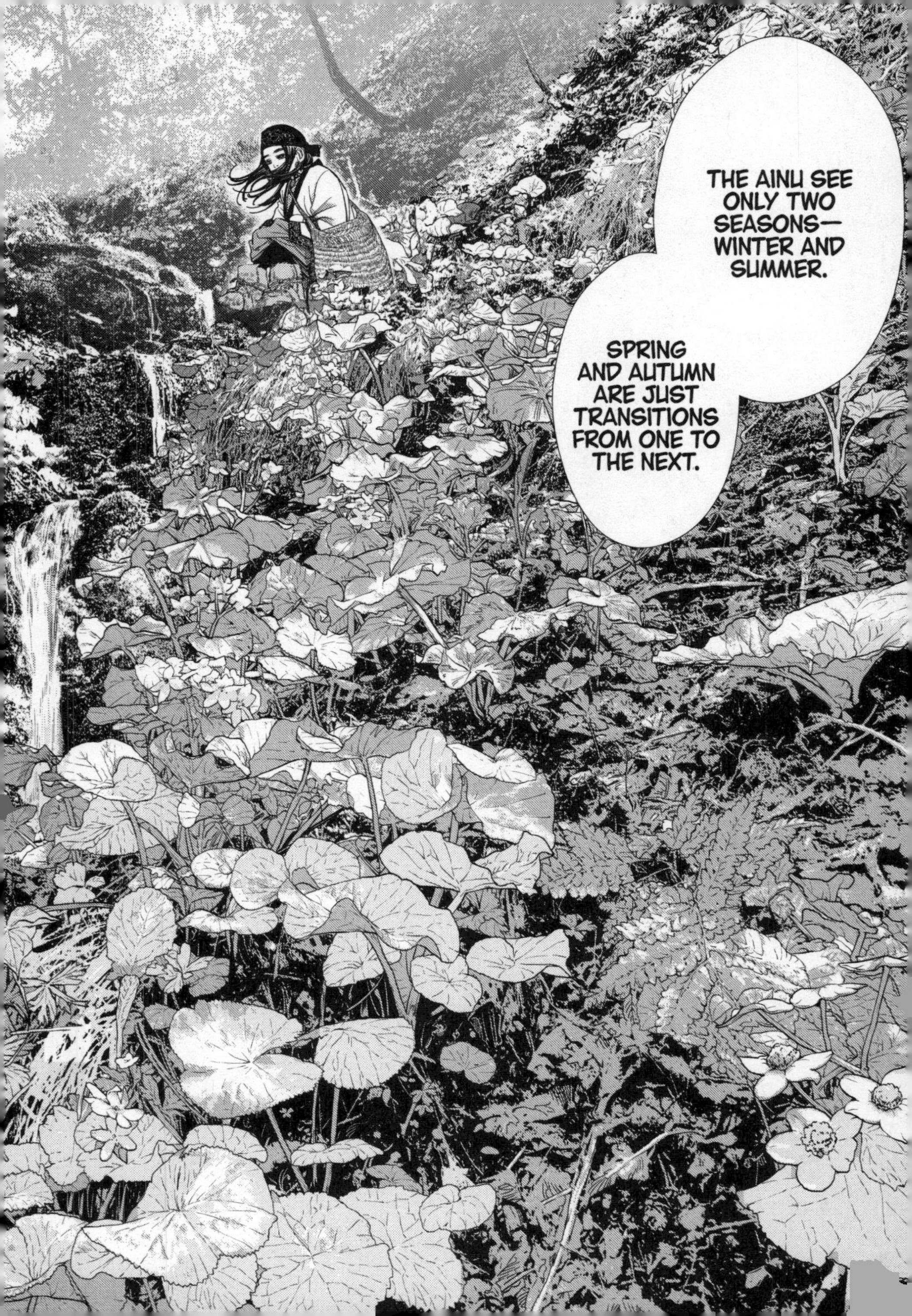
THE AINU SEE ONLY TWO SEASONS— WINTER AND SUMMER.
SPRING AND AUTUMN ARE JUST TRANSITIONS FROM ONE TO THE NEXT.

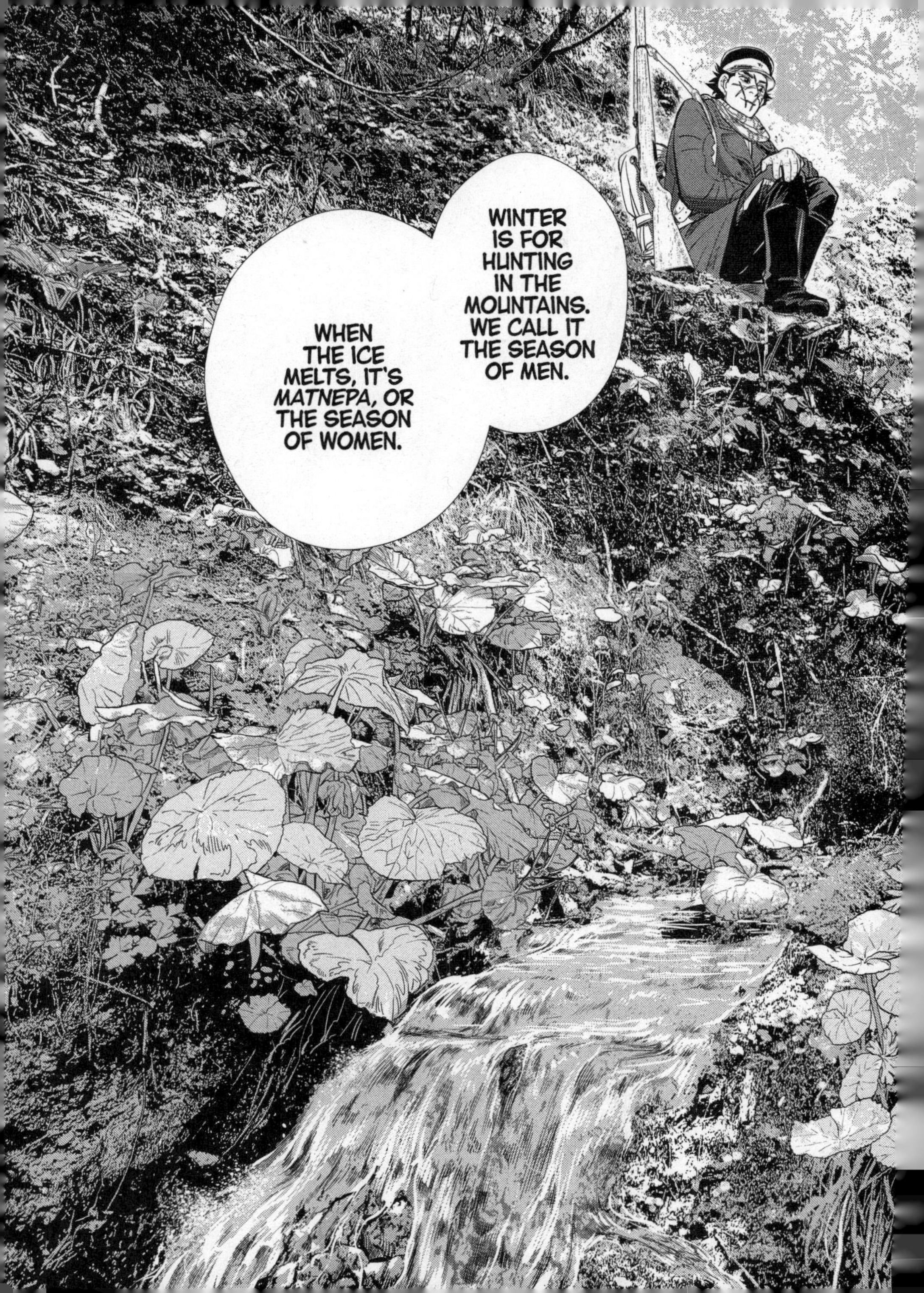
WINTER IS FOR HUNTING IN THE MOUNTAINS. WE CALL IT THE SEASON OF MEN.
WHEN THE ICE MELTS, IT'S *MATNEPA*, OR THE SEASON OF WOMEN.

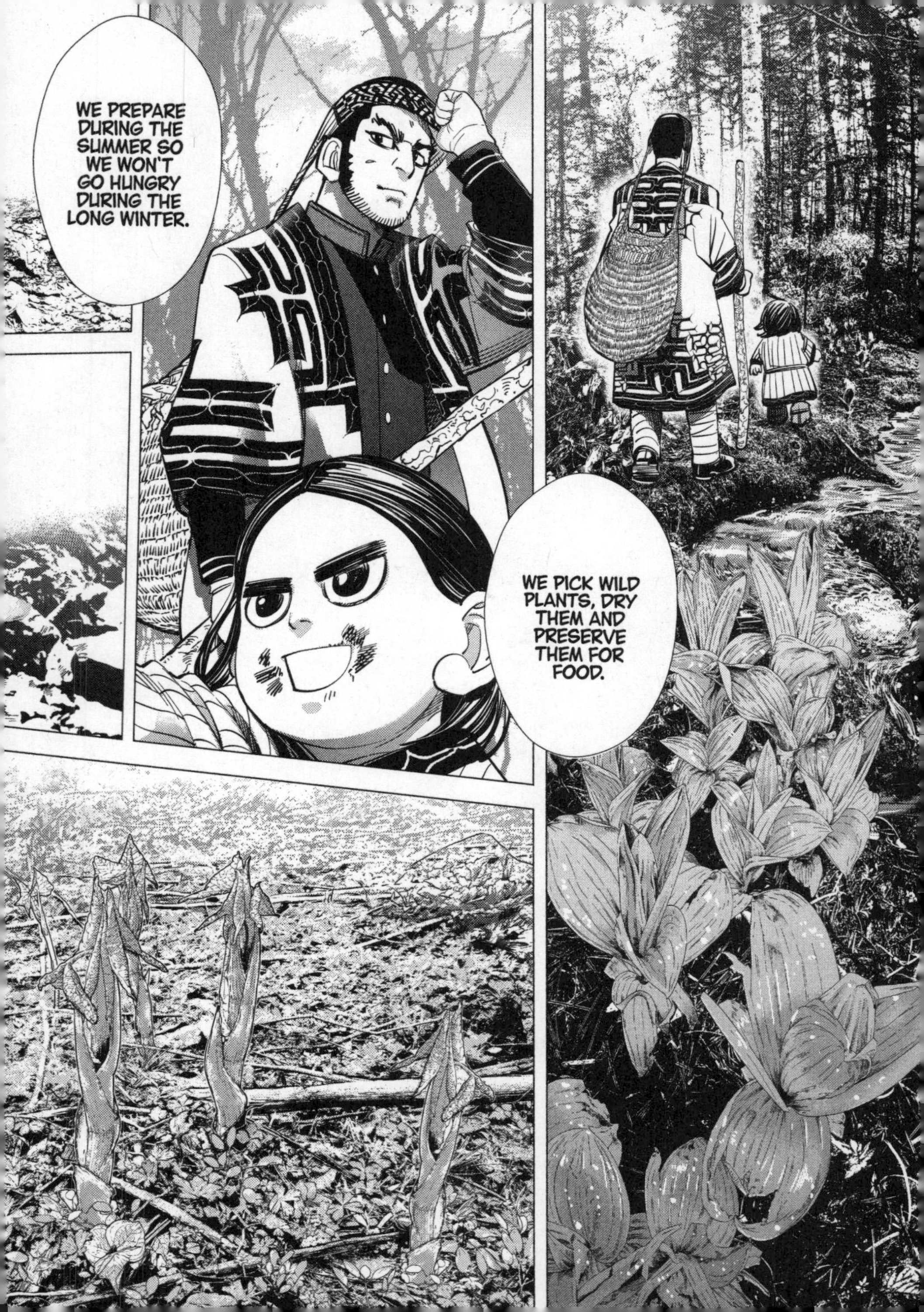
WE PREPARE DURING THE SUMMER SO WE WON'T GO HUNGRY DURING THE LONG WINTER.
WE PICK WILD PLANTS, DRY THEM AND PRESERVE THEM FOR FOOD.

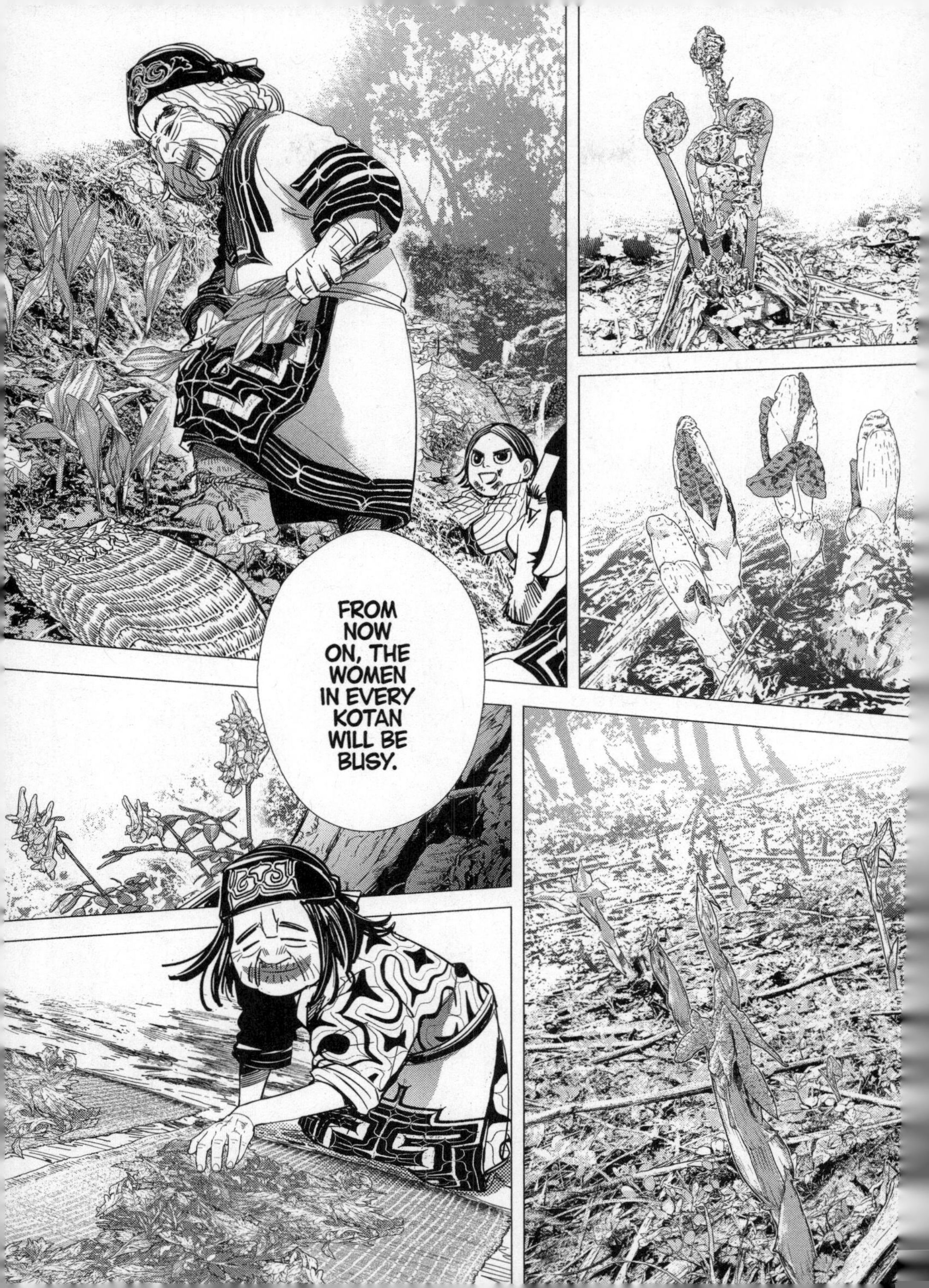
FROM NOW ON, THE WOMEN IN EVERY KOTAN WILL BE BUSY.

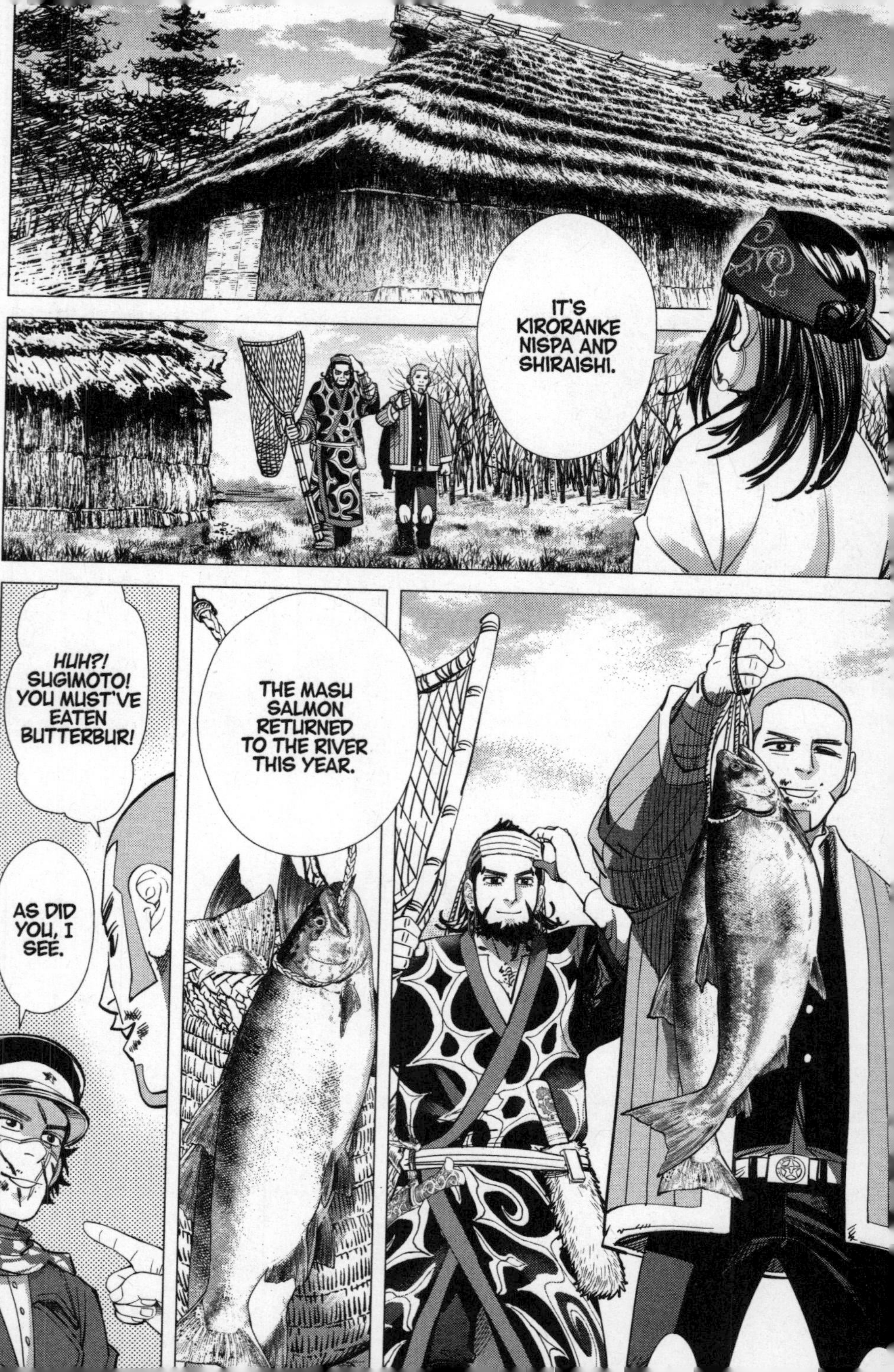
IT'S KIRORANKE NISPA AND SHIRAISHI.
THE MASU SALMON RETURNED TO THE RIVER THIS YEAR.
HUH?! SUGIMOTO! YOU MUST'VE EATEN BUTTERBUR!
AS DID YOU, I SEE.

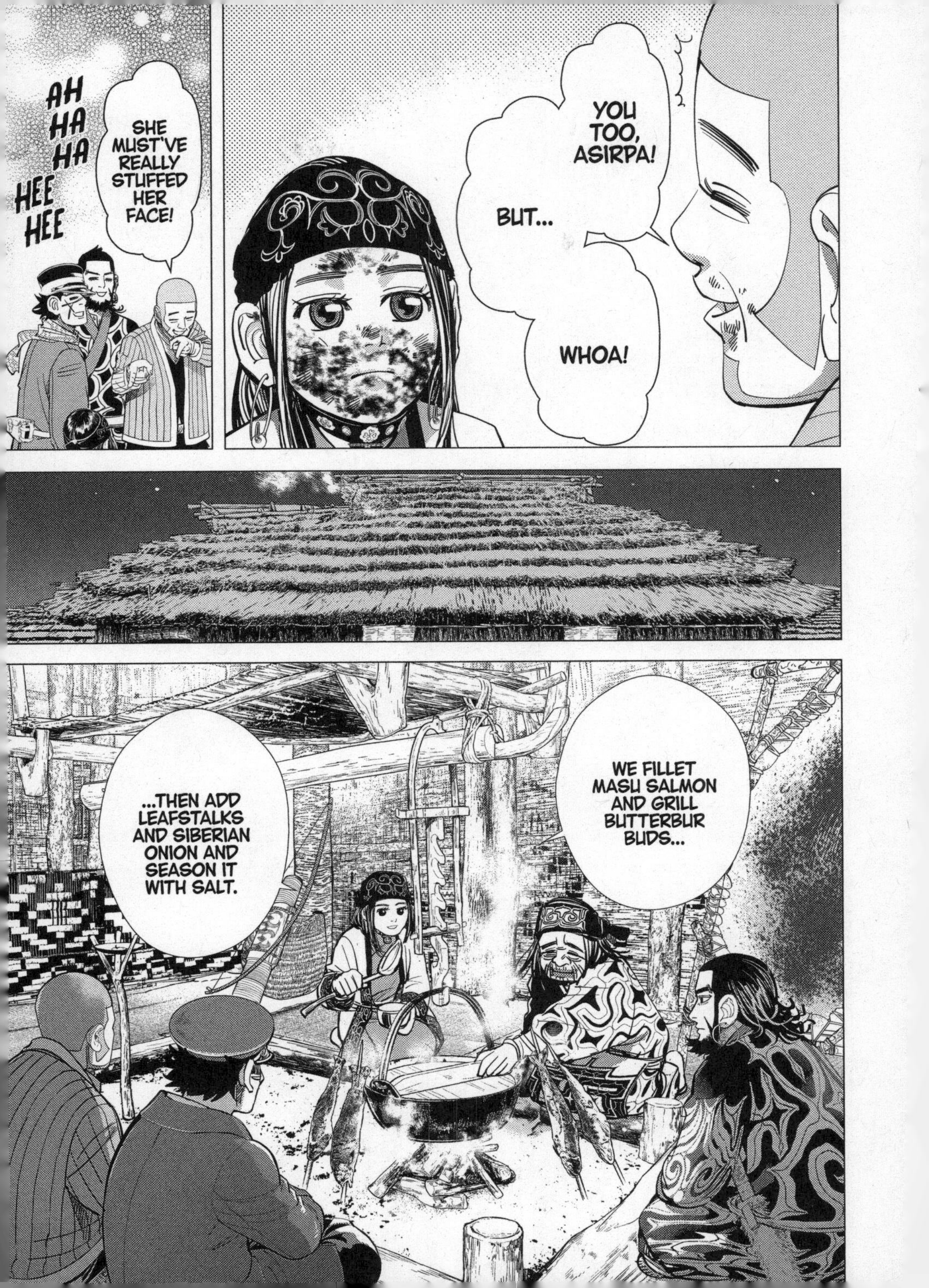
YOU TOO, ASIRPA!
BUT...
WHOA!
AH HA HA
HEE HEE
SHE MUST'VE REALLY STUFFED HER FACE!
WE FILLET MASU SALMON AND GRILL BUTTERBUR BUDS...
...THEN ADD LEAFSTALKS AND SIBERIAN ONION AND SEASON IT WITH SALT.

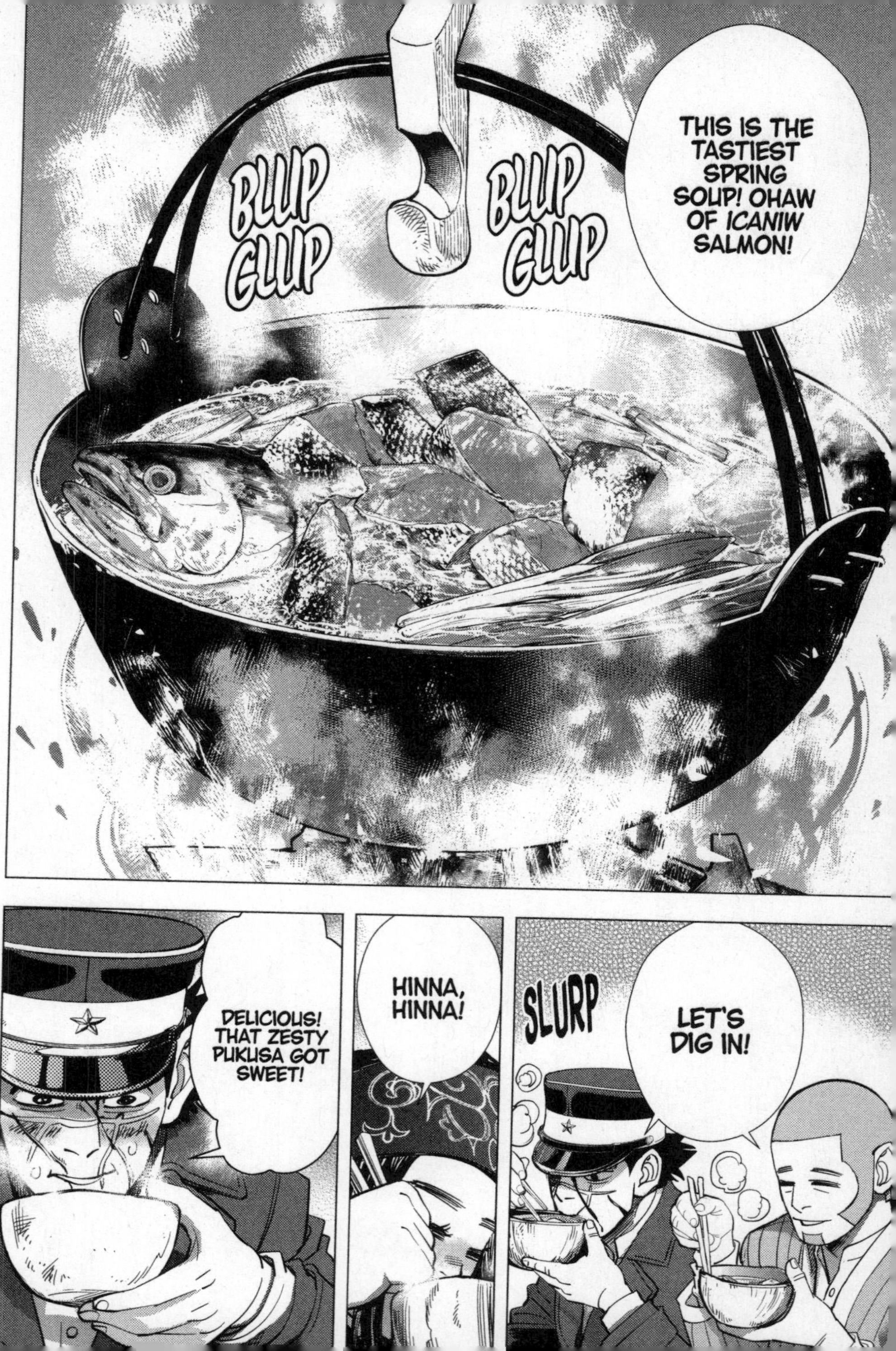
THIS IS THE TASTIEST SPRING SOUP! OHAW OF ICANIW SALMON!
BLUP GLUP
BLUP GLUP
LET'S DIG IN!
SLURP
HINNA, HINNA!
DELICIOUS! THAT ZESTY PUKUSA GOT SWEET!

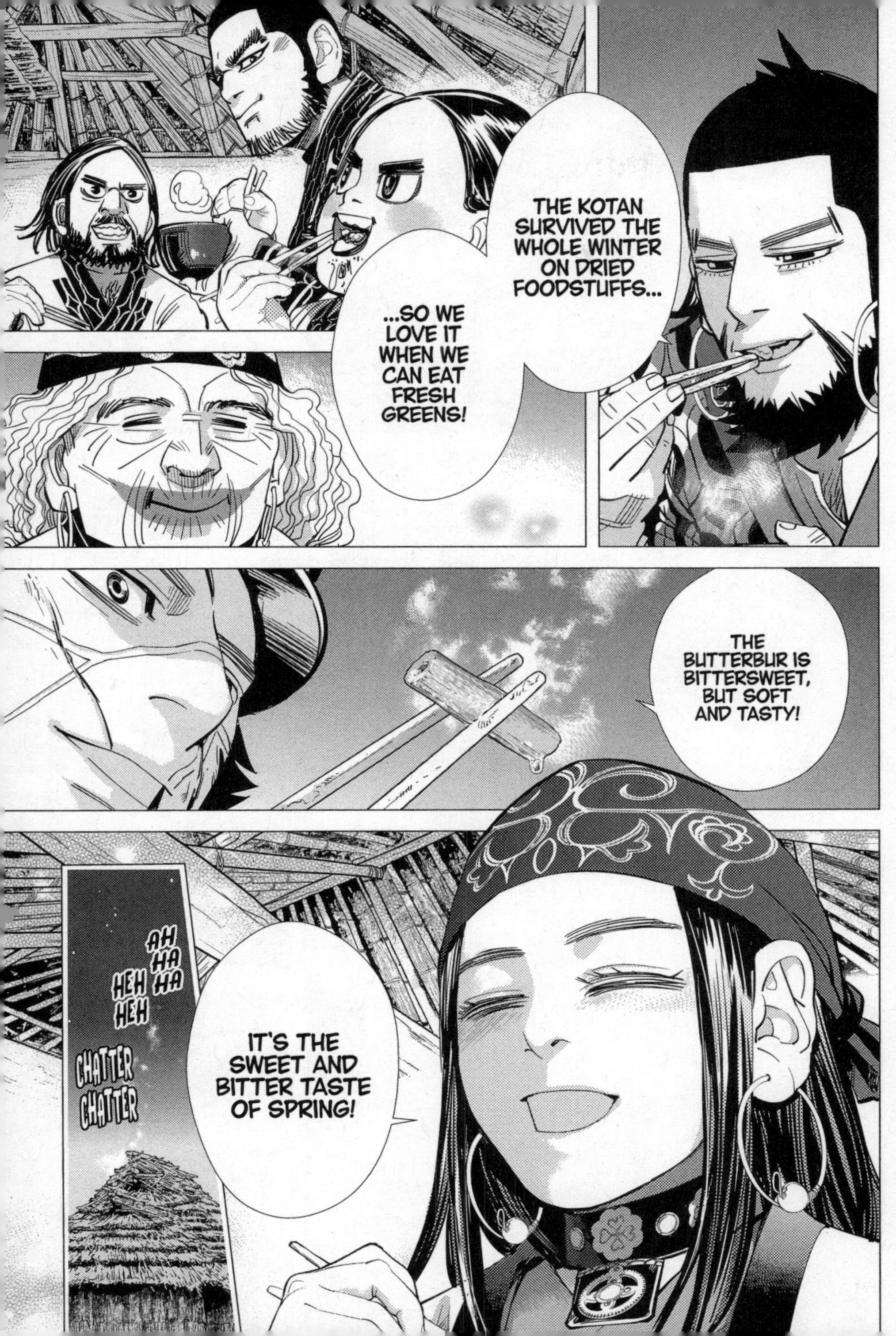
THE KOTAN SURVIVED THE WHOLE WINTER ON DRIED FOODSTUFFS...
...SO WE LOVE IT WHEN WE CAN EAT FRESH GREENS!
THE BUTTERBUR IS BITTERSWEET, BUT SOFT AND TASTY!
IT'S THE SWEET AND BITTER TASTE OF SPRING!
AH HA HA
HEH HEH
CHATTER CHATTER

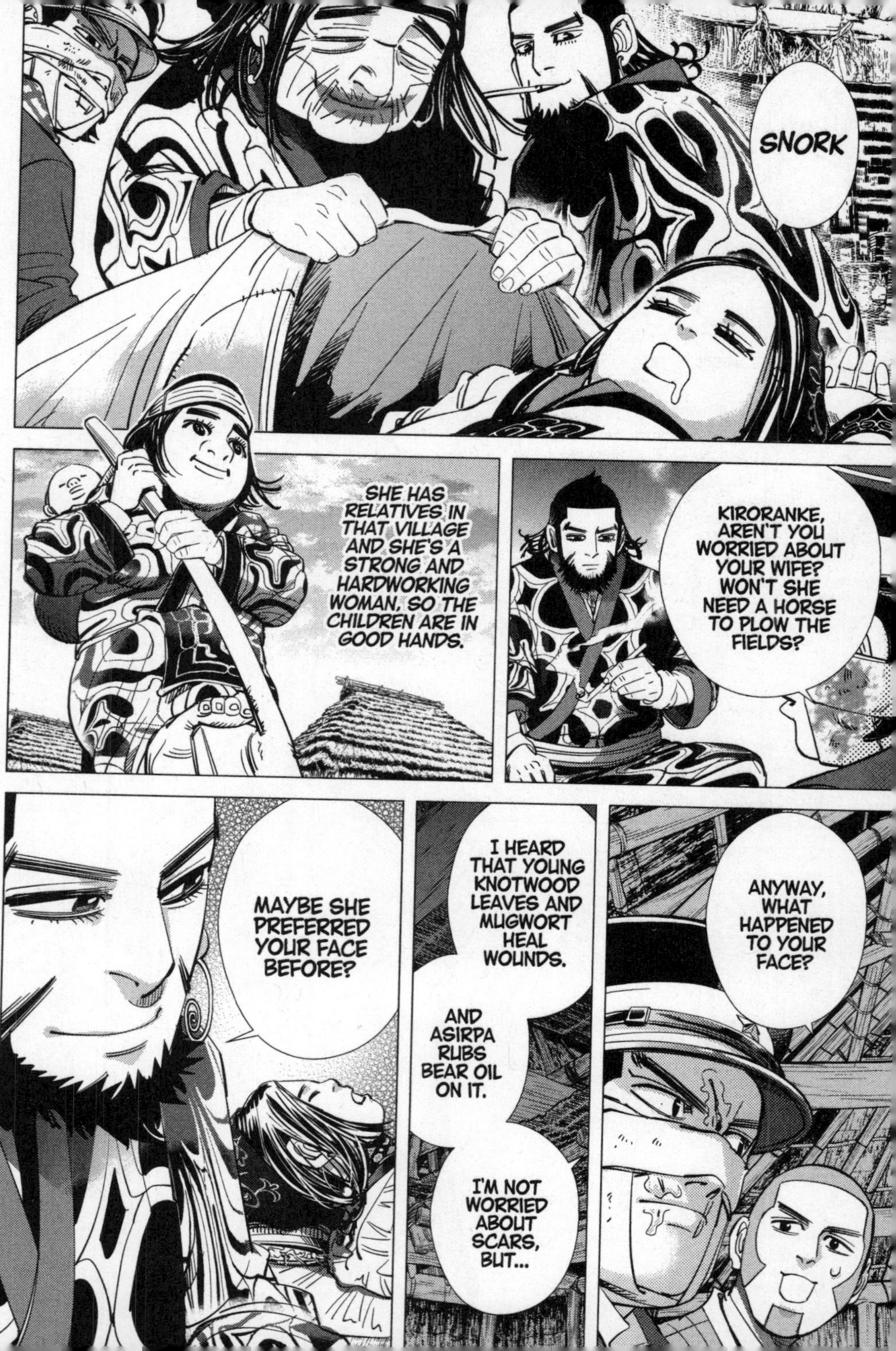
SNORK
KIRORANKE, AREN'T YOU WORRIED ABOUT YOUR WIFE? WON'T SHE NEED A HORSE TO PLOW THE FIELDS?
SHE HAS RELATIVES IN THAT VILLAGE AND SHE'S A STRONG AND HARDWORKING WOMAN, SO THE CHILDREN ARE IN GOOD HANDS.
ANYWAY, WHAT HAPPENED TO YOUR FACE?
I HEARD THAT YOUNG KNOTWOOD LEAVES AND MUGWORT HEAL WOUNDS.
AND ASIRPA RUBS BEAR OIL ON IT.
I'M NOT WORRIED ABOUT SCARS, BUT...
MAYBE SHE PREFERRED YOUR FACE BEFORE?

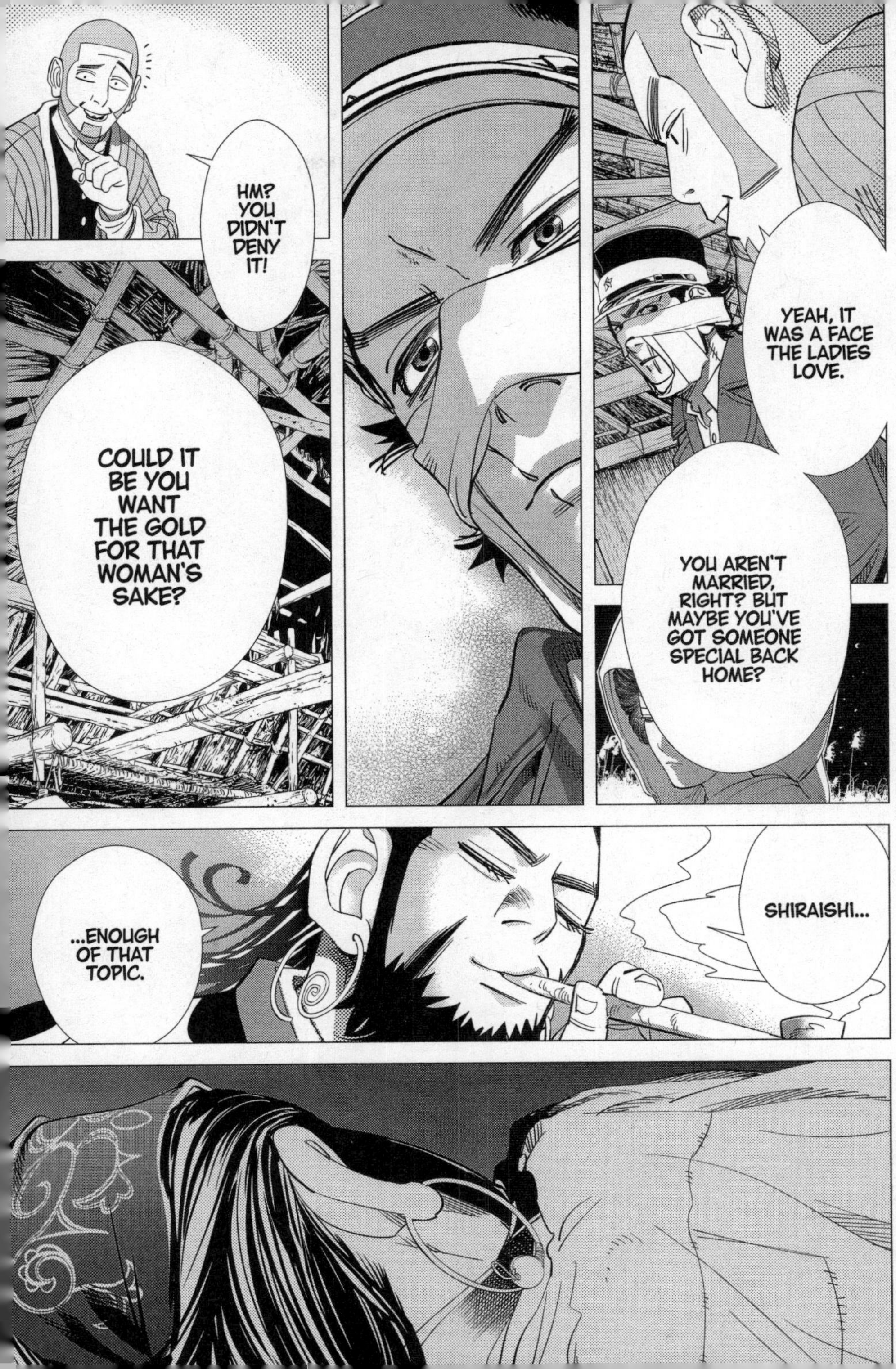
YEAH, IT WAS A FACE THE LADIES LOVE.
YOU AREN'T MARRIED, RIGHT? BUT MAYBE YOU'VE GOT SOMEONE SPECIAL BACK HOME?
HM? YOU DIDN'T DENY IT!
COULD IT BE YOU WANT THE GOLD FOR THAT WOMAN'S SAKE?
SHIRAISHI...
...ENOUGH OF THAT TOPIC.

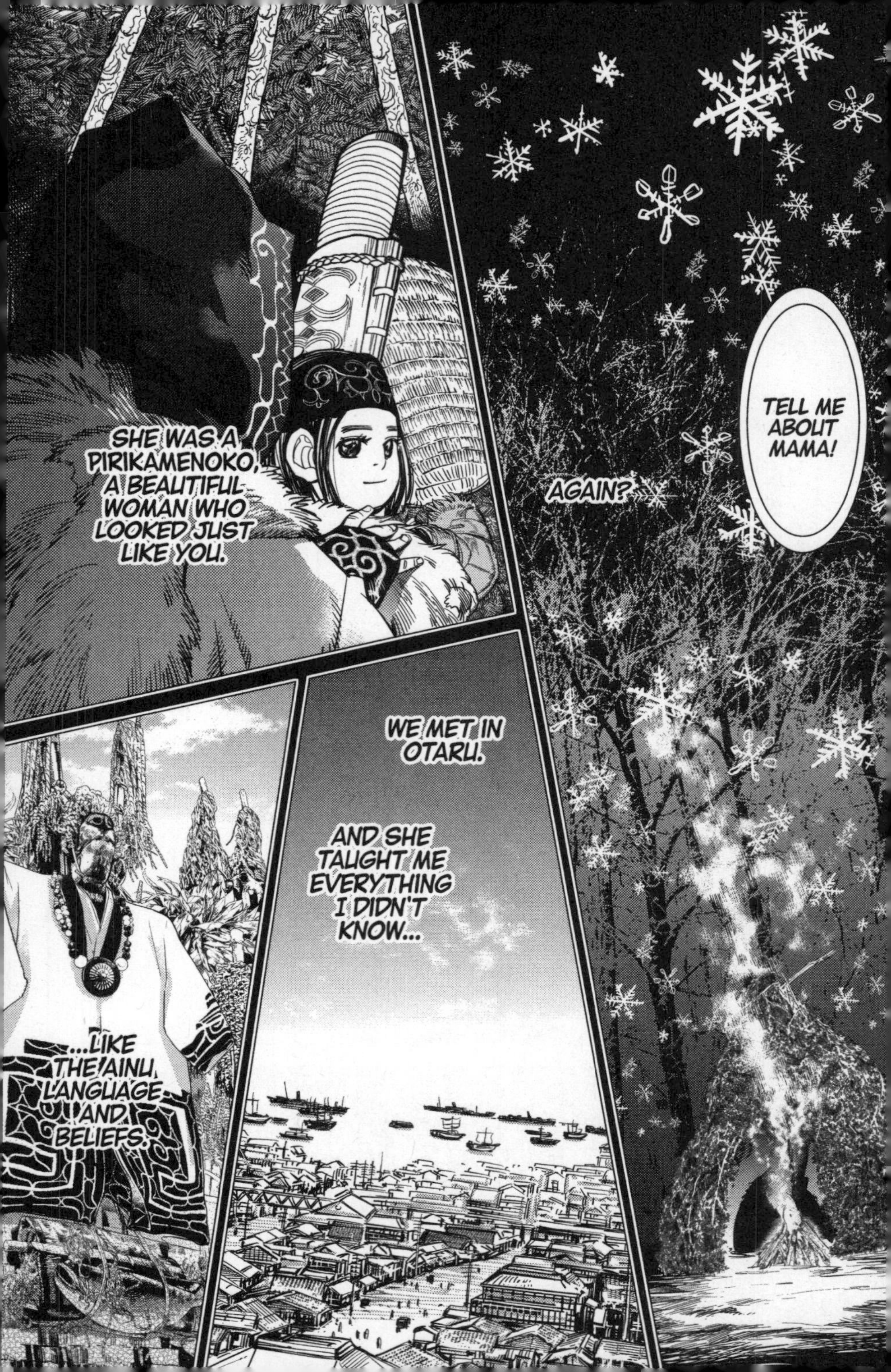
TELL ME ABOUT MAMA!
AGAIN?
SHE WAS A PIRIKAMENOKO, A BEAUTIFUL WOMAN WHO LOOKED JUST LIKE YOU.
WE MET IN OTARU.
AND SHE TAUGHT ME EVERYTHING I DIDN'T KNOW...
...LIKE THE AINU LANGUAGE AND BELIEFS.

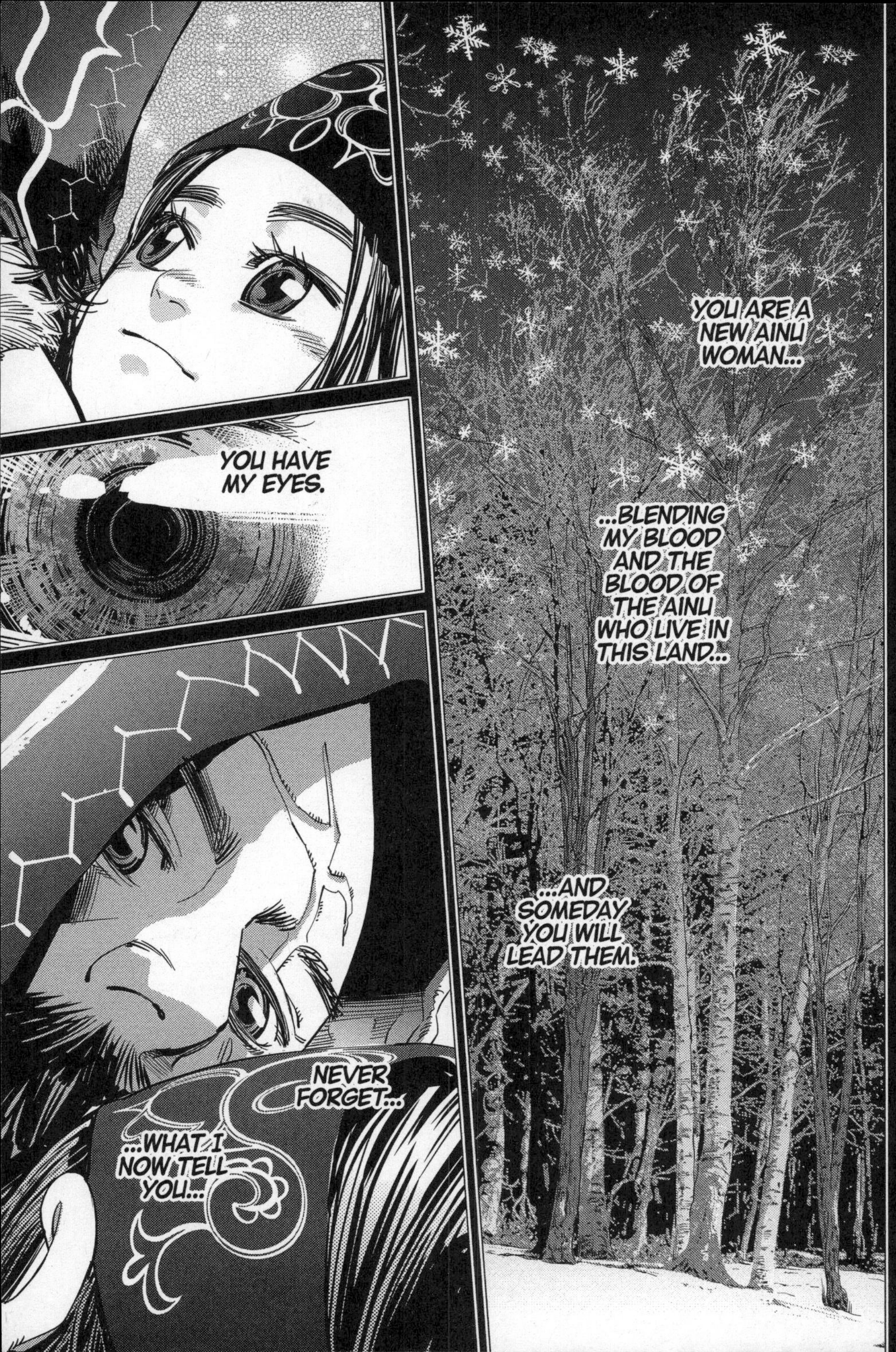
YOU ARE A NEW AINU WOMAN...
...BLENDING MY BLOOD AND THE BLOOD OF THE AINU WHO LIVE IN THIS LAND...
...AND SOMEDAY YOU WILL LEAD THEM.
YOU HAVE MY EYES.
NEVER FORGET...
...WHAT I NOW TELL YOU...

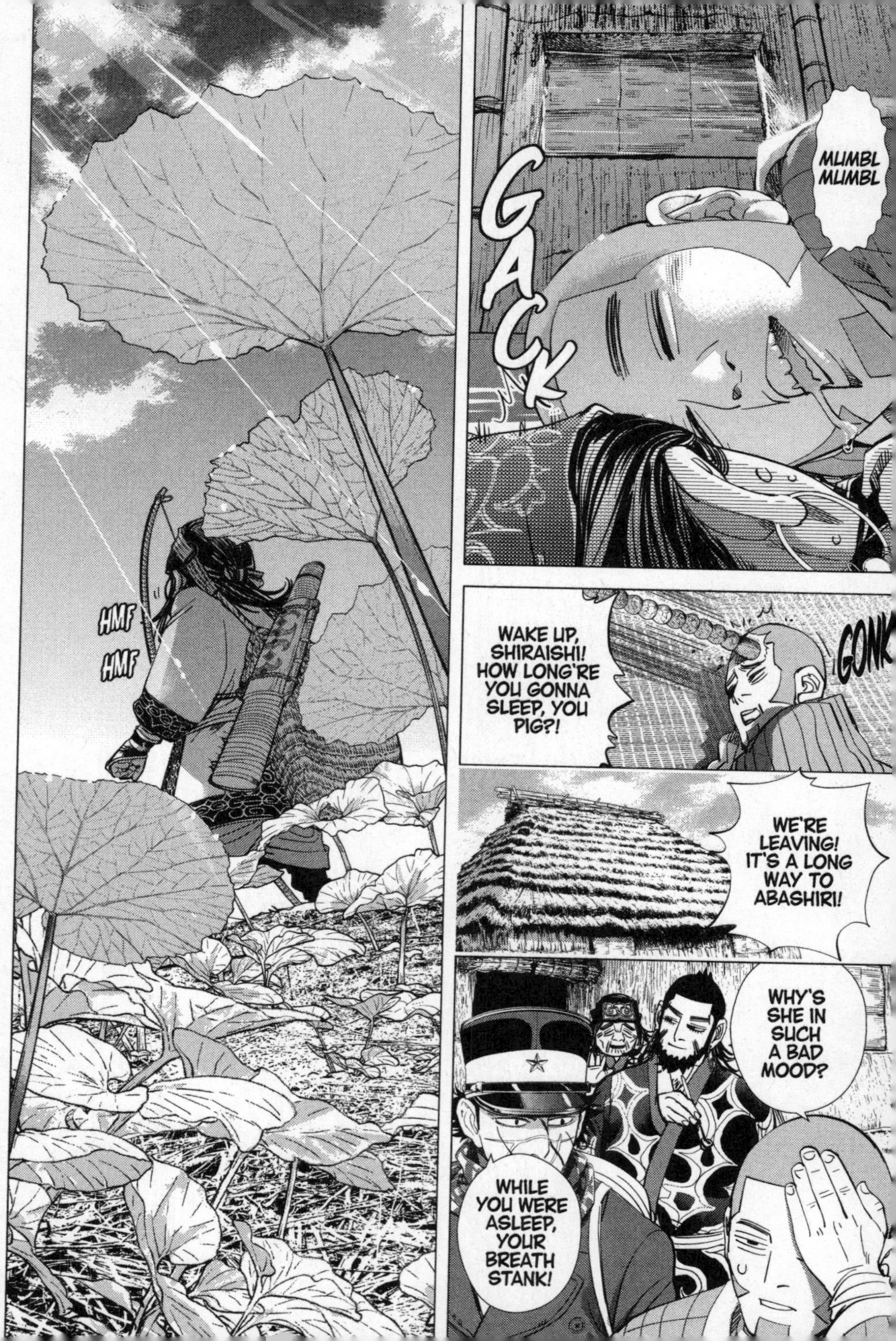
MUMBL MUMBL
GACK
GONK
WAKE UP, SHIRAISHI! HOW LONG'RE YOU GONNA SLEEP, YOU PIG?!
WE'RE LEAVING! IT'S A LONG WAY TO ABASHIRI!
WHY'S SHE IN SUCH A BAD MOOD?
WHILE YOU WERE ASLEEP, YOUR BREATH STANK!
HMF
HMF

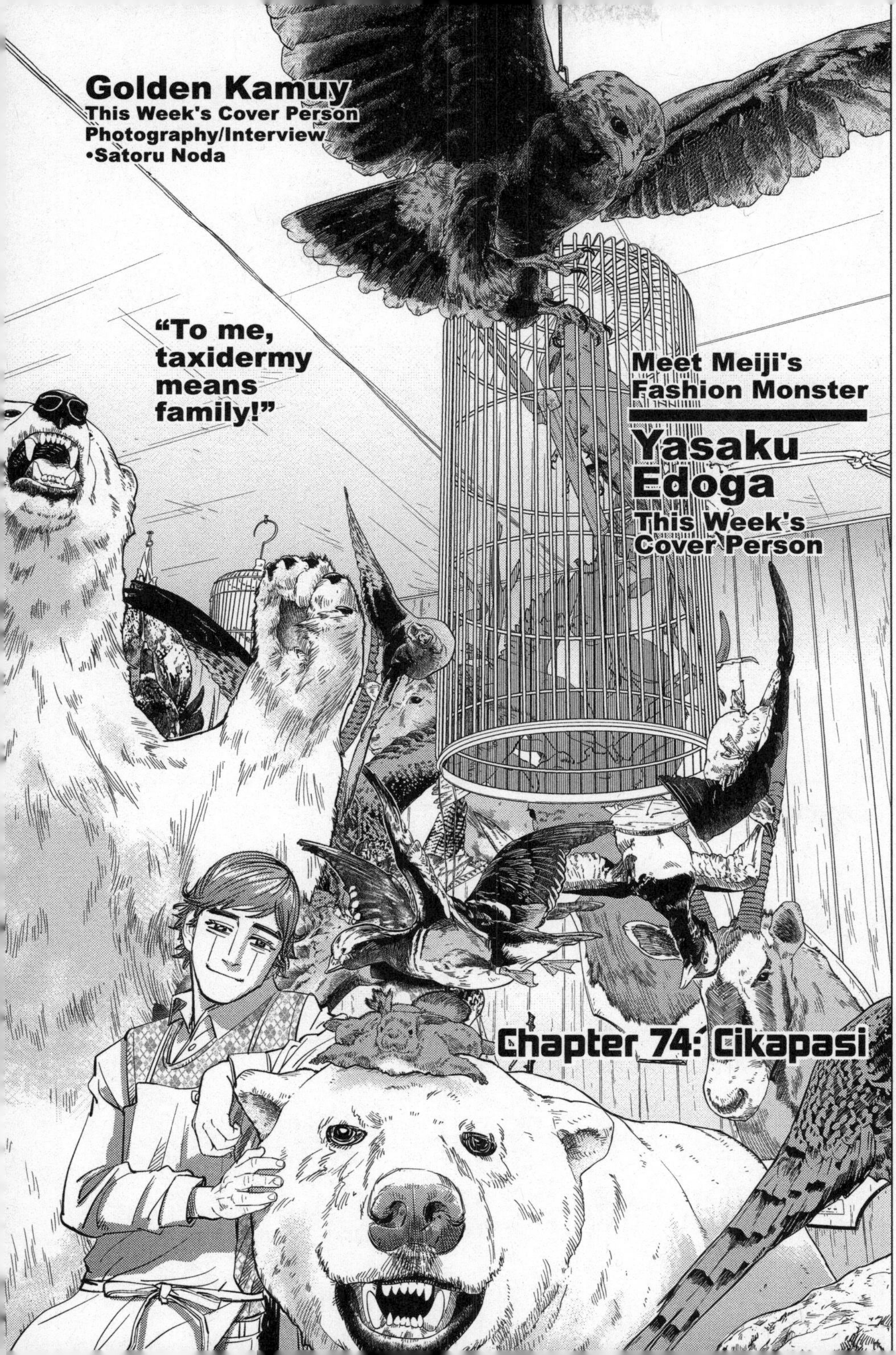
Golden Kamuy
This Week's Cover Person
Photography/Interview
•Satoru Noda
Meet Meiji's
Fashion Monster
Yasaku
Edoga
This Week's
Cover Person
“To me,
taxidermy
means
family!”
Chapter 74: Cikapasi

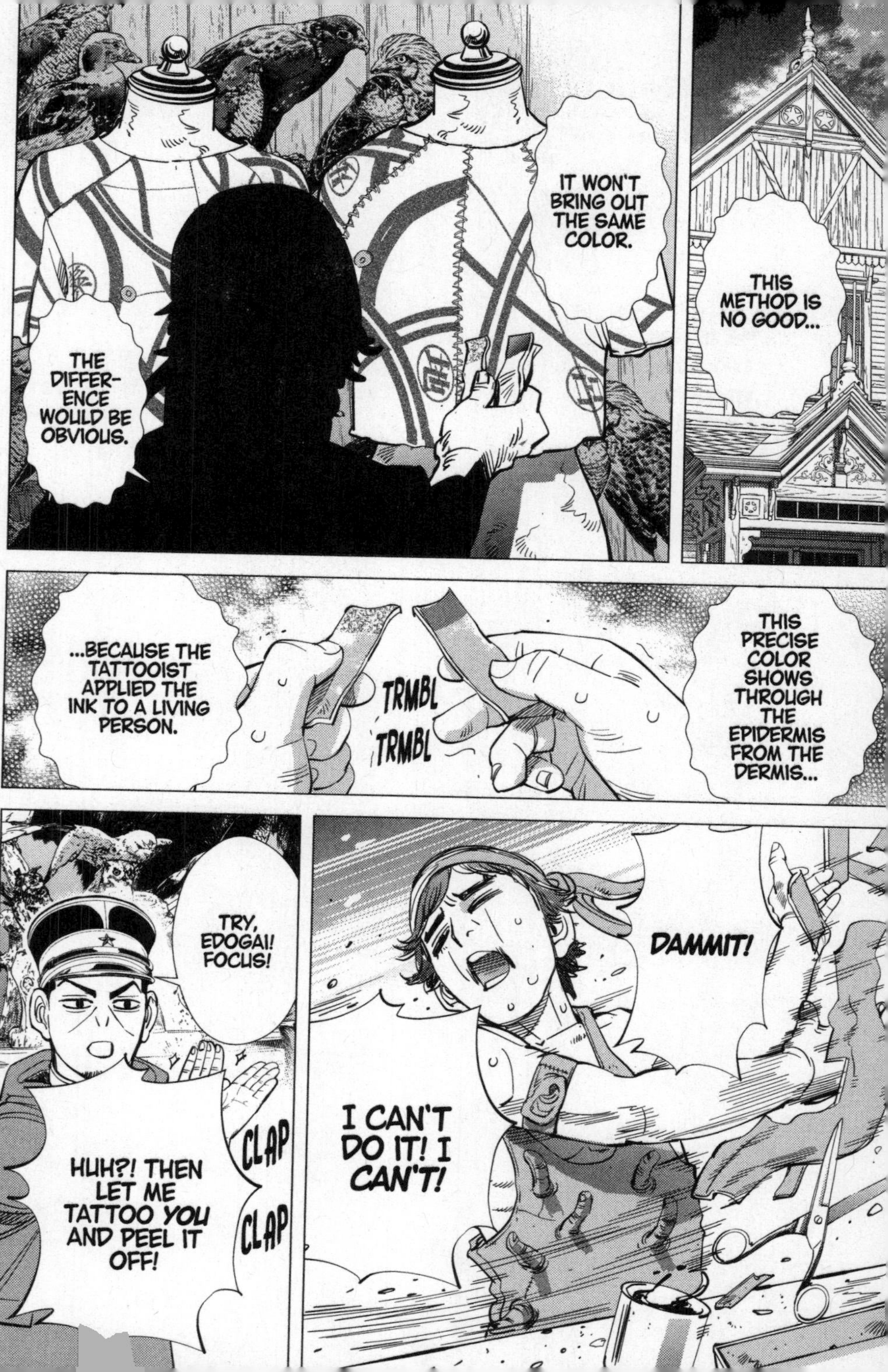
THIS METHOD IS NO GOOD...
IT WON'T BRING OUT THE SAME COLOR.
THE DIFFERENCE WOULD BE OBVIOUS.
THIS PRECISE COLOR SHOWS THROUGH THE EPIDERMIS FROM THE DERMIS...
TRMBL
TRMBL
...BECAUSE THE TATTOOIST APPLIED THE INK TO A LIVING PERSON.
DAMMIT!
I CAN'T DO IT! I *CAN'T*!
TRY, EDOGAI! FOCUS!
CLAP
CLAP
HUH?! THEN LET ME TATTOO *YOU* AND PEEL IT OFF!

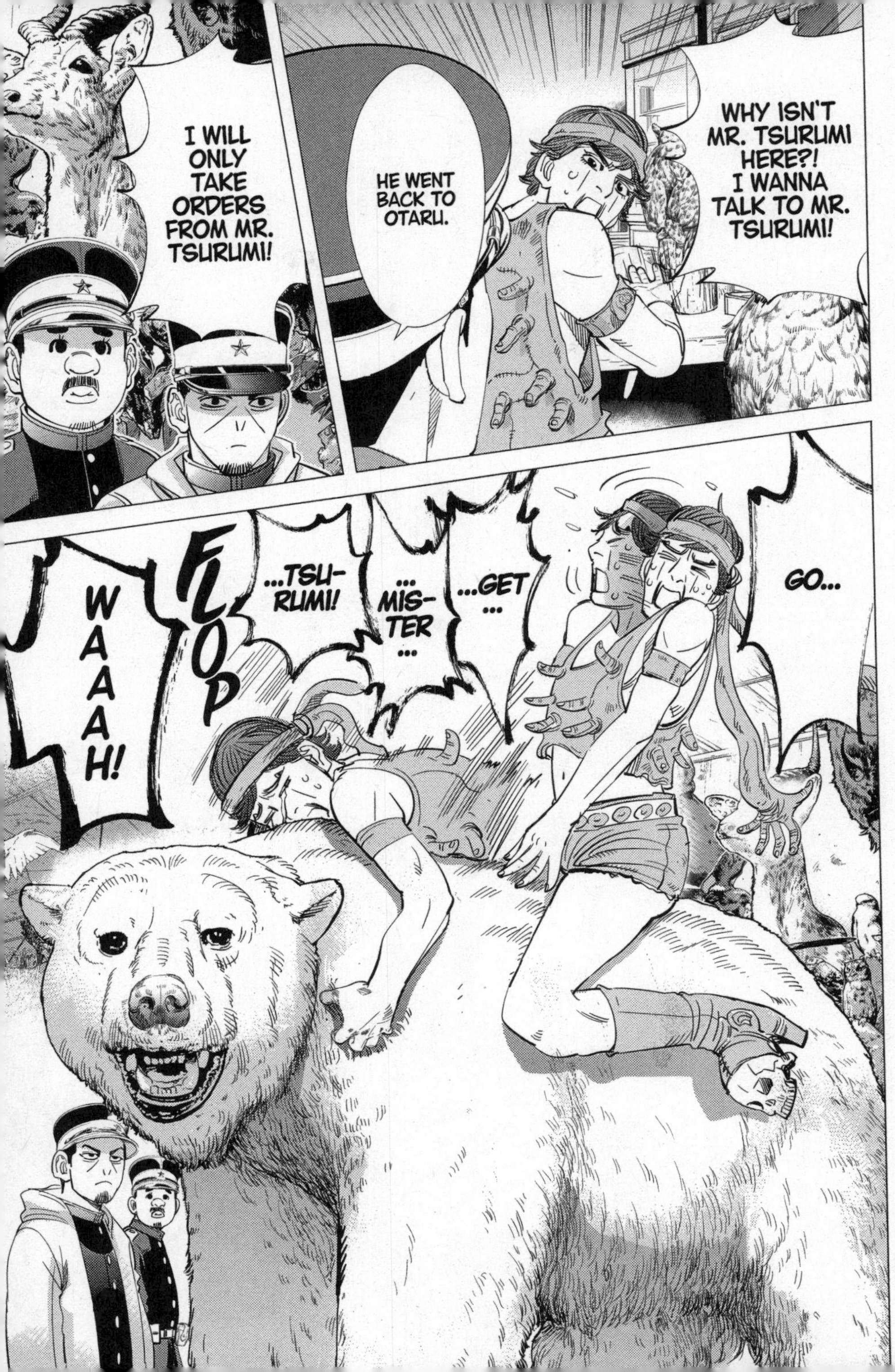
WHY ISN'T MR. TSURUMI HERE?! I WANNA TALK TO MR. TSURUMI!
HE WENT BACK TO OTARU.
I WILL ONLY TAKE ORDERS FROM MR. TSURUMI!
GO...
...GET...
...MISTER...
...TSU-RUMI!
FLOP
WAAAAH!

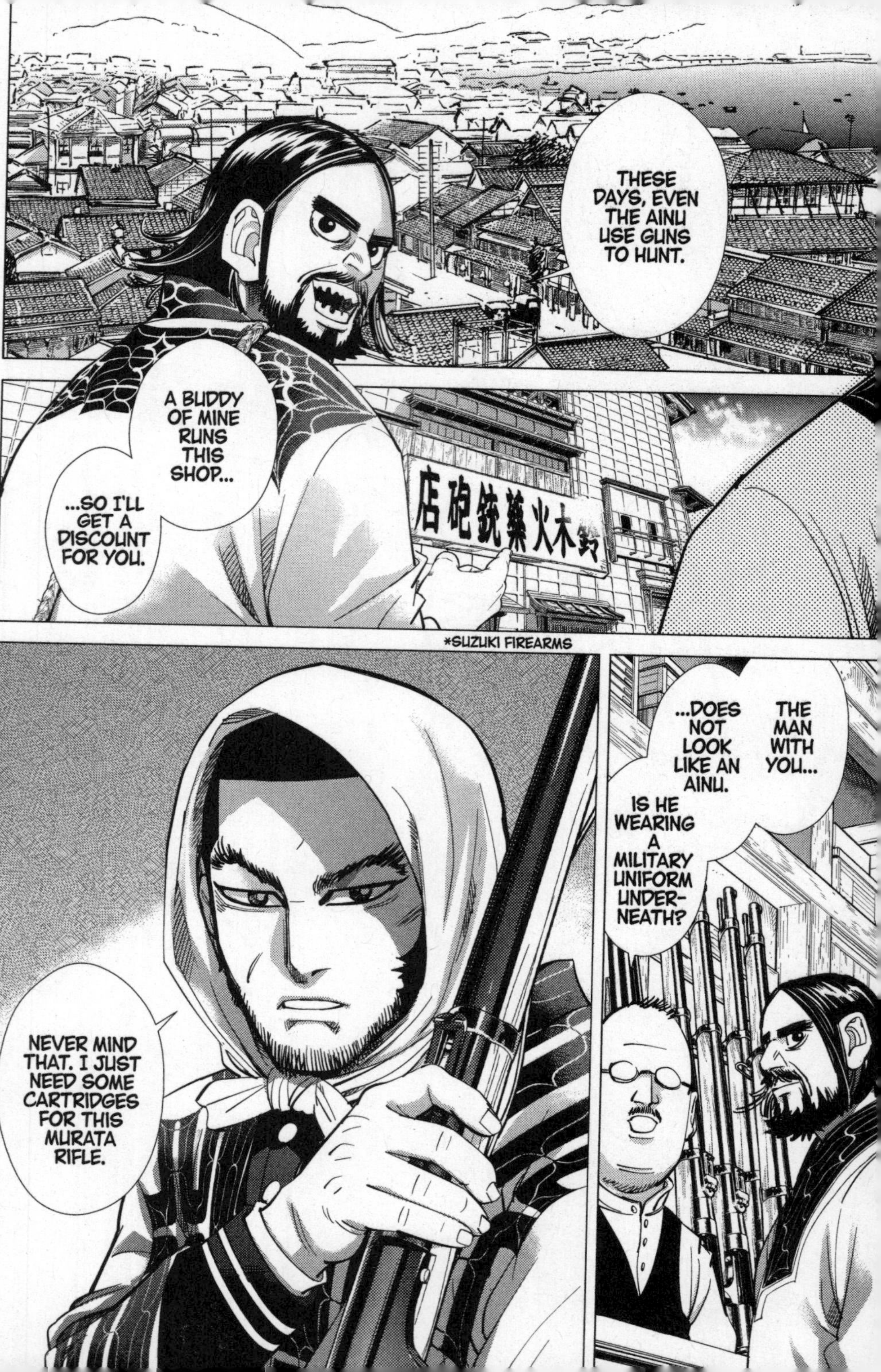
THESE DAYS, EVEN THE AINU USE GUNS TO HUNT.
A BUDDY OF MINE RUNS THIS SHOP...
...SO I'LL GET A DISCOUNT FOR YOU.
鈴木火藥銃砲店
*SUZUKI FIREARMS
THE MAN WITH YOU...
...DOES NOT LOOK LIKE AN AINU.
IS HE WEARING A MILITARY UNIFORM UNDER-NEATH?
NEVER MIND THAT. I JUST NEED SOME CARTRIDGES FOR THIS MURATA RIFLE.

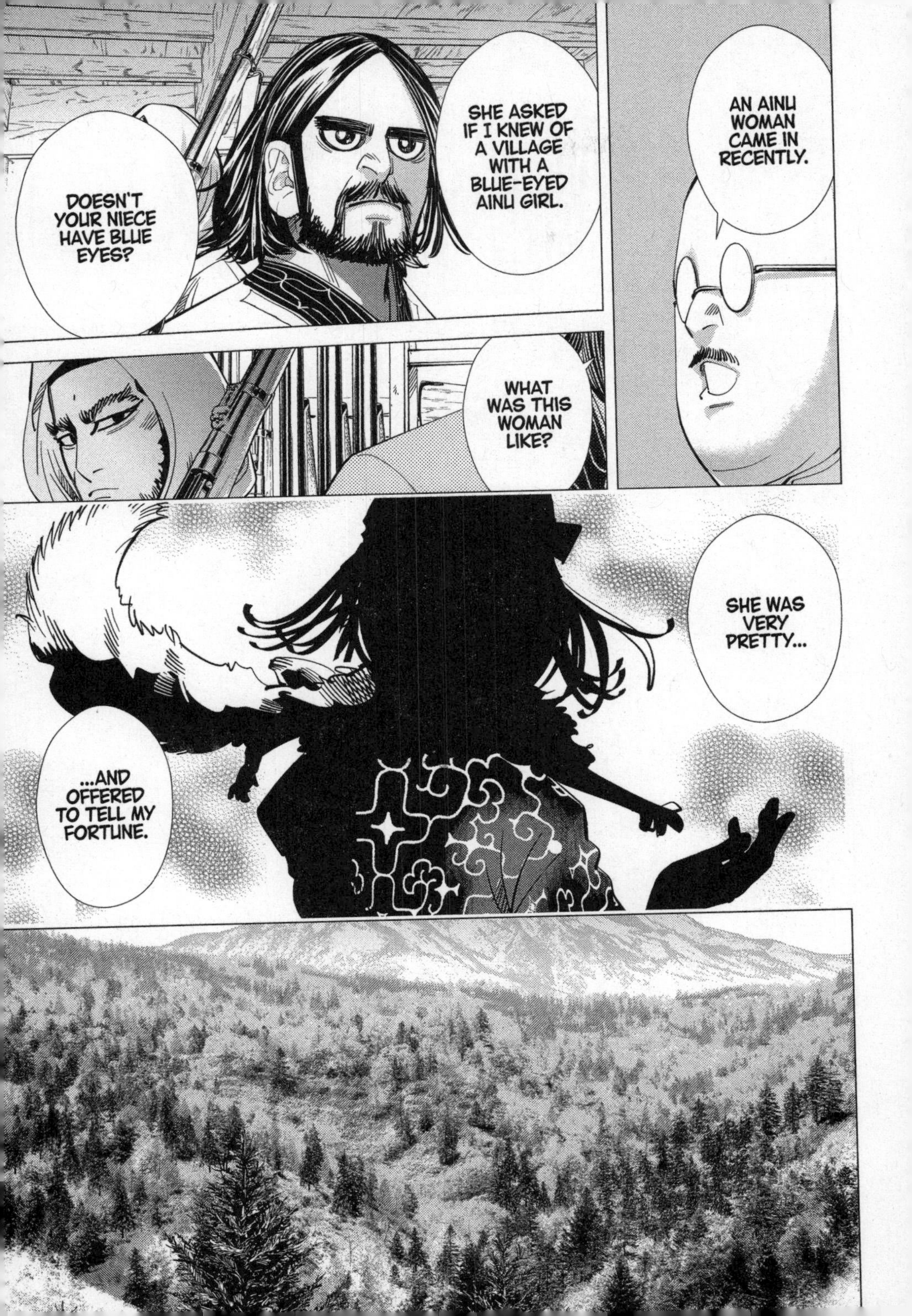
AN AINU WOMAN CAME IN RECENTLY.
SHE ASKED IF I KNEW OF A VILLAGE WITH A BLUE-EYED AINU GIRL.
DOESN'T YOUR NIECE HAVE BLUE EYES?
WHAT WAS THIS WOMAN LIKE?
SHE WAS VERY PRETTY...
...AND OFFERED TO TELL MY FORTUNE.

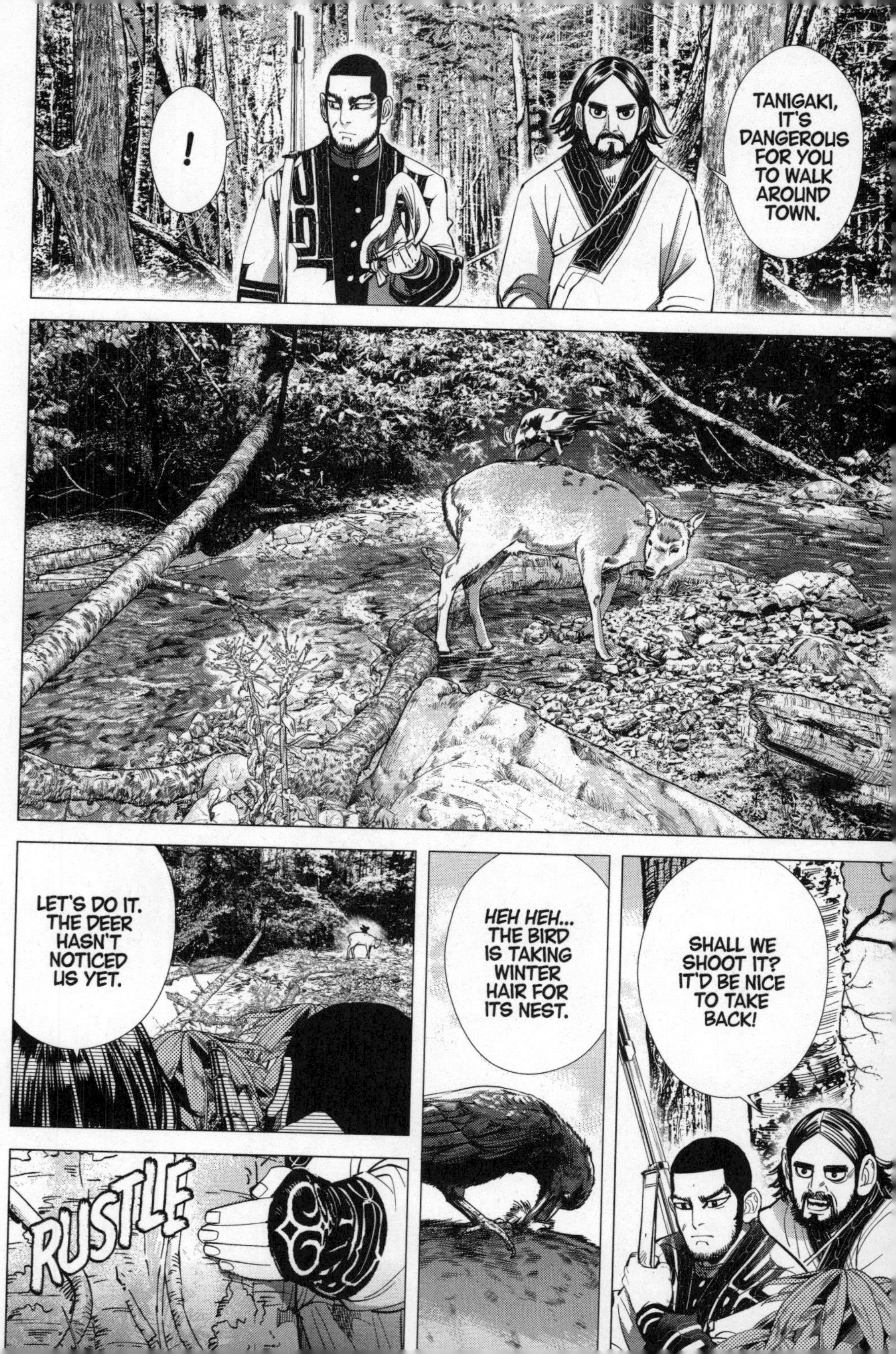
TANIGAKI, IT'S DANGEROUS FOR YOU TO WALK AROUND TOWN.
!
SHALL WE SHOOT IT? IT'D BE NICE TO TAKE BACK!
HEH HEH... THE BIRD IS TAKING WINTER HAIR FOR ITS NEST.
LET'S DO IT. THE DEER HASN'T NOTICED US YET.
RUSTLE

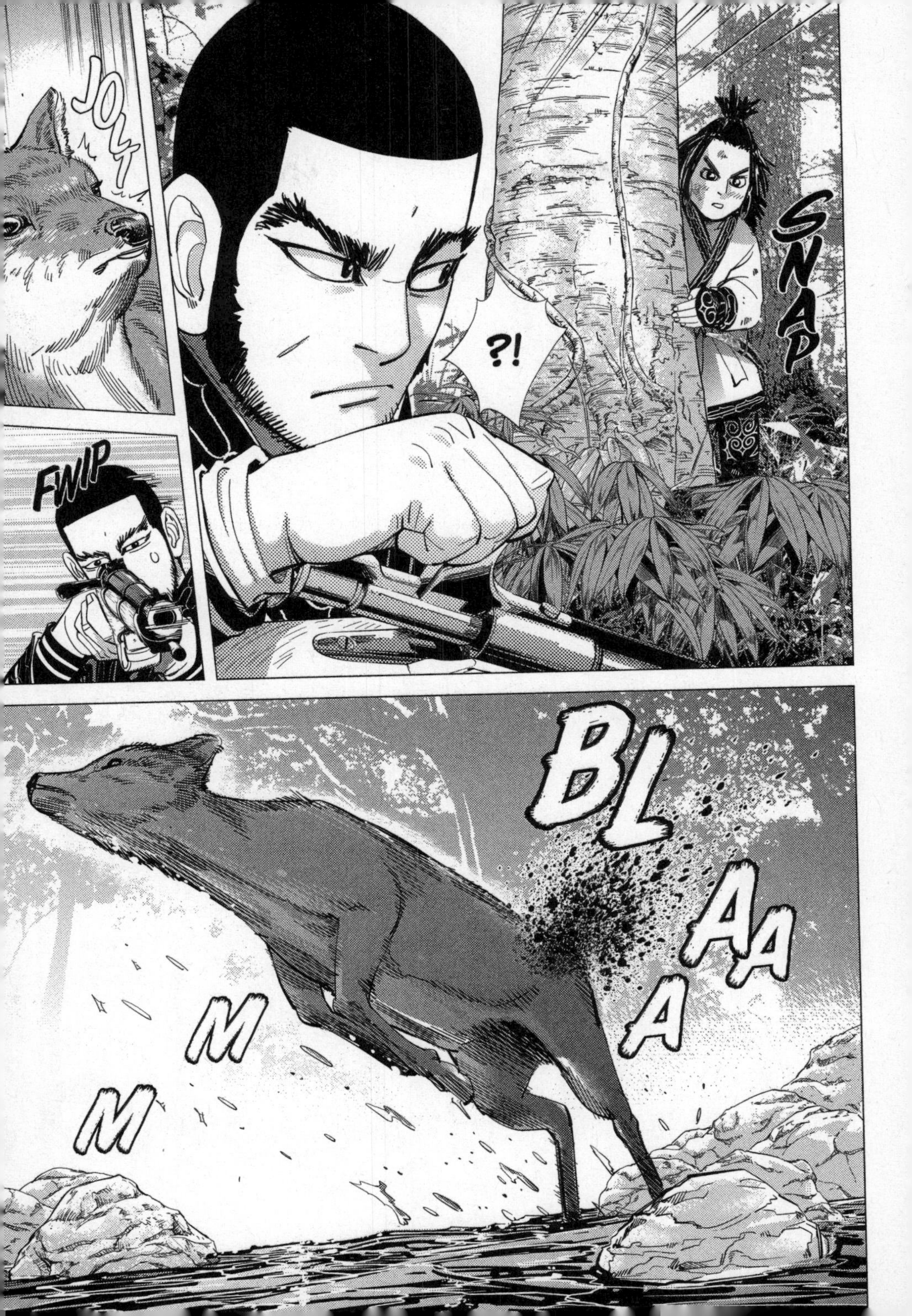
SNAP
?!
JOLT
FWIP
BLAAAAMM

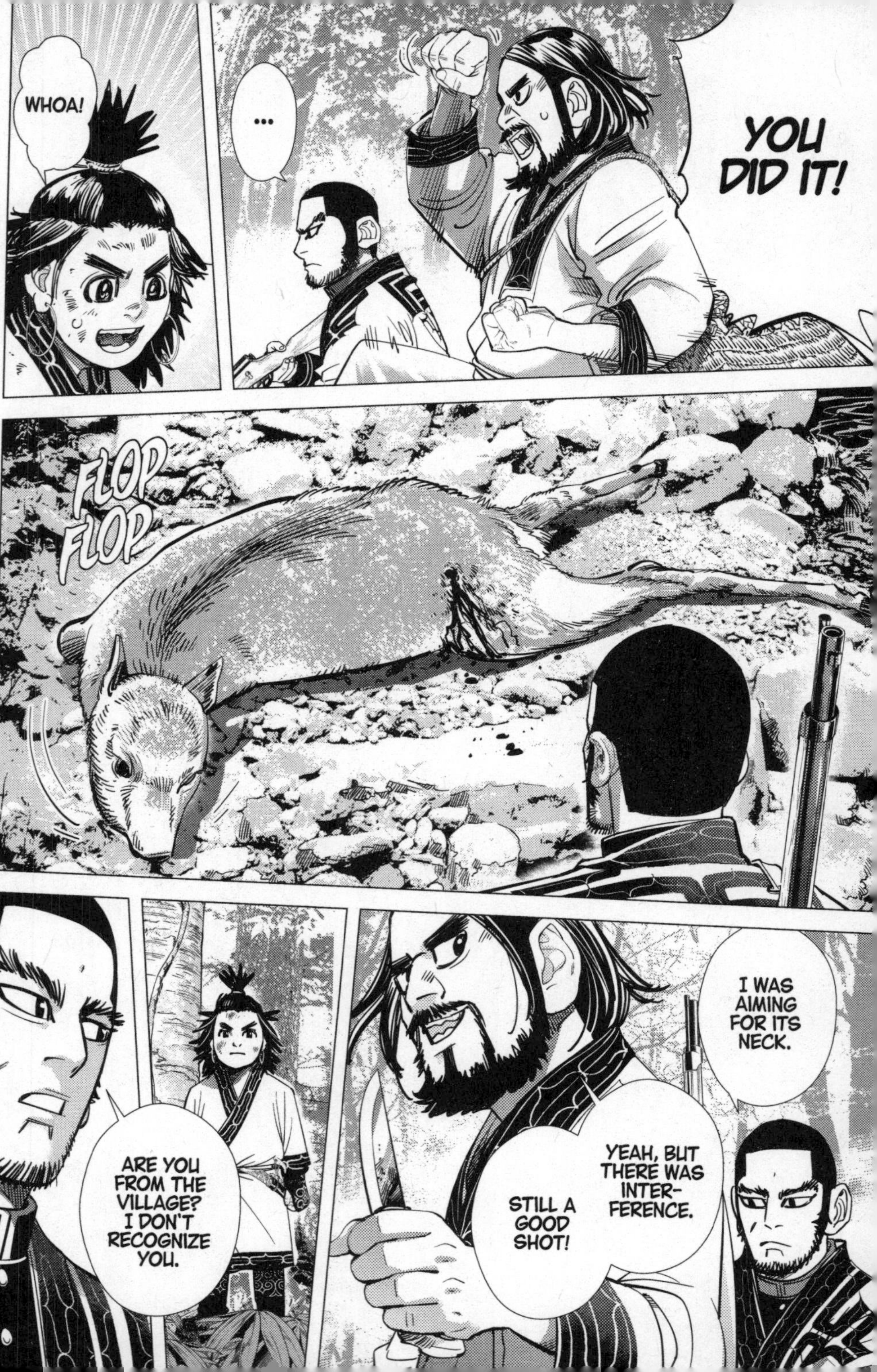
YOU DID IT!
...
WHOA!
FLOP FLOP
I WAS AIMING FOR ITS NECK.
YEAH, BUT THERE WAS INTER- FERENCE.
STILL A GOOD SHOT!
ARE YOU FROM THE VILLAGE? I DON'T RECOGNIZE YOU.

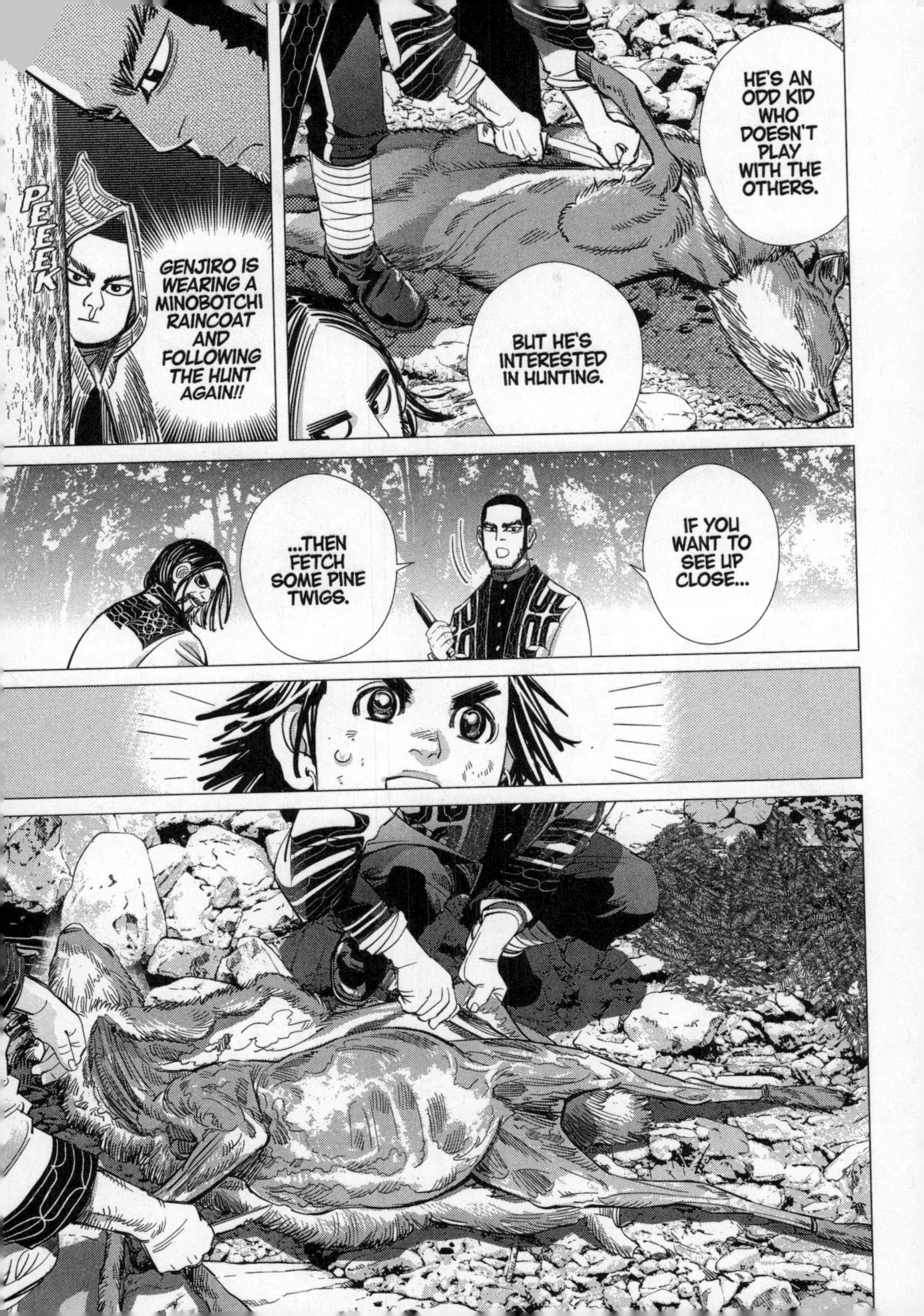
HE'S AN ODD KID WHO DOESN'T PLAY WITH THE OTHERS.
BUT HE'S INTERESTED IN HUNTING.
PEEEK
GENJIRO IS WEARING A MINOBOTCHI RAINCOAT AND FOLLOWING THE HUNT AGAIN!!
IF YOU WANT TO SEE UP CLOSE...
...THEN FETCH SOME PINE TWIGS.

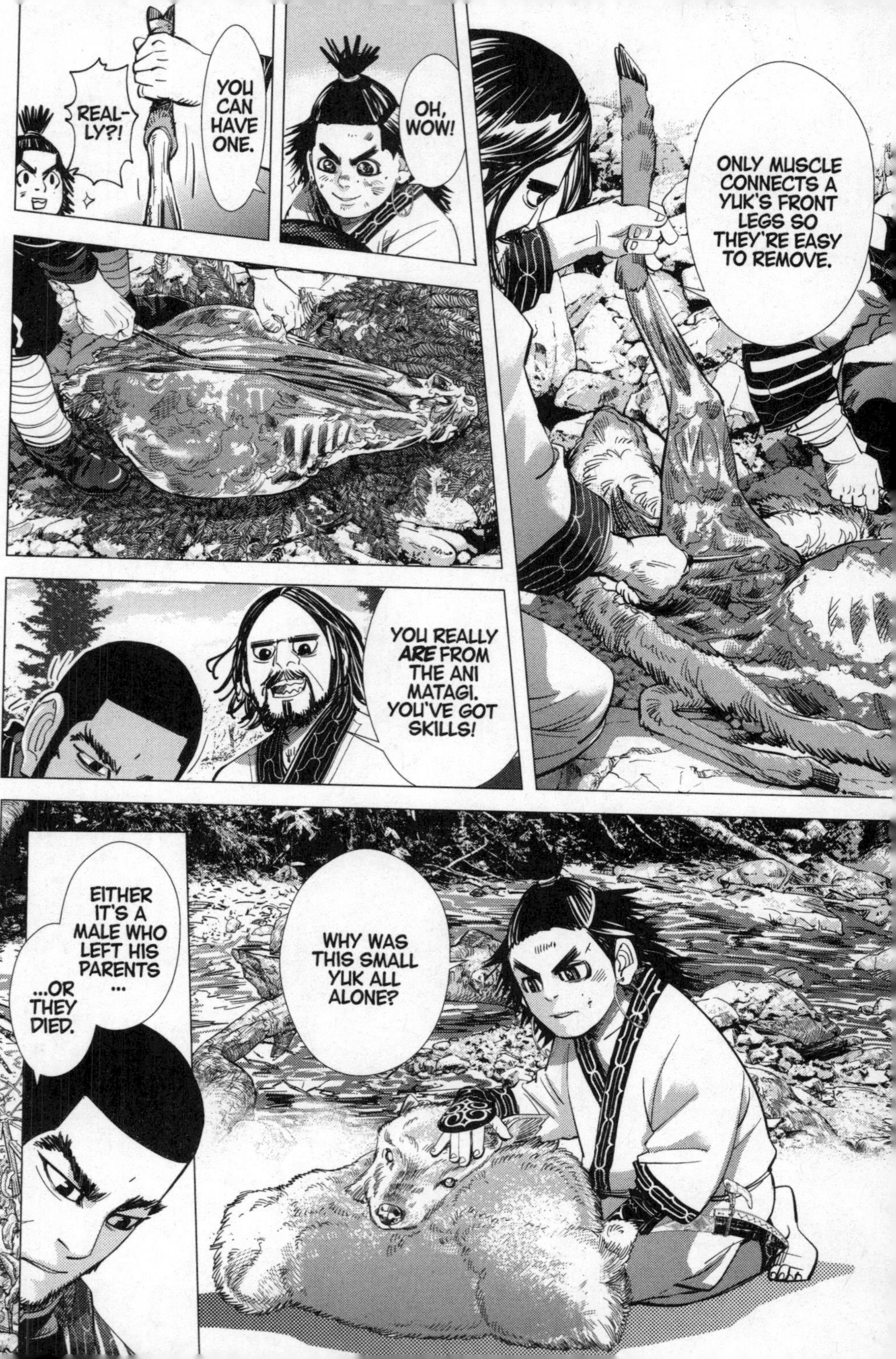
ONLY MUSCLE CONNECTS A YUK'S FRONT LEGS SO THEY'RE EASY TO REMOVE.
OH, WOW!
YOU CAN HAVE ONE.
REAL-LY?!
YOU REALLY *ARE* FROM THE ANI MATAGI. YOU'VE GOT SKILLS!
WHY WAS THIS SMALL YUK ALL ALONE?
EITHER IT'S A MALE WHO LEFT HIS PARENTS ...
...OR THEY DIED.

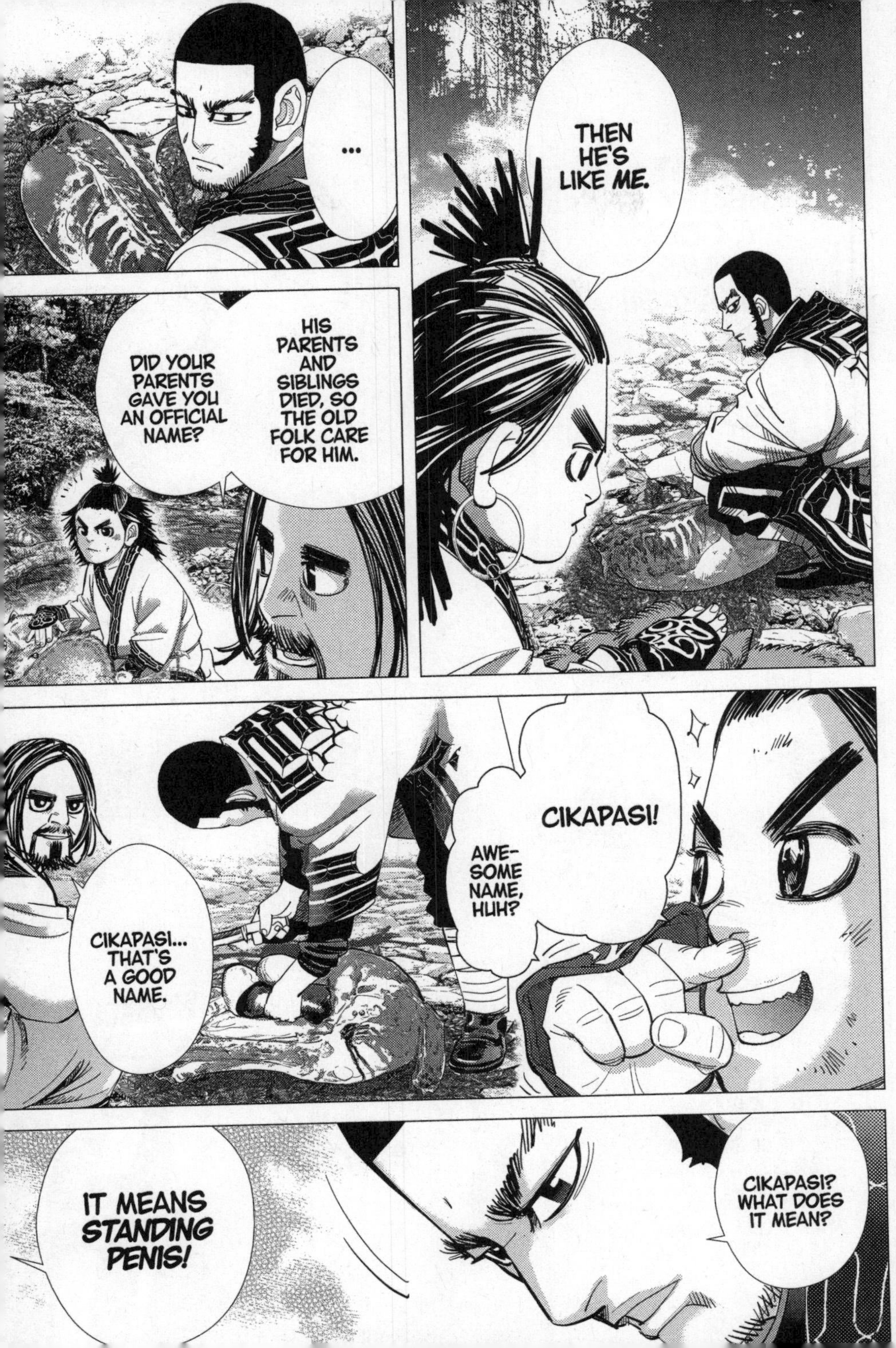
THEN HE'S LIKE ME.
...
HIS PARENTS AND SIBLINGS DIED, SO THE OLD FOLK CARE FOR HIM.
DID YOUR PARENTS GAVE YOU AN OFFICIAL NAME?
CIKAPASI!
AWE-SOME NAME, HUH?
CIKAPASI... THAT'S A GOOD NAME.
CIKAPASI? WHAT DOES IT MEAN?
IT MEANS STANDING PENIS!

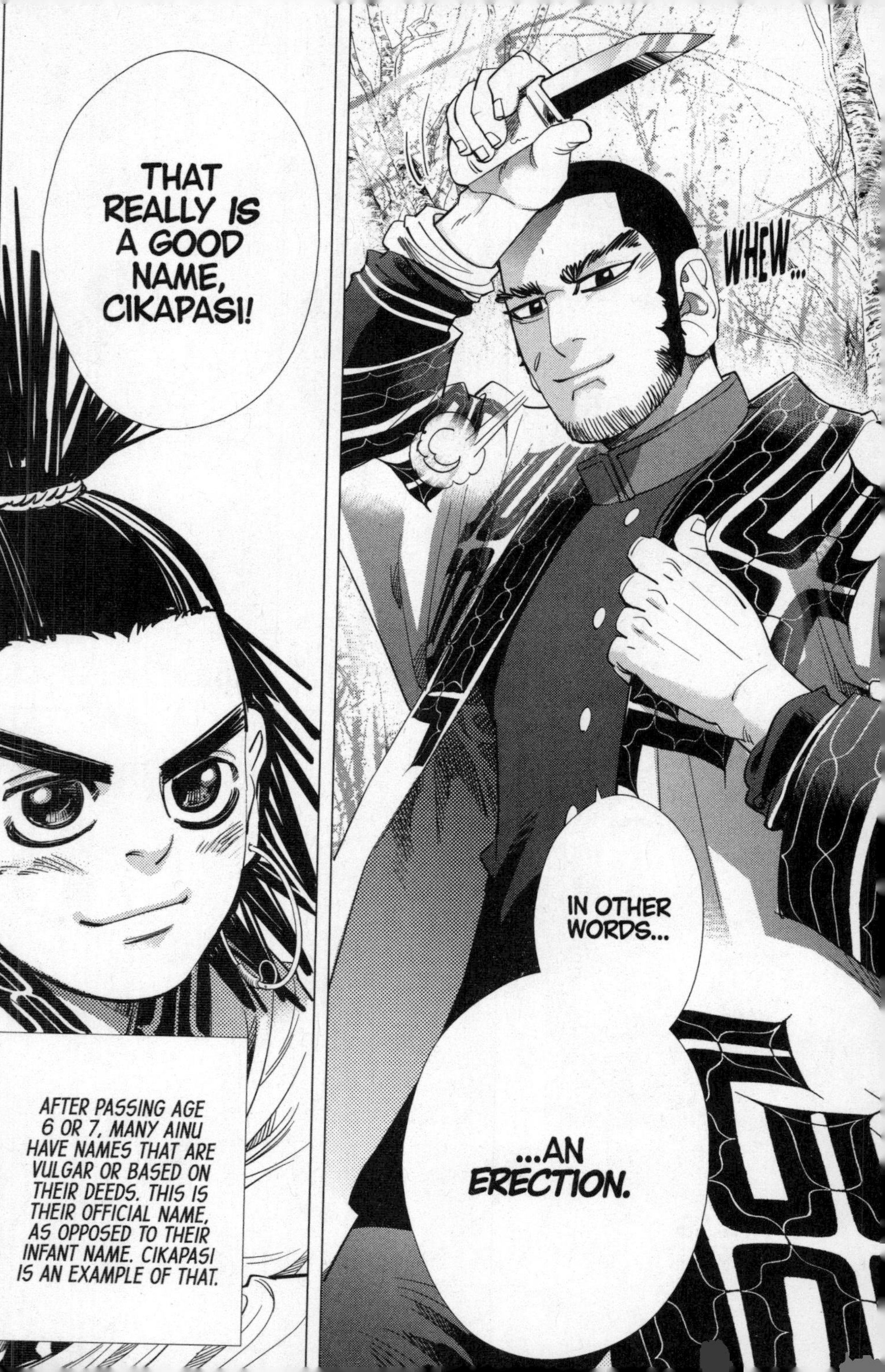
WHEW...
IN OTHER WORDS...
...AN ERECTION.
THAT REALLY IS A GOOD NAME, CIKAPASI!
AFTER PASSING AGE 6 OR 7, MANY AINU HAVE NAMES THAT ARE VULGAR OR BASED ON THEIR DEEDS. THIS IS THEIR OFFICIAL NAME, AS OPPOSED TO THEIR INFANT NAME. CIKAPASI IS AN EXAMPLE OF THAT.

CIKAP
SUALLY
MEANS
BIRD.
ENIS IS
KIND OF
TAPHOR.

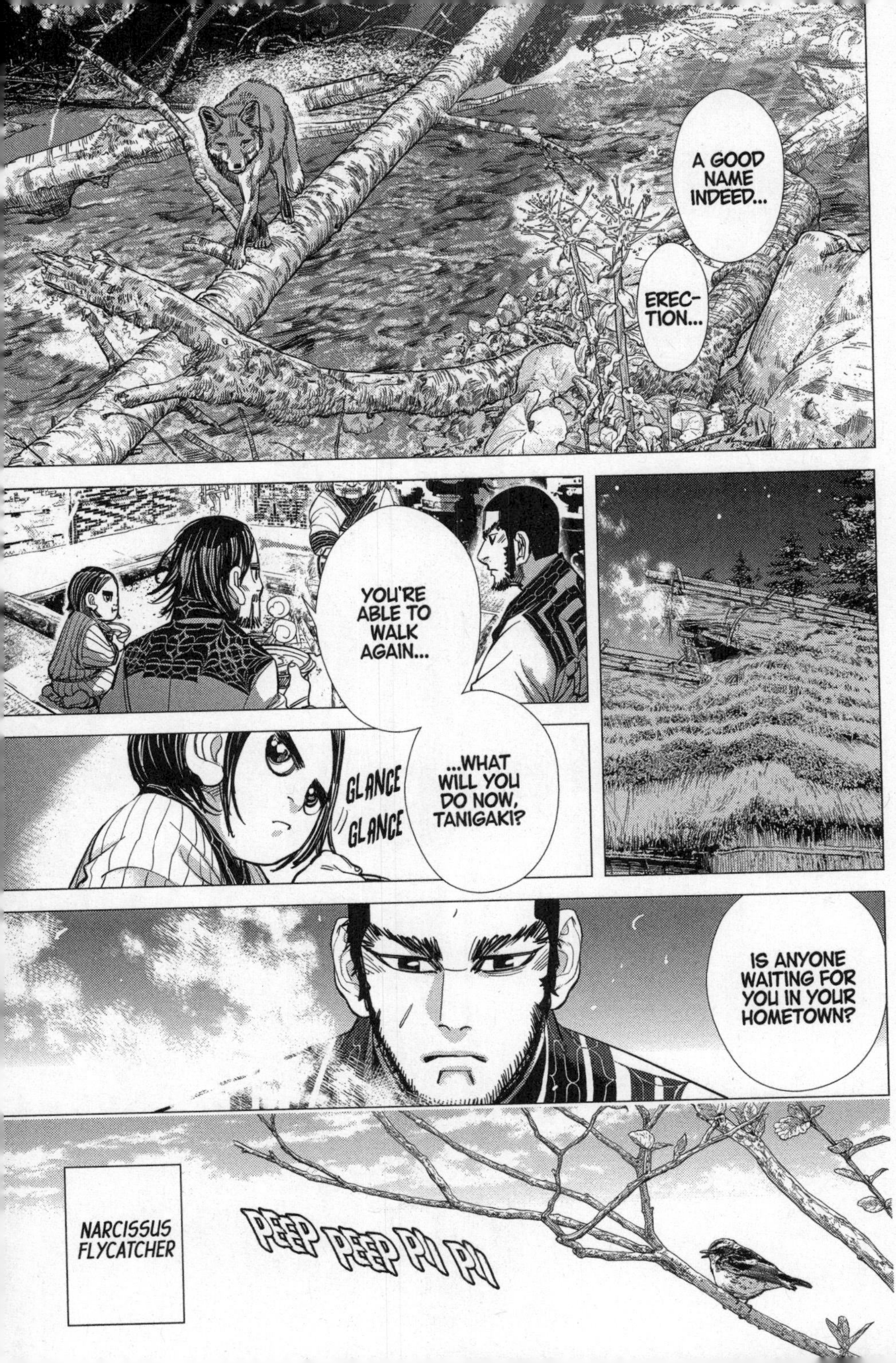
A GOOD NAME INDEED...
ERECTION...
YOU'RE ABLE TO WALK AGAIN...
...WHAT WILL YOU DO NOW, TANIGAKI?
GLANCE GLANCE
IS ANYONE WAITING FOR YOU IN YOUR HOMETOWN?
PEEP PEEP PI PI
NARCISSUS FLYCATCHER

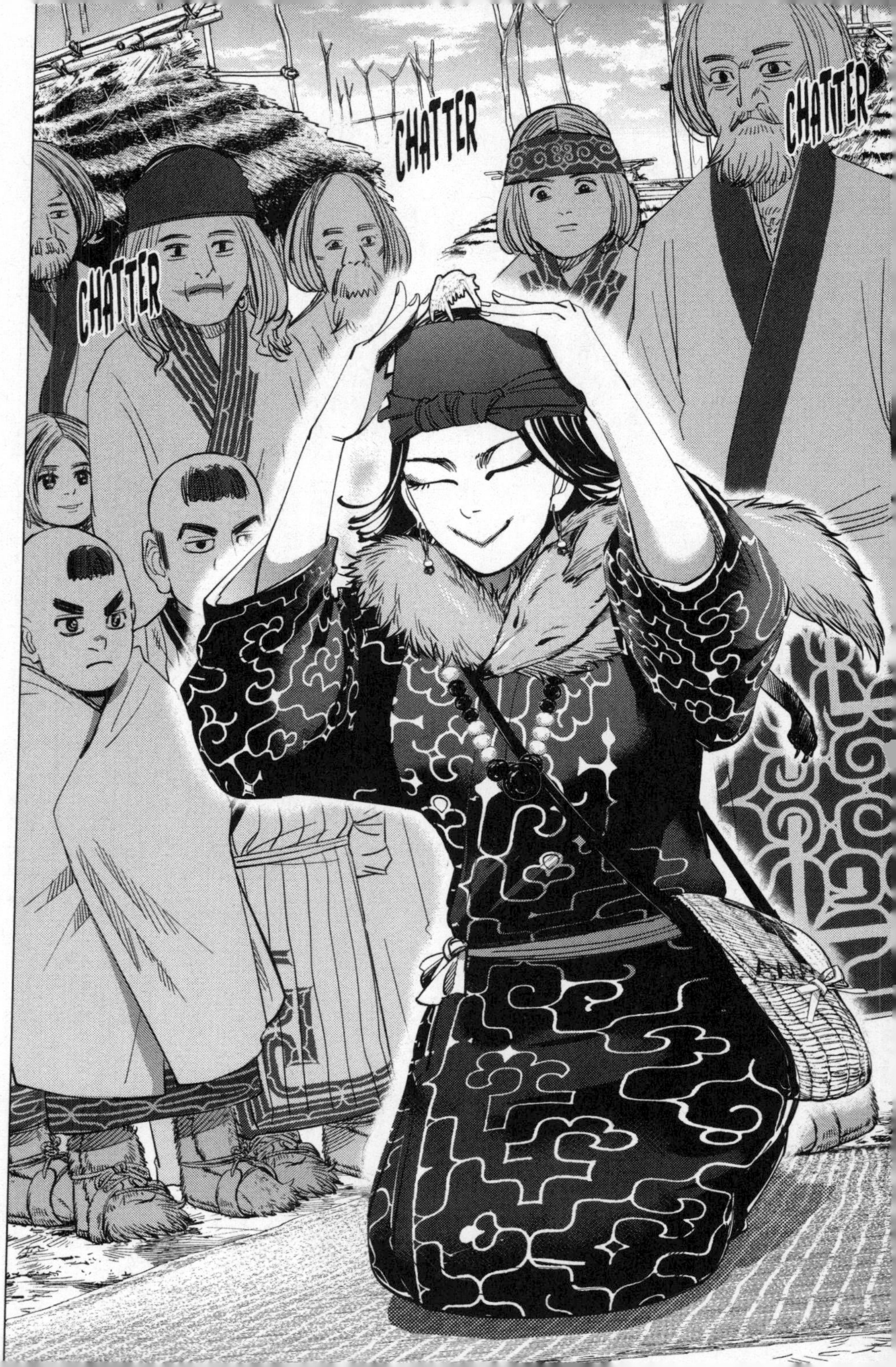
CHATTER
CHATTER
CHATTER

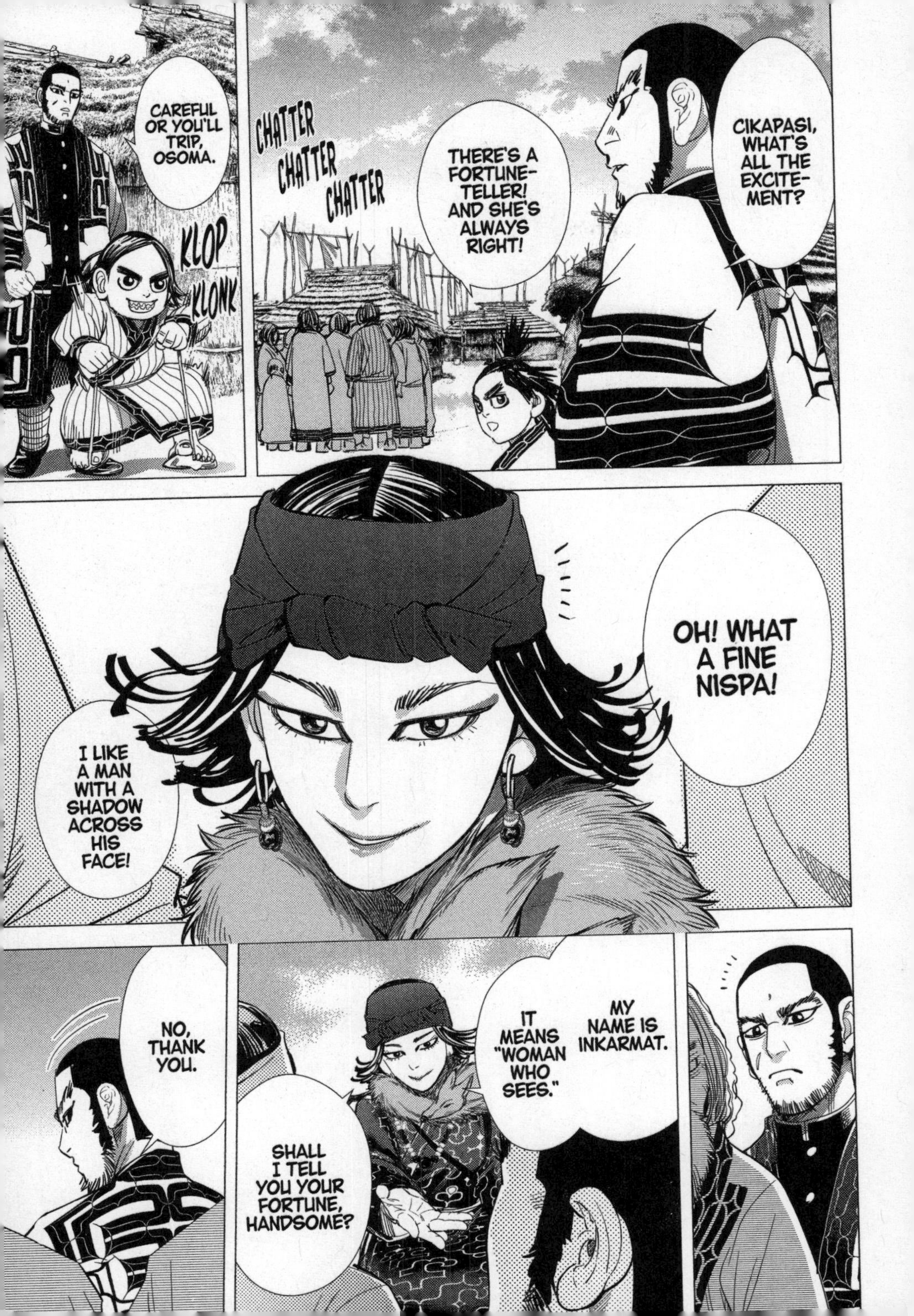
CIKAPASI, WHAT'S ALL THE EXCITEMENT?
THERE'S A FORTUNE-TELLER! AND SHE'S ALWAYS RIGHT!
CHATTER CHATTER CHATTER
CAREFUL OR YOU'LL TRIP, OSOMA.
KLOP KLONK
OH! WHAT A FINE NISPA!
I LIKE A MAN WITH A SHADOW ACROSS HIS FACE!
MY NAME IS INKARMAT.
IT MEANS "WOMAN WHO SEES."
SHALL I TELL YOU YOUR FORTUNE, HANDSOME?
NO, THANK YOU.

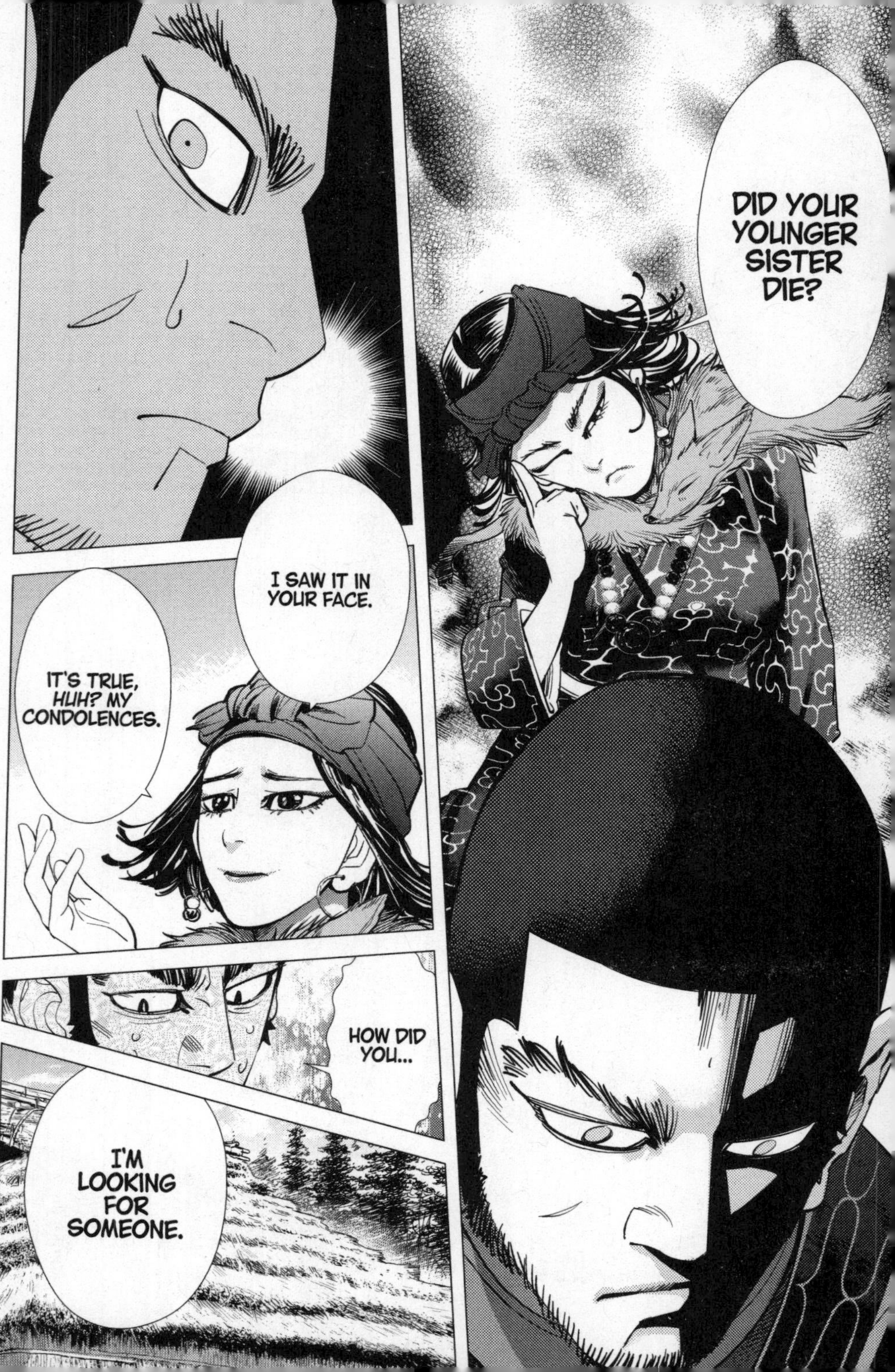
DID YOUR YOUNGER SISTER DIE?
I SAW IT IN YOUR FACE.
IT'S TRUE, HUH? MY CONDOLENCES.
HOW DID YOU...
I'M LOOKING FOR SOMEONE.

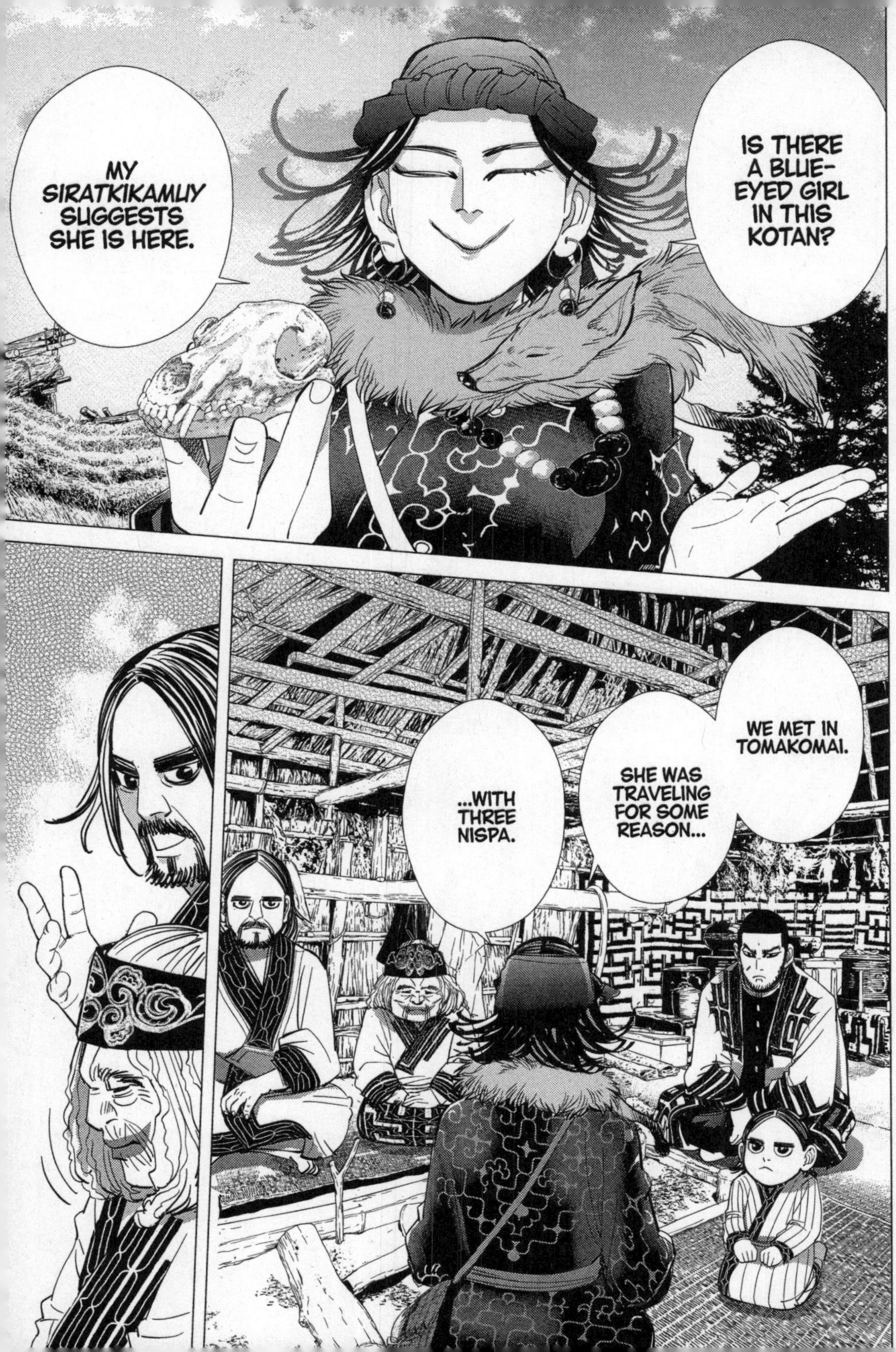
IS THERE A BLUE-EYED GIRL IN THIS KOTAN?
MY SIRATKIKAMUY SUGGESTS SHE IS HERE.
WE MET IN TOMAKOMAI.
SHE WAS TRAVELING FOR SOME REASON...
...WITH THREE NISPA.

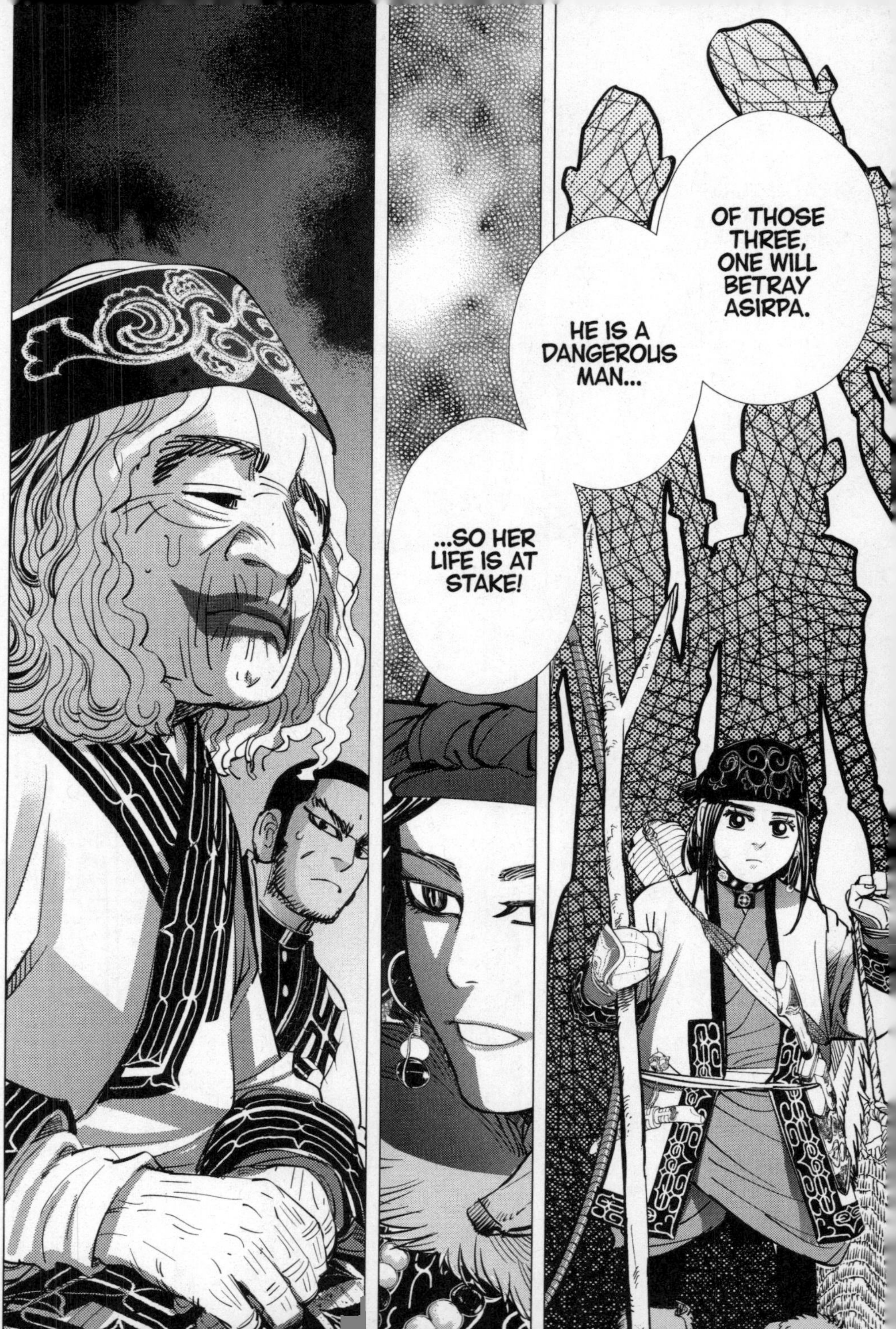
OF THOSE THREE, ONE WILL BETRAY ASIRPA.
HE IS A DANGEROUS MAN...
...SO HER LIFE IS AT STAKE!

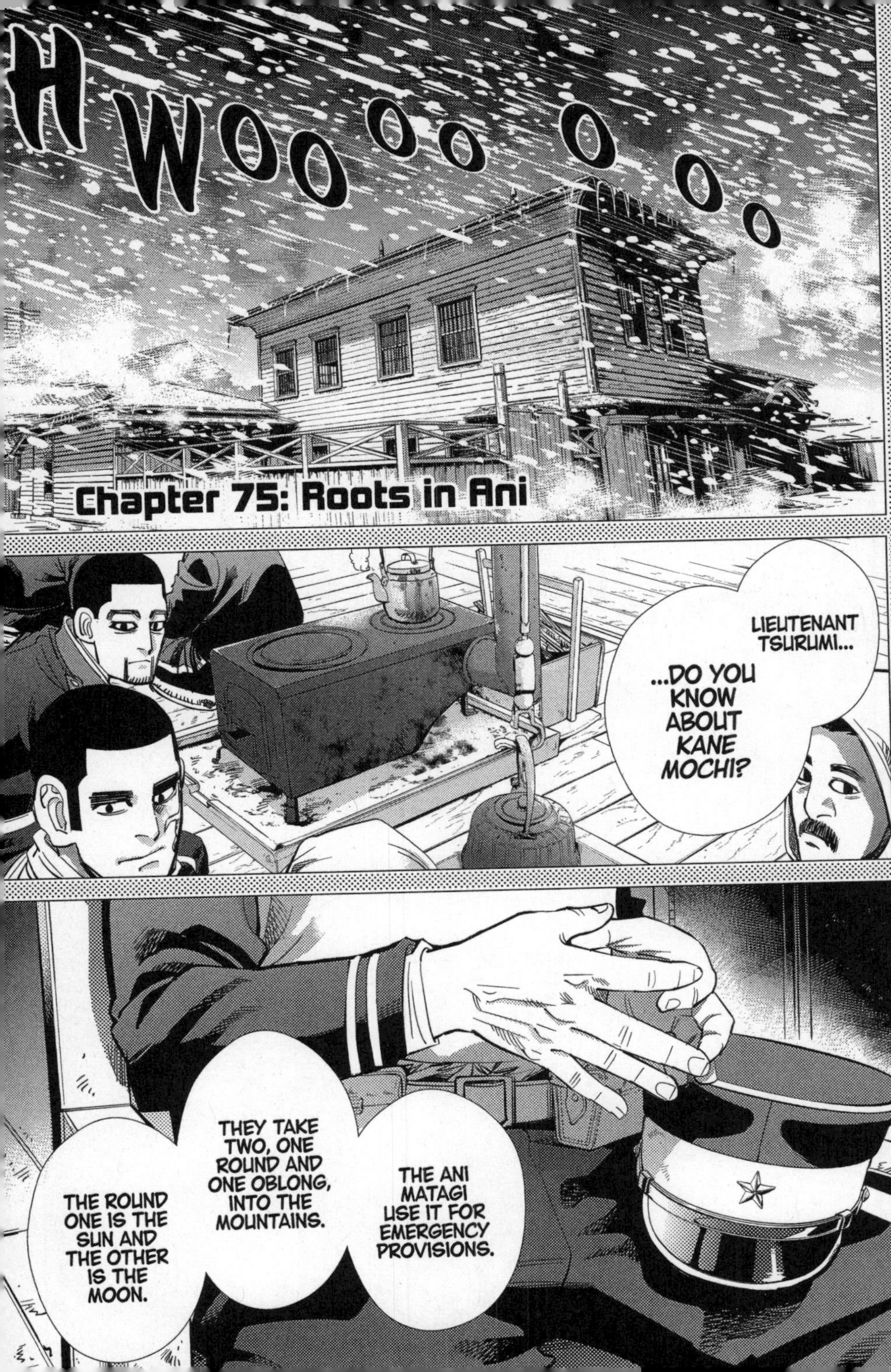
HWOOOOO...
Chapter 75: Roots in Ani
LIEUTENANT TSURUMI...
...DO YOU KNOW ABOUT KANE MOCHI?
THE ANI MATAGI USE IT FOR EMERGENCY PROVISIONS.
THEY TAKE TWO, ONE ROUND AND ONE OBLONG, INTO THE MOUNTAINS.
THE ROUND ONE IS THE SUN AND THE OTHER IS THE MOON.

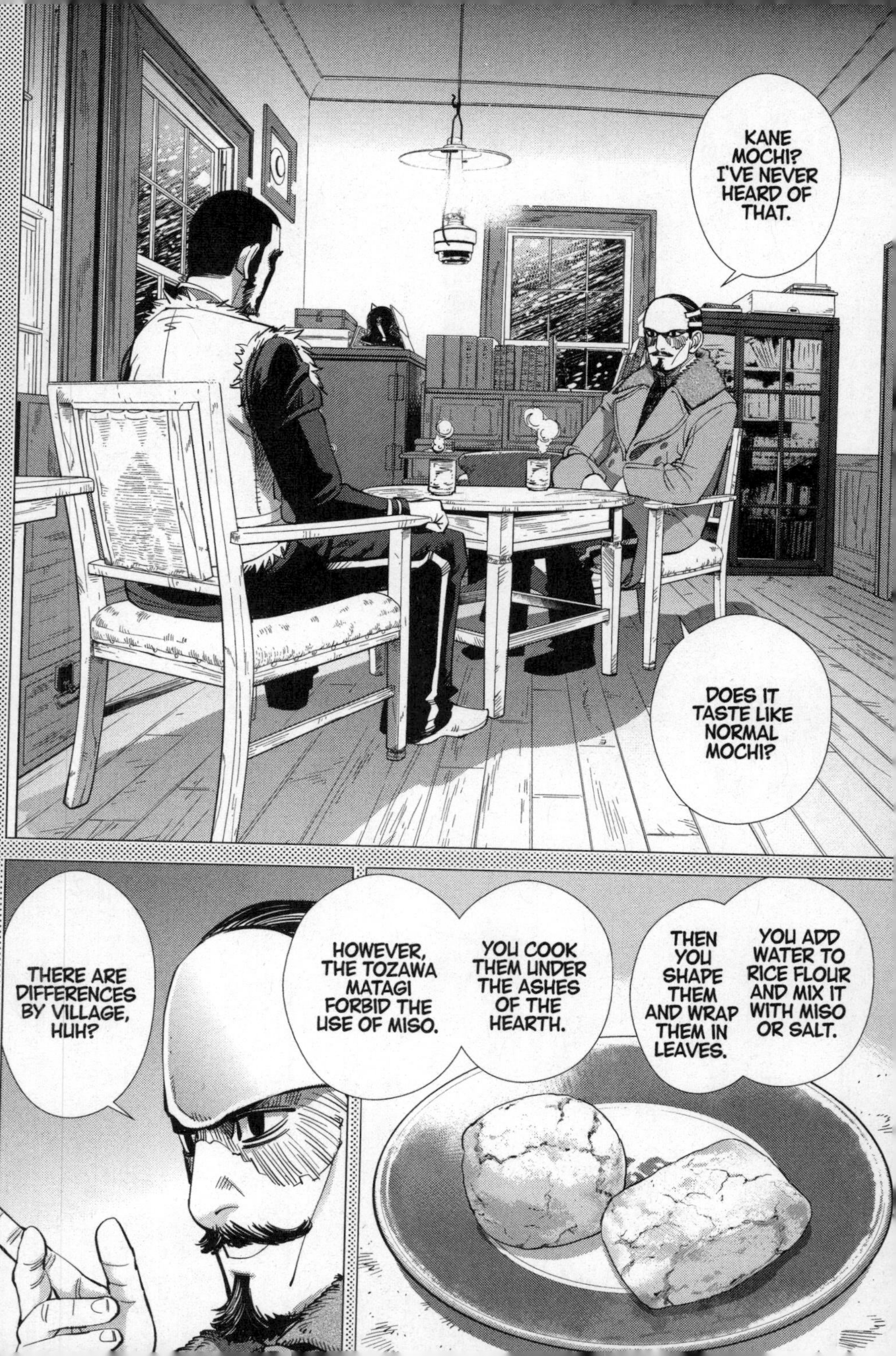
KANE MOCHI? I'VE NEVER HEARD OF THAT.
DOES IT TASTE LIKE NORMAL MOCHI?
YOU ADD WATER TO RICE FLOUR AND MIX IT WITH MISO OR SALT.
THEN YOU SHAPE THEM AND WRAP THEM IN LEAVES.
YOU COOK THEM UNDER THE ASHES OF THE HEARTH.
HOWEVER, THE TOZAWA MATAGI FORBID THE USE OF MISO.
THERE ARE DIFFERENCES BY VILLAGE, HUH?

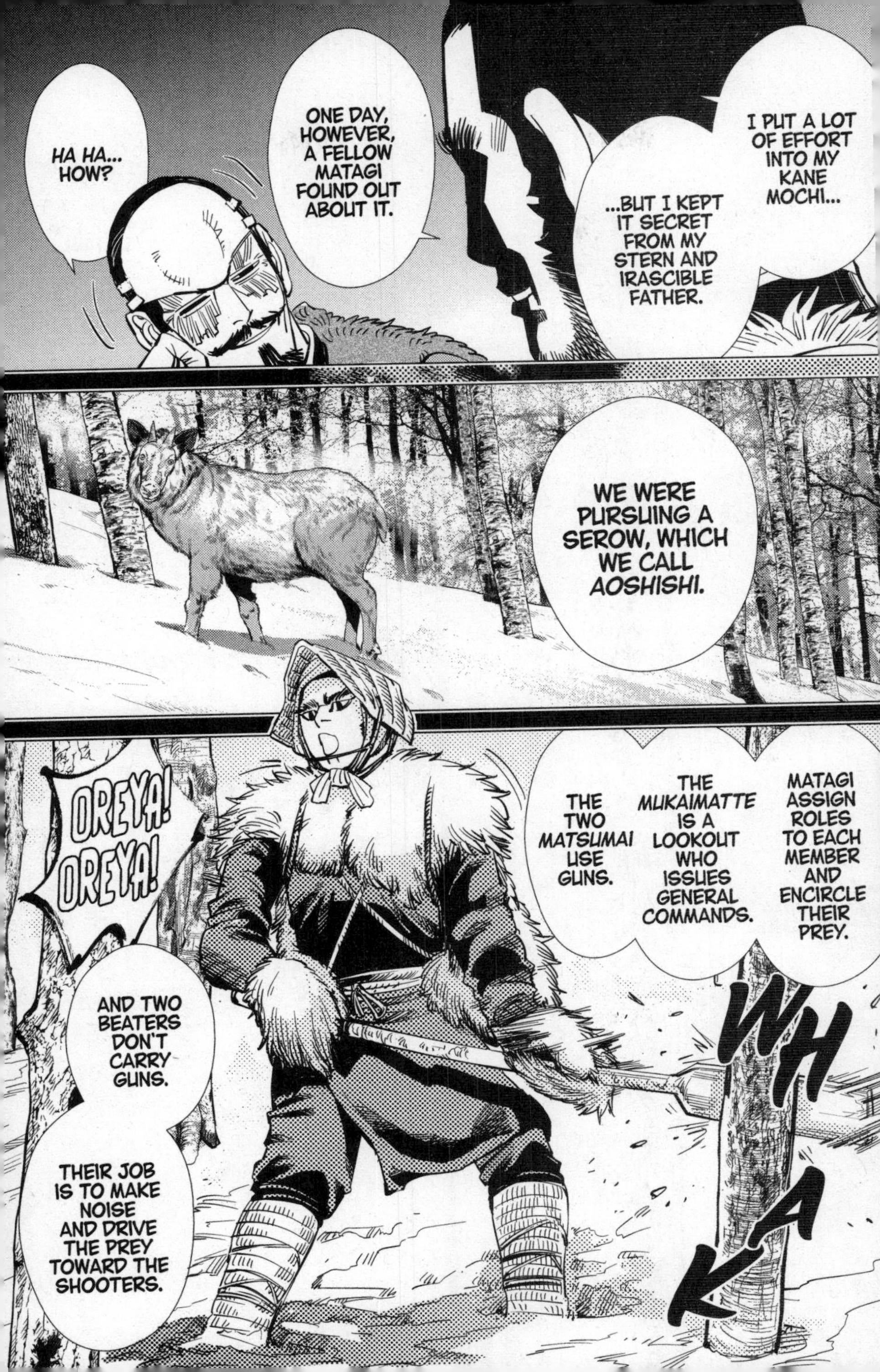
I PUT A LOT OF EFFORT INTO MY KANE MOCHI...
...BUT I KEPT IT SECRET FROM MY STERN AND IRASCIBLE FATHER.
ONE DAY, HOWEVER, A FELLOW MATAGI FOUND OUT ABOUT IT.
HA HA... HOW?
WE WERE PURSUING A SEROW, WHICH WE CALL AOSHISHI.
MATAGI ASSIGN ROLES TO EACH MEMBER AND ENCIRCLE THEIR PREY.
THE *MUKAIMATTE* IS A LOOKOUT WHO ISSUES GENERAL COMMANDS.
THE TWO *MATSUMAI* USE GUNS.
OREYA! OREYA!
WHAK
AND TWO BEATERS DON'T CARRY GUNS.
THEIR JOB IS TO MAKE NOISE AND DRIVE THE PREY TOWARD THE SHOOTERS.

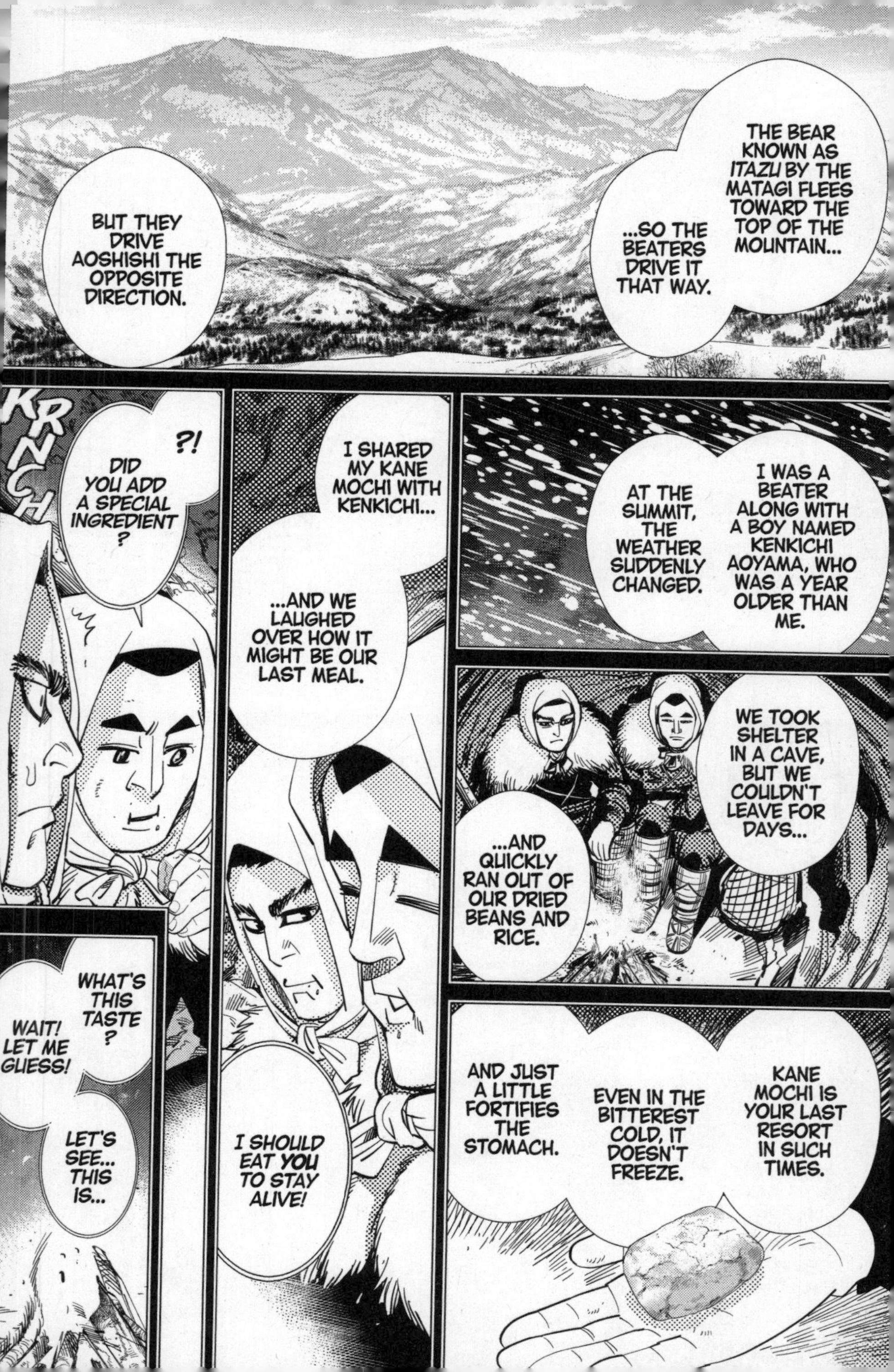
THE BEAR KNOWN AS ITAZU BY THE MATAGI FLEES TOWARD THE TOP OF THE MOUNTAIN...
...SO THE BEATERS DRIVE IT THAT WAY.
BUT THEY DRIVE AOSHISHI THE OPPOSITE DIRECTION.
I WAS A BEATER ALONG WITH A BOY NAMED KENKICHI AOYAMA, WHO WAS A YEAR OLDER THAN ME.
AT THE SUMMIT, THE WEATHER SUDDENLY CHANGED.
WE TOOK SHELTER IN A CAVE, BUT WE COULDN'T LEAVE FOR DAYS...
...AND QUICKLY RAN OUT OF OUR DRIED BEANS AND RICE.
KANE MOCHI IS YOUR LAST RESORT IN SUCH TIMES.
EVEN IN THE BITTEREST COLD, IT DOESN'T FREEZE.
AND JUST A LITTLE FORTIFIES THE STOMACH.
I SHARED MY KANE MOCHI WITH KENKICHI...
...AND WE LAUGHED OVER HOW IT MIGHT BE OUR LAST MEAL.
I SHOULD EAT *YOU* TO STAY ALIVE!
KRNCH
?!
DID YOU ADD A SPECIAL INGREDIENT?
WHAT'S THIS TASTE?
WAIT! LET ME GUESS!
LET'S SEE... THIS IS...

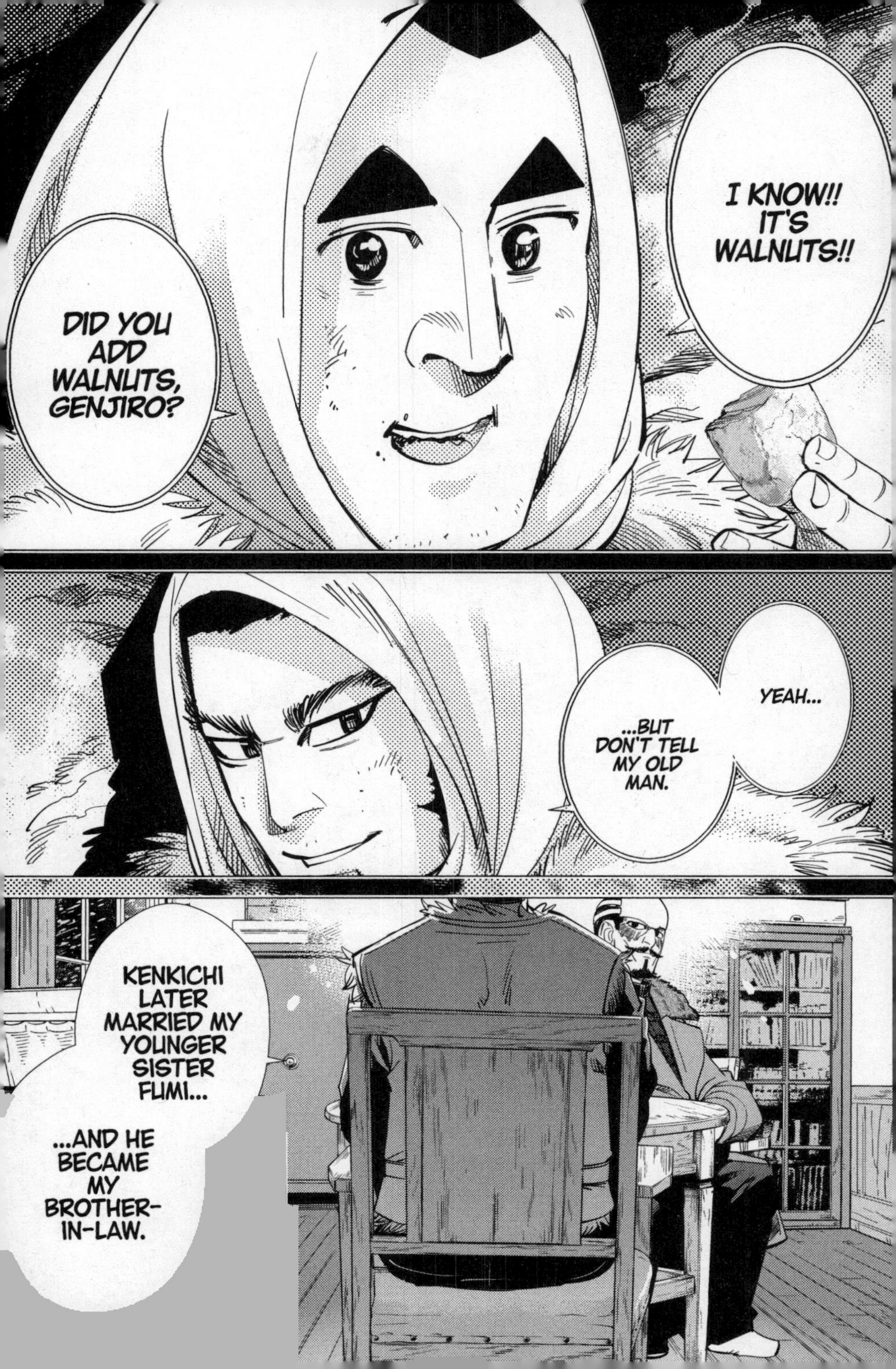
I KNOW!! IT'S WALNUTS!!
DID YOU ADD WALNUTS, GENJIRO?
YEAH...
...BUT DON'T TELL MY OLD MAN.
KENKICHI LATER MARRIED MY YOUNGER SISTER FUMI...
...AND HE BECAME MY BROTHER-IN-LAW.

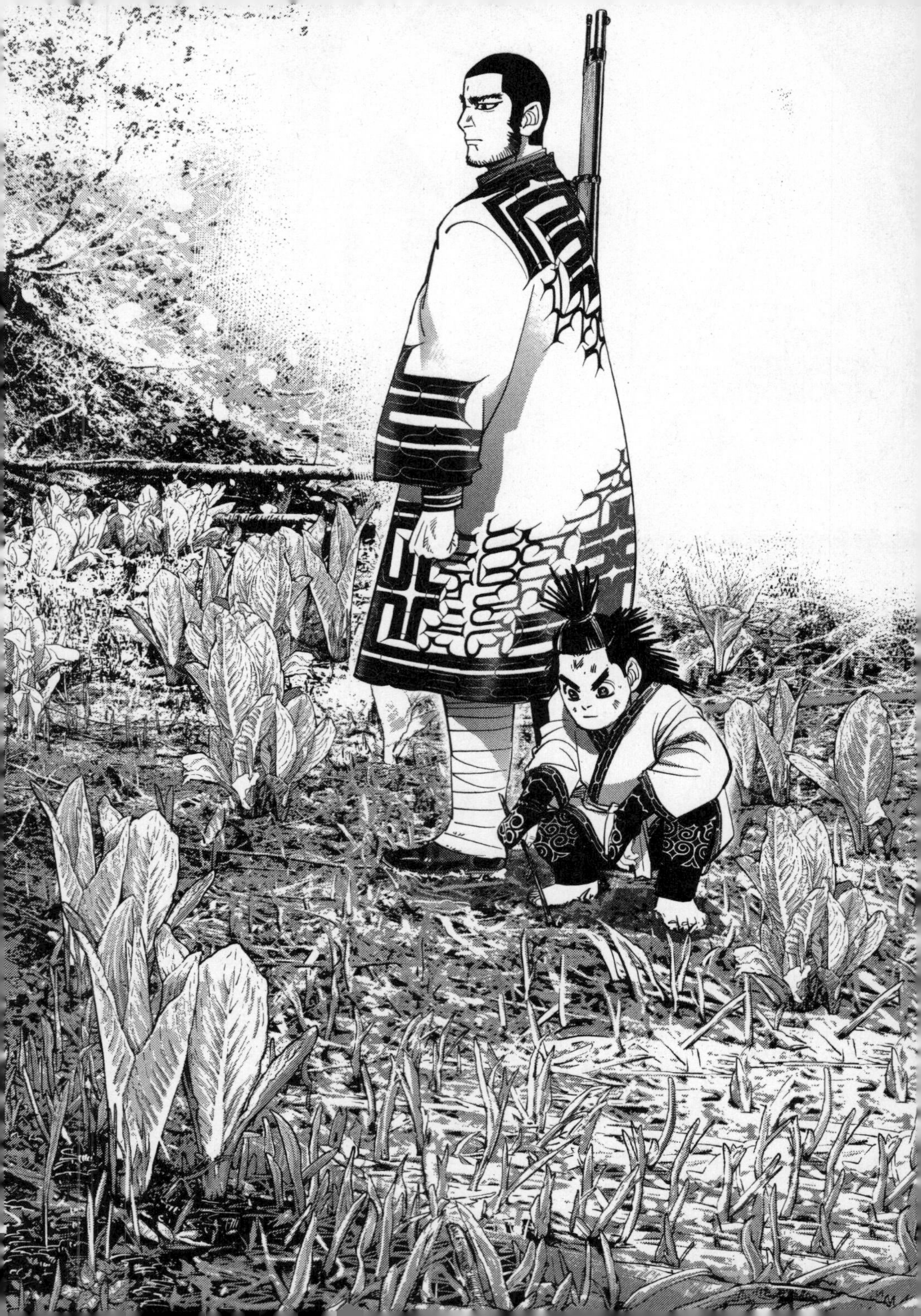

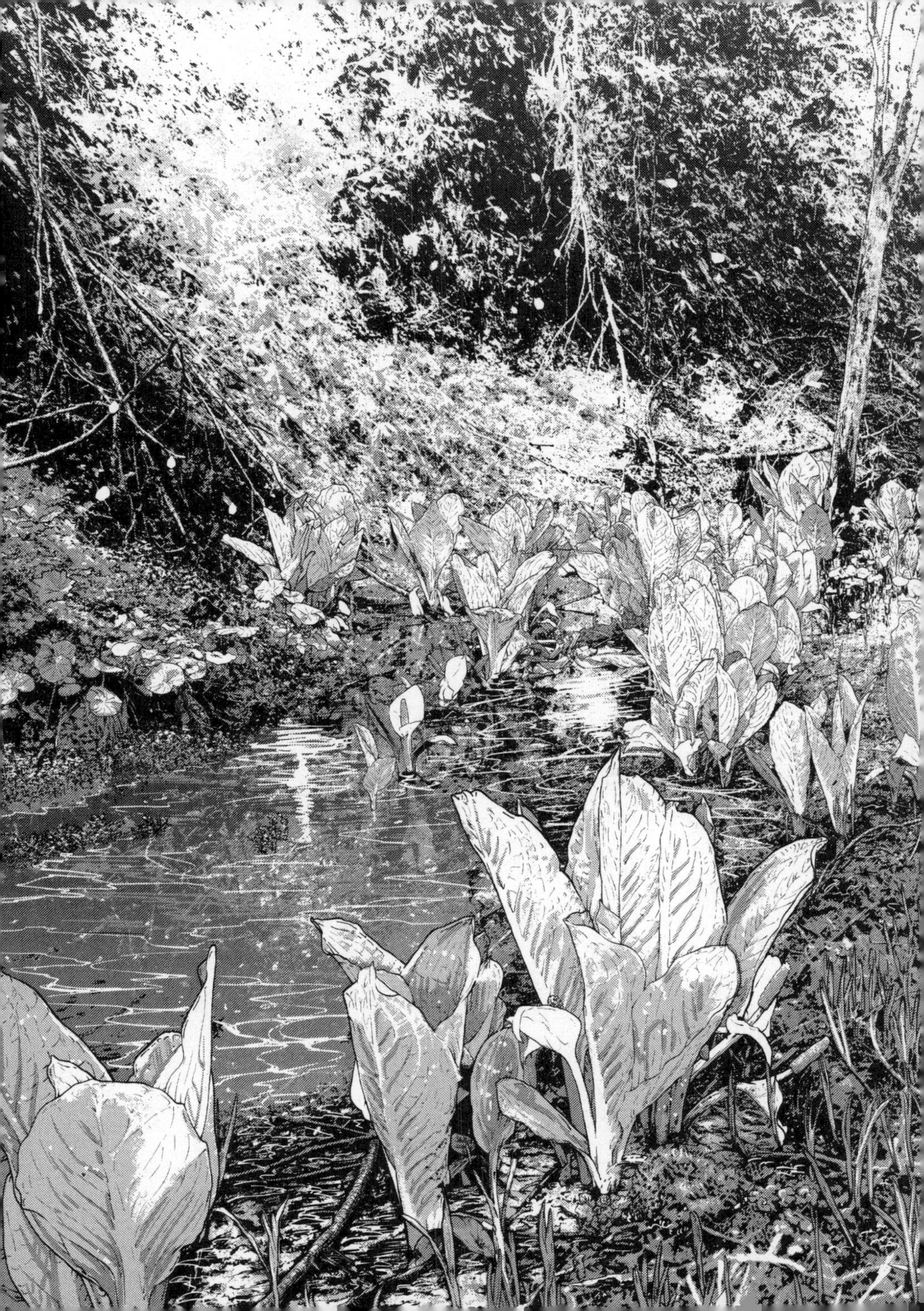

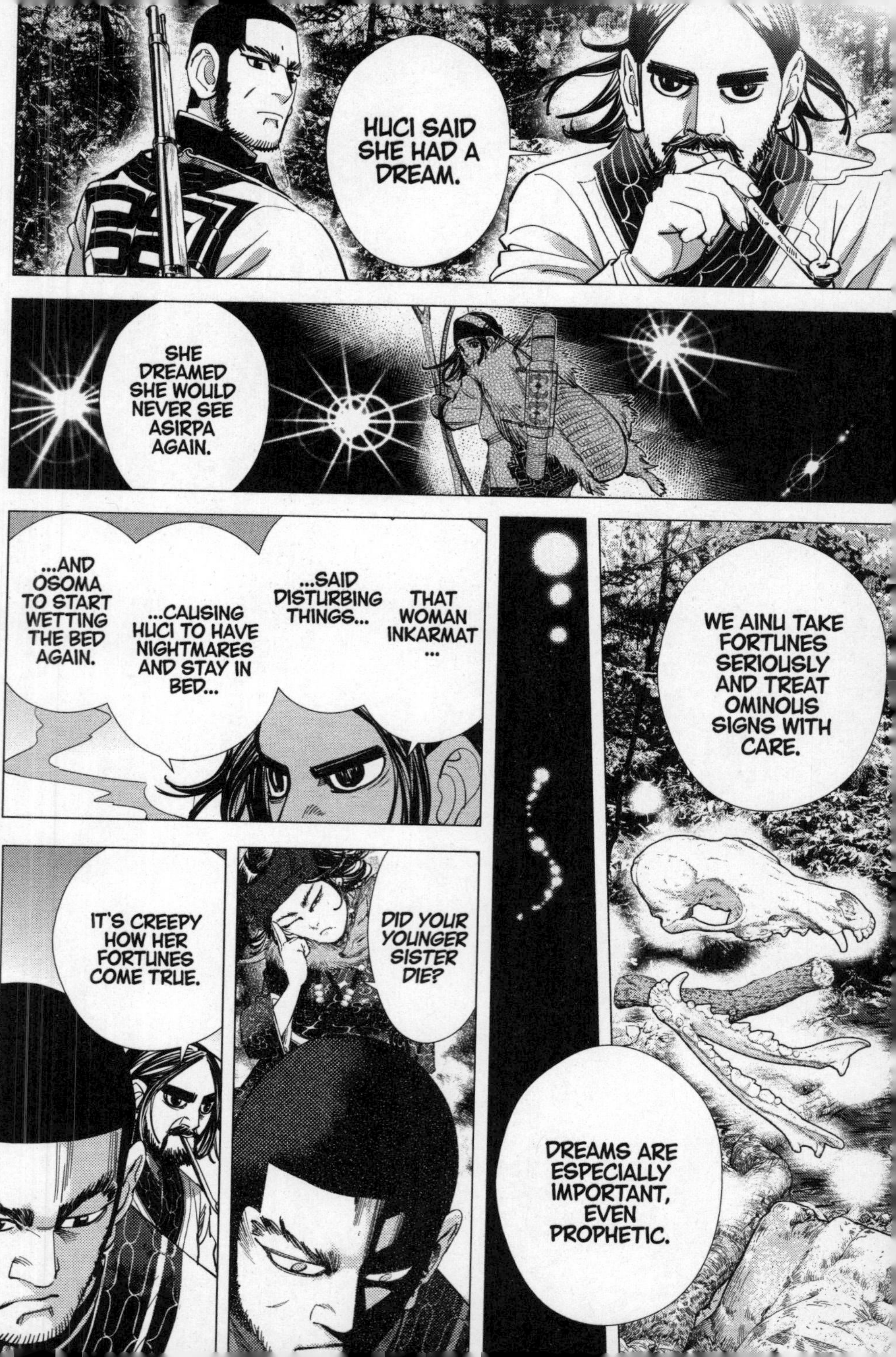
HUCI SAID SHE HAD A DREAM.
SHE DREAMED SHE WOULD NEVER SEE ASIRPA AGAIN.
WE AINU TAKE FORTUNES SERIOUSLY AND TREAT OMINOUS SIGNS WITH CARE.
DREAMS ARE ESPECIALLY IMPORTANT, EVEN PROPHETIC.
THAT WOMAN INKARMAT ...
...SAID DISTURBING THINGS...
...CAUSING HUCI TO HAVE NIGHTMARES AND STAY IN BED...
...AND OSOMA TO START WETTING THE BED AGAIN.
DID YOUR YOUNGER SISTER DIE?
IT'S CREEPY HOW HER FORTUNES COME TRUE.

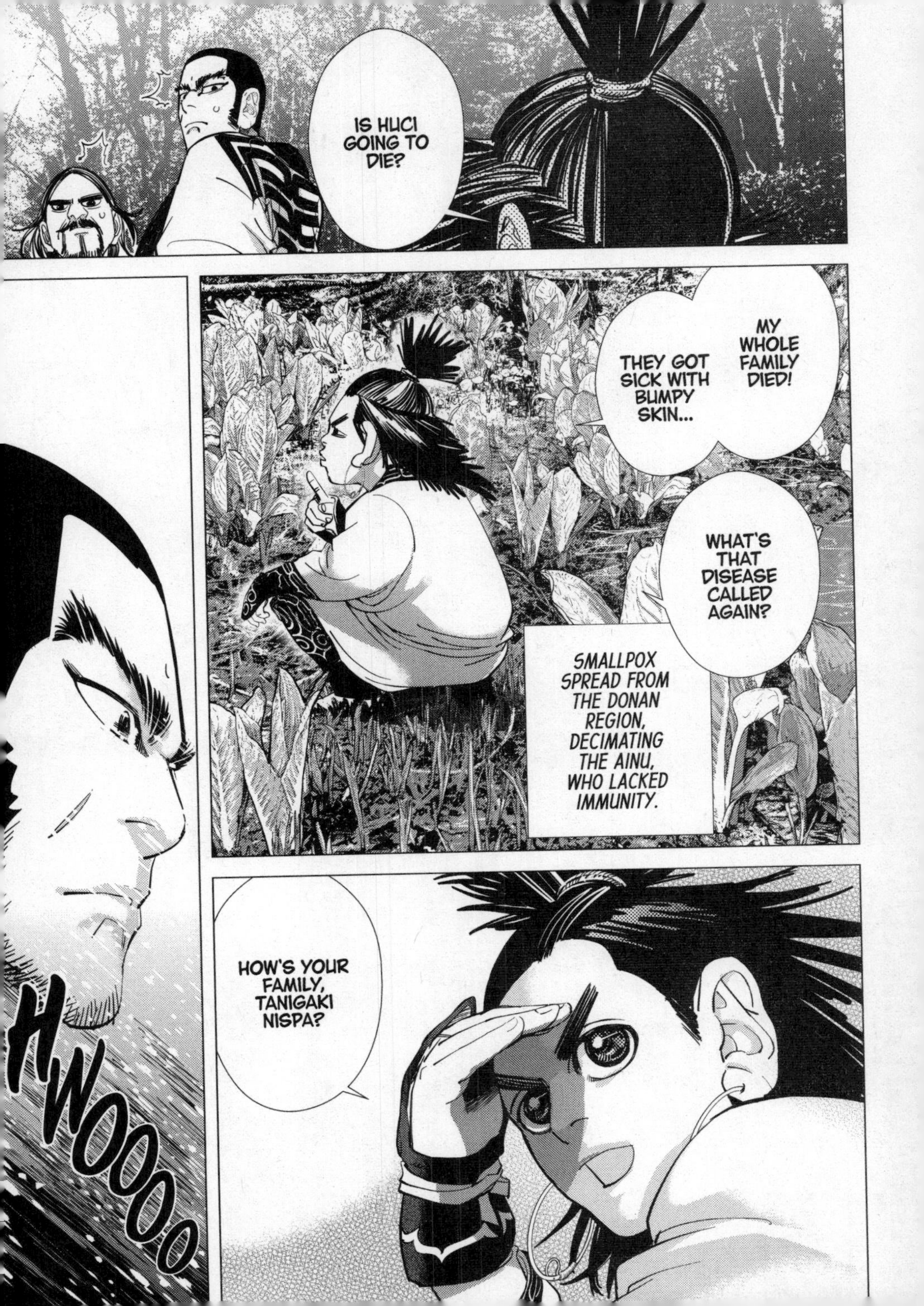
IS HUCI GOING TO DIE?
MY WHOLE FAMILY DIED!
THEY GOT SICK WITH BUMPY SKIN...
WHAT'S THAT DISEASE CALLED AGAIN?
SMALLPOX SPREAD FROM THE DONAN REGION, DECIMATING THE AINU, WHO LACKED IMMUNITY.
HOW'S YOUR FAMILY, TANIGAKI NISPA?
HWOOOO

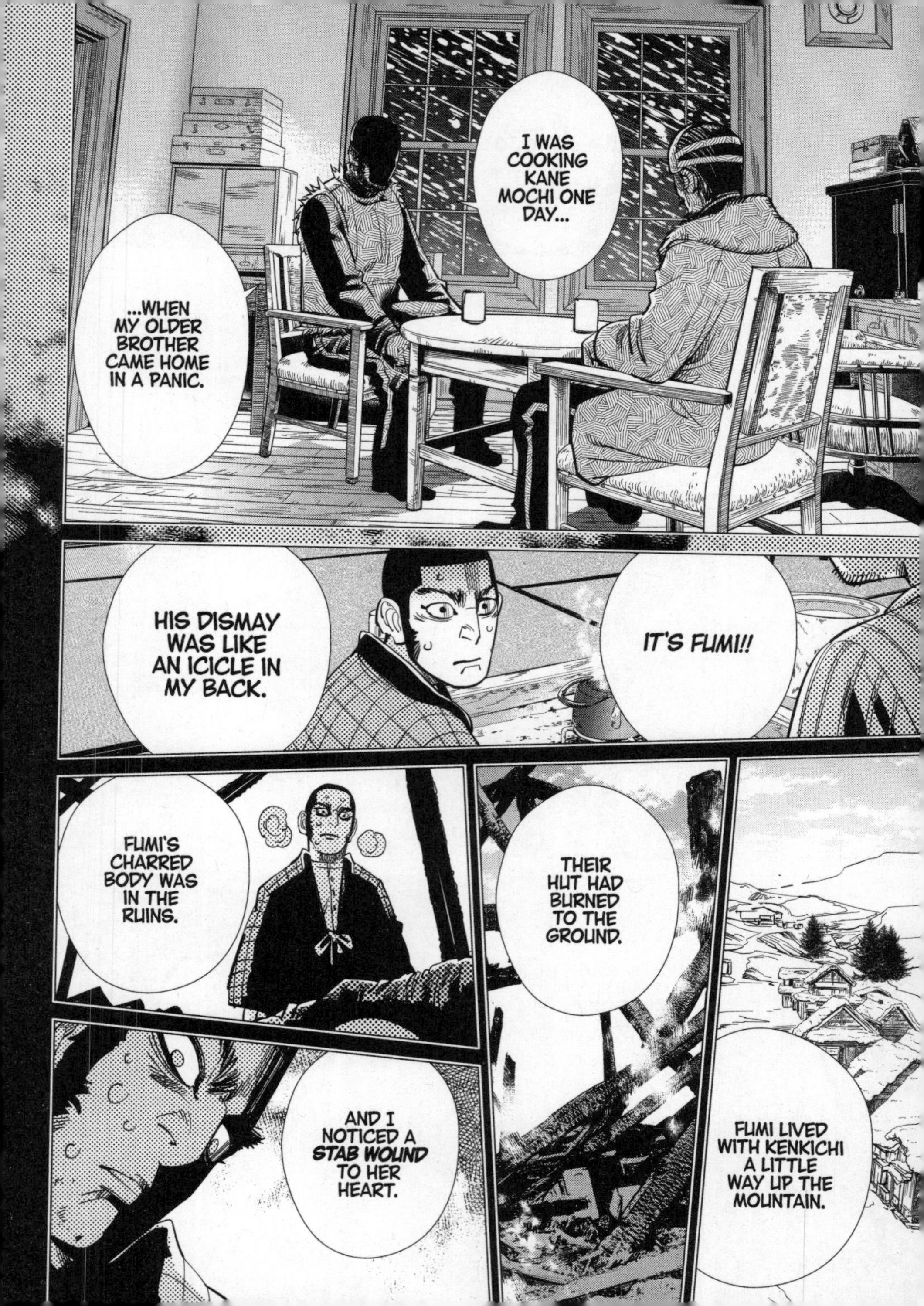
I WAS COOKING KANE MOCHI ONE DAY...
...WHEN MY OLDER BROTHER CAME HOME IN A PANIC.
IT'S FUMI!!
HIS DISMAY WAS LIKE AN ICICLE IN MY BACK.
FUMI LIVED WITH KENKICHI A LITTLE WAY UP THE MOUNTAIN.
THEIR HUT HAD BURNED TO THE GROUND.
FUMI'S CHARRED BODY WAS IN THE RUINS.
AND I NOTICED A *STAB WOUND* TO HER HEART.

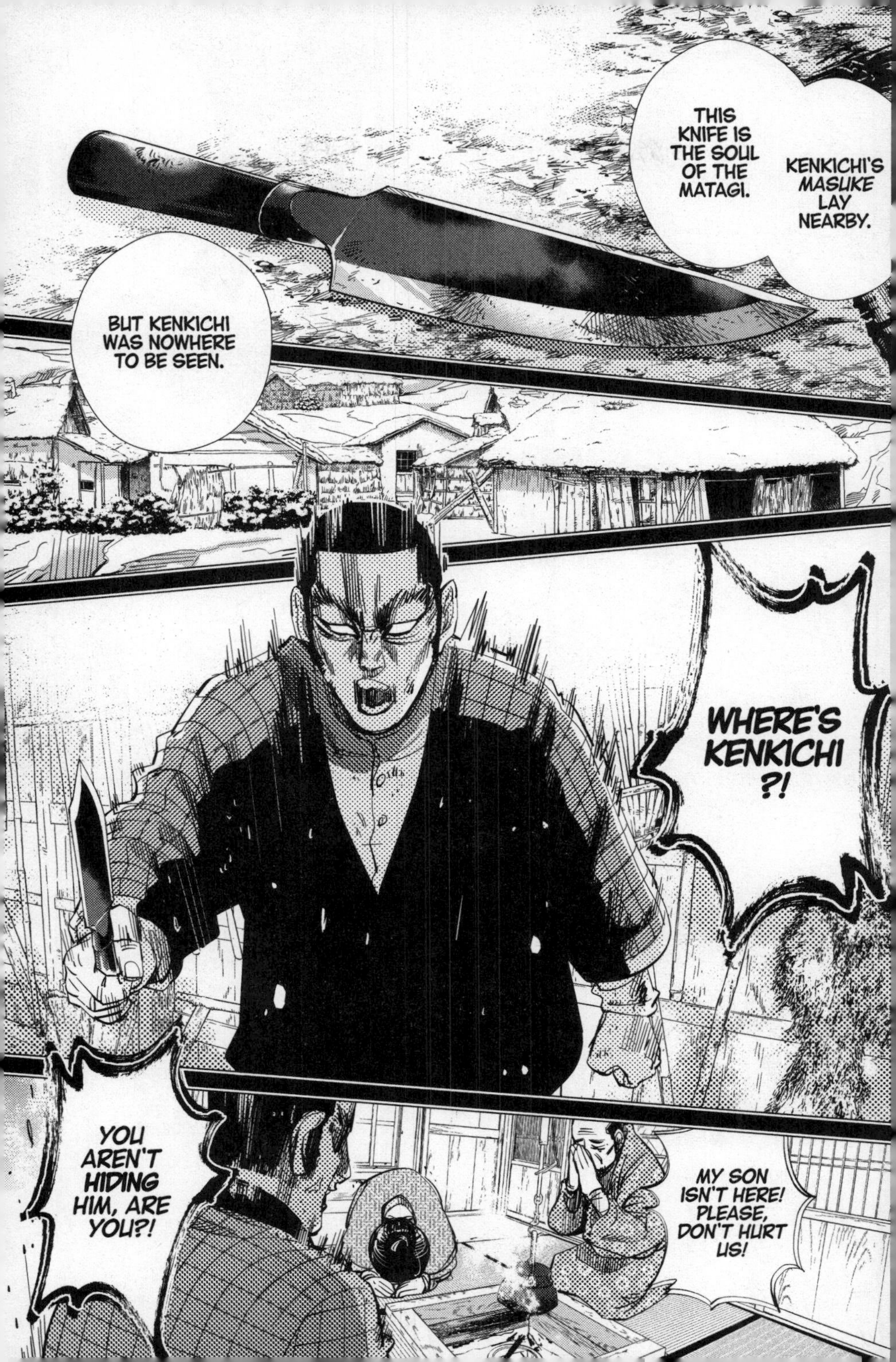
KENKICHI'S MASUKE LAY NEARBY.
THIS KNIFE IS THE SOUL OF THE MATAGI.
BUT KENKICHI WAS NOWHERE TO BE SEEN.
WHERE'S KENKICHI ?!
MY SON ISN'T HERE! PLEASE, DON'T HURT US!
YOU AREN'T HIDING HIM, ARE YOU?!

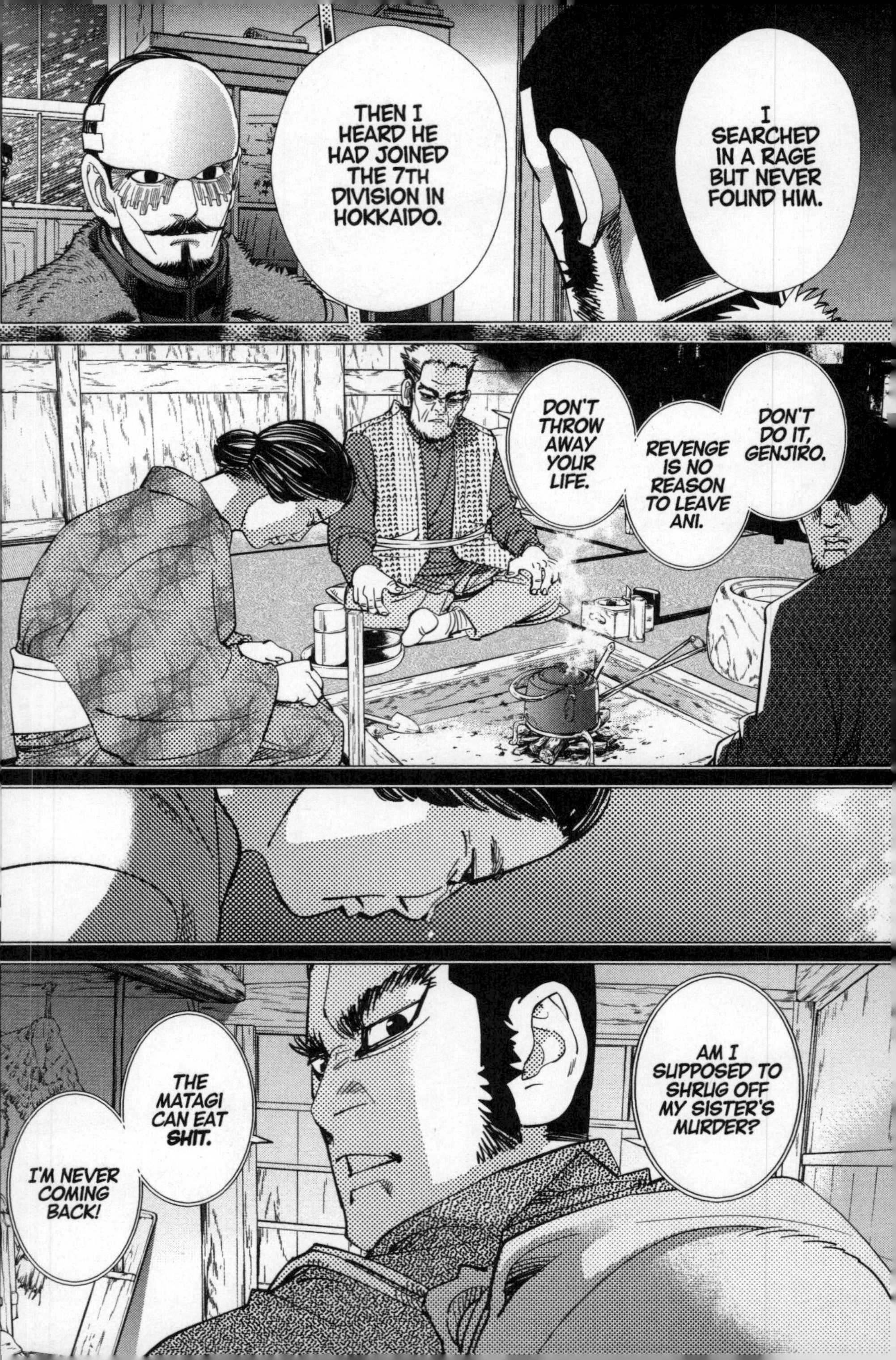
I SEARCHED IN A RAGE BUT NEVER FOUND HIM.
THEN I HEARD HE HAD JOINED THE 7TH DIVISION IN HOKKAIDO.
DON'T DO IT, GENJIRO.
REVENGE IS NO REASON TO LEAVE ANI.
DON'T THROW AWAY YOUR LIFE.
AM I SUPPOSED TO SHRUG OFF MY SISTER'S MURDER?
THE MATAGI CAN EAT SHIT.
I'M NEVER COMING BACK!

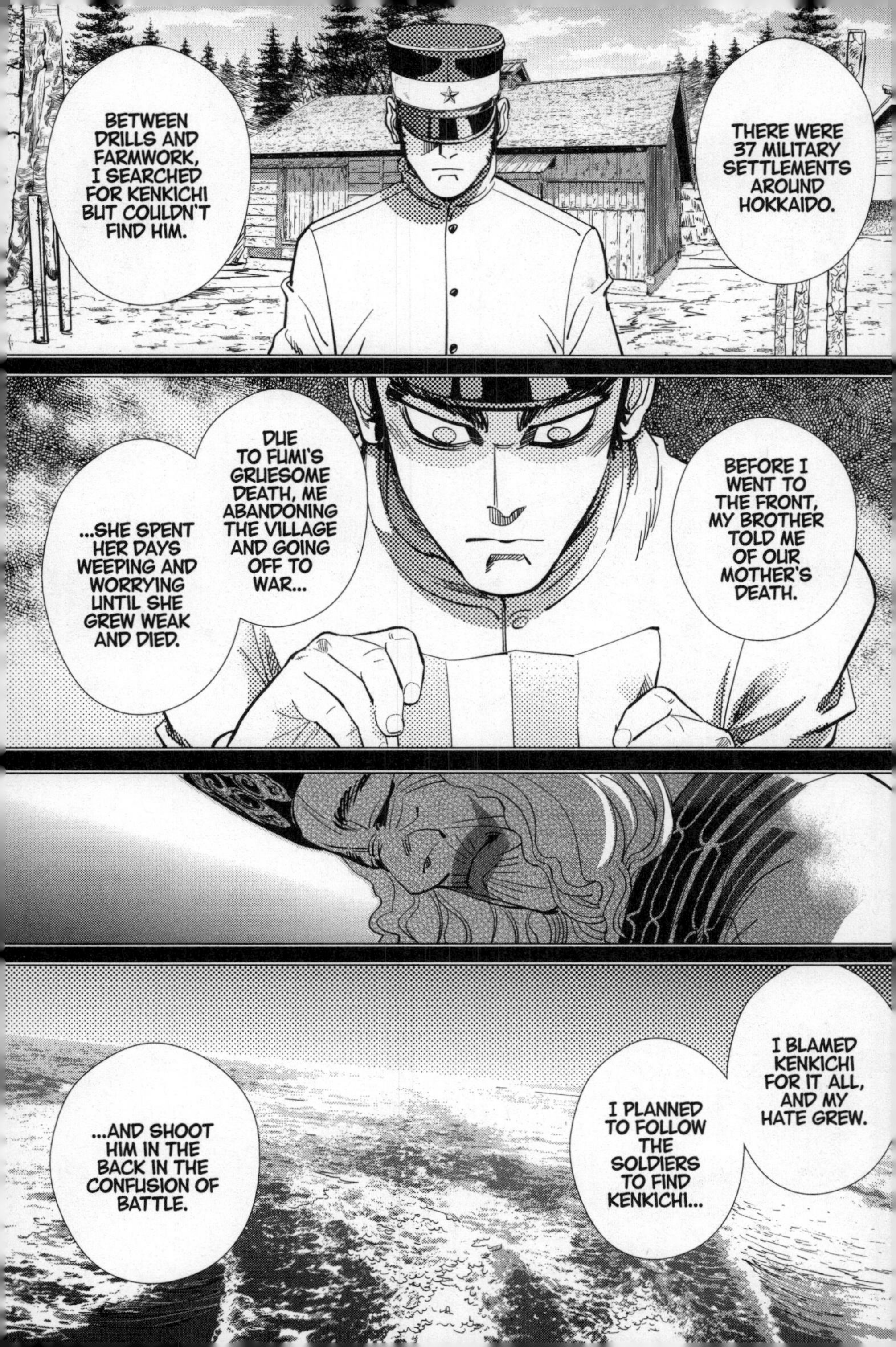
THERE WERE 37 MILITARY SETTLEMENTS AROUND HOKKAIDO.
BETWEEN DRILLS AND FARMWORK, I SEARCHED FOR KENKICHI BUT COULDN'T FIND HIM.
BEFORE I WENT TO THE FRONT, MY BROTHER TOLD ME OF OUR MOTHER'S DEATH.
DUE TO FUMI'S GRUESOME DEATH, ME ABANDONING THE VILLAGE AND GOING OFF TO WAR...
...SHE SPENT HER DAYS WEEPING AND WORRYING UNTIL SHE GREW WEAK AND DIED.
I BLAMED KENKICHI FOR IT ALL, AND MY HATE GREW.
I PLANNED TO FOLLOW THE SOLDIERS TO FIND KENKICHI...
...AND SHOOT HIM IN THE BACK IN THE CONFUSION OF BATTLE.

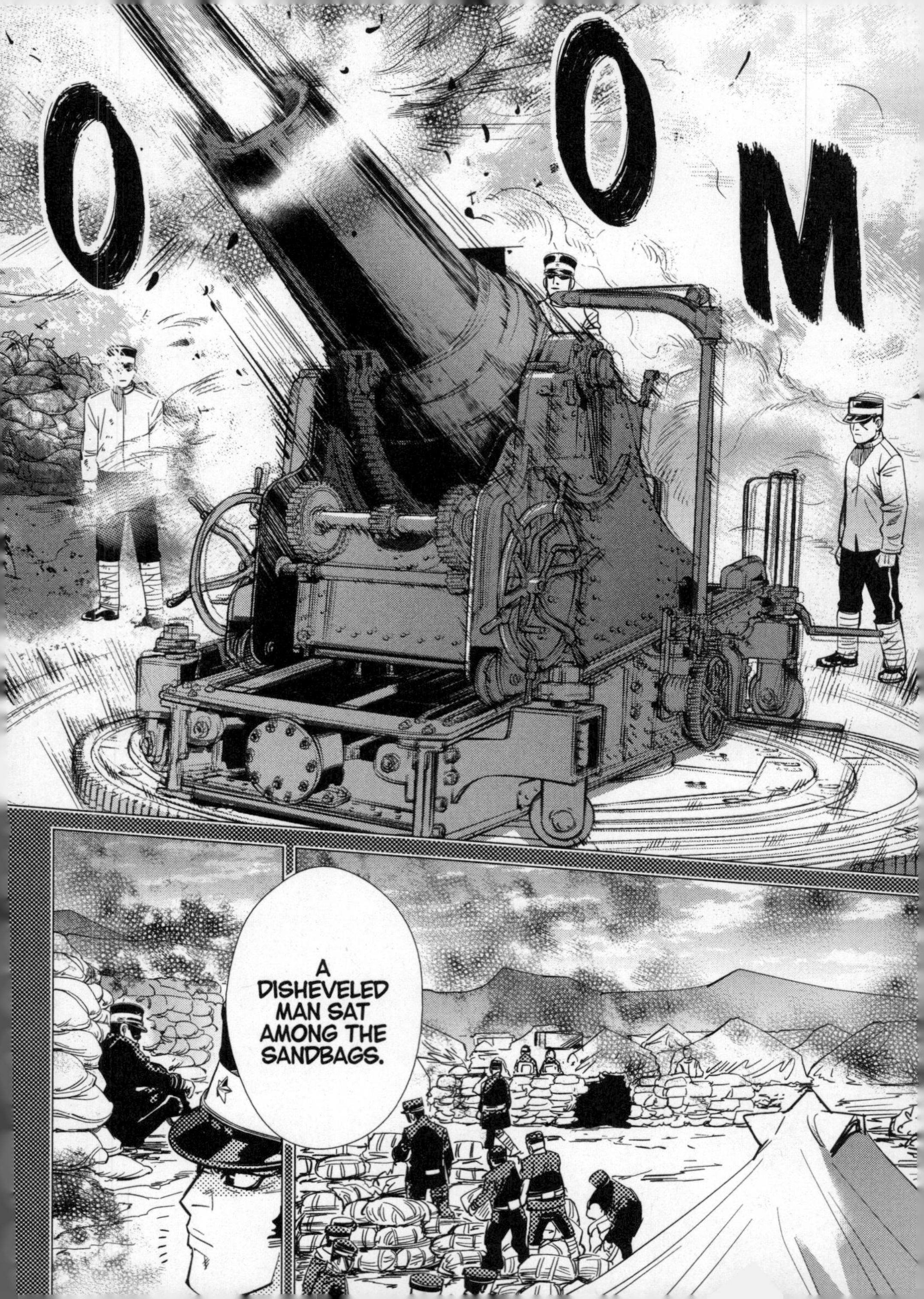
OOM
A DISHEVELED MAN SAT AMONG THE SANDBAGS.

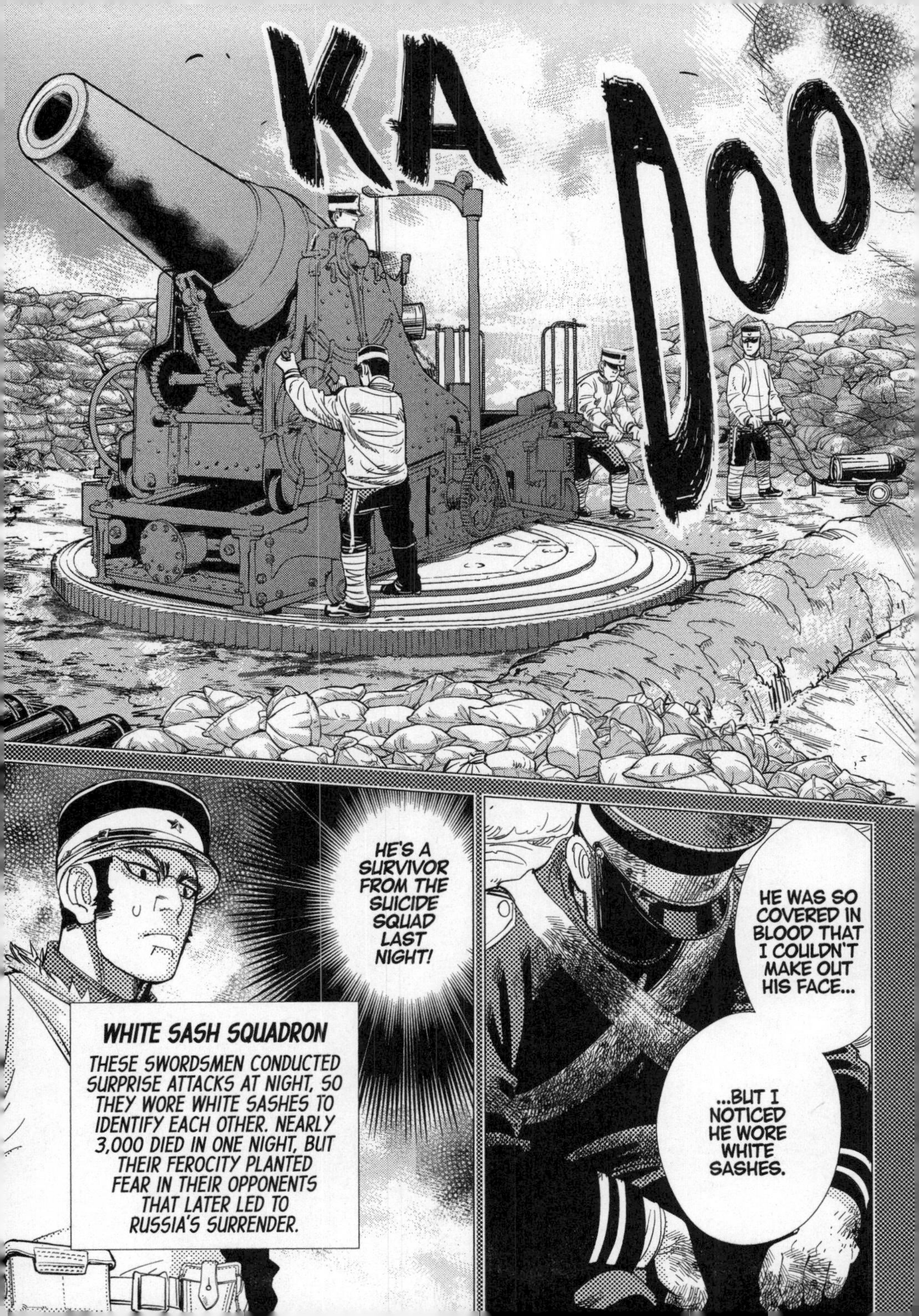
KA DOO
HE WAS SO COVERED IN BLOOD THAT I COULDN'T MAKE OUT HIS FACE...
...BUT I NOTICED HE WORE WHITE SASHES.
HE'S A SURVIVOR FROM THE SUICIDE SQUAD LAST NIGHT!
WHITE SASH SQUADRON
THESE SWORDSMEN CONDUCTED SURPRISE ATTACKS AT NIGHT, SO THEY WORE WHITE SASHES TO IDENTIFY EACH OTHER. NEARLY 3,000 DIED IN ONE NIGHT, BUT THEIR FEROCITY PLANTED FEAR IN THEIR OPPONENTS THAT LATER LED TO RUSSIA'S SURRENDER.

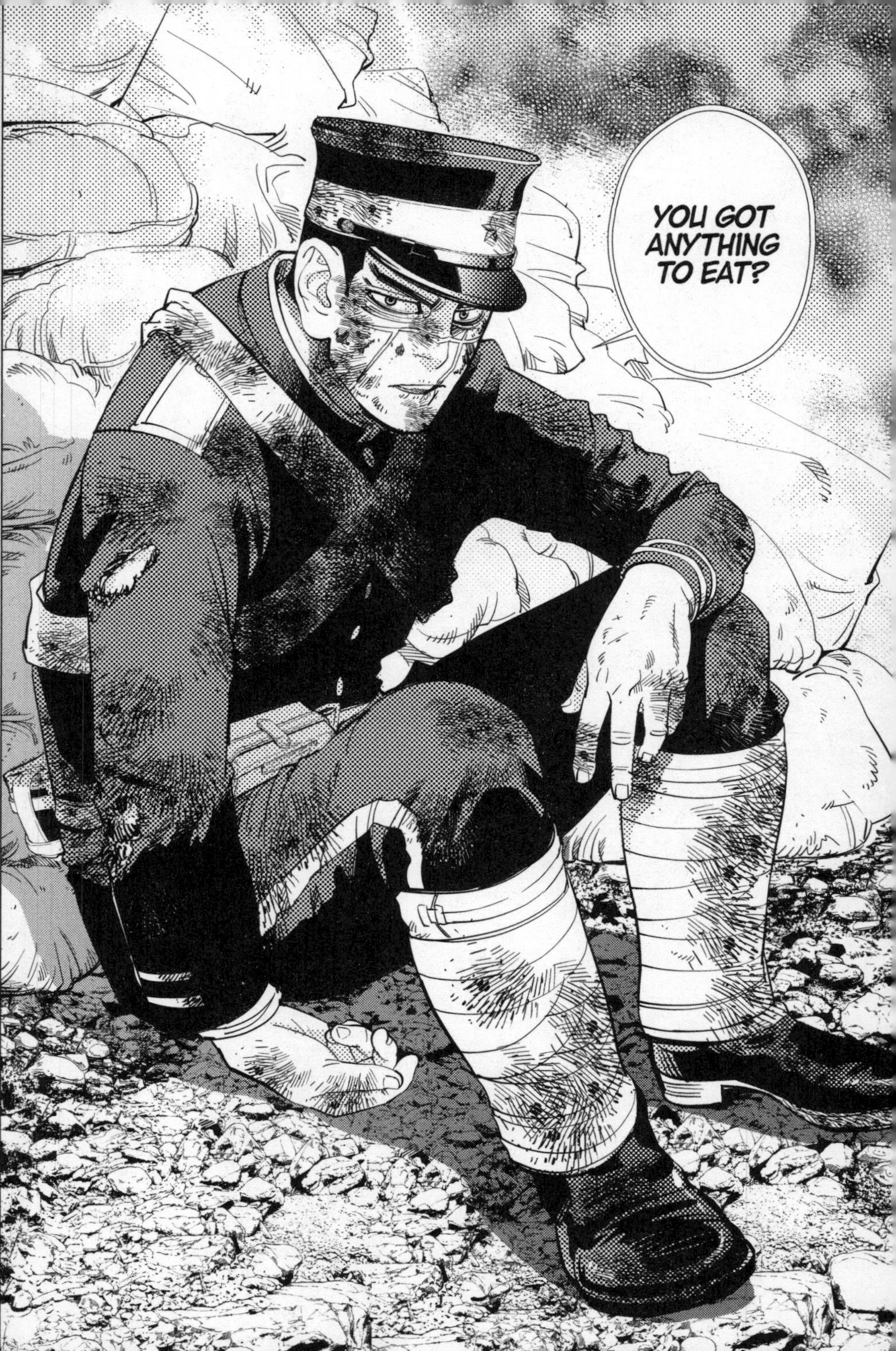
YOU GOT ANYTHING TO EAT?

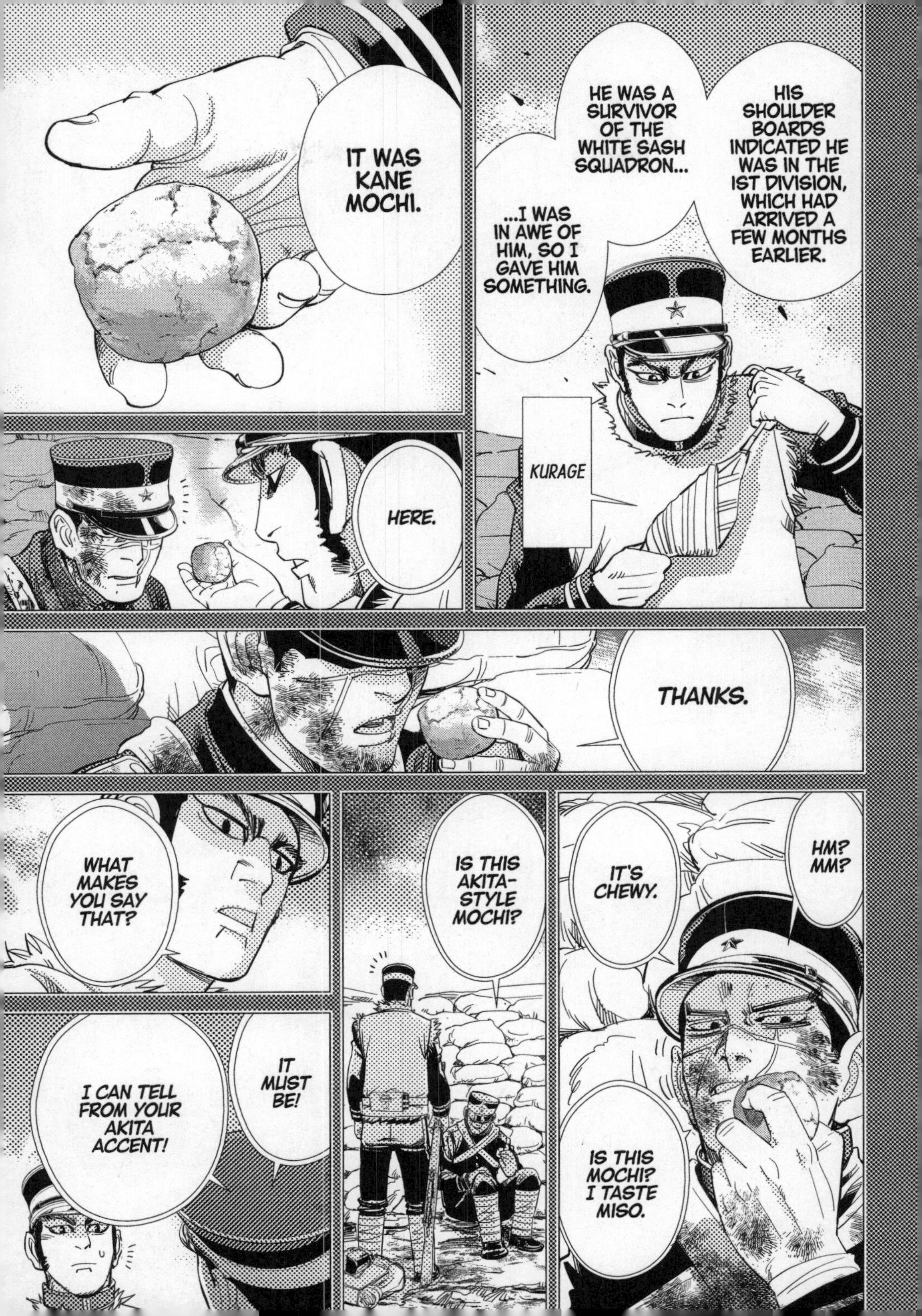
HIS SHOULDER BOARDS INDICATED HE WAS IN THE 1ST DIVISION, WHICH HAD ARRIVED A FEW MONTHS EARLIER.
HE WAS A SURVIVOR OF THE WHITE SASH SQUADRON...
...I WAS IN AWE OF HIM, SO I GAVE HIM SOMETHING.
KURAGE
IT WAS KANE MOCHI.
HERE.
THANKS.
HM? MM?
IT'S CHEWY.
IS THIS MOCHI? I TASTE MISO.
IS THIS AKITA-STYLE MOCHI?
WHAT MAKES YOU SAY THAT?
IT MUST BE!
I CAN TELL FROM YOUR AKITA ACCENT!

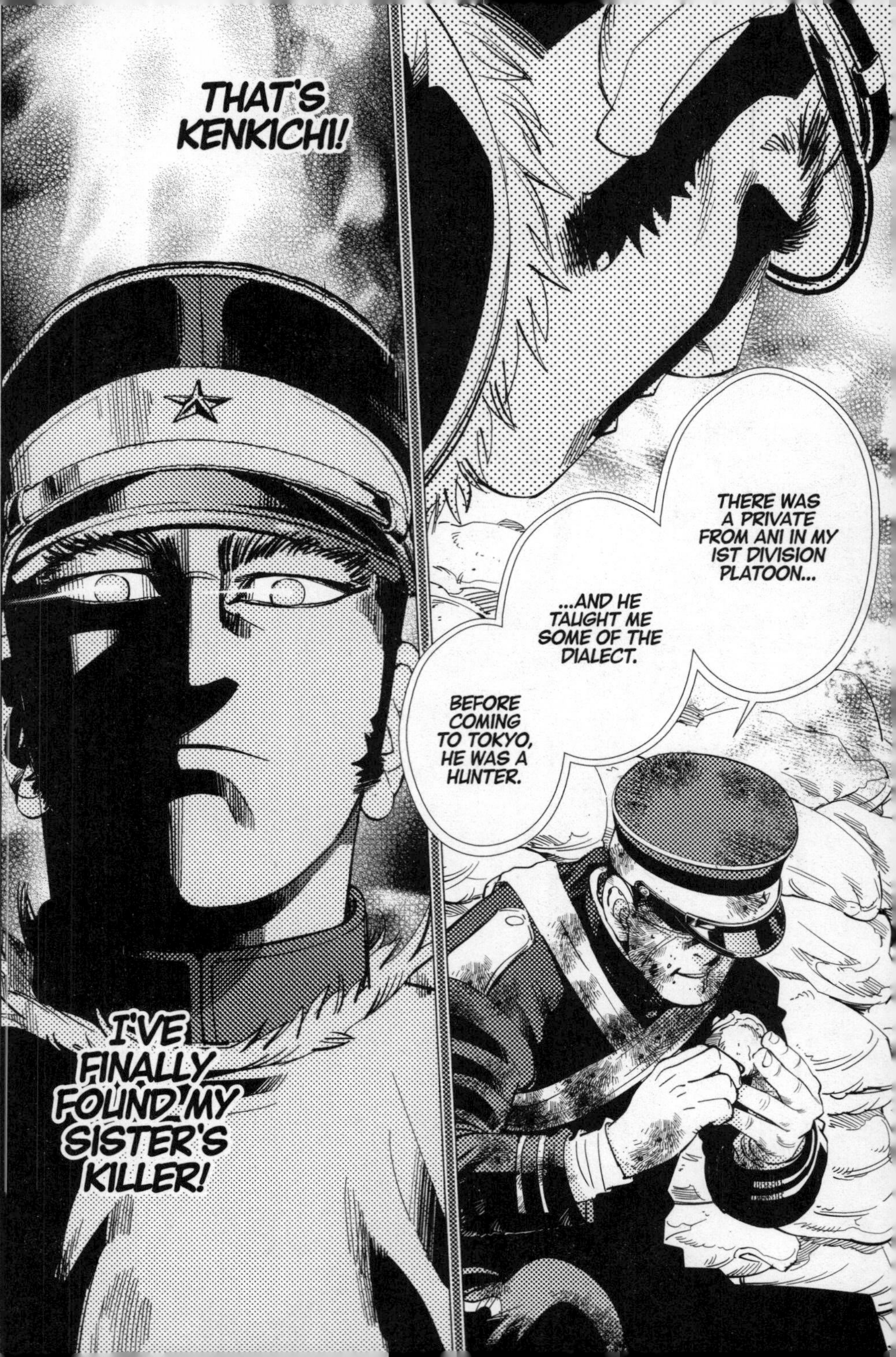
THERE WAS A PRIVATE FROM ANI IN MY 1ST DIVISION PLATOON...
...AND HE TAUGHT ME SOME OF THE DIALECT.
BEFORE COMING TO TOKYO, HE WAS A HUNTER.
THAT'S KENKICHI!
I'VE FINALLY FOUND MY SISTER'S KILLER!

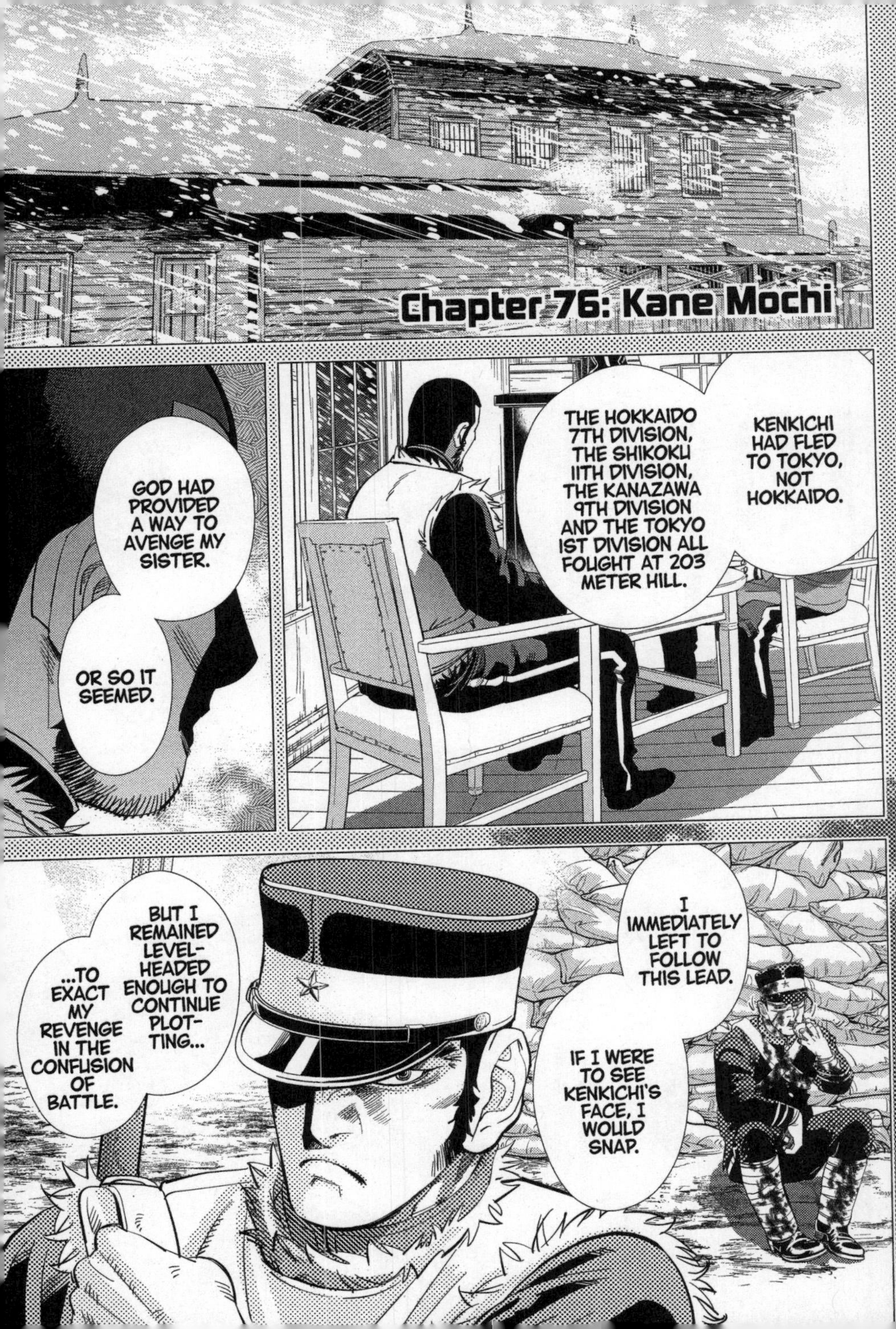
Chapter 76: Kane Mochi
KENKICHI HAD FLED TO TOKYO, NOT HOKKAIDO.
THE HOKKAIDO 7TH DIVISION, THE SHIKOKU 11TH DIVISION, THE KANAZAWA 9TH DIVISION AND THE TOKYO 1ST DIVISION ALL FOUGHT AT 203 METER HILL.
GOD HAD PROVIDED A WAY TO AVENGE MY SISTER.
OR SO IT SEEMED.
I IMMEDIATELY LEFT TO FOLLOW THIS LEAD.
IF I WERE TO SEE KENKICHI'S FACE, I WOULD SNAP.
BUT I REMAINED LEVEL-HEADED ENOUGH TO CONTINUE PLOT-TING...
...TO EXACT MY REVENGE IN THE CONFUSION OF BATTLE.

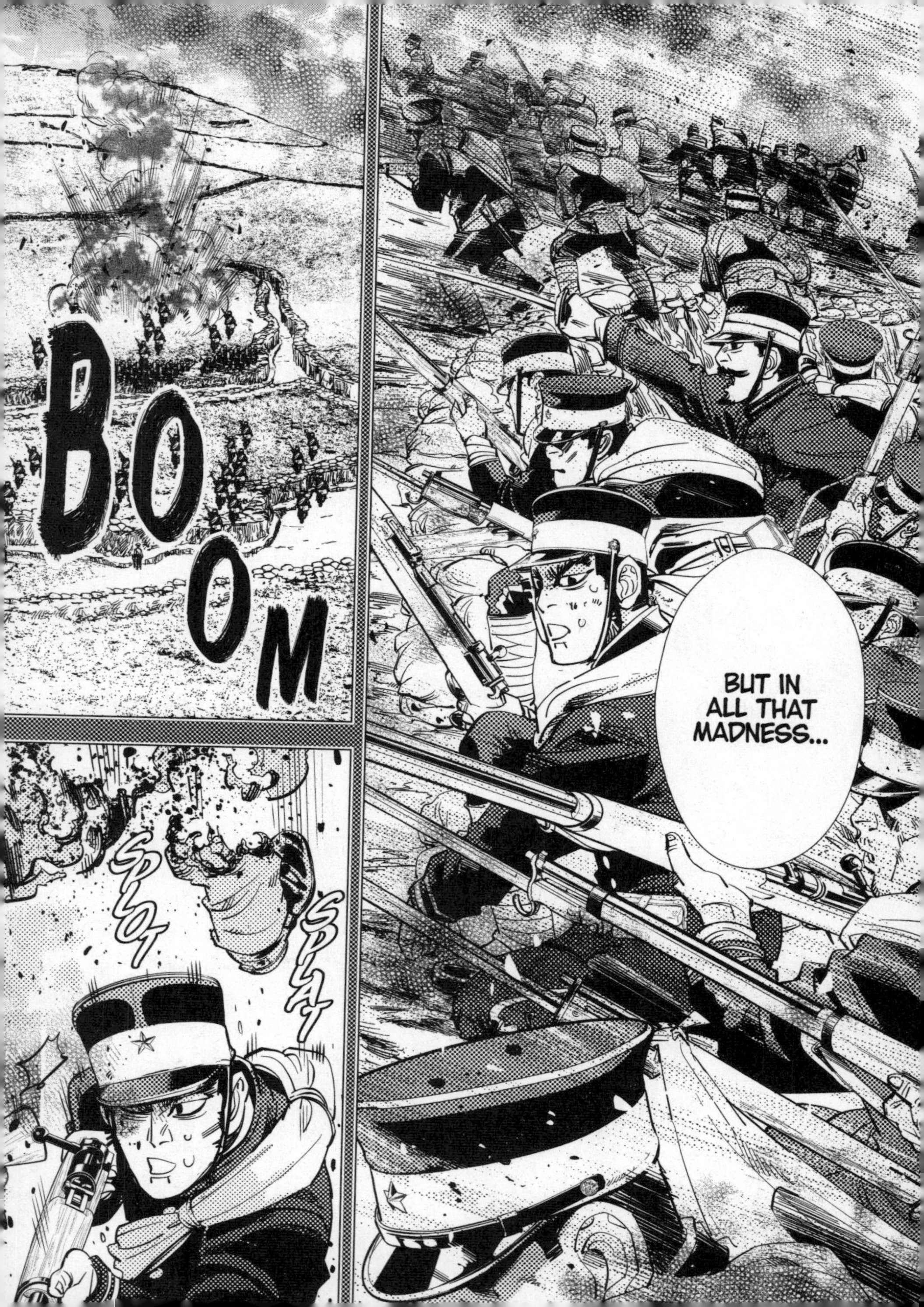
BUT IN ALL THAT MADNESS...
BOOM
SPLAT
SPLOT

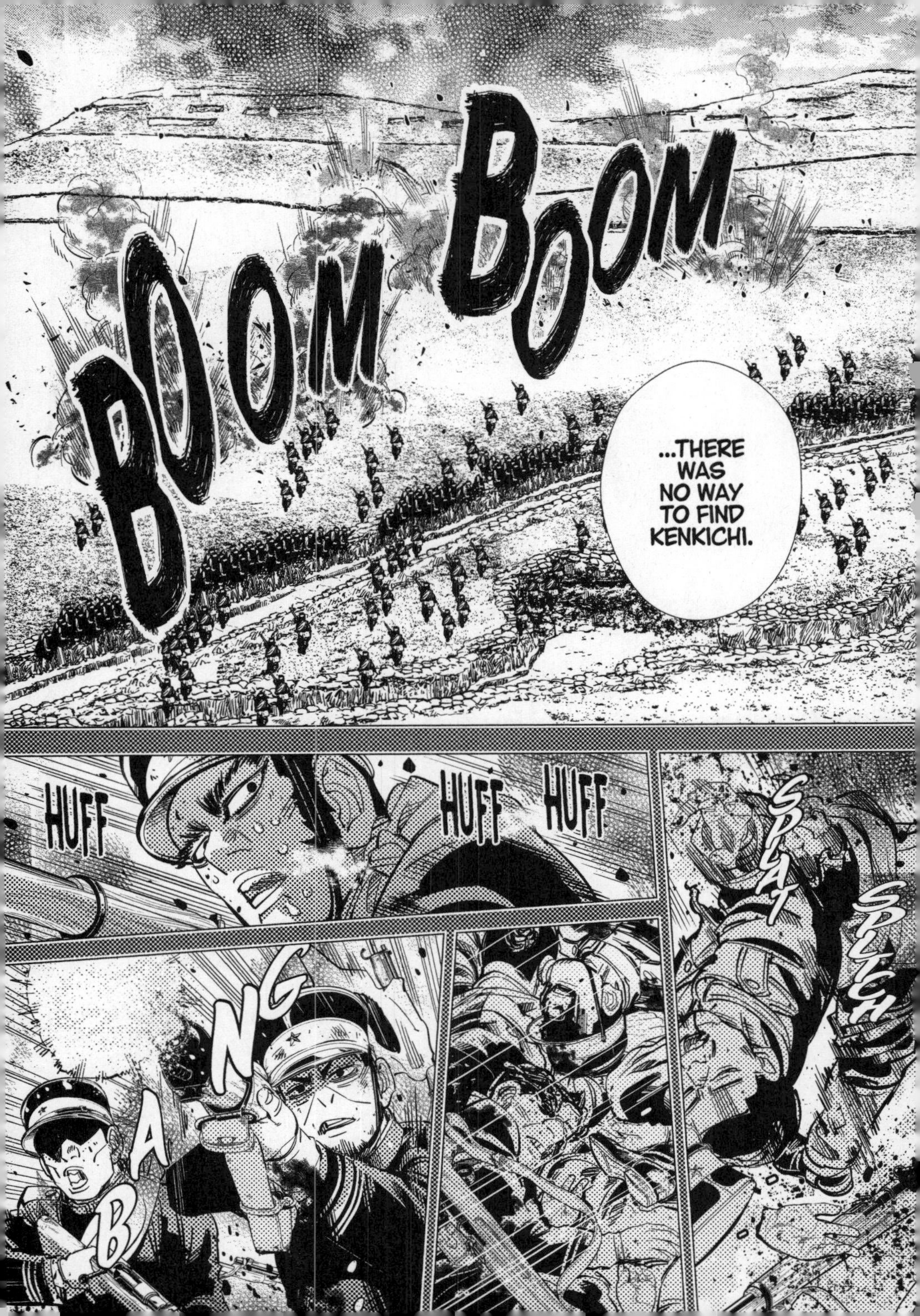
BOOM BOOM
...THERE WAS NO WAY TO FIND KENKICHI.
SPLAT
SPLUCH
HUFF HUFF HUFF
BANG

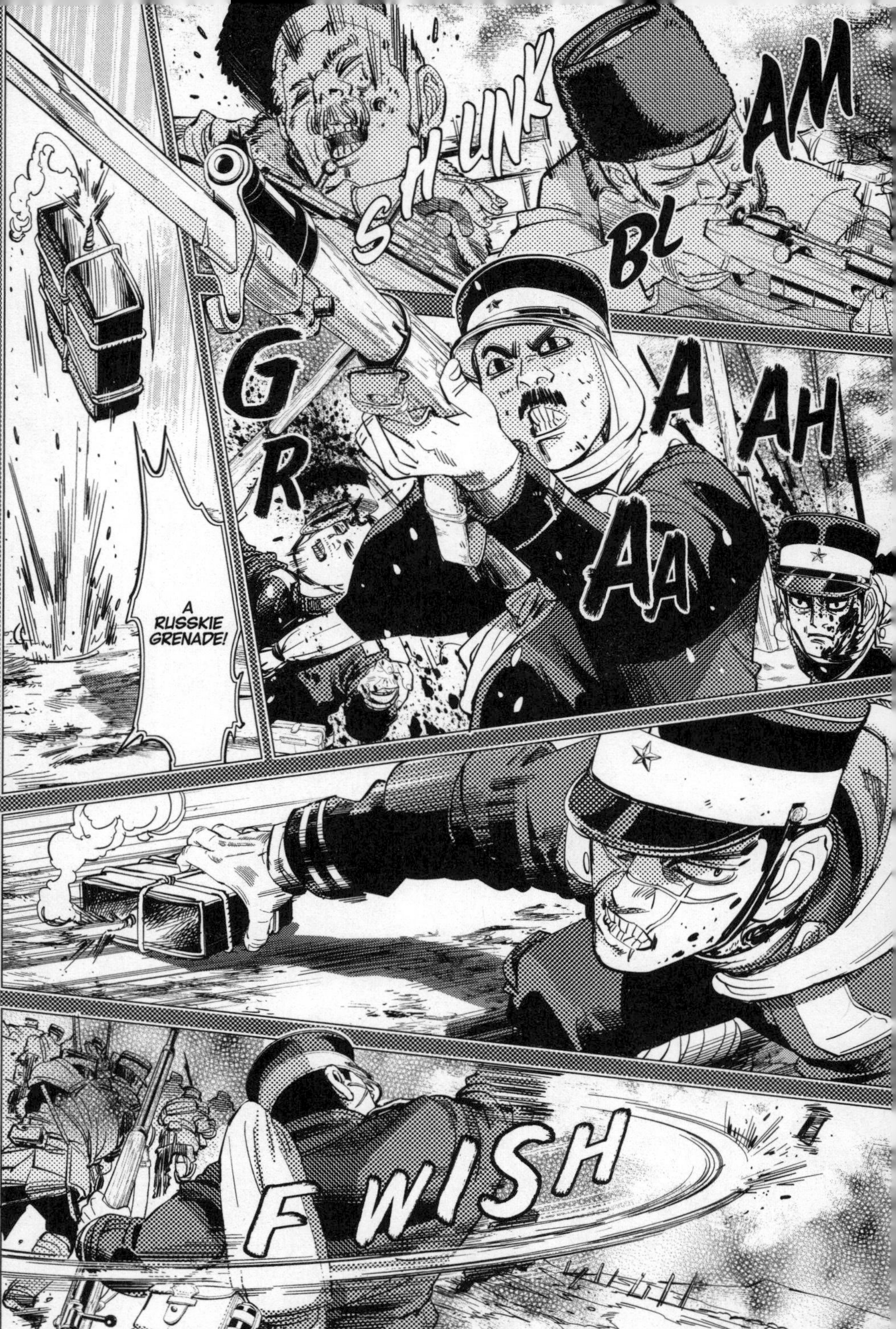
BLAM
SHUNK
GRAAAAH
A RUSSKIE GRENADE!
FWISH

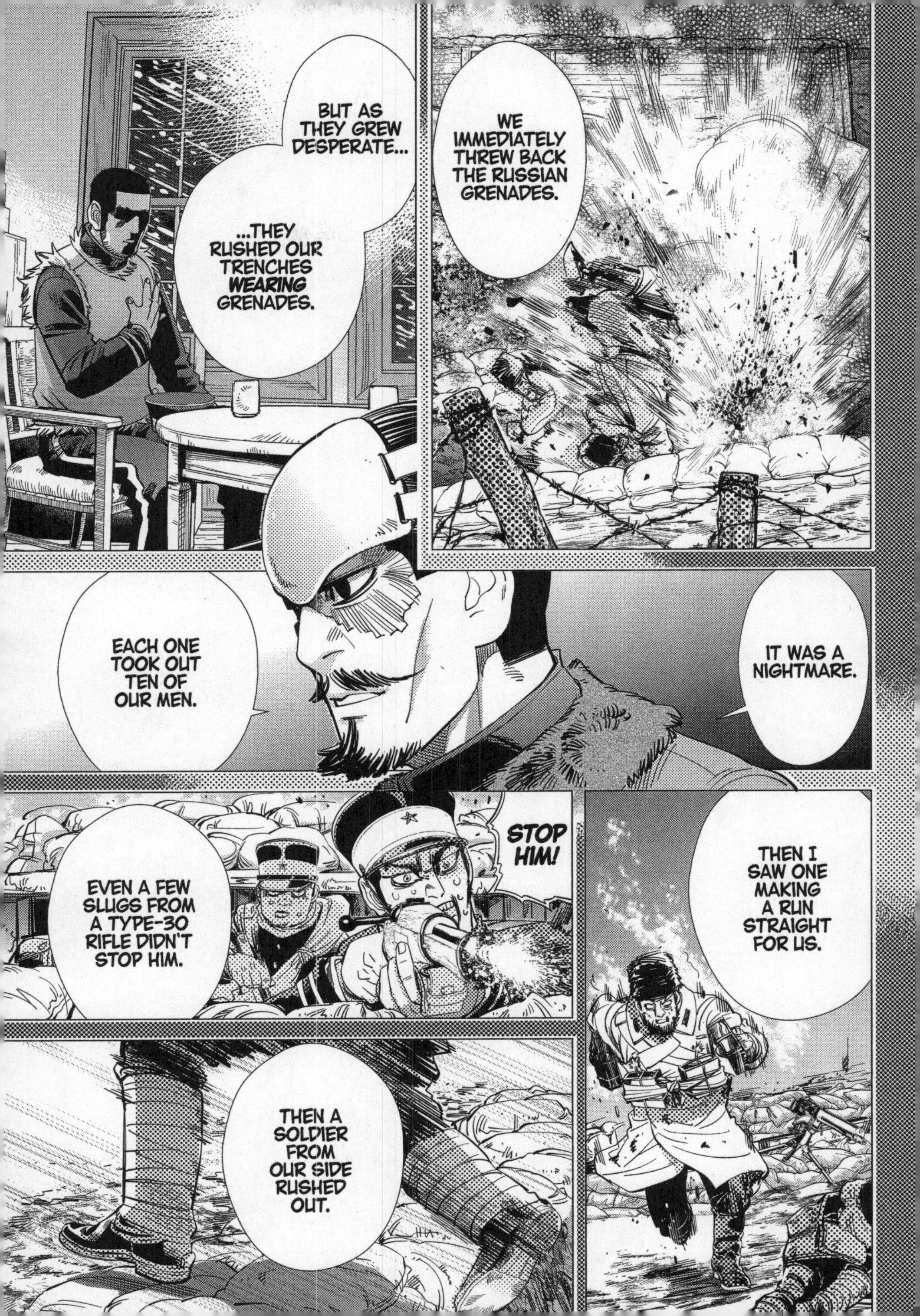
WE IMMEDIATELY THREW BACK THE RUSSIAN GRENADES.
BUT AS THEY GREW DESPERATE...
...THEY RUSHED OUR TRENCHES *WEARING* GRENADES.
IT WAS A NIGHTMARE.
EACH ONE TOOK OUT TEN OF OUR MEN.
THEN I SAW ONE MAKING A RUN STRAIGHT FOR US.
STOP HIM!
EVEN A FEW SLUGS FROM A TYPE-30 RIFLE DIDN'T STOP HIM.
THEN A SOLDIER FROM OUR SIDE RUSHED OUT.

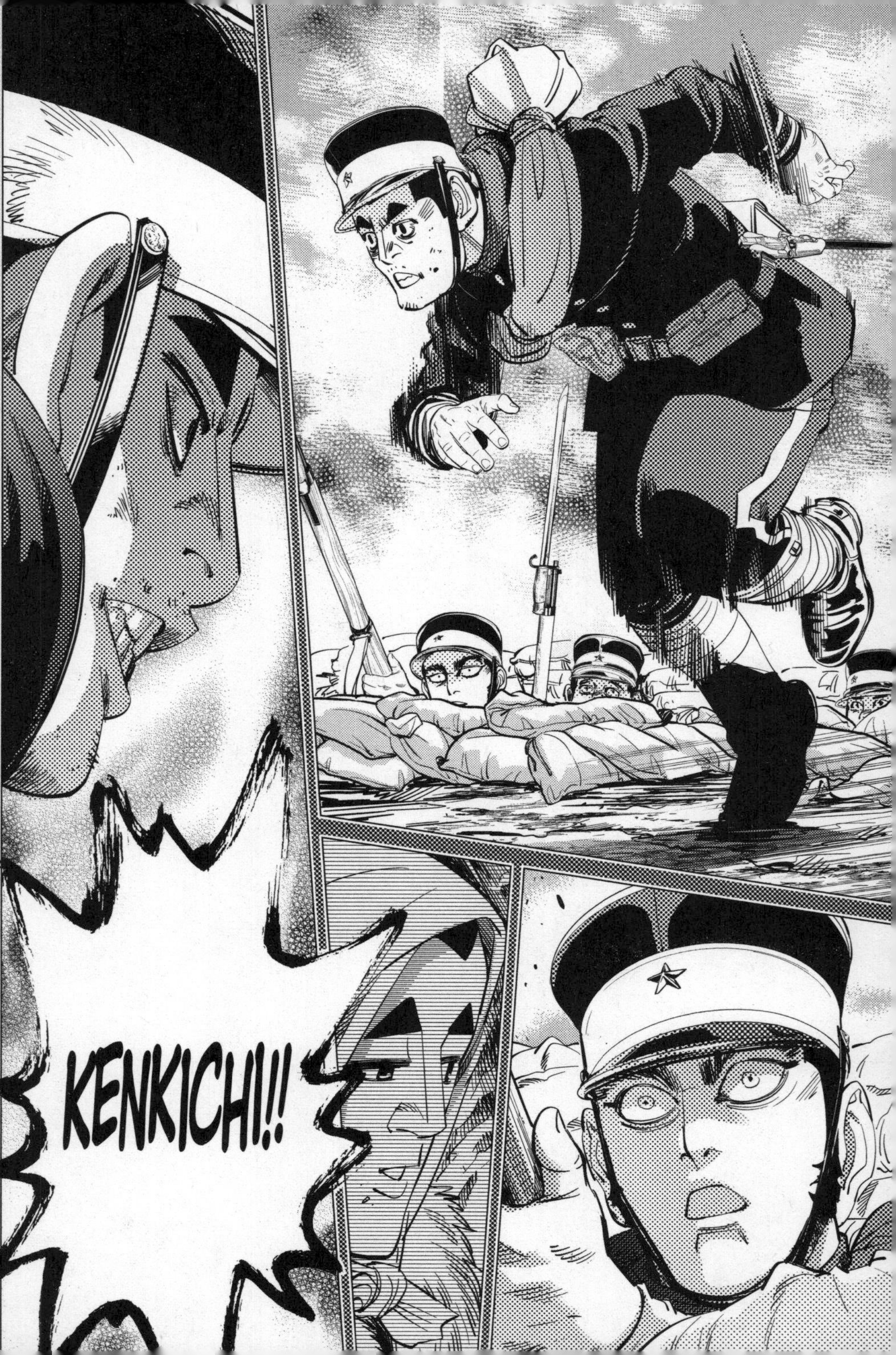
KENKICHI!!

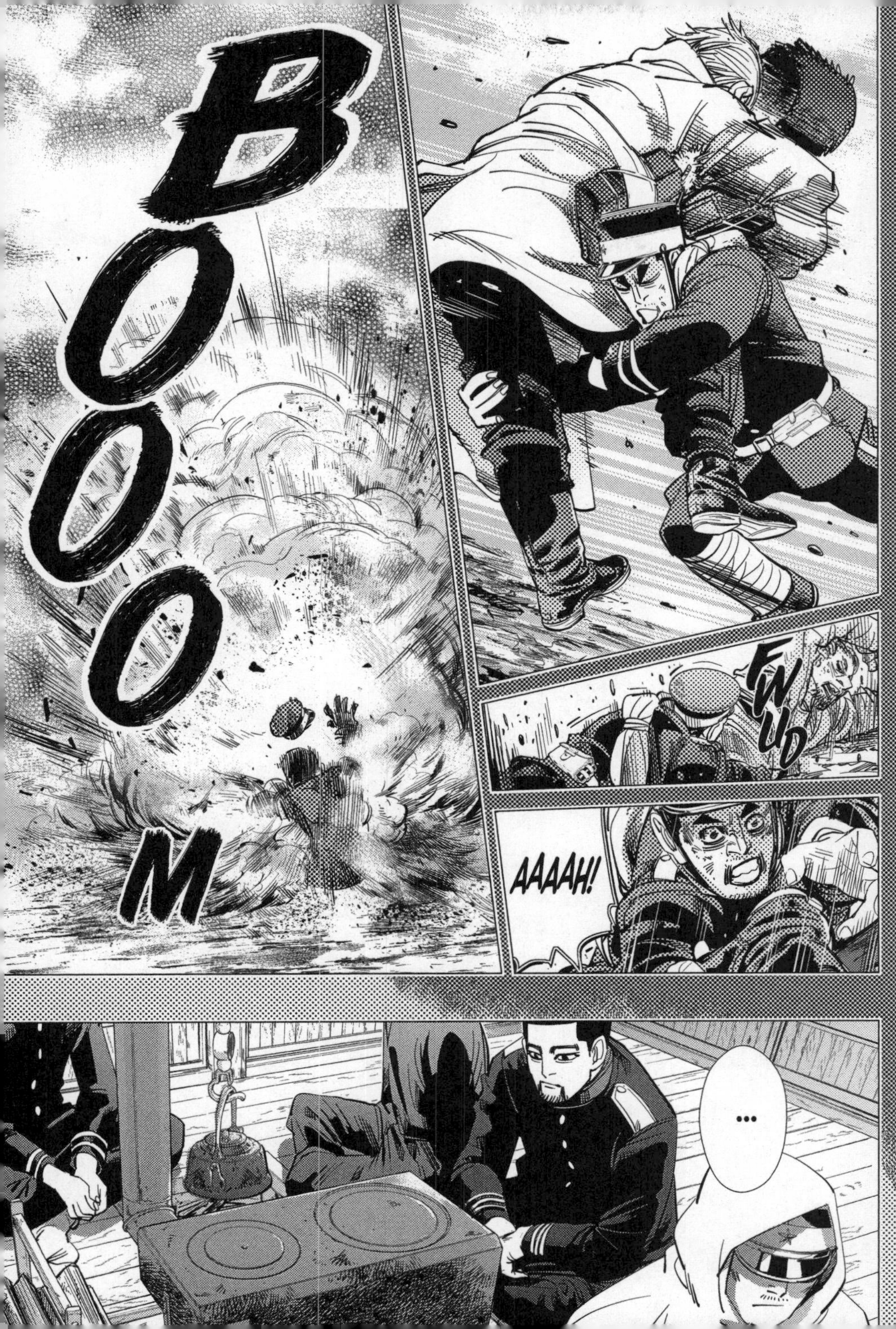
FWUD
AAAAH!
BOOOOM
...

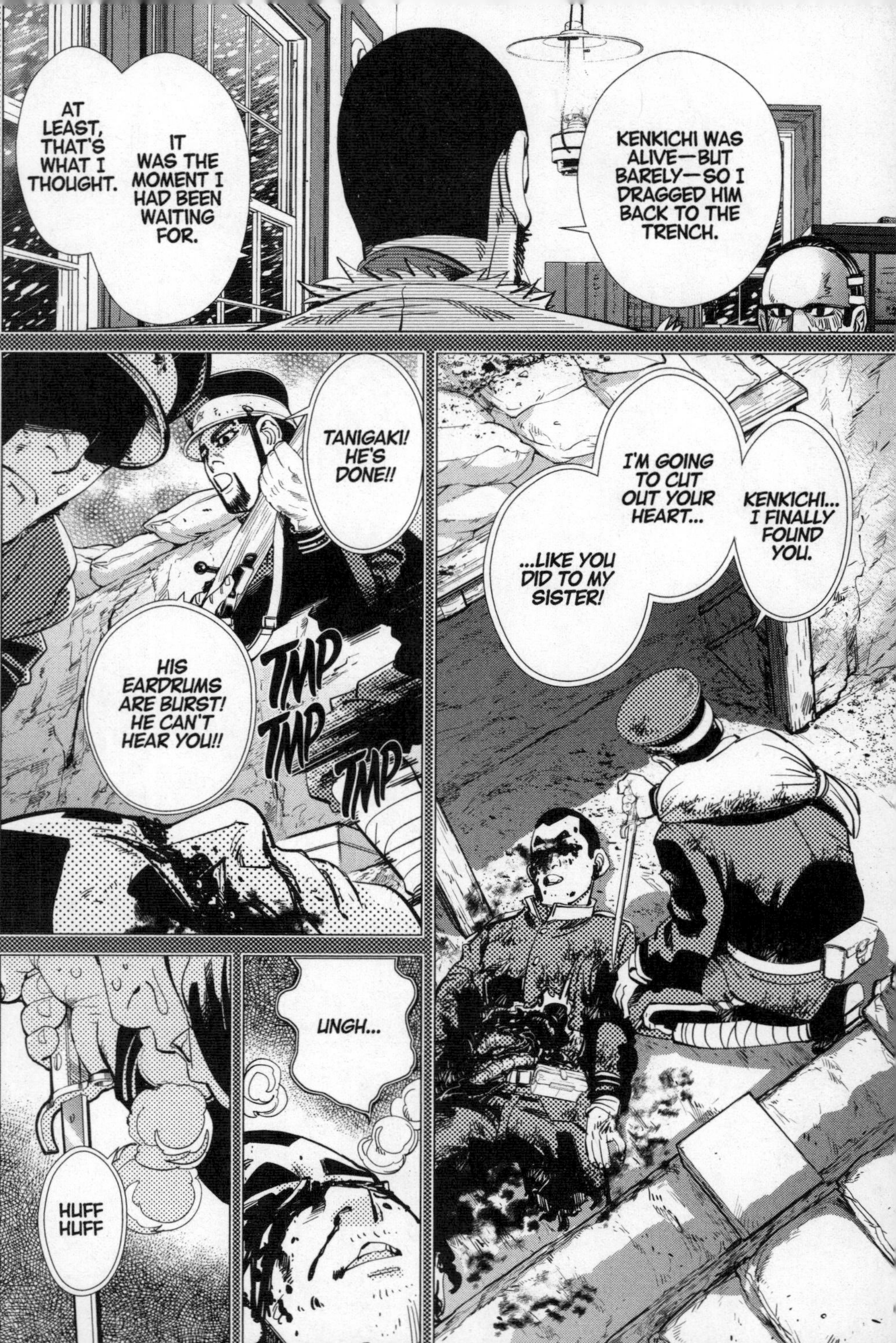
KENKICHI WAS ALIVE—BUT BARELY—SO I DRAGGED HIM BACK TO THE TRENCH.
IT WAS THE MOMENT I HAD BEEN WAITING FOR.
AT LEAST, THAT'S WHAT I THOUGHT.
KENKICHI... I FINALLY FOUND YOU.
I'M GOING TO CUT OUT YOUR HEART...
...LIKE YOU DID TO MY SISTER!
TANIGAKI! HE'S DONE!!
HIS EARDRUMS ARE BURST! HE CAN'T HEAR YOU!!
TMP TMP TMP
UNGH...
HUFF HUFF

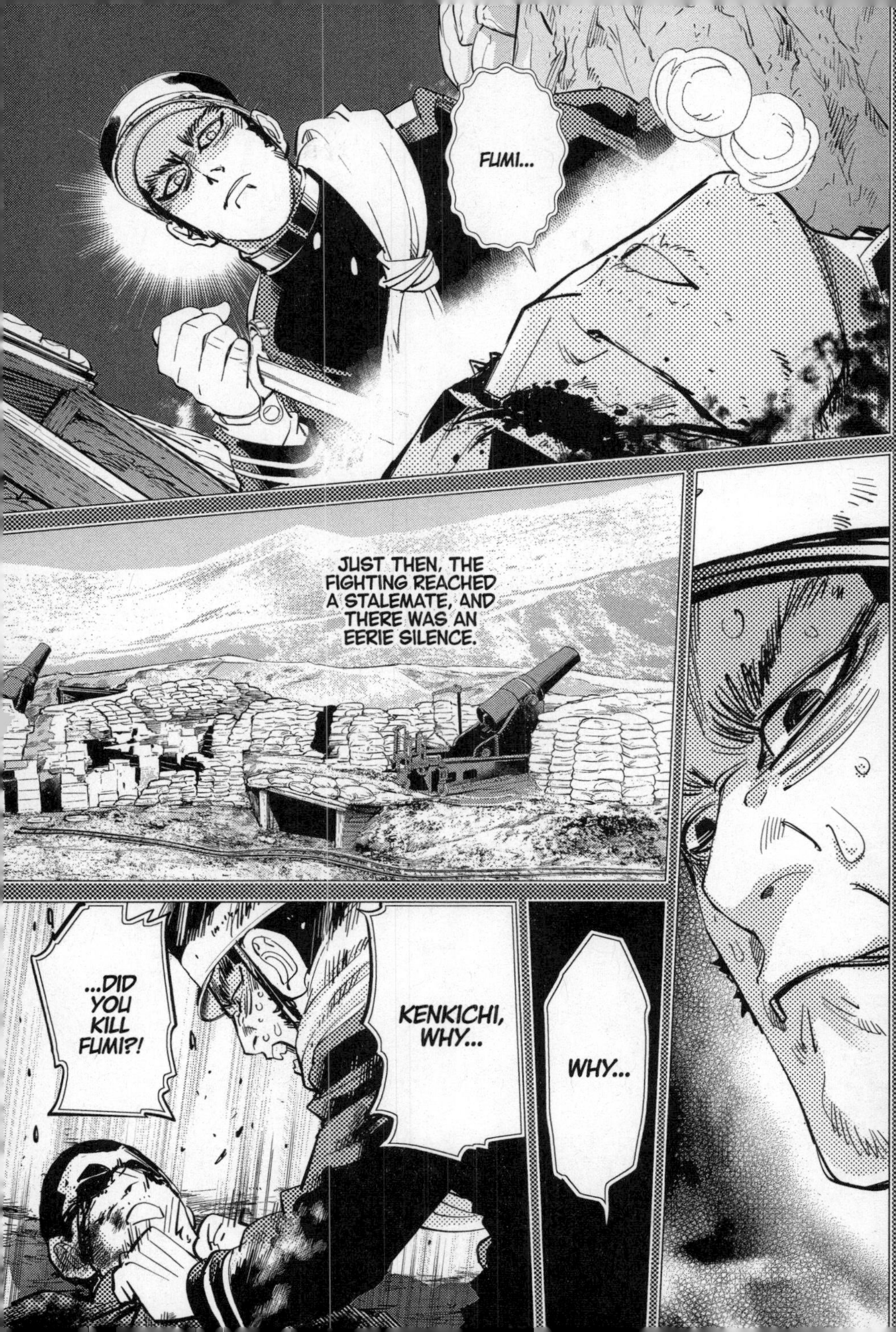
FUMI...
JUST THEN, THE FIGHTING REACHED A STALEMATE, AND THERE WAS AN EERIE SILENCE.
WHY...
KENKICHI, WHY...
...DID YOU KILL FUMI?!

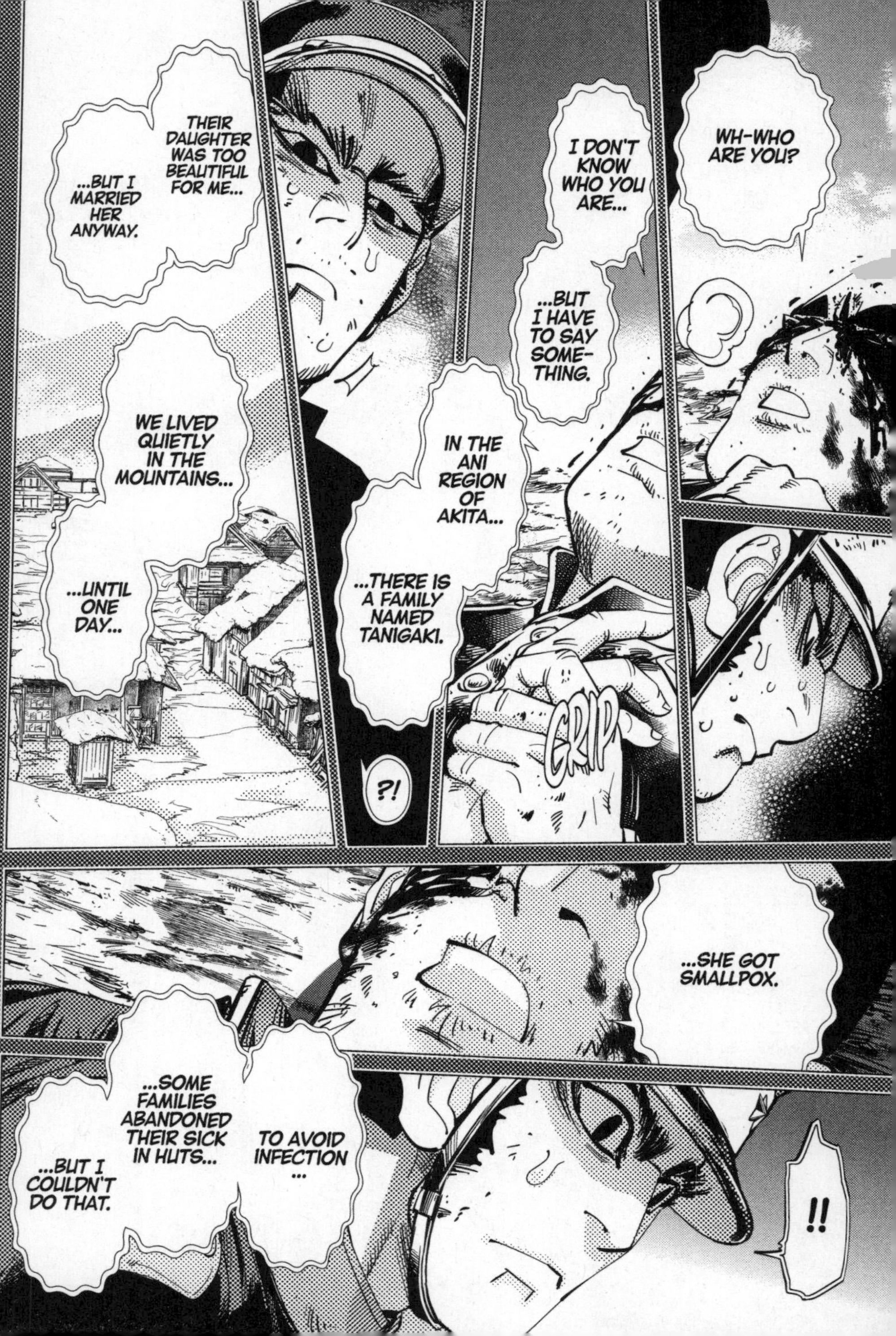
WH-WHO ARE YOU?
I DON'T KNOW WHO YOU ARE...
...BUT I HAVE TO SAY SOME-THING.
IN THE ANI REGION OF AKITA...
...THERE IS A FAMILY NAMED TANIGAKI.
GRIP
?!
THEIR DAUGHTER WAS TOO BEAUTIFUL FOR ME...
...BUT I MARRIED HER ANYWAY.
WE LIVED QUIETLY IN THE MOUNTAINS...
...UNTIL ONE DAY...
...SHE GOT SMALLPOX.
!!
TO AVOID INFECTION...
...SOME FAMILIES ABANDONED THEIR SICK IN HUTS...
...BUT I COULDN'T DO THAT.

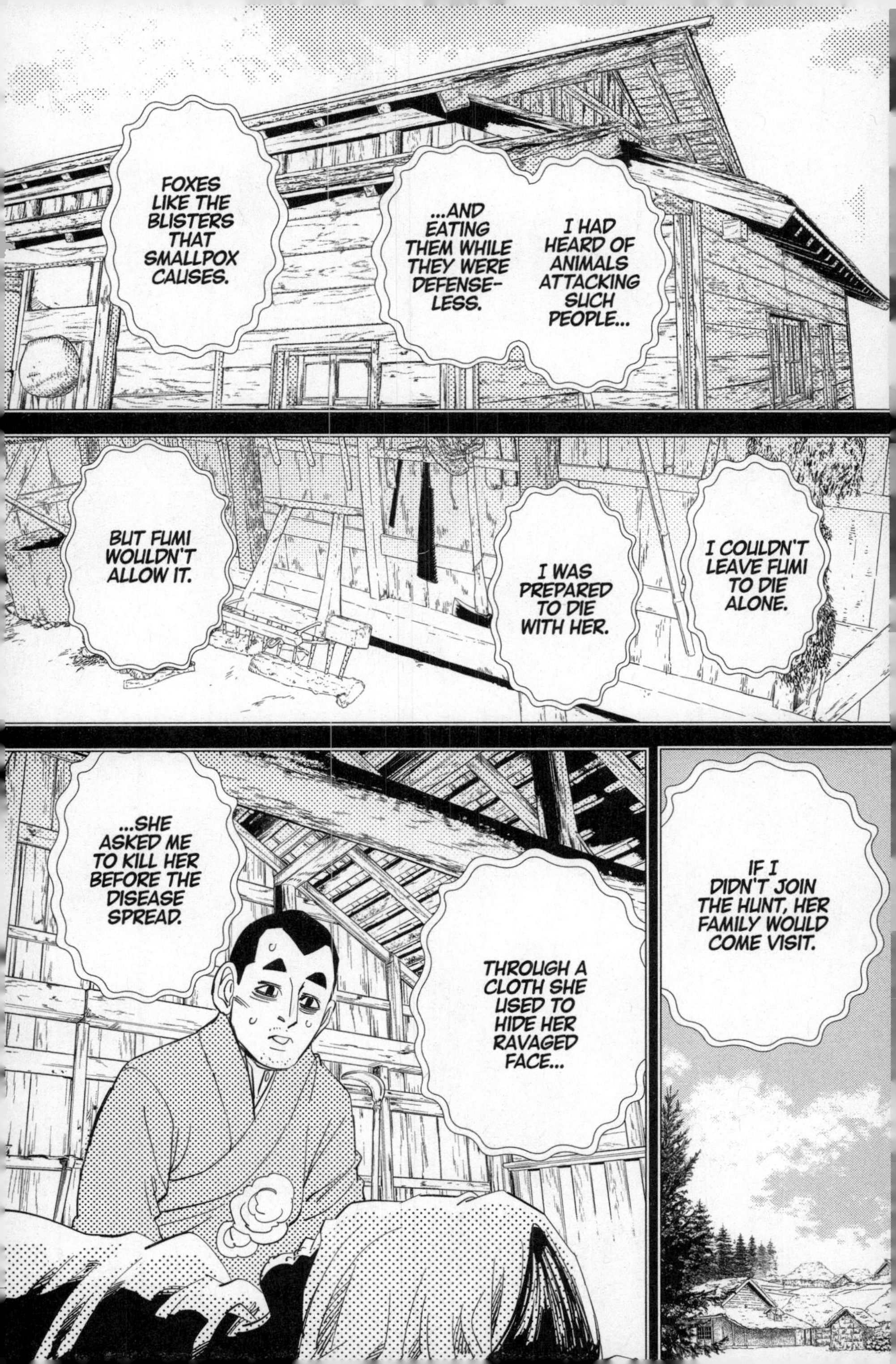
I HAD HEARD OF ANIMALS ATTACKING SUCH PEOPLE...
...AND EATING THEM WHILE THEY WERE DEFENSE-LESS.
FOXES LIKE THE BLISTERS THAT SMALLPOX CAUSES.
I COULDN'T LEAVE FUMI TO DIE ALONE.
I WAS PREPARED TO DIE WITH HER.
BUT FUMI WOULDN'T ALLOW IT.
IF I DIDN'T JOIN THE HUNT, HER FAMILY WOULD COME VISIT.
THROUGH A CLOTH SHE USED TO HIDE HER RAVAGED FACE...
...SHE ASKED ME TO KILL HER BEFORE THE DISEASE SPREAD.

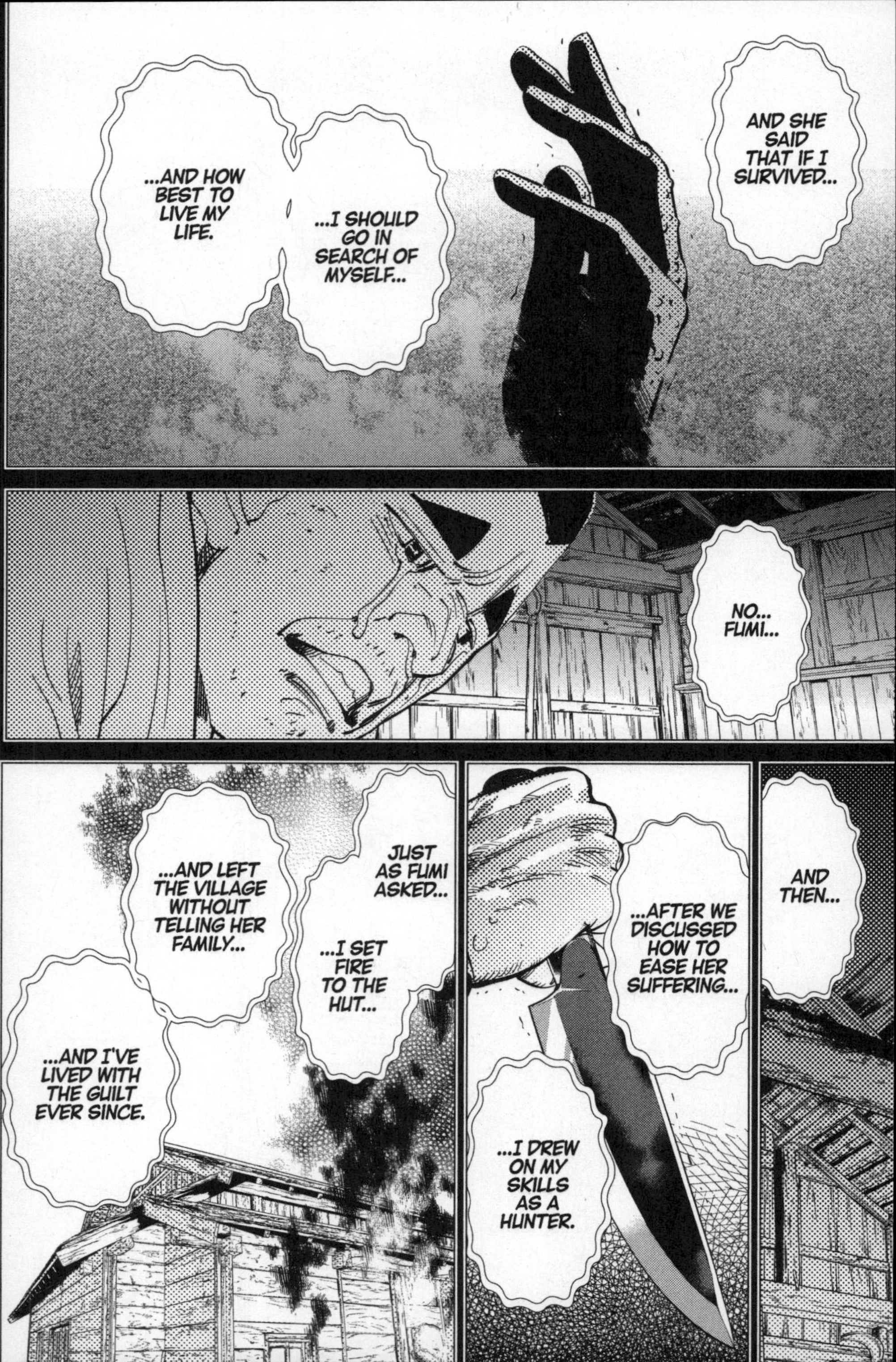
AND SHE SAID THAT IF I SURVIVED...
...I SHOULD GO IN SEARCH OF MYSELF...
...AND HOW BEST TO LIVE MY LIFE.
NO... FUMI...
AND THEN...
...AFTER WE DISCUSSED HOW TO EASE HER SUFFERING...
...I DREW ON MY SKILLS AS A HUNTER.
JUST AS FUMI ASKED...
...I SET FIRE TO THE HUT...
...AND LEFT THE VILLAGE WITHOUT TELLING HER FAMILY...
...AND I'VE LIVED WITH THE GUILT EVER SINCE.

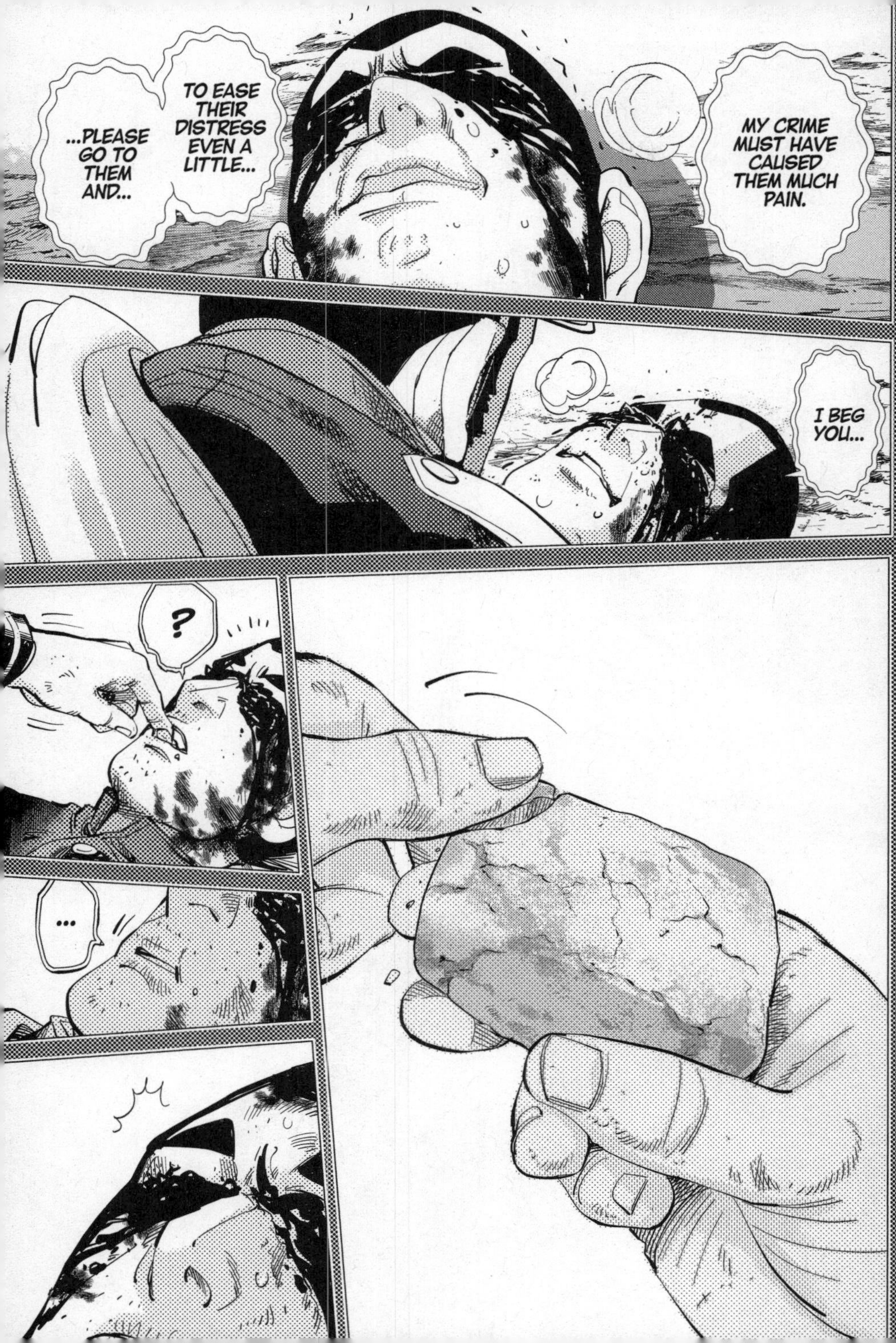
MY CRIME MUST HAVE CAUSED THEM MUCH PAIN.
TO EASE THEIR DISTRESS EVEN A LITTLE...
...PLEASE GO TO THEM AND...
I BEG YOU...
?
...

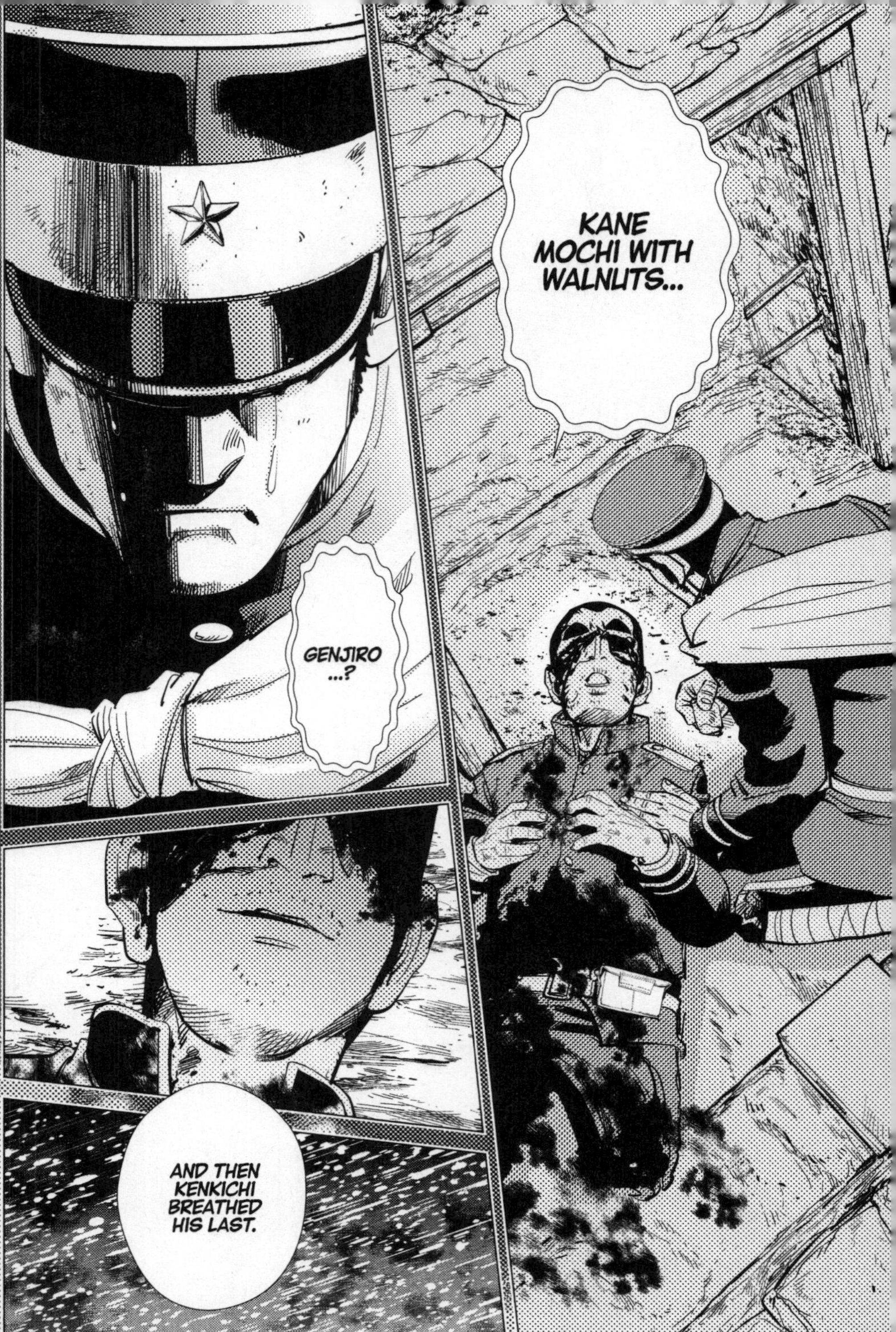
KANE MOCHI WITH WALNUTS...
GENJIRO ...?
AND THEN KENKICHI BREATHED HIS LAST.

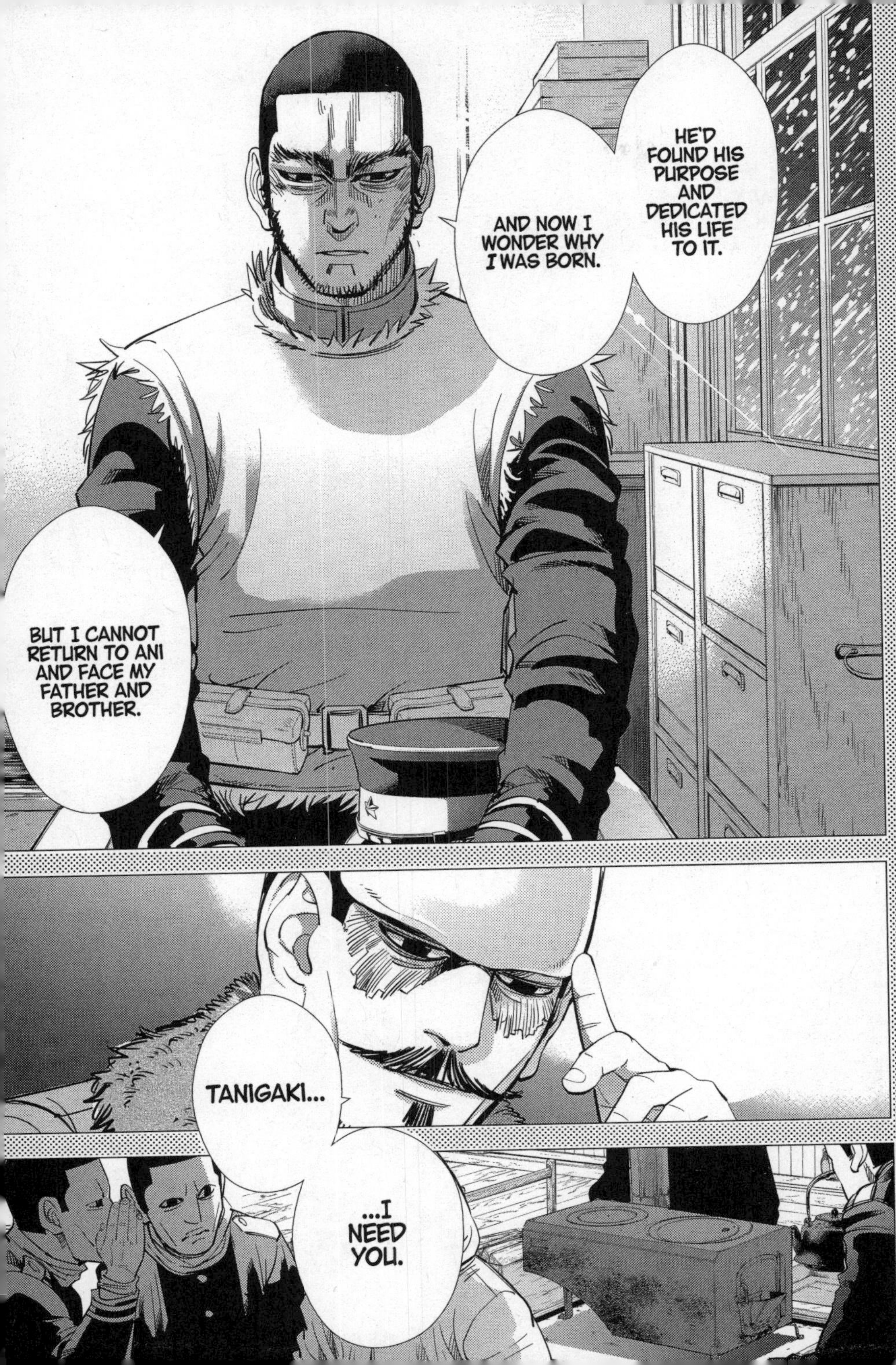
HE'D FOUND HIS PURPOSE AND DEDICATED HIS LIFE TO IT.
AND NOW I WONDER WHY I WAS BORN.
BUT I CANNOT RETURN TO ANI AND FACE MY FATHER AND BROTHER.
TANIGAKI...
...I NEED YOU.

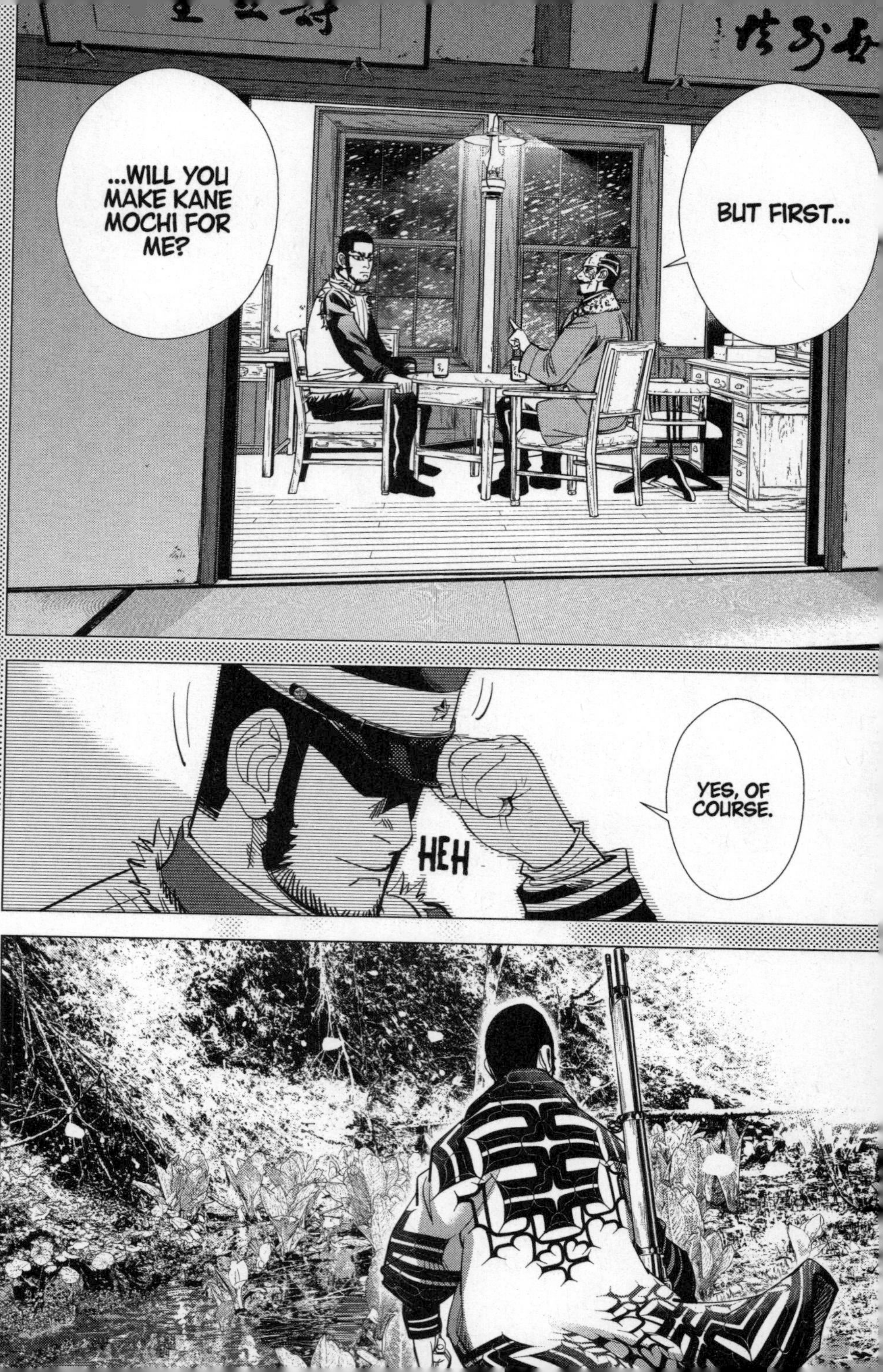
BUT FIRST...
...WILL YOU MAKE KANE MOCHI FOR ME?
YES, OF COURSE.
HEH

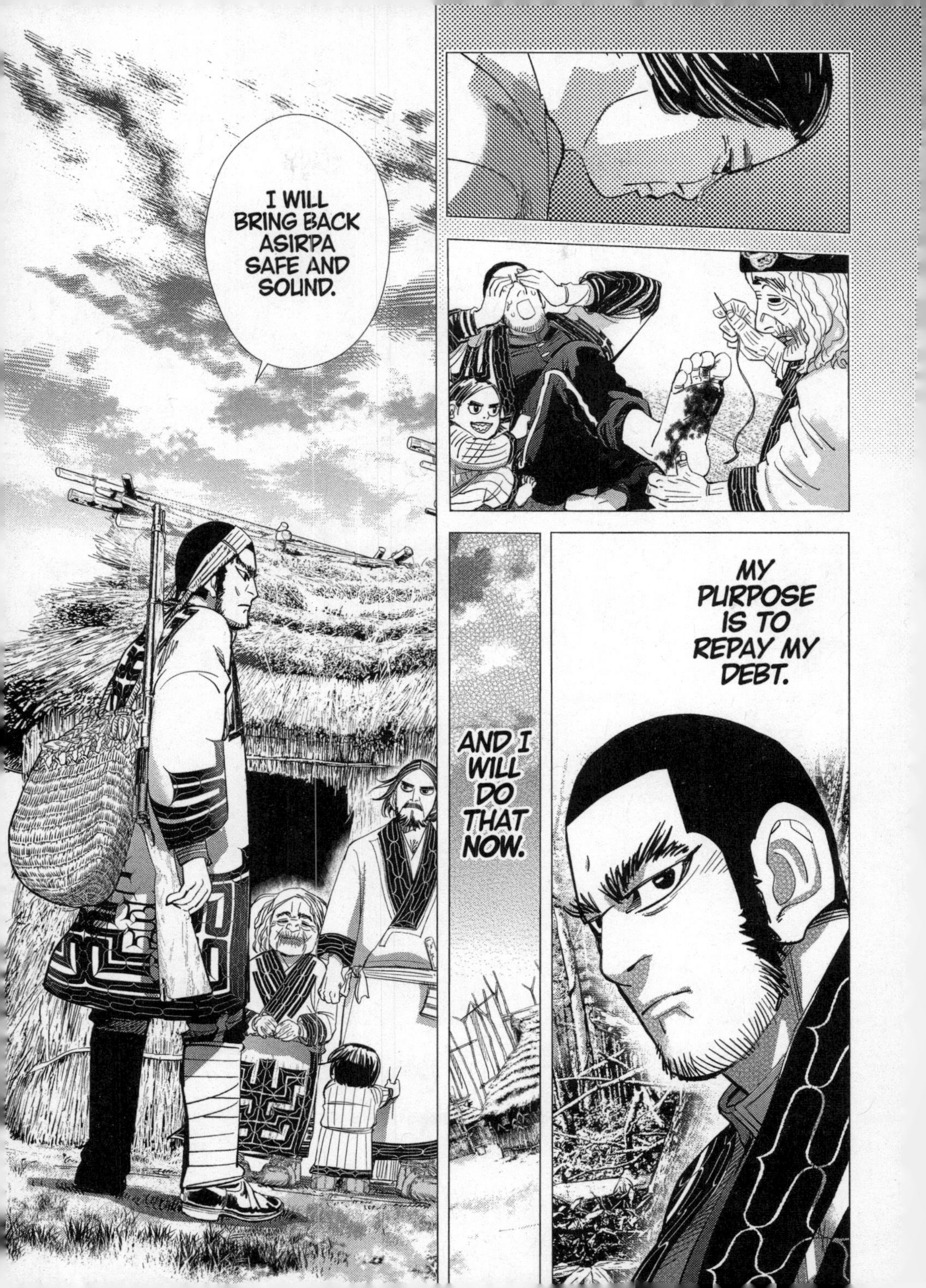
MY PURPOSE IS TO REPAY MY DEBT.
AND I WILL DO THAT NOW.
I WILL BRING BACK ASIRPA SAFE AND SOUND.

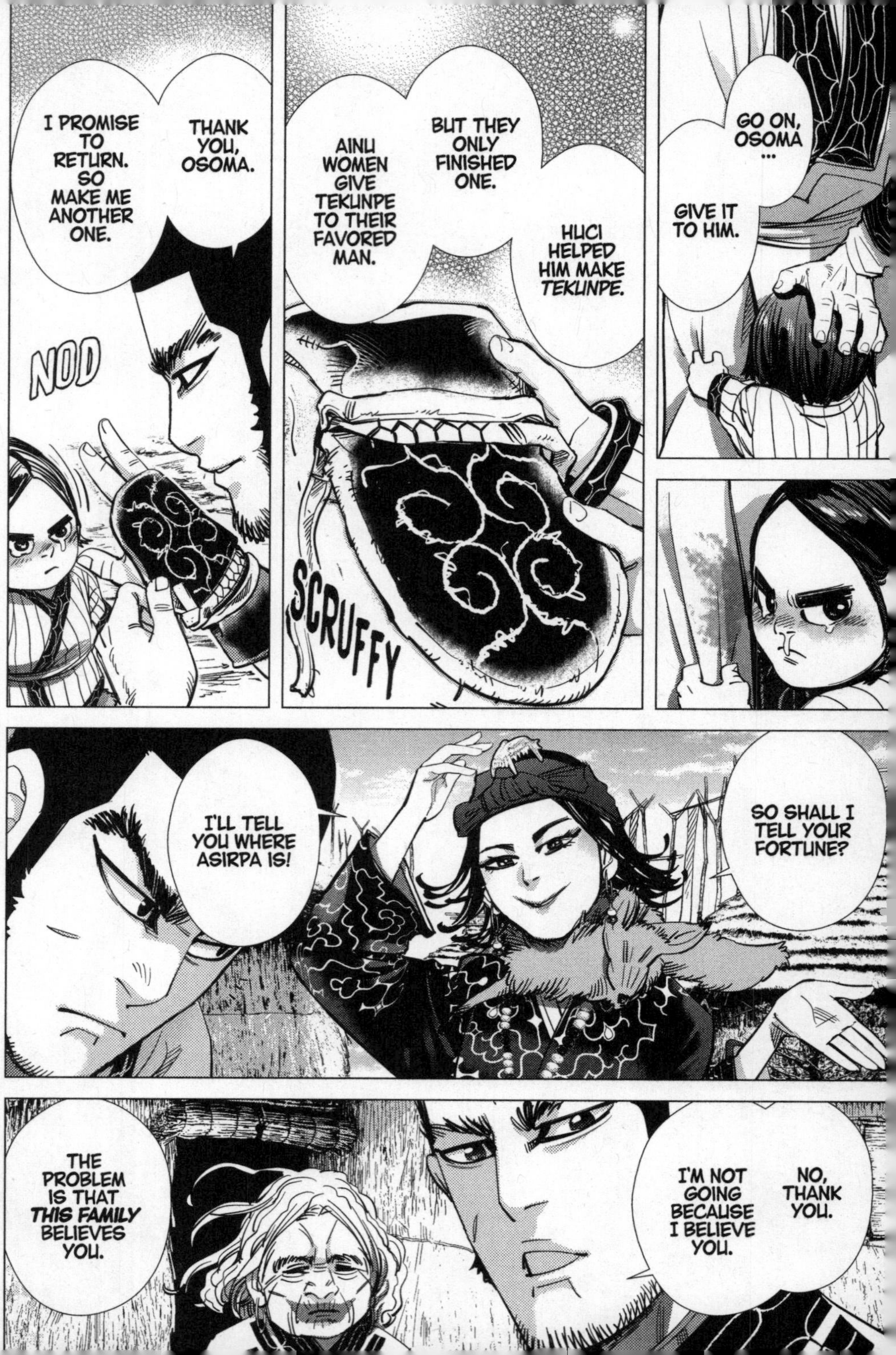
GO ON, OSOMA...
GIVE IT TO HIM.
HUCI HELPED HIM MAKE *TEKUNPE*.
AINU WOMEN GIVE TEKUNPE TO THEIR FAVORED MAN.
BUT THEY ONLY FINISHED ONE.
SCRUFFY
THANK YOU, OSOMA.
I PROMISE TO RETURN. SO MAKE ME ANOTHER ONE.
NOD
SO SHALL I TELL YOUR FORTUNE?
I'LL TELL YOU WHERE ASIRPA IS!
NO, THANK YOU.
I'M NOT GOING BECAUSE I BELIEVE YOU.
THE PROBLEM IS THAT ***THIS FAMILY*** BELIEVES YOU.

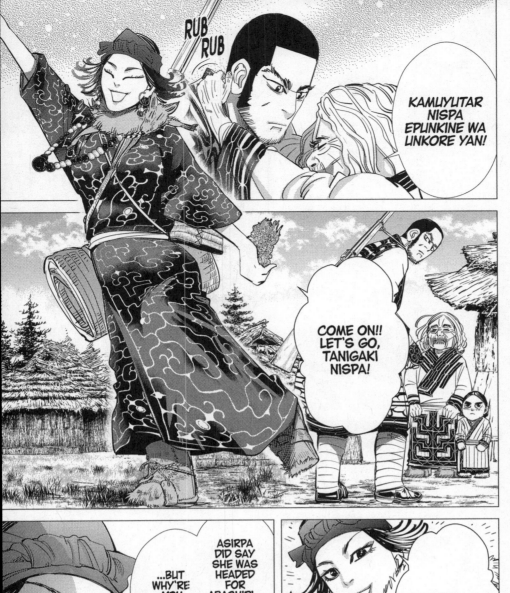

KAMUYUTAR NISPA EPUNKINE WA UNKORE YAN!
RUB RUB
COME ON!! LET'S GO, TANIGAKI NISPA!
THE SIRATKIKAMUY SAYS EAST IS FORTUITOUS!!
ASIRPA DID SAY SHE WAS HEADED FOR ABASHIRI...
...BUT WHY'RE YOU COMING?
WELL...

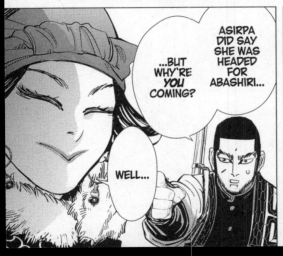

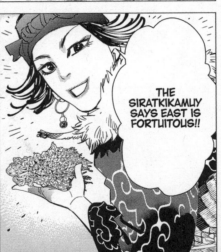

...I JUST HAVE A SOFT SPOT FOR MEN WITH SCARRED FACES.

HMM... I SEE...

THERE'S A MAN IN THAT KOTAN NAMED TANIGAKI THAT I WANT YOU TO MANIPULATE.

HIS FEET WILL BE RECOVERED SOON.

Chapter 77: Fake

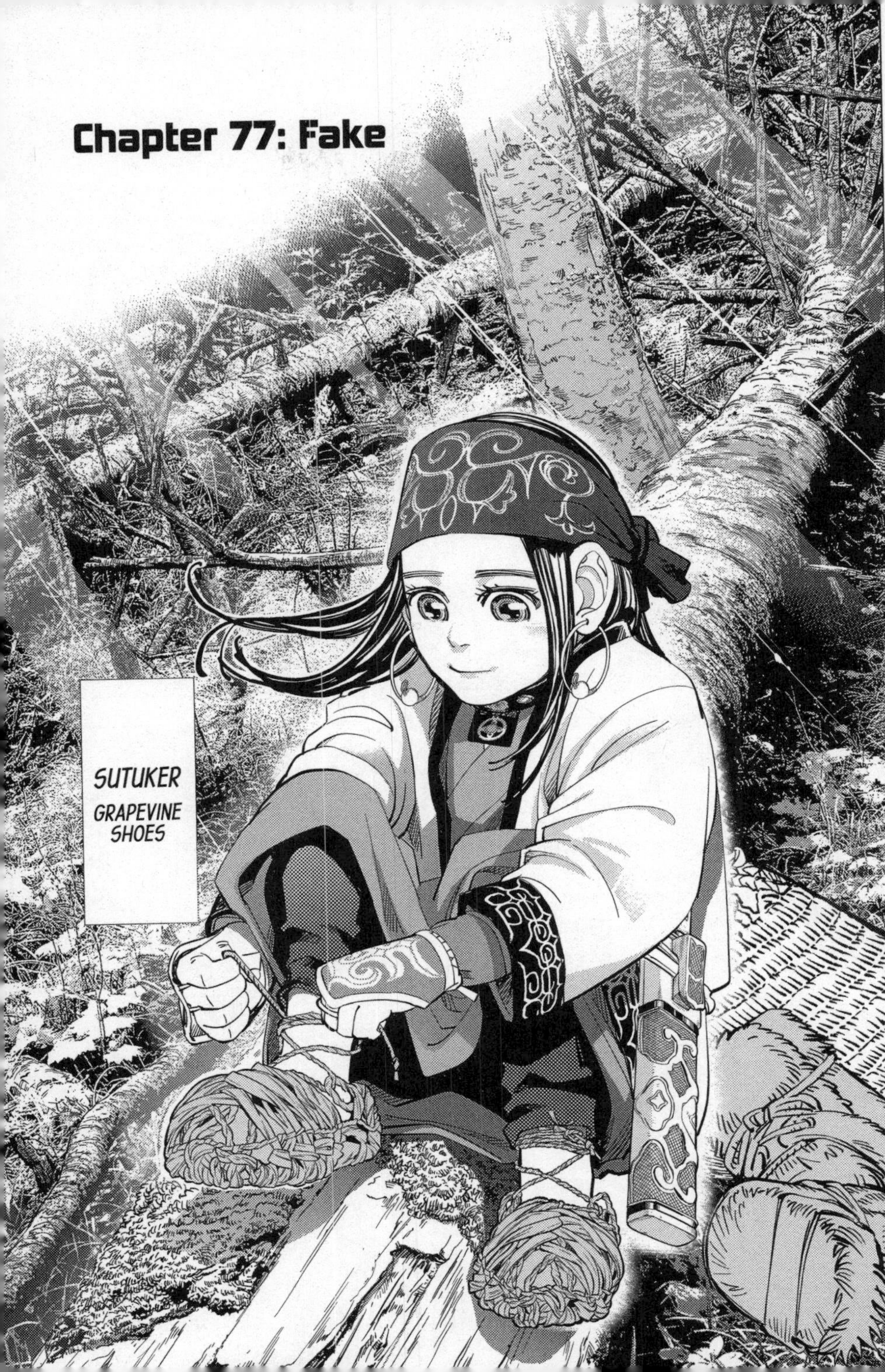
SUTUKER
GRAPEVINE SHOES

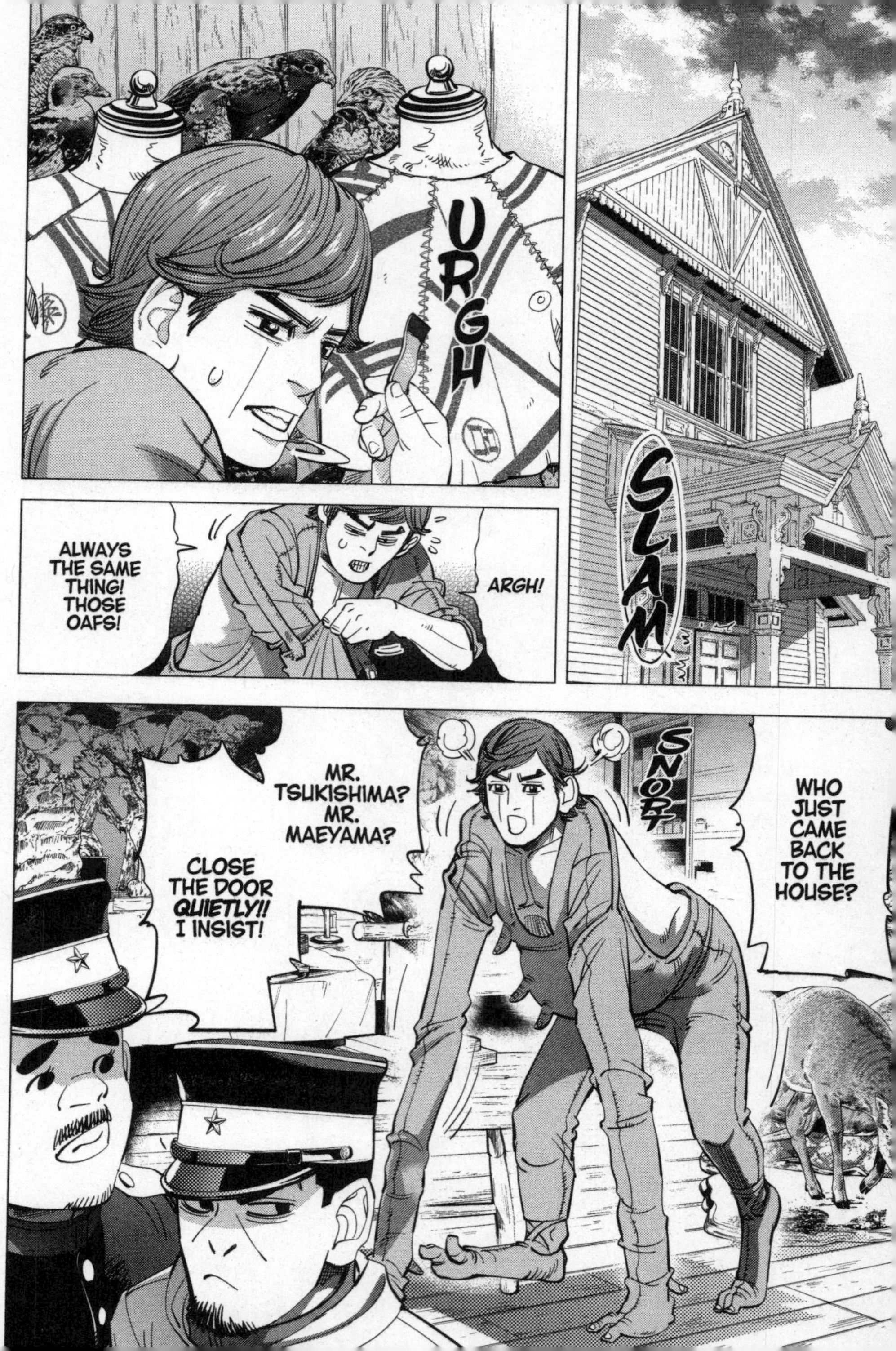
SLAM
URGH
ARGH!
ALWAYS THE SAME THING! THOSE OAFS!
WHO JUST CAME BACK TO THE HOUSE?
SNORT
MR. TSUKISHIMA? MR. MAEYAMA?
CLOSE THE DOOR QUIETLY!! I INSIST!

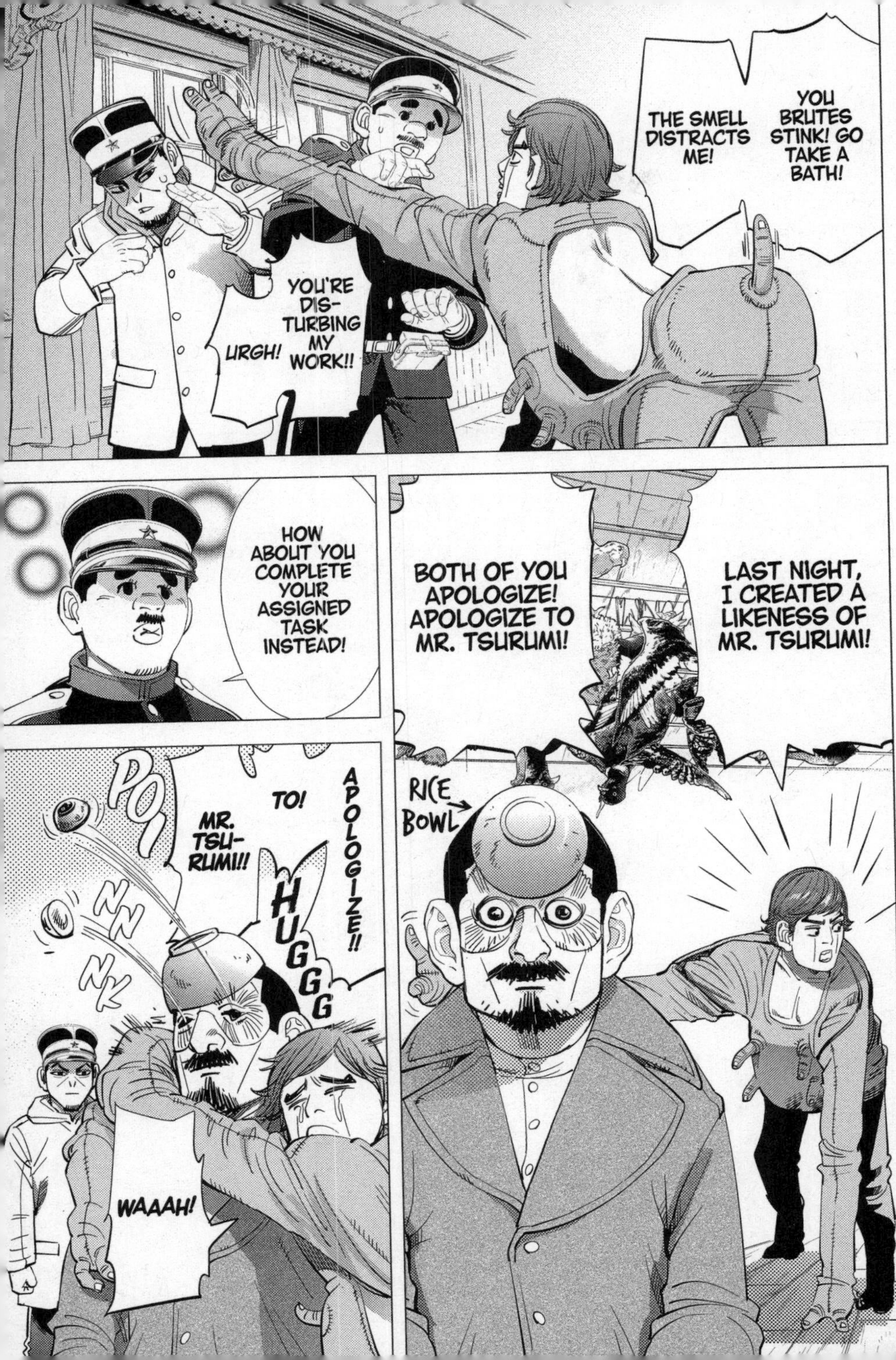
YOU BRUTES STINK! GO TAKE A BATH!
THE SMELL DISTRACTS ME!
YOU'RE DIS-TURBING MY WORK!!
URGH!
LAST NIGHT, I CREATED A LIKENESS OF MR. TSURUMI!
BOTH OF YOU APOLOGIZE! APOLOGIZE TO MR. TSURUMI!
HOW ABOUT YOU COMPLETE YOUR ASSIGNED TASK INSTEAD!
RICE BOWL
APOLOGIZE!!
TO!
MR. TSU-RUMI!!
HUGGG
POI
NNNK
WAAAH!

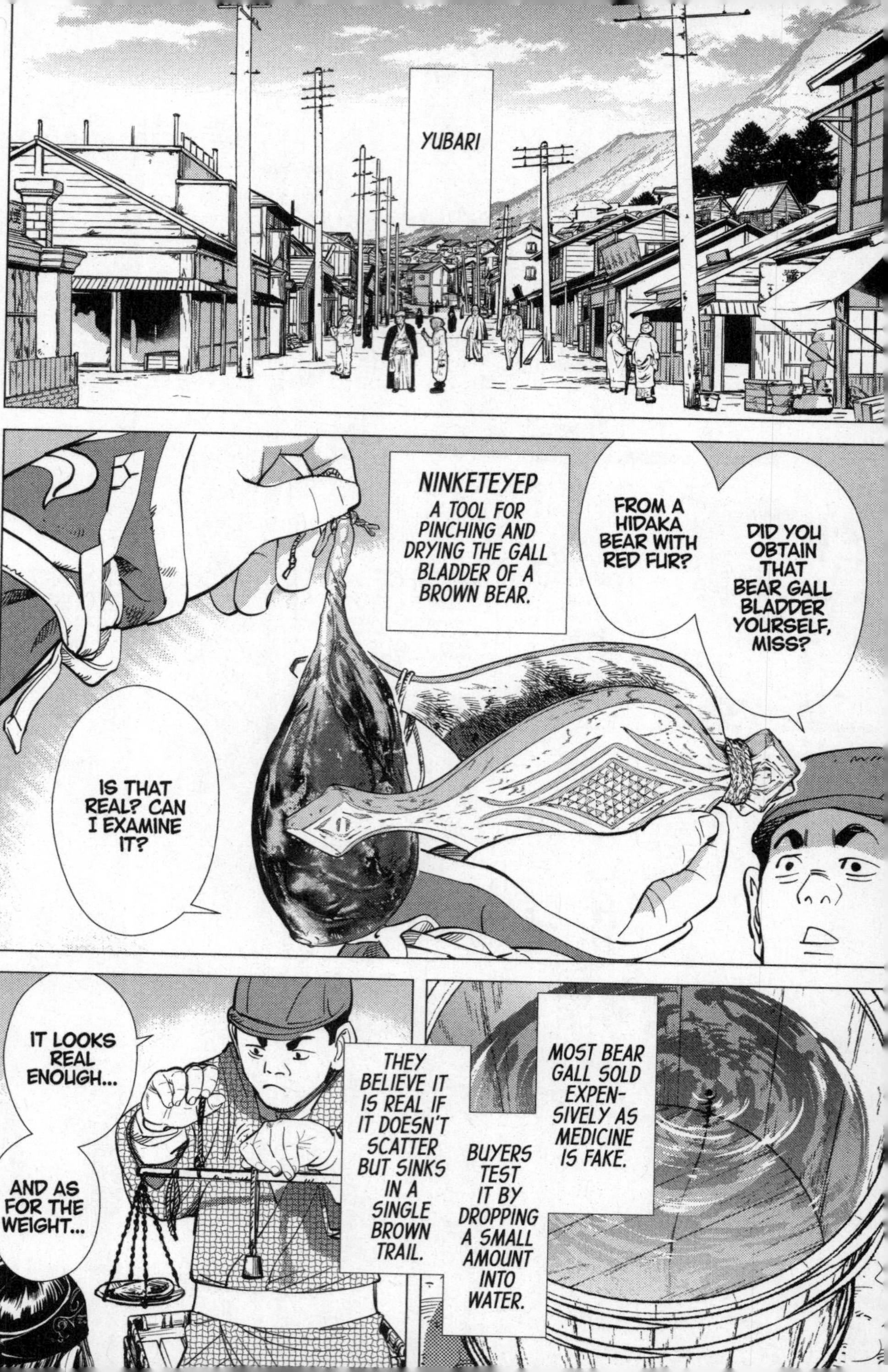
YUBARI
DID YOU OBTAIN THAT BEAR GALL BLADDER YOURSELF, MISS?
FROM A HIDAKA BEAR WITH RED FUR?
NINKETEYEP
A TOOL FOR PINCHING AND DRYING THE GALL BLADDER OF A BROWN BEAR.
IS THAT REAL? CAN I EXAMINE IT?
MOST BEAR GALL SOLD EXPEN-SIVELY AS MEDICINE IS FAKE.
BUYERS TEST IT BY DROPPING A SMALL AMOUNT INTO WATER.
THEY BELIEVE IT IS REAL IF IT DOESN'T SCATTER BUT SINKS IN A SINGLE BROWN TRAIL.
IT LOOKS REAL ENOUGH...
AND AS FOR THE WEIGHT...

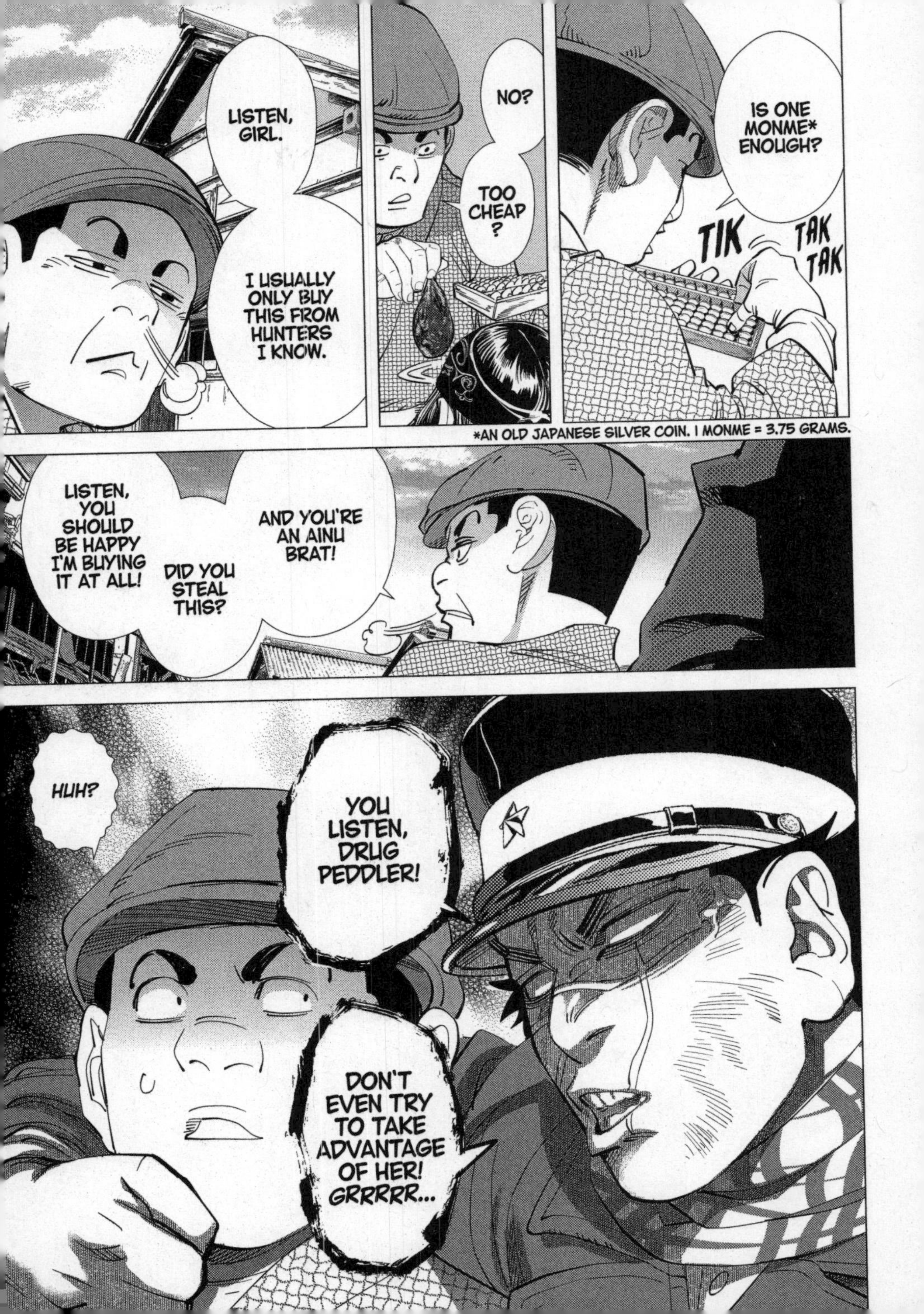
IS ONE MONME* ENOUGH?
TIK
TAK TAK
NO?
TOO CHEAP?
LISTEN, GIRL.
I USUALLY ONLY BUY THIS FROM HUNTERS I KNOW.
*AN OLD JAPANESE SILVER COIN. 1 MONME = 3.75 GRAMS.
AND YOU'RE AN AINU BRAT!
LISTEN, YOU SHOULD BE HAPPY I'M BUYING IT AT ALL!
DID YOU STEAL THIS?
YOU LISTEN, DRUG PEDDLER!
HUH?
DON'T EVEN TRY TO TAKE ADVANTAGE OF HER! GRRRRR...

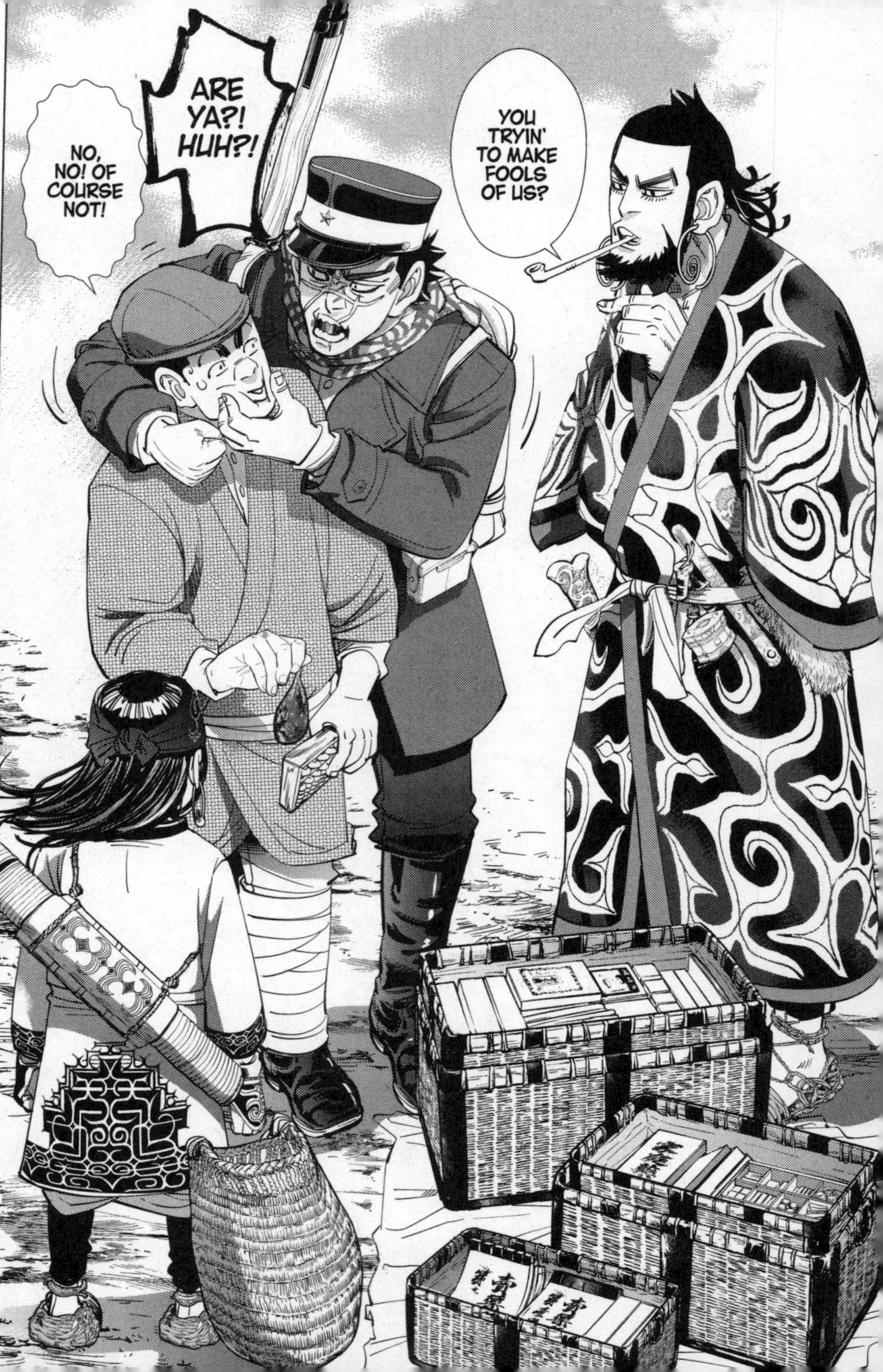
YOU TRYIN' TO MAKE FOOLS OF US?
ARE YA?! HUH?!
NO, NO! OF COURSE NOT!

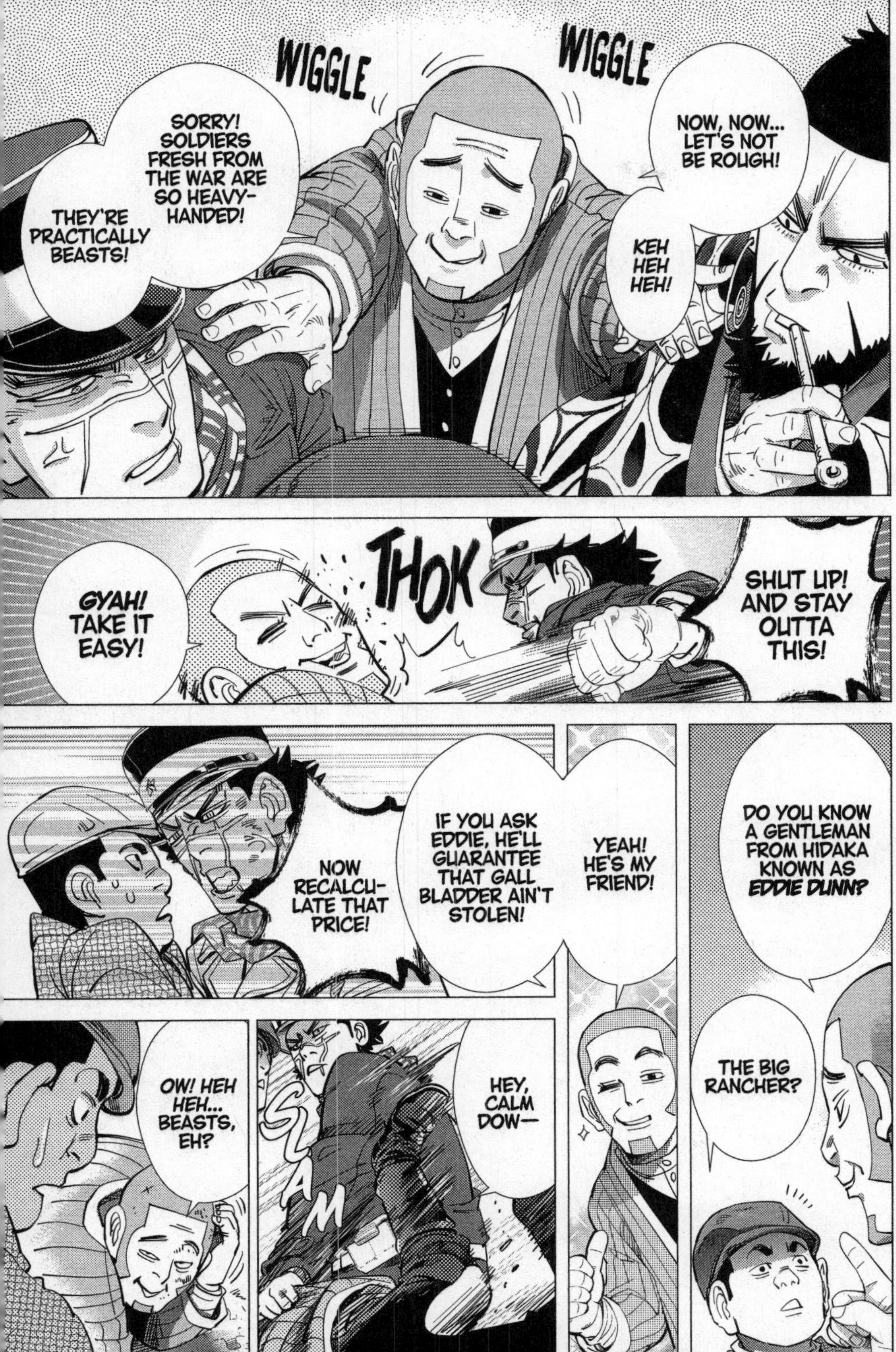
NOW, NOW... LET'S NOT BE ROUGH!
WIGGLE
KEH HEH HEH!
WIGGLE
SORRY! SOLDIERS FRESH FROM THE WAR ARE SO HEAVY-HANDED!
THEY'RE PRACTICALLY BEASTS!
SHUT UP! AND STAY OUTTA THIS!
THOK
GYAH! TAKE IT EASY!
DO YOU KNOW A GENTLEMAN FROM HIDAKA KNOWN AS EDDIE DUNN?
THE BIG RANCHER?
YEAH! HE'S MY FRIEND!
IF YOU ASK EDDIE, HE'LL GUARANTEE THAT GALL BLADDER AIN'T STOLEN!
NOW RECALCULATE THAT PRICE!
HEY, CALM DOW—
SLAM
OW! HEH HEH... BEASTS, EH?

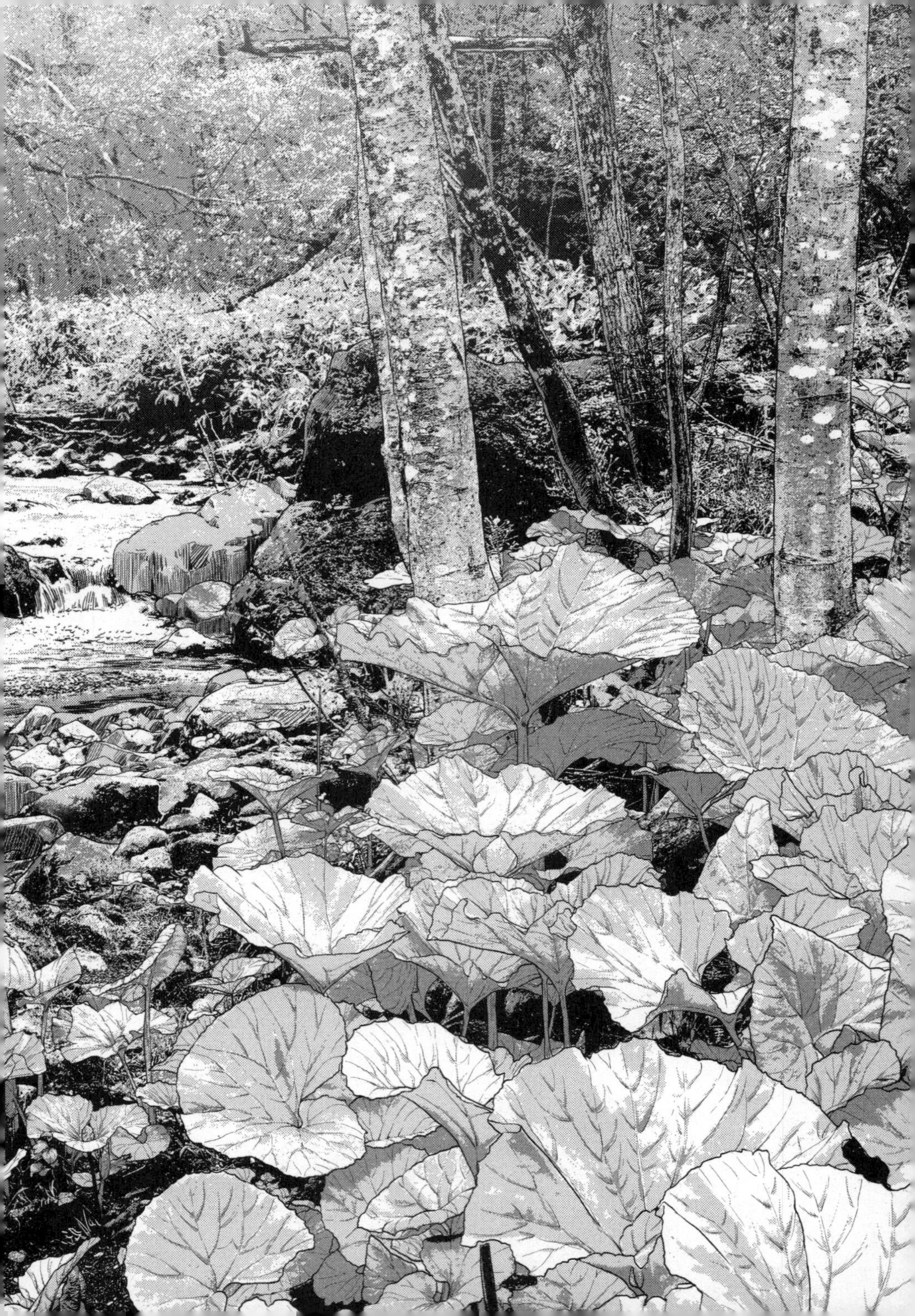

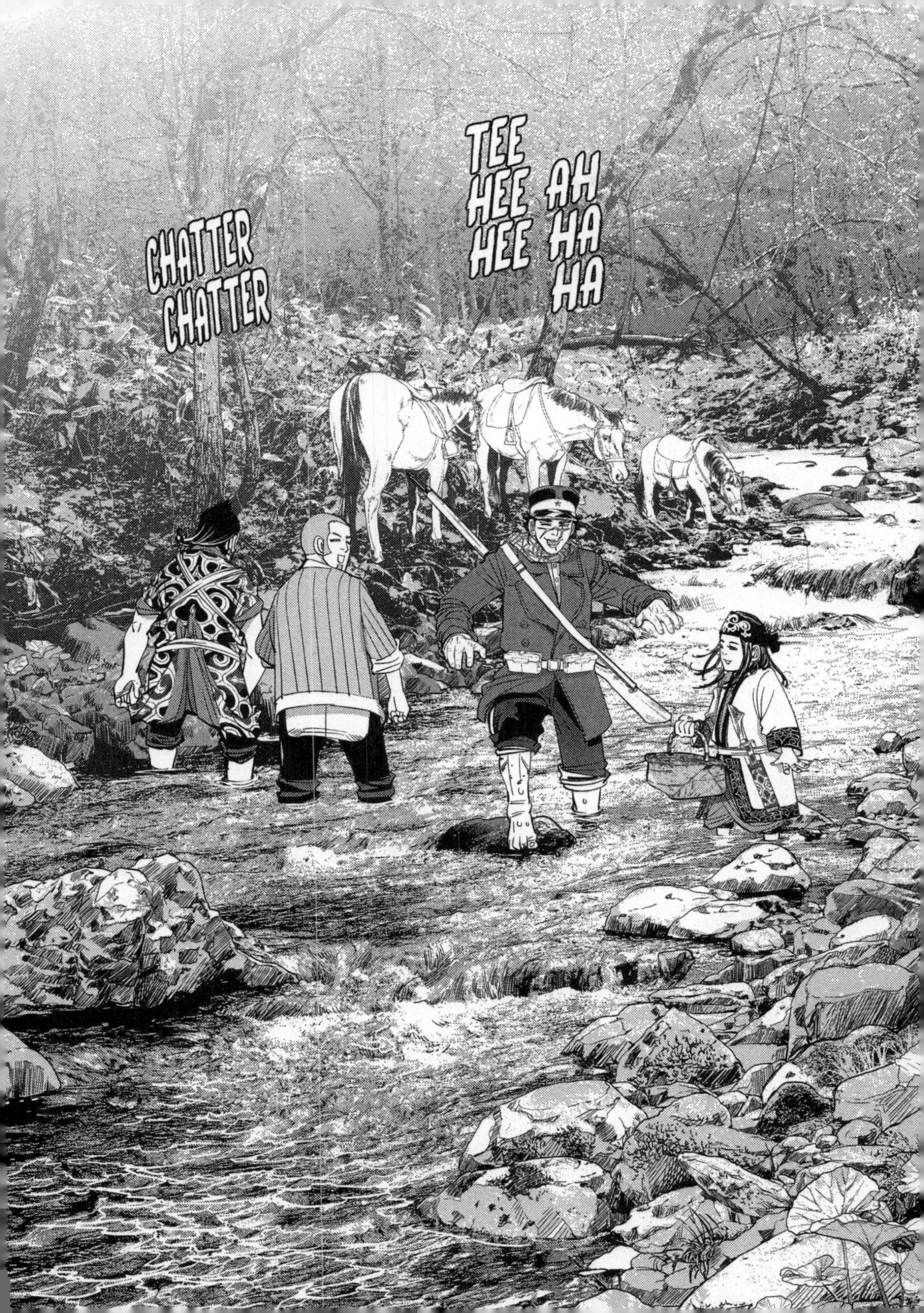
TEE HEE HEE
AH HA HA
CHATTER CHATTER

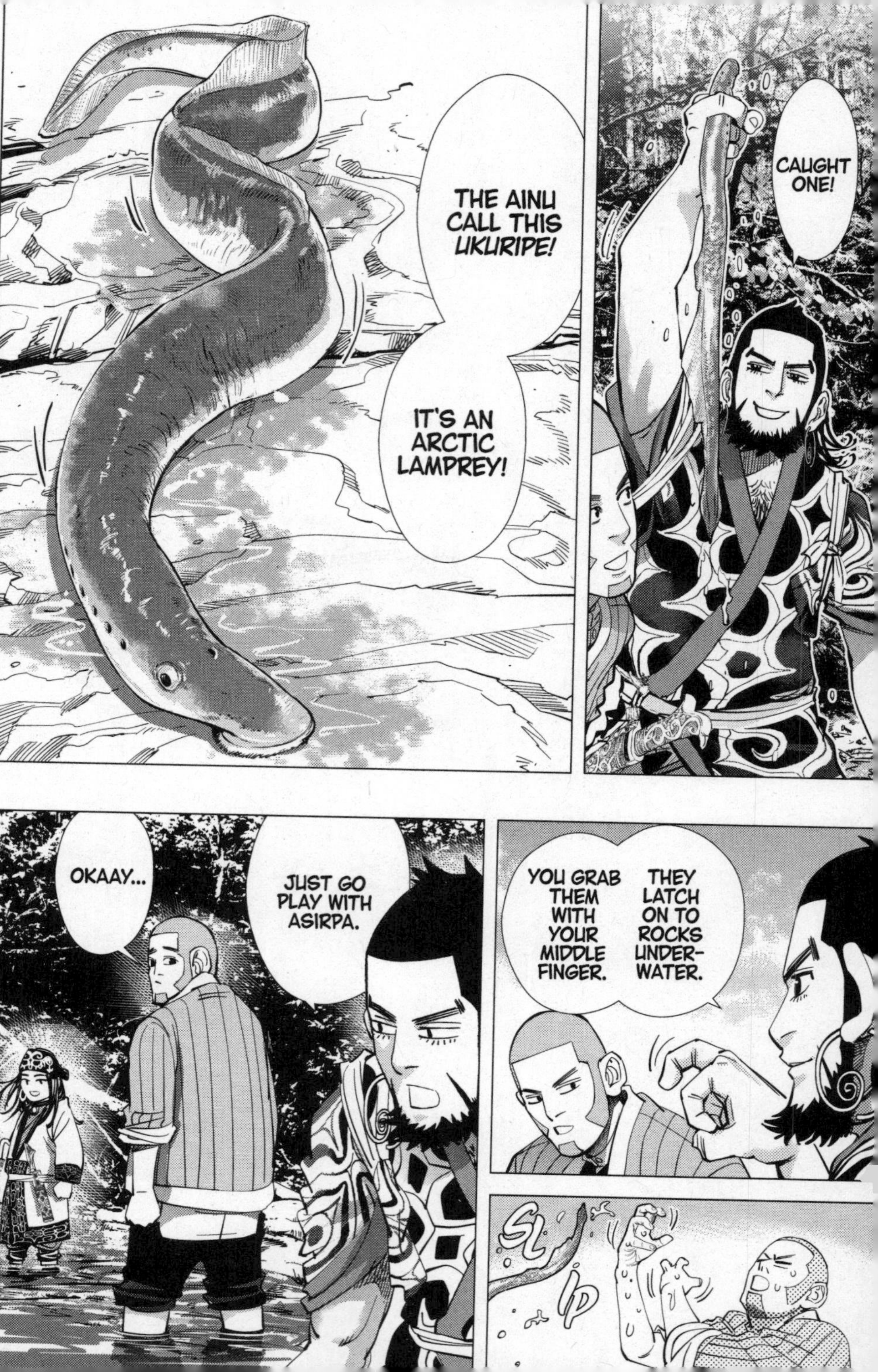
CAUGHT ONE!
THE AINU CALL THIS UKURIPE!
IT'S AN ARCTIC LAMPREY!
THEY LATCH ON TO ROCKS UNDERWATER.
YOU GRAB THEM WITH YOUR MIDDLE FINGER.
SLIP
JUST GO PLAY WITH ASIRPA.
OKAAY...

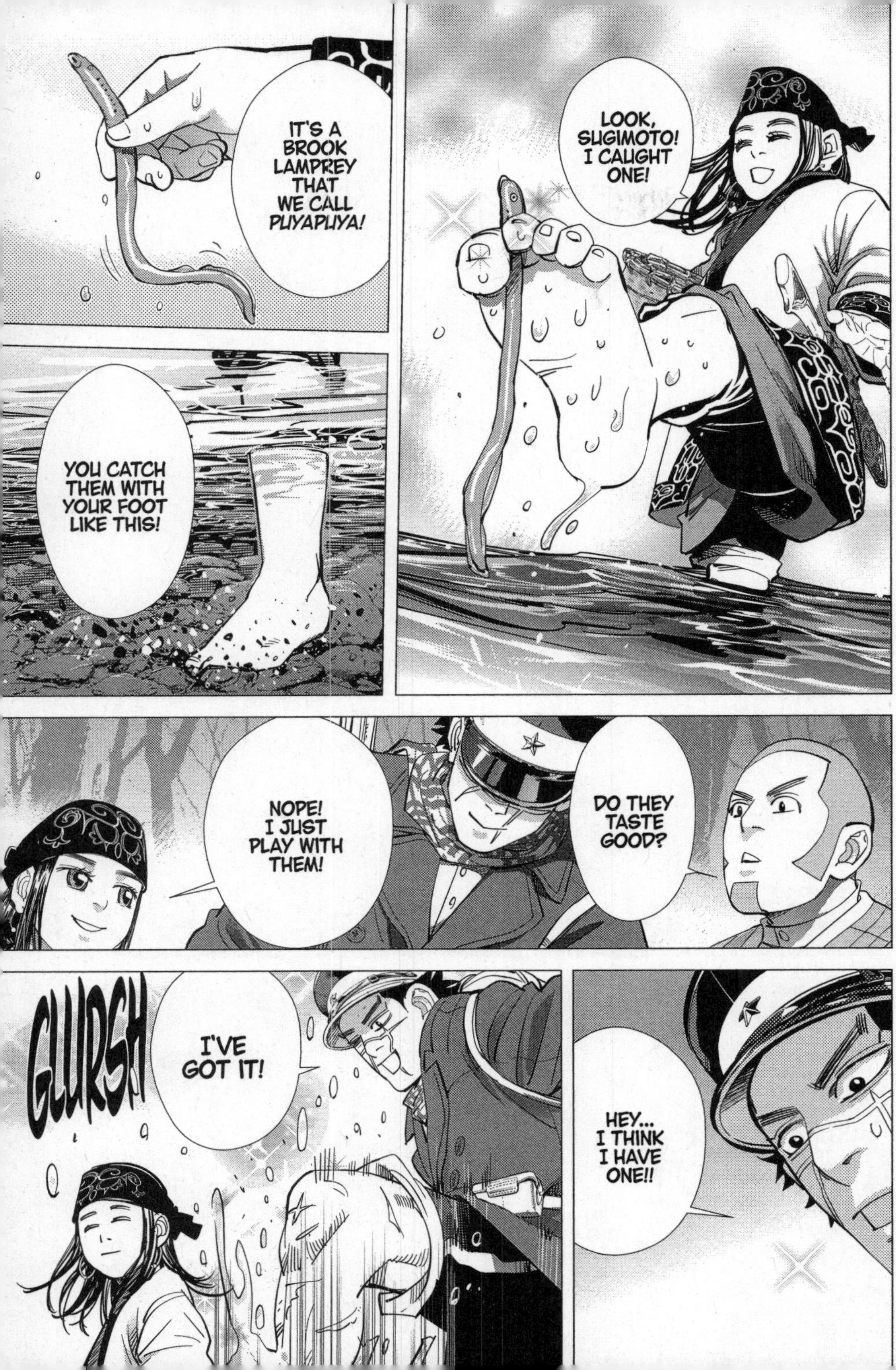
LOOK, SUGIMOTO! I CAUGHT ONE!
IT'S A BROOK LAMPREY THAT WE CALL *PUYAPUYA*!
YOU CATCH THEM WITH YOUR FOOT LIKE THIS!
DO THEY TASTE GOOD?
NOPE! I JUST PLAY WITH THEM!
HEY... I THINK I HAVE ONE!!
I'VE GOT IT!
GLURSH

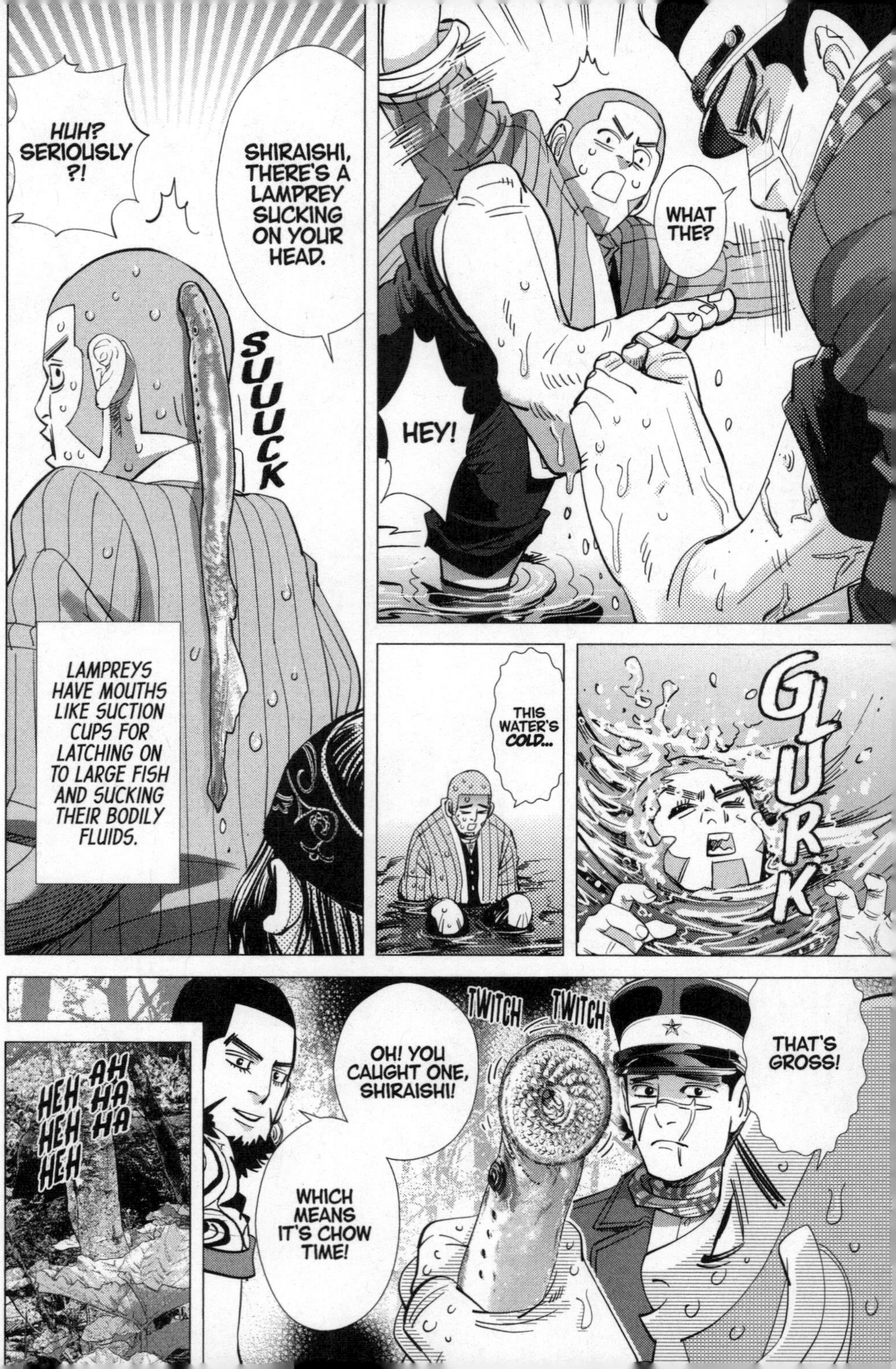
WHAT THE?
HEY!
GLURK
THIS WATER'S COLD...
SHIRAISHI, THERE'S A LAMPREY SUCKING ON YOUR HEAD.
HUH? SERIOUSLY ?!
SUUUUCK
LAMPREYS HAVE MOUTHS LIKE SUCTION CUPS FOR LATCHING ON TO LARGE FISH AND SUCKING THEIR BODILY FLUIDS.
THAT'S GROSS!
TWITCH TWITCH
OH! YOU CAUGHT ONE, SHIRAISHI!
WHICH MEANS IT'S CHOW TIME!
AH HA HA
HEH HEH HEH HEH

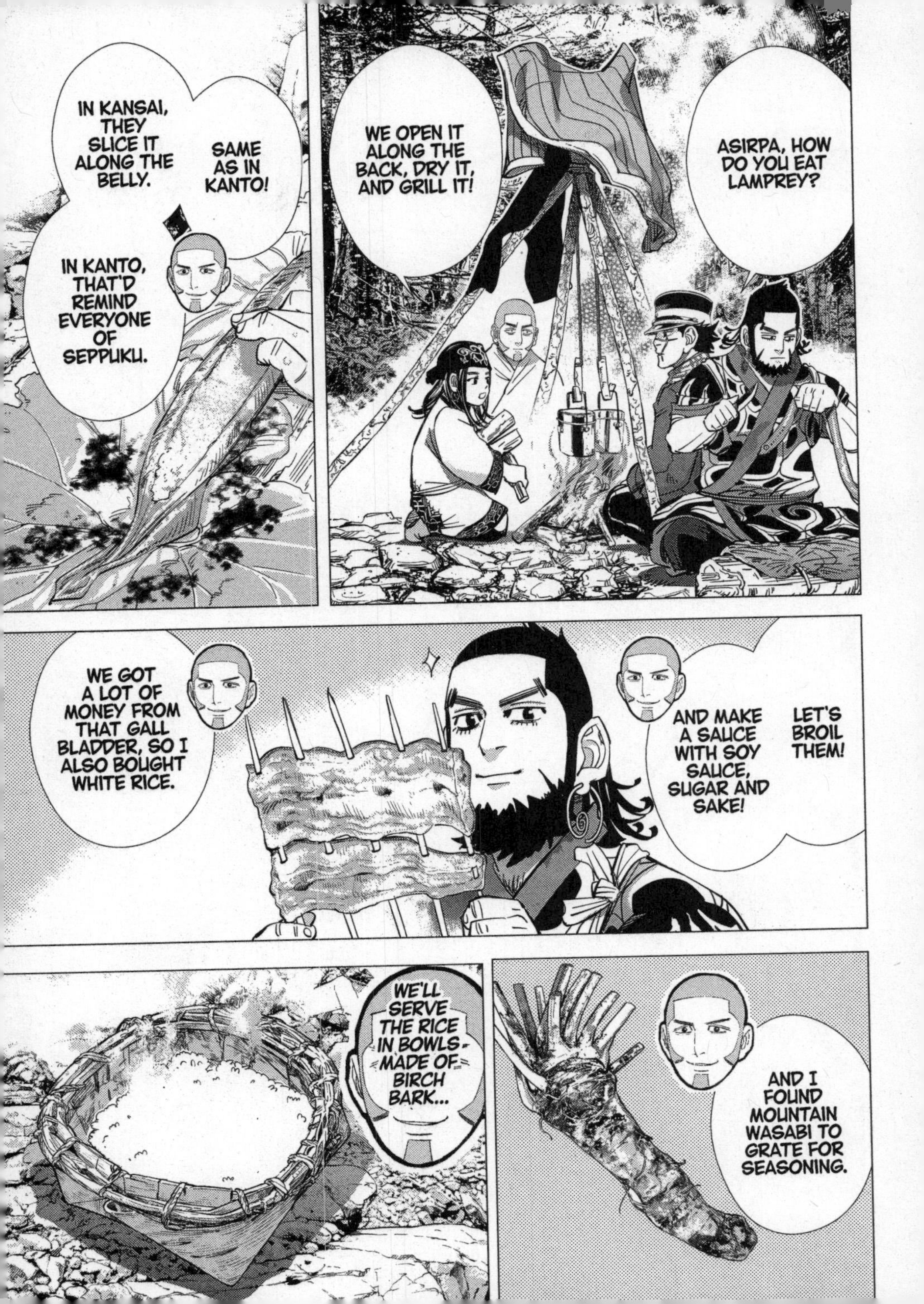
ASIRPA, HOW DO YOU EAT LAMPREY?
WE OPEN IT ALONG THE BACK, DRY IT, AND GRILL IT!
SAME AS IN KANTO!
IN KANSAI, THEY SLICE IT ALONG THE BELLY.
IN KANTO, THAT'D REMIND EVERYONE OF SEPPUKU.
LET'S BROIL THEM!
AND MAKE A SAUCE WITH SOY SAUCE, SUGAR AND SAKE!
WE GOT A LOT OF MONEY FROM THAT GALL BLADDER, SO I ALSO BOUGHT WHITE RICE.
AND I FOUND MOUNTAIN WASABI TO GRATE FOR SEASONING.
WE'LL SERVE THE RICE IN BOWLS MADE OF BIRCH BARK...

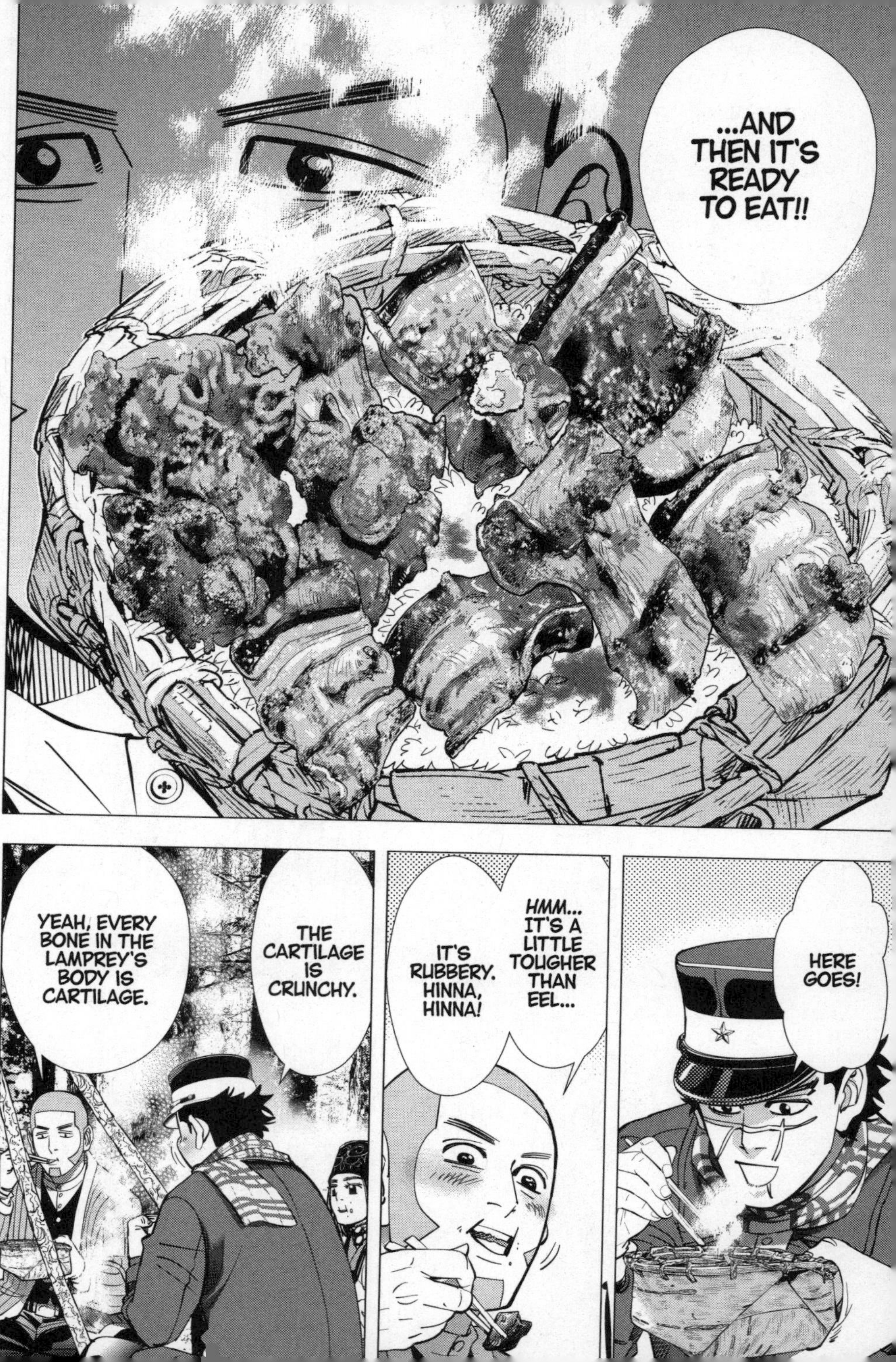
...AND THEN IT'S READY TO EAT!!
HERE GOES!
HMM... IT'S A LITTLE TOUGHER THAN EEL...
IT'S RUBBERY. HINNA, HINNA!
THE CARTILAGE IS CRUNCHY.
YEAH, EVERY BONE IN THE LAMPREY'S BODY IS CARTILAGE.

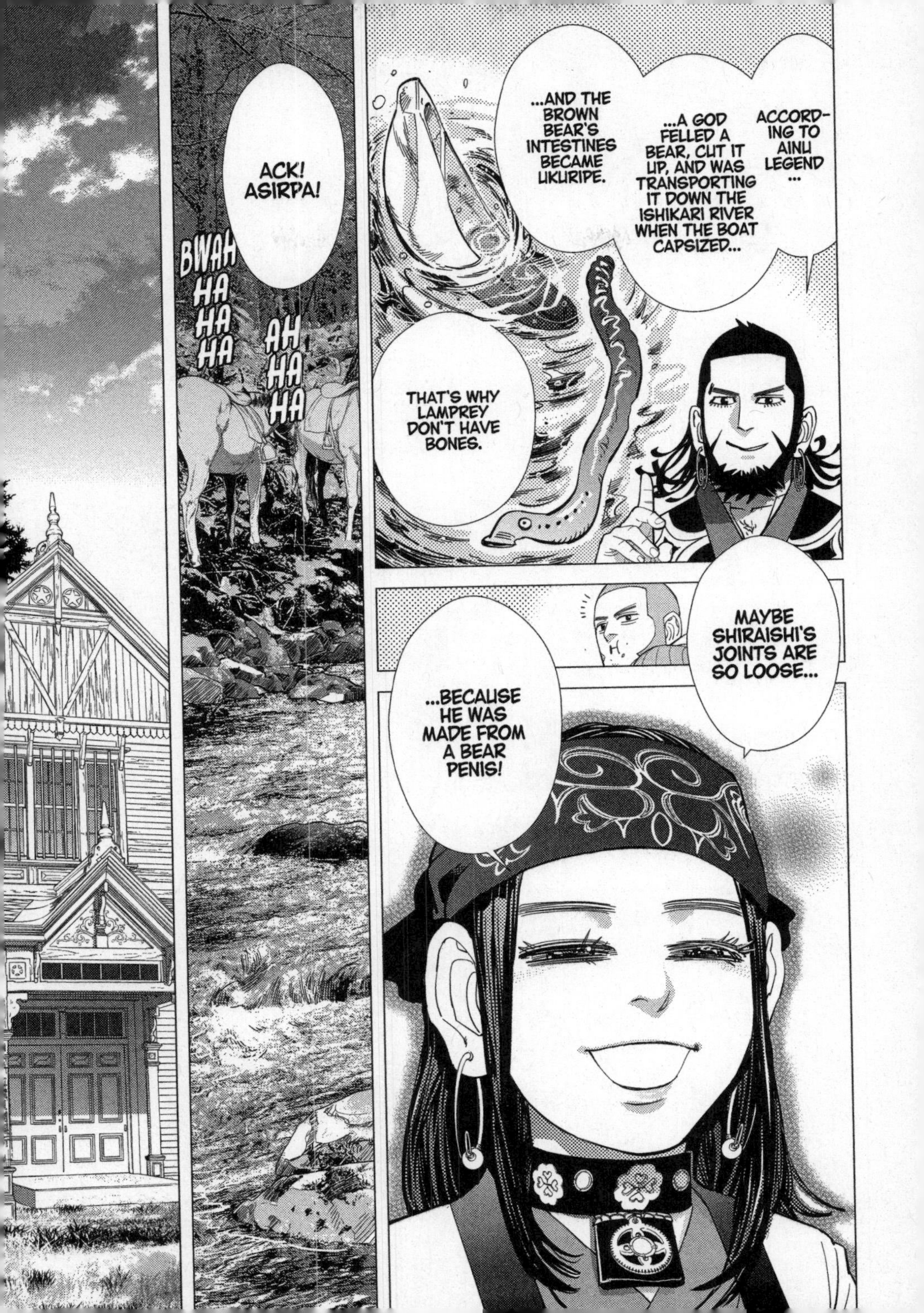

ACCORDING TO AINU LEGEND...
...A GOD FELLED A BEAR, CUT IT UP, AND WAS TRANSPORTING IT DOWN THE ISHIKARI RIVER WHEN THE BOAT CAPSIZED...
...AND THE BROWN BEAR'S INTESTINES BECAME UKURIPE.
THAT'S WHY LAMPREY DON'T HAVE BONES.
MAYBE SHIRAISHI'S JOINTS ARE SO LOOSE...
...BECAUSE HE WAS MADE FROM A BEAR PENIS!
ACK! ASIRPA!
AH HA HA HA
BWAH HA HA HA

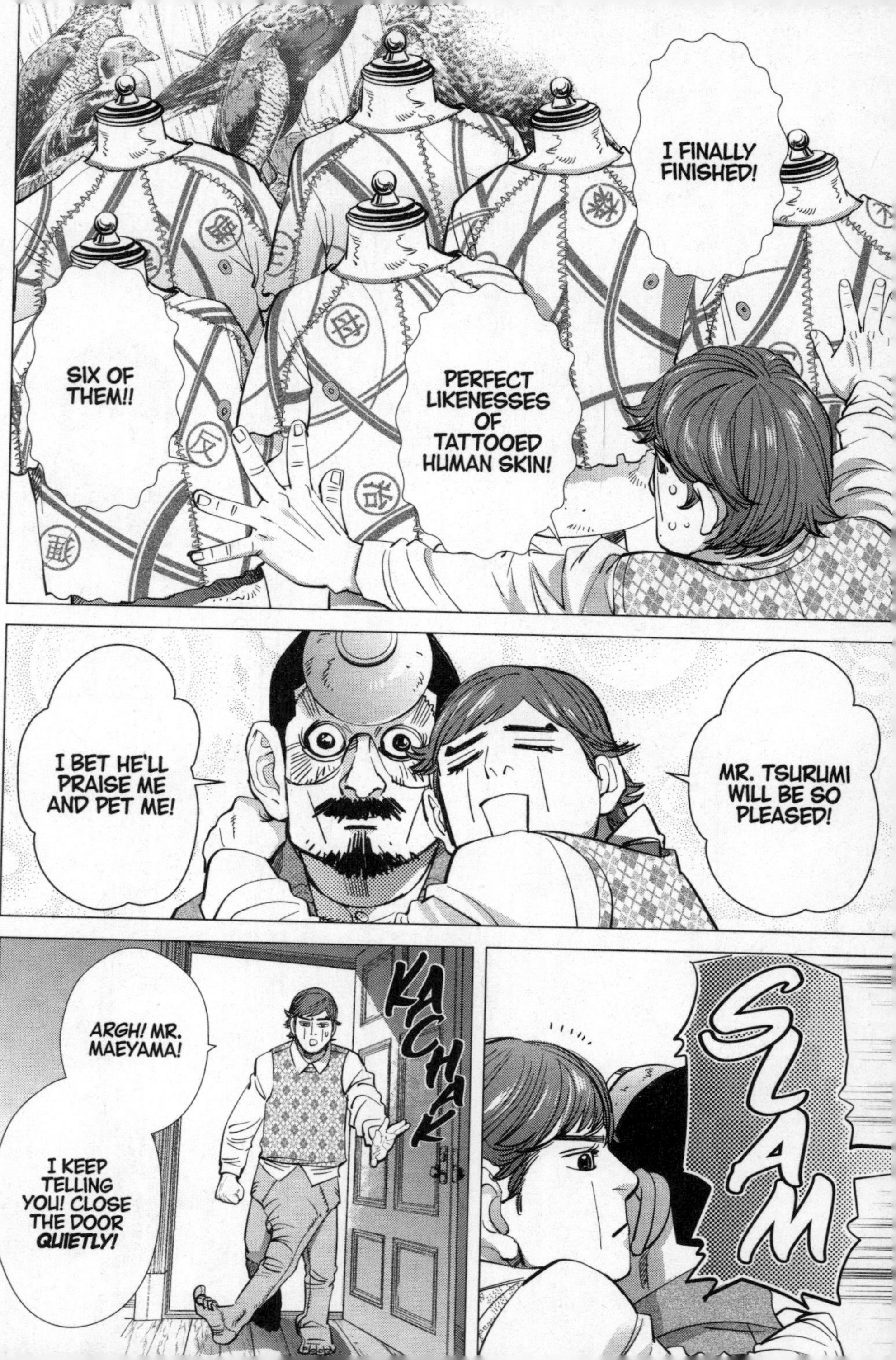
I FINALLY FINISHED!
PERFECT LIKENESSES OF TATTOOED HUMAN SKIN!
SIX OF THEM!!
MR. TSURUMI WILL BE SO PLEASED!
I BET HE'LL PRAISE ME AND PET ME!
SLAM
KACHAK
ARGH! MR. MAEYAMA!
I KEEP TELLING YOU! CLOSE THE DOOR *QUIETLY*!

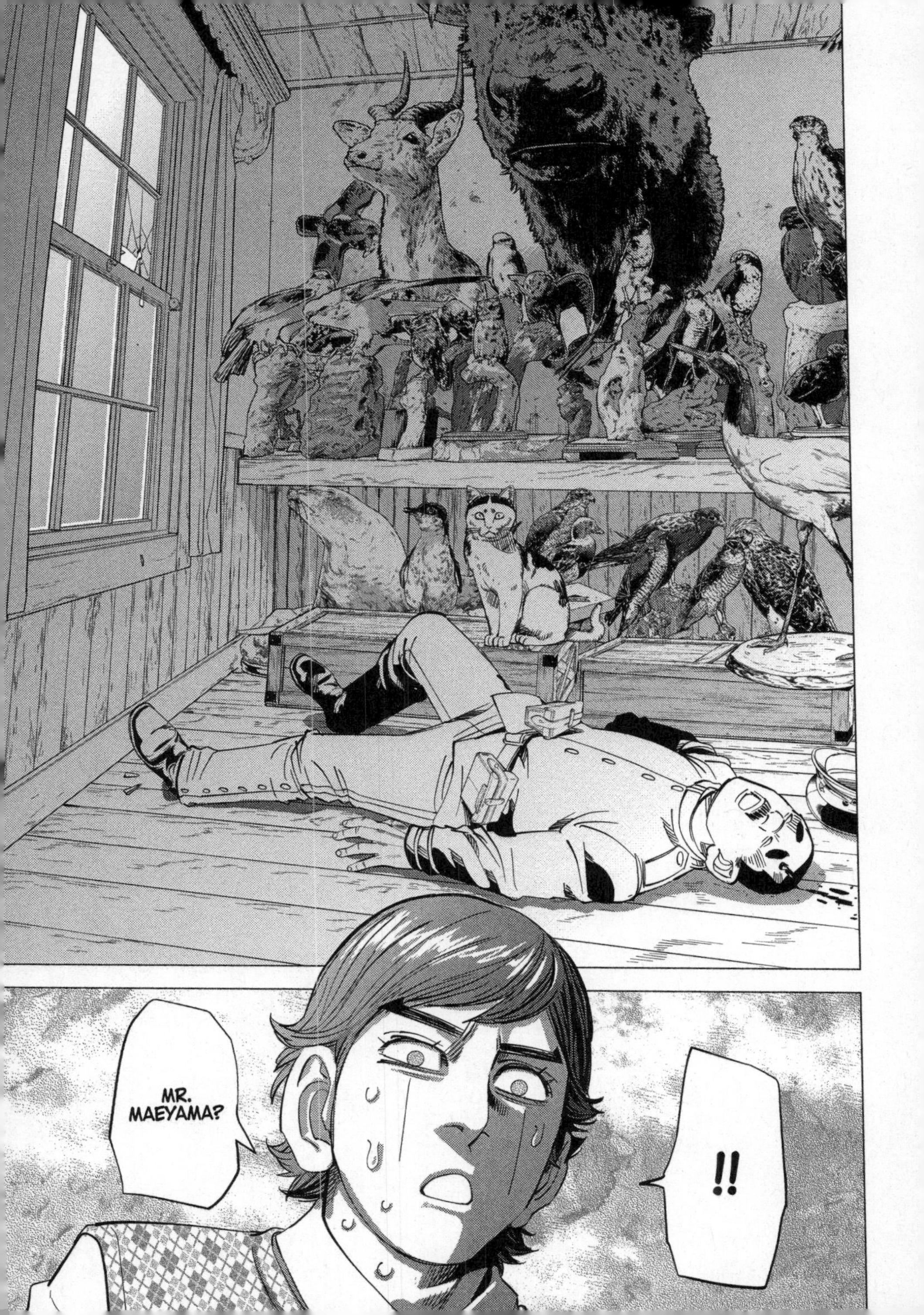
!!
MR. MAEYAMA?

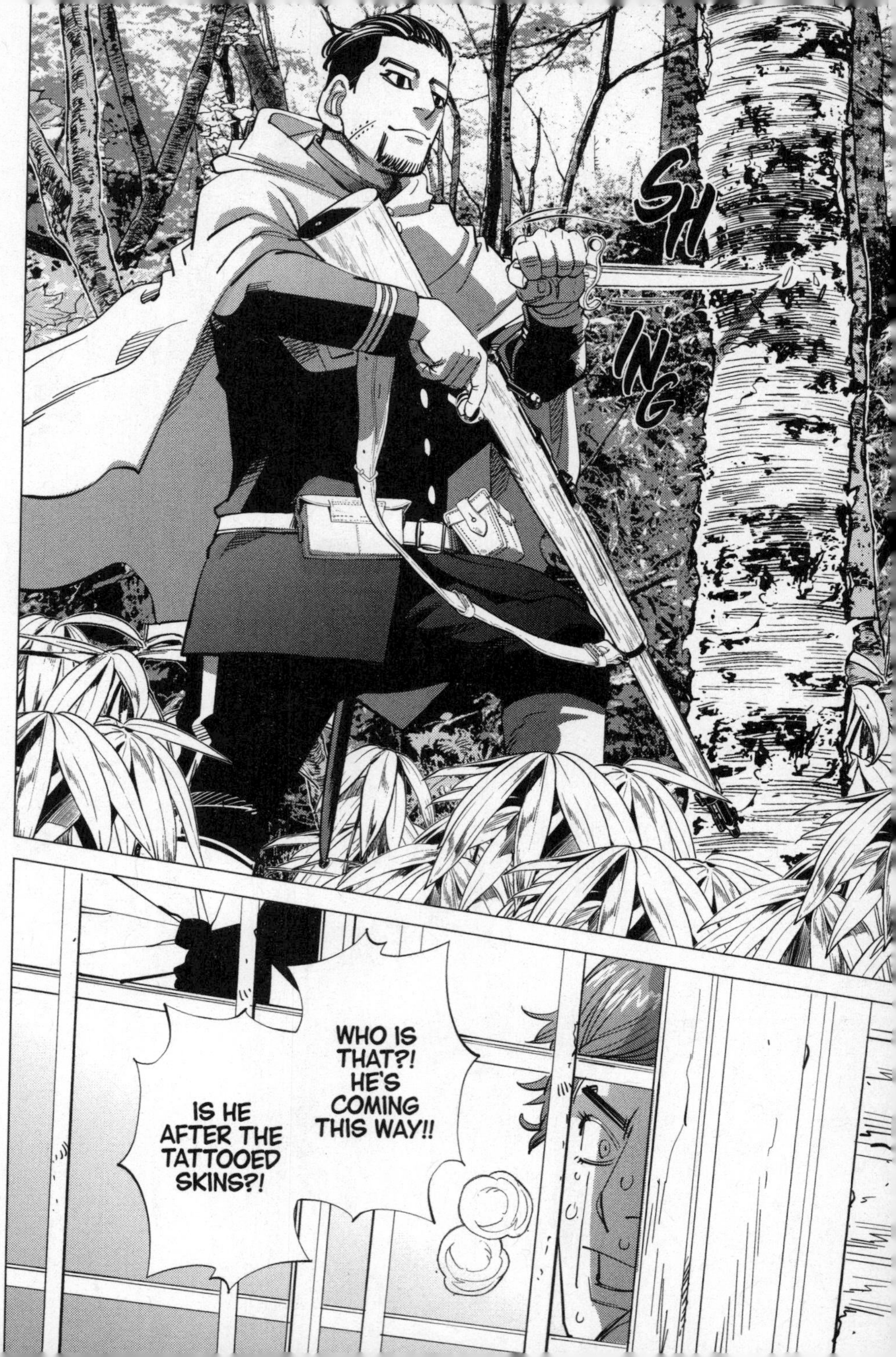
SHING
WHO IS THAT?! HE'S COMING THIS WAY!!
IS HE AFTER THE TATTOOED SKINS?!

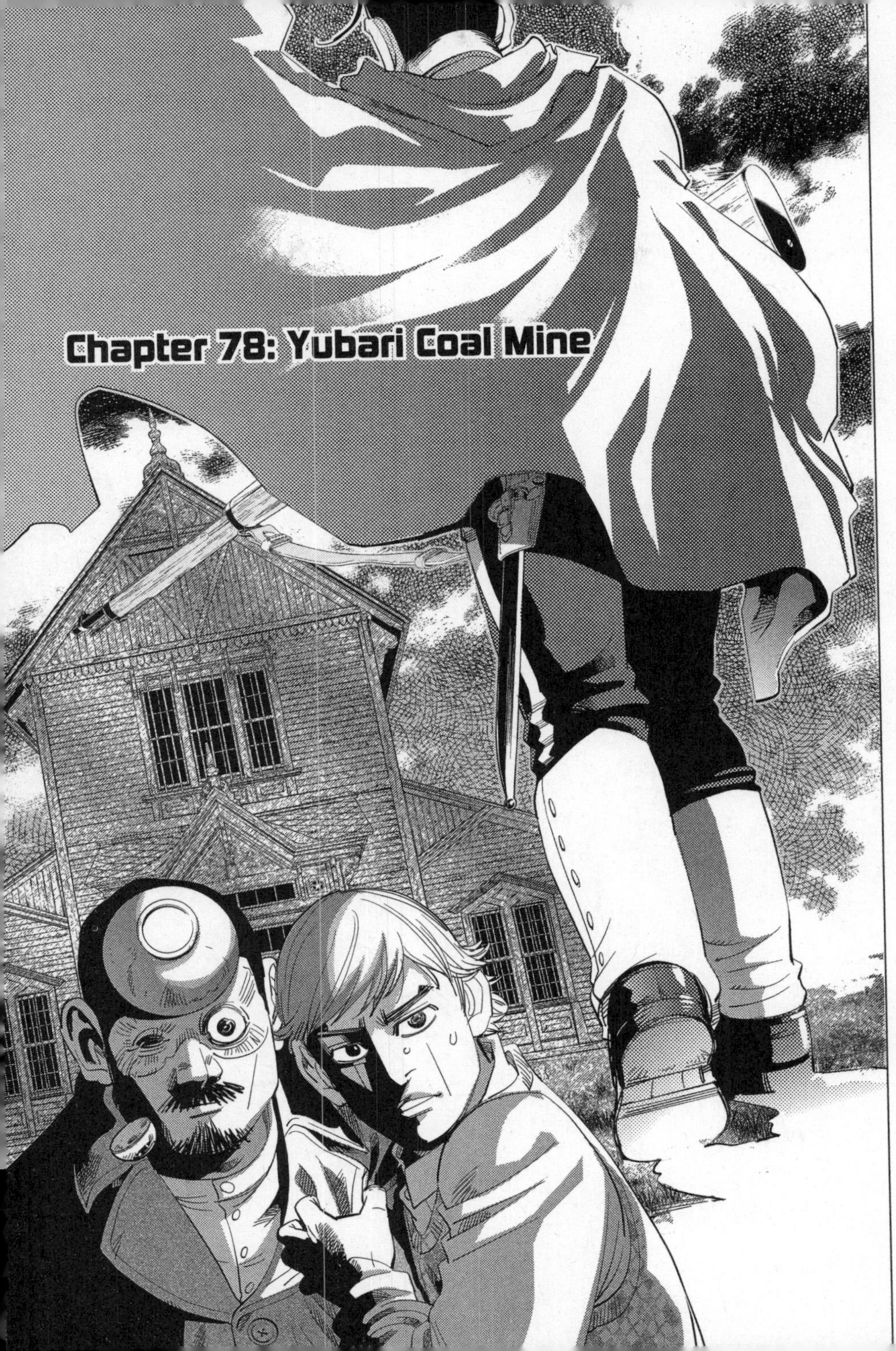
Chapter 78: Yubari Coal Mine

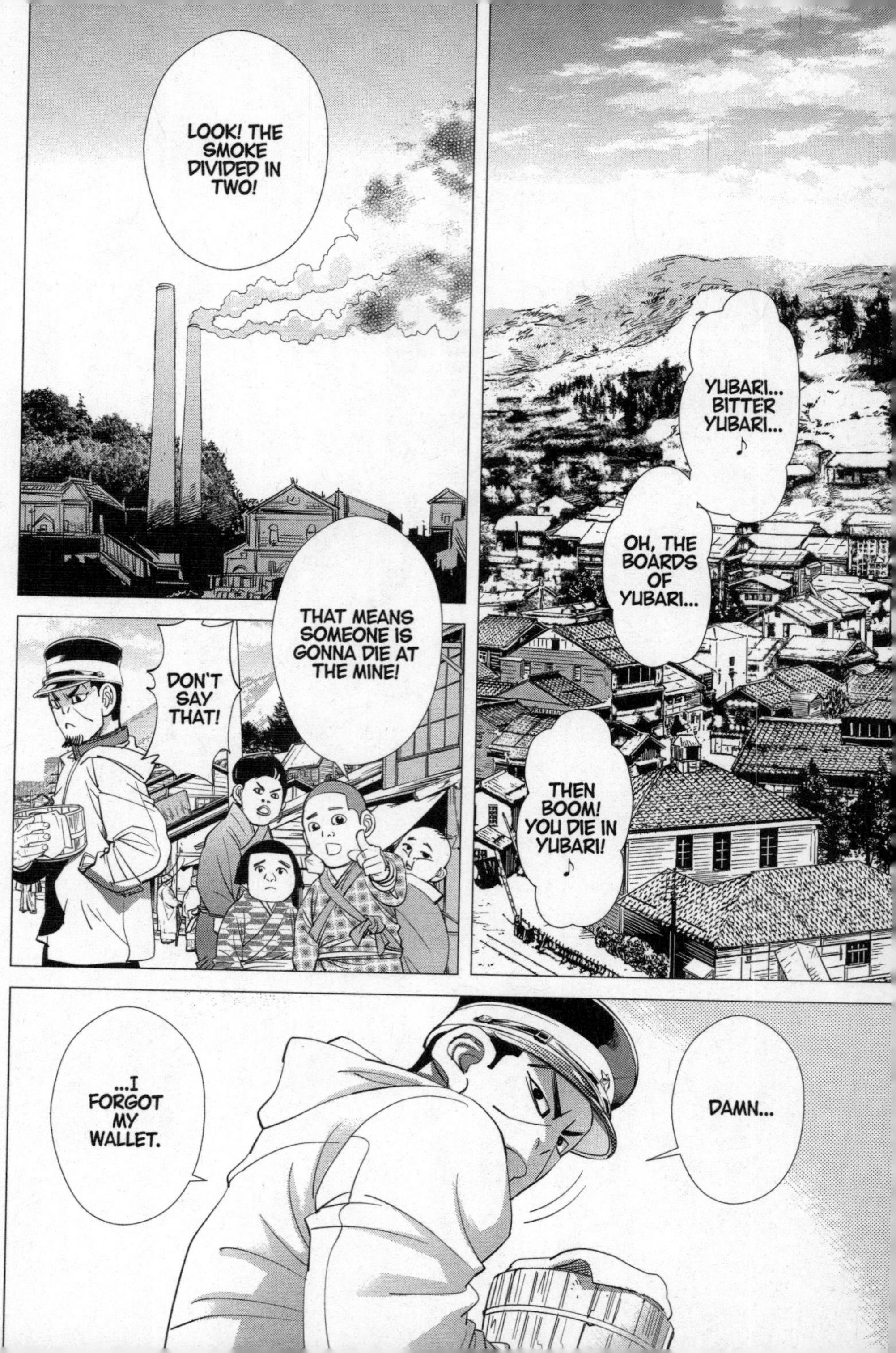
YUBARI... BITTER YUBARI... ♪
OH, THE BOARDS OF YUBARI...
THEN BOOM! YOU DIE IN YUBARI! ♪
LOOK! THE SMOKE DIVIDED IN TWO!
THAT MEANS SOMEONE IS GONNA DIE AT THE MINE!
DON'T SAY THAT!
DAMN...
...I FORGOT MY WALLET.

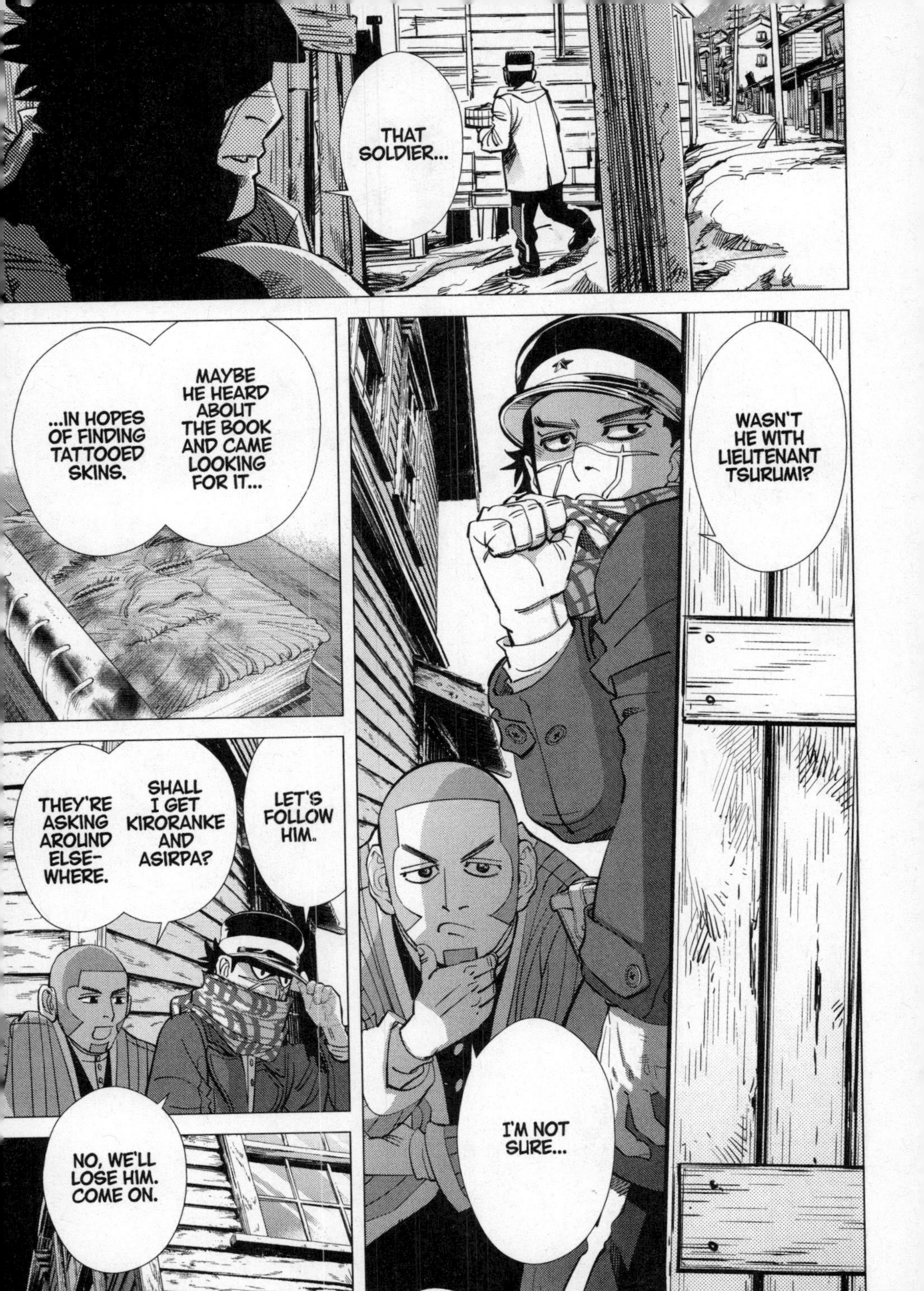
THAT SOLDIER...
WASN'T HE WITH LIEUTENANT TSURUMI?
I'M NOT SURE...
MAYBE HE HEARD ABOUT THE BOOK AND CAME LOOKING FOR IT...
...IN HOPES OF FINDING TATTOOED SKINS.
LET'S FOLLOW HIM.
SHALL I GET KIRORANKE AND ASIRPA?
THEY'RE ASKING AROUND ELSE-WHERE.
NO, WE'LL LOSE HIM. COME ON.

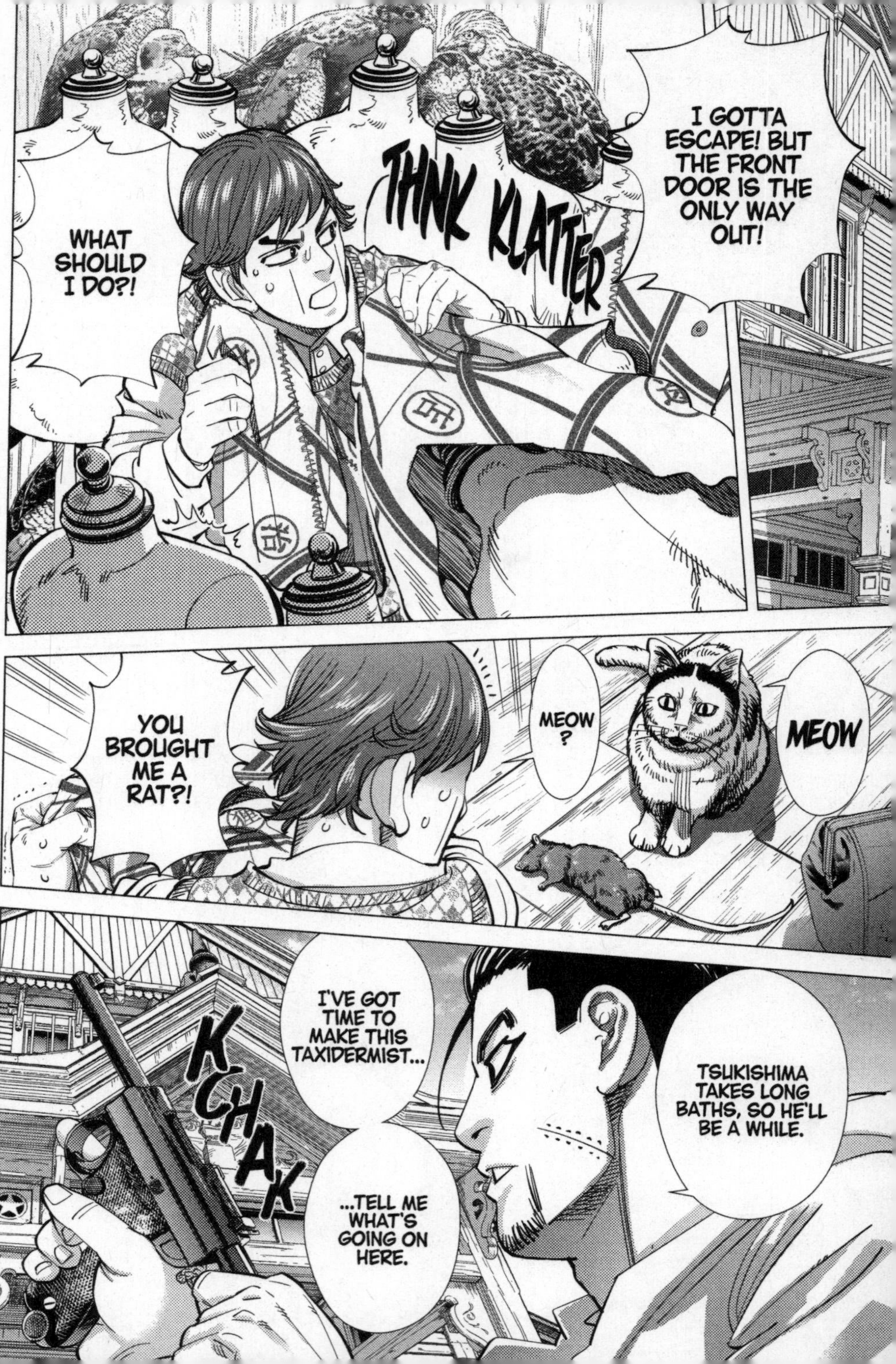
I GOTTA ESCAPE! BUT THE FRONT DOOR IS THE ONLY WAY OUT!
THNK KLATTER
WHAT SHOULD I DO?!
MEOW
MEOW?
YOU BROUGHT ME A RAT?!
TSUKISHIMA TAKES LONG BATHS, SO HE'LL BE A WHILE.
I'VE GOT TIME TO MAKE THIS TAXIDERMIST...
...TELL ME WHAT'S GOING ON HERE.
KCHAK

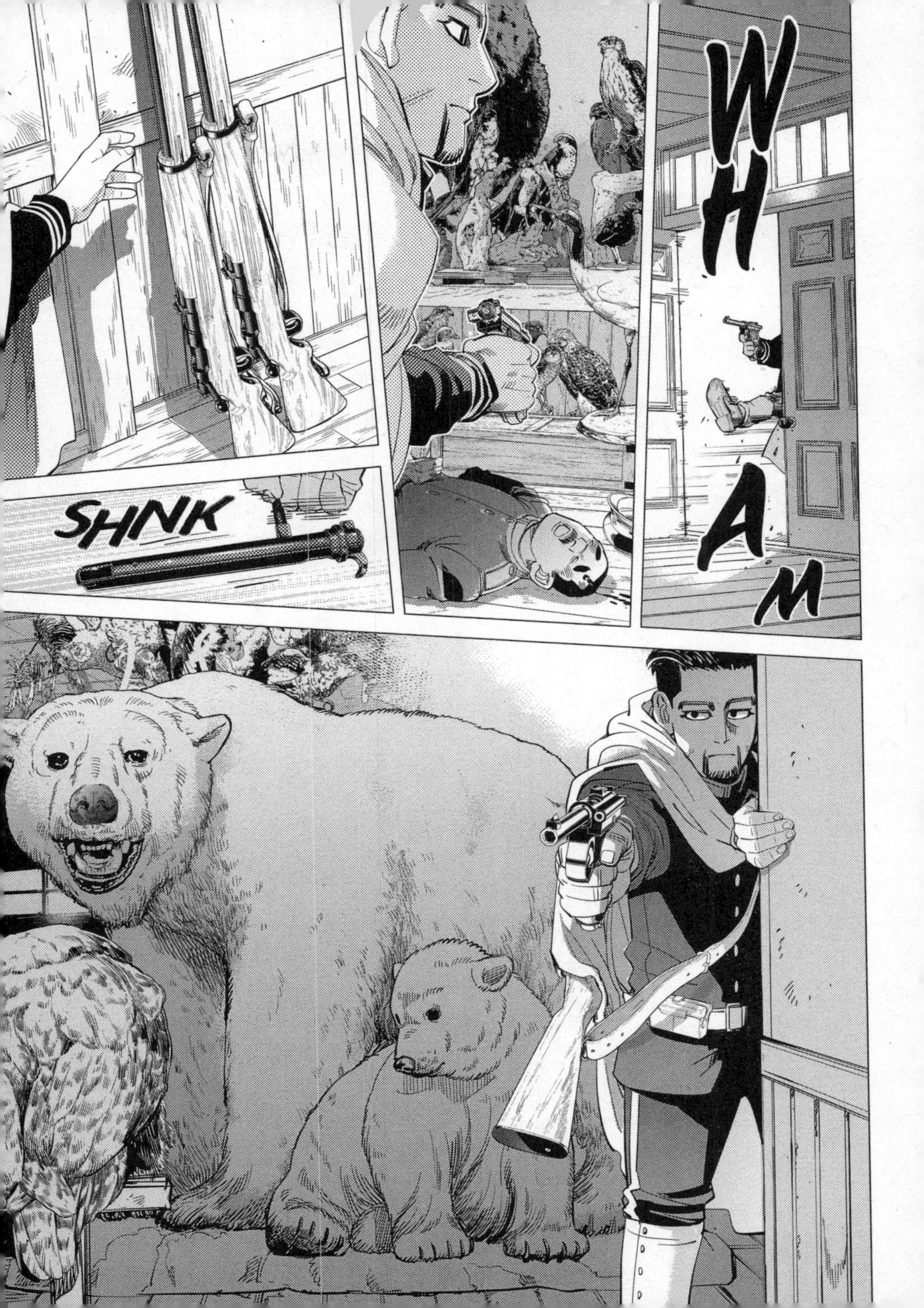
WHAM
SHNK

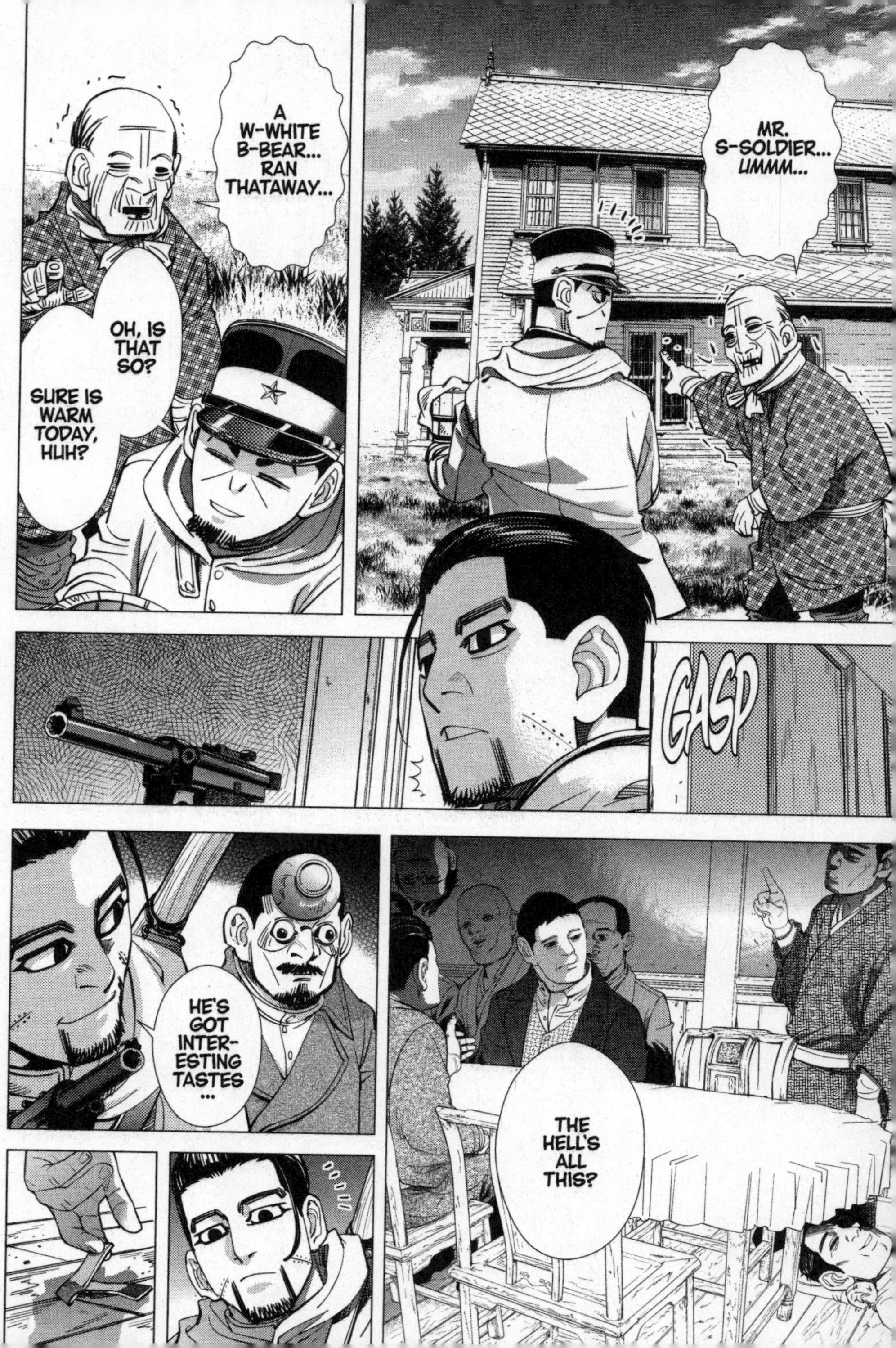
MR. S-SOLDIER... UMMM...
A W-WHITE B-BEAR... RAN THATAWAY...
OH, IS THAT SO?
SURE IS WARM TODAY, HUH?
GASP
THE HELL'S ALL THIS?
HE'S GOT INTER-ESTING TASTES...

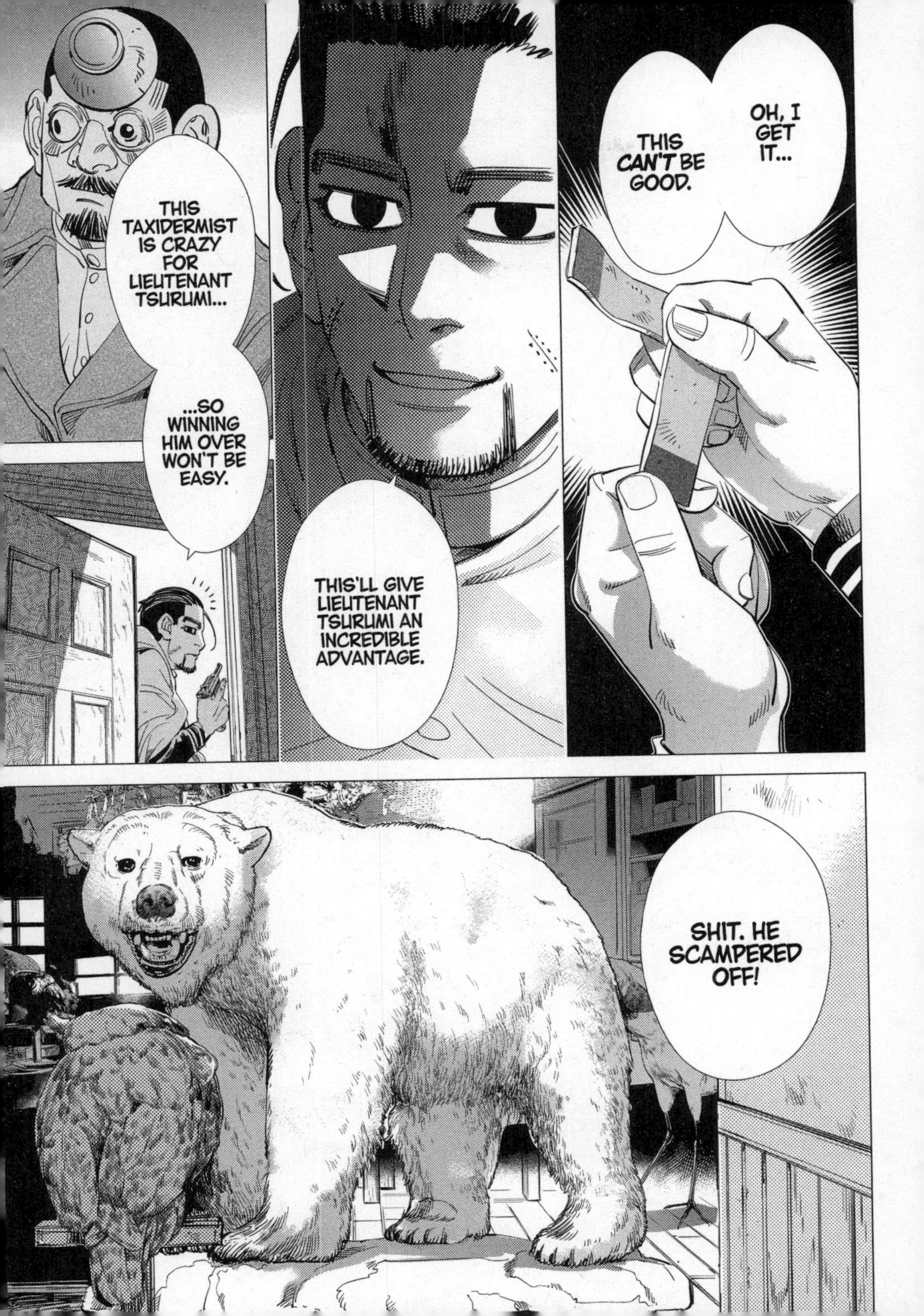
OH, I GET IT...
THIS CAN'T BE GOOD.
THIS'LL GIVE LIEUTENANT TSURUMI AN INCREDIBLE ADVANTAGE.
THIS TAXIDERMIST IS CRAZY FOR LIEUTENANT TSURUMI...
...SO WINNING HIM OVER WON'T BE EASY.
SHIT. HE SCAMPERED OFF!

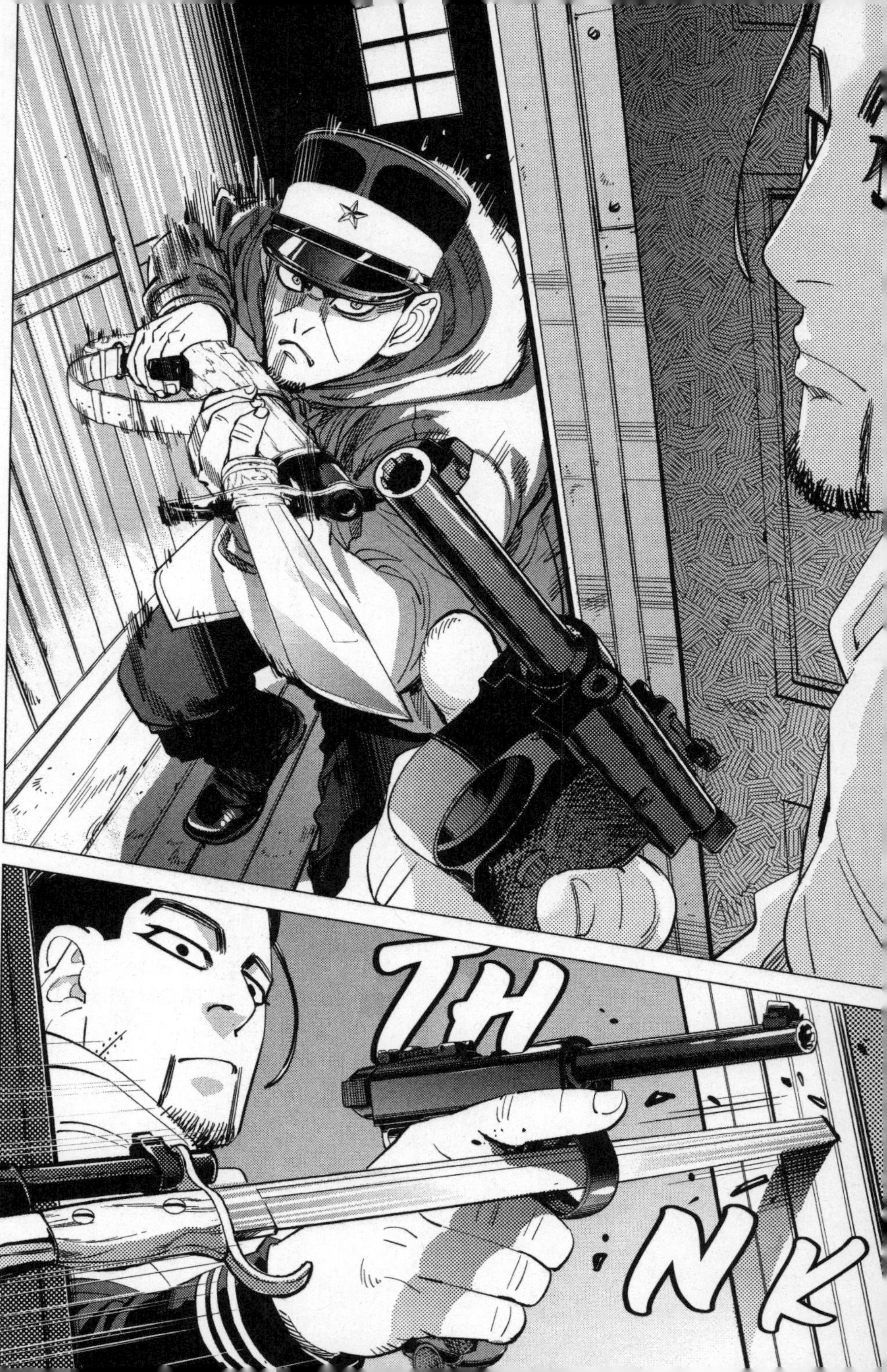
THUNK

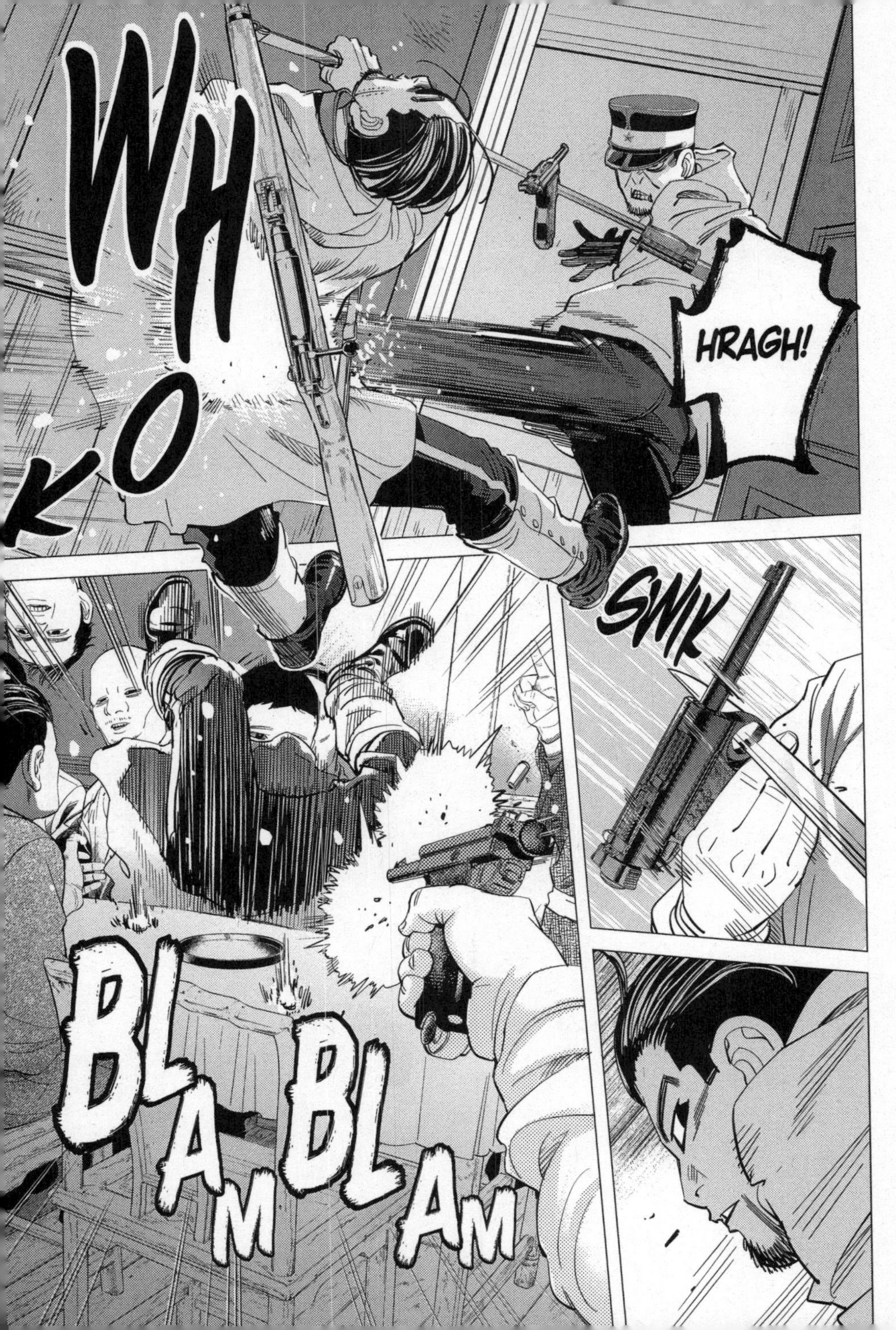
HRAGH!
WHOK
SWIK
BLAM BLAM

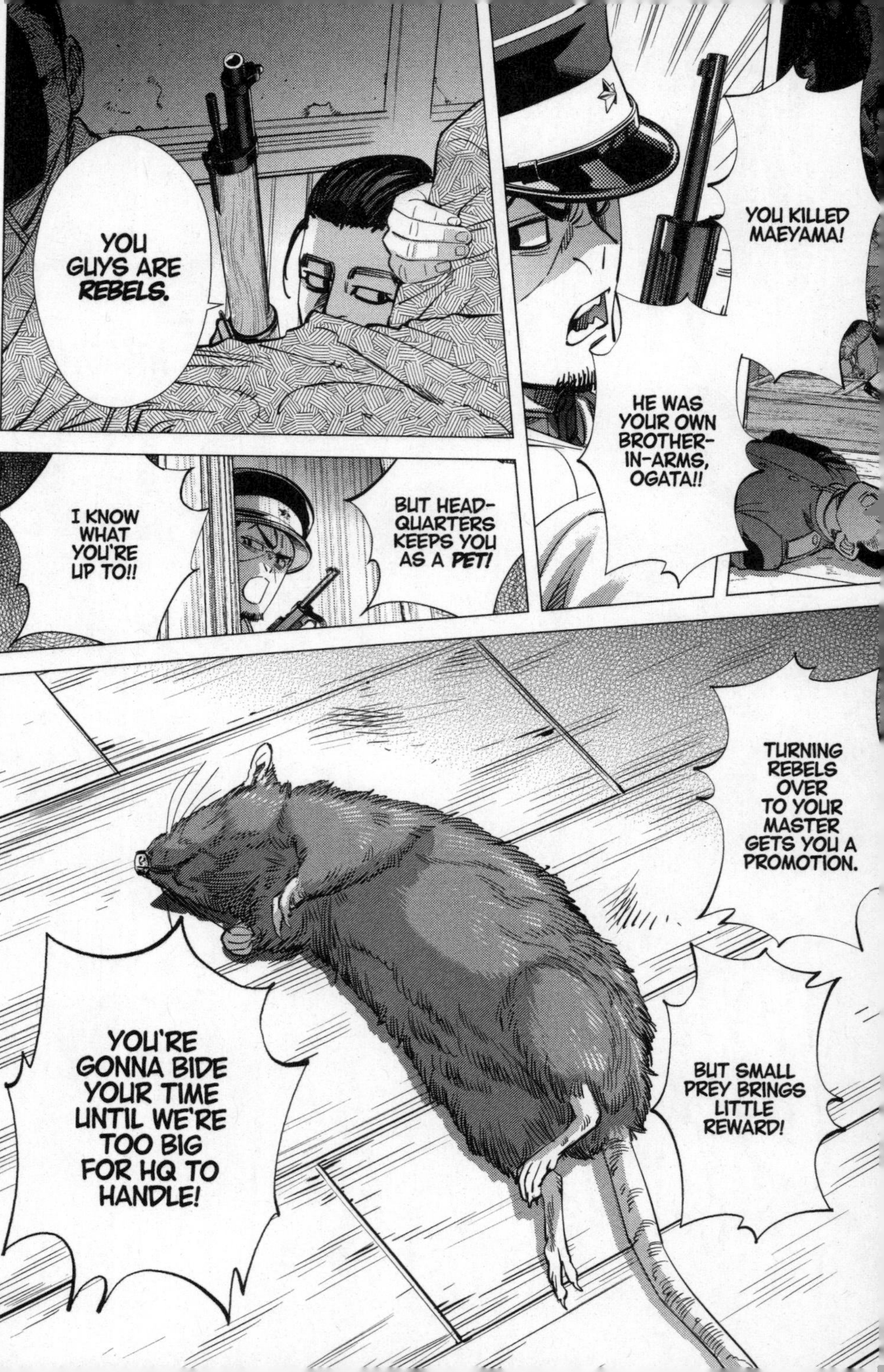
YOU KILLED MAEYAMA!
HE WAS YOUR OWN BROTHER-IN-ARMS, OGATA!!
YOU GUYS ARE REBELS.
BUT HEAD-QUARTERS KEEPS YOU AS A PET!
I KNOW WHAT YOU'RE UP TO!!
TURNING REBELS OVER TO YOUR MASTER GETS YOU A PROMOTION.
BUT SMALL PREY BRINGS LITTLE REWARD!
YOU'RE GONNA BIDE YOUR TIME UNTIL WE'RE TOO BIG FOR HQ TO HANDLE!

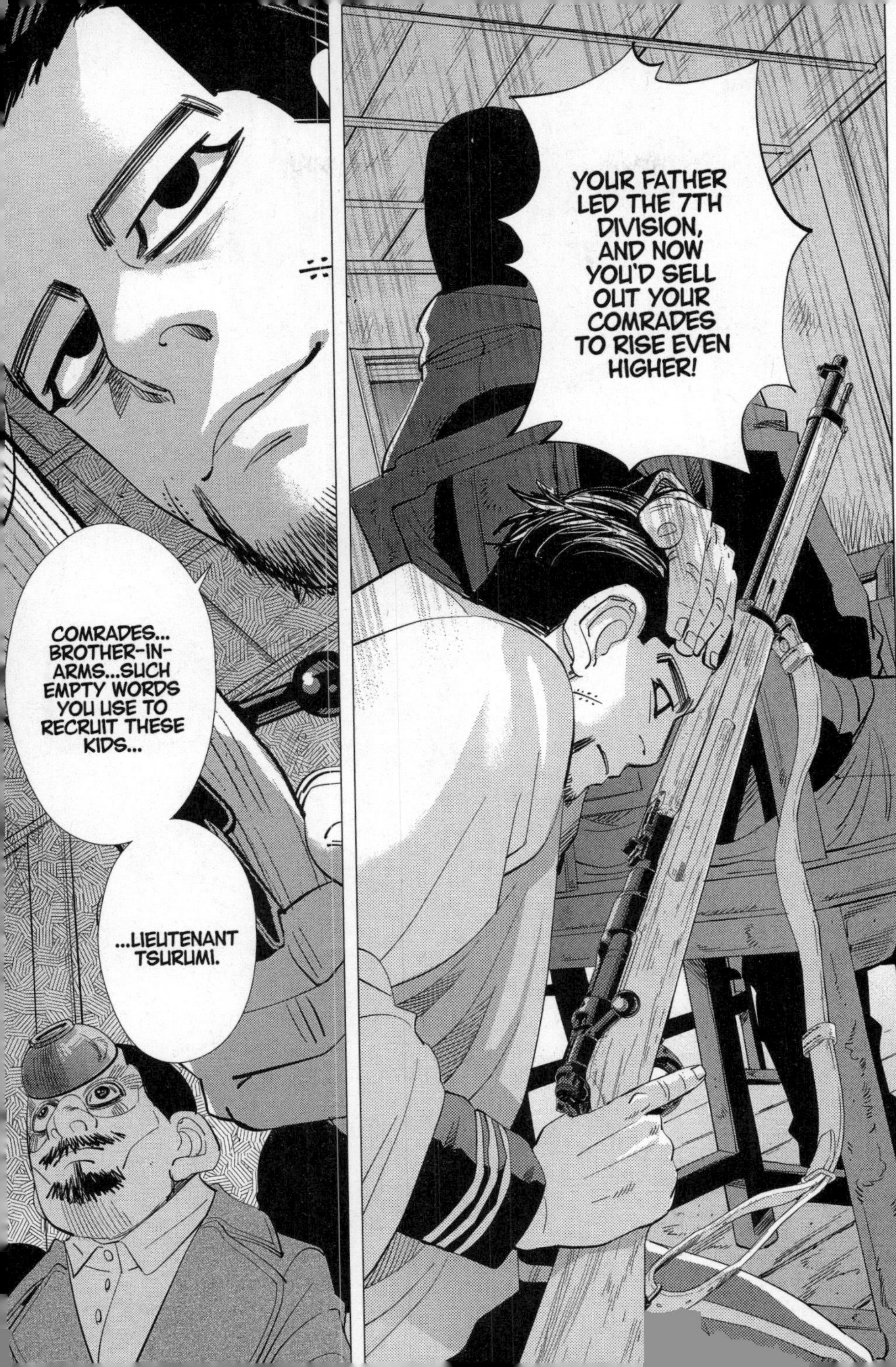
YOUR FATHER LED THE 7TH DIVISION, AND NOW YOU'D SELL OUT YOUR COMRADES TO RISE EVEN HIGHER!
COMRADES... BROTHER-IN-ARMS...SUCH EMPTY WORDS YOU USE TO RECRUIT THESE KIDS...
...LIEUTENANT TSURUMI.

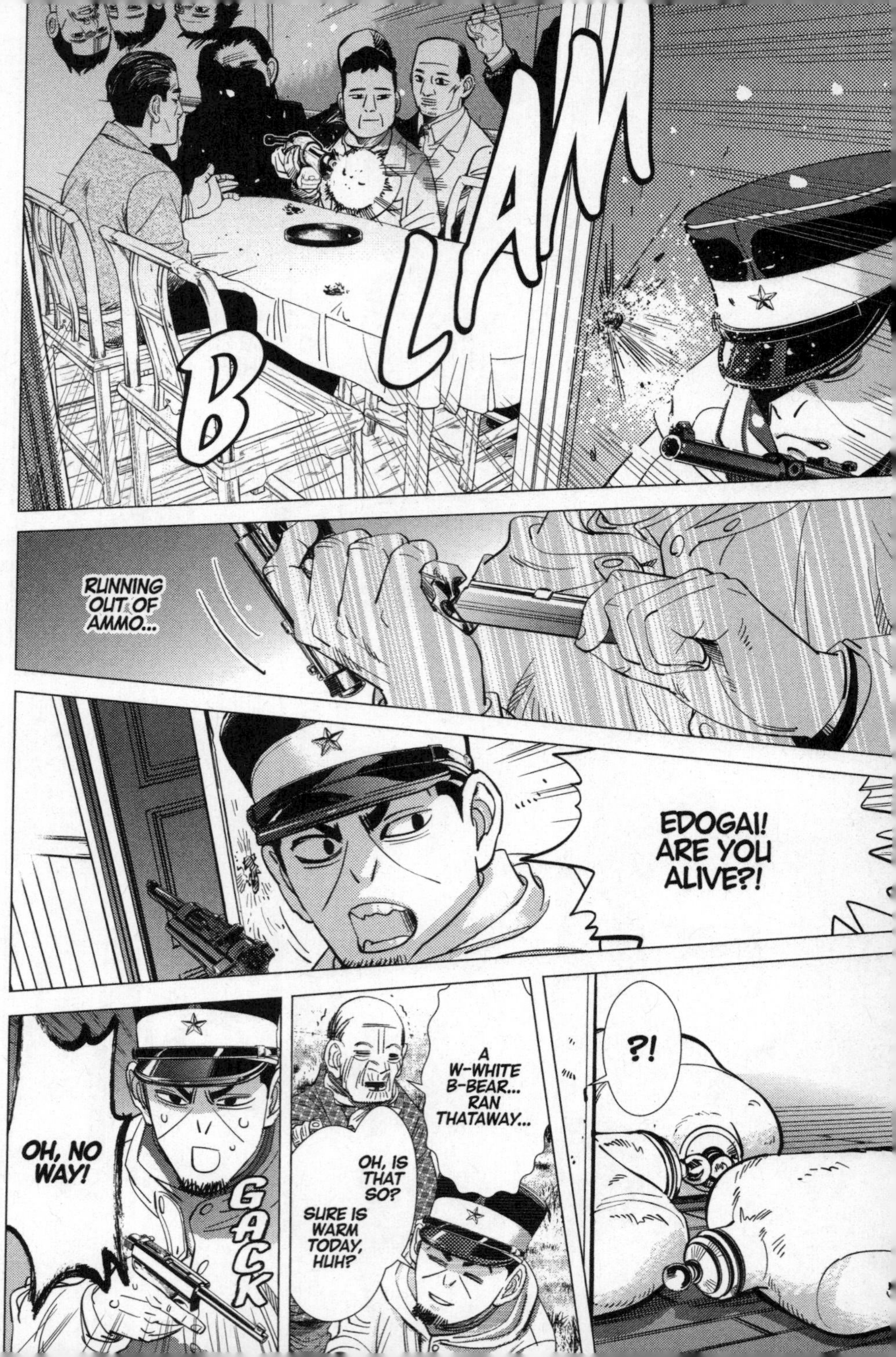
BLAM
RUNNING OUT OF AMMO...
EDOGAI! ARE YOU ALIVE?!
?!
A W-WHITE B-BEAR... RAN THATAWAY...
OH, IS THAT SO?
SURE IS WARM TODAY, HUH?
OH, NO WAY!
GACK

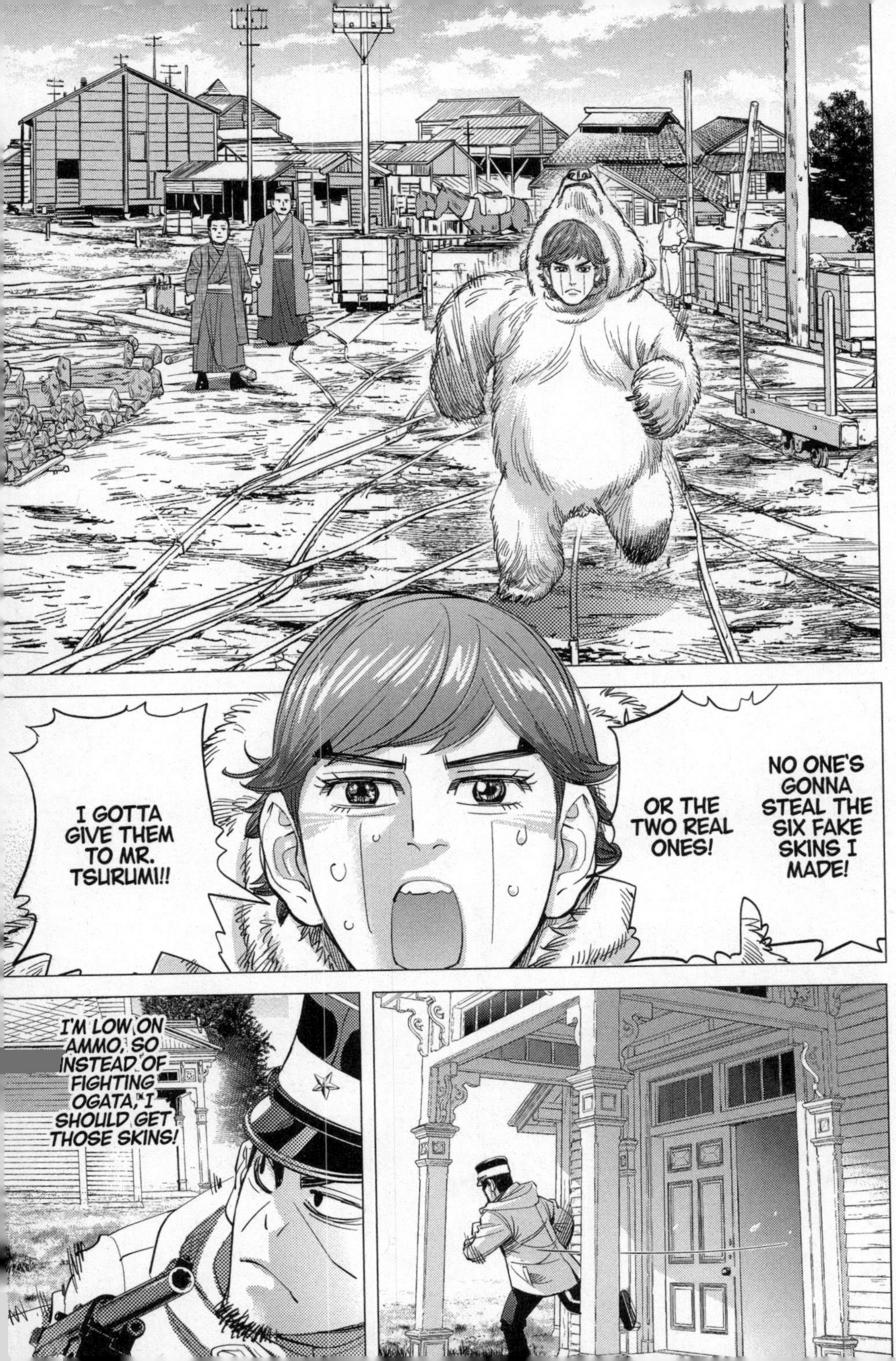
NO ONE'S GONNA STEAL THE SIX FAKE SKINS I MADE!
OR THE TWO REAL ONES!
I GOTTA GIVE THEM TO MR. TSURUMI!!
I'M LOW ON AMMO, SO INSTEAD OF FIGHTING OGATA, I SHOULD GET THOSE SKINS!

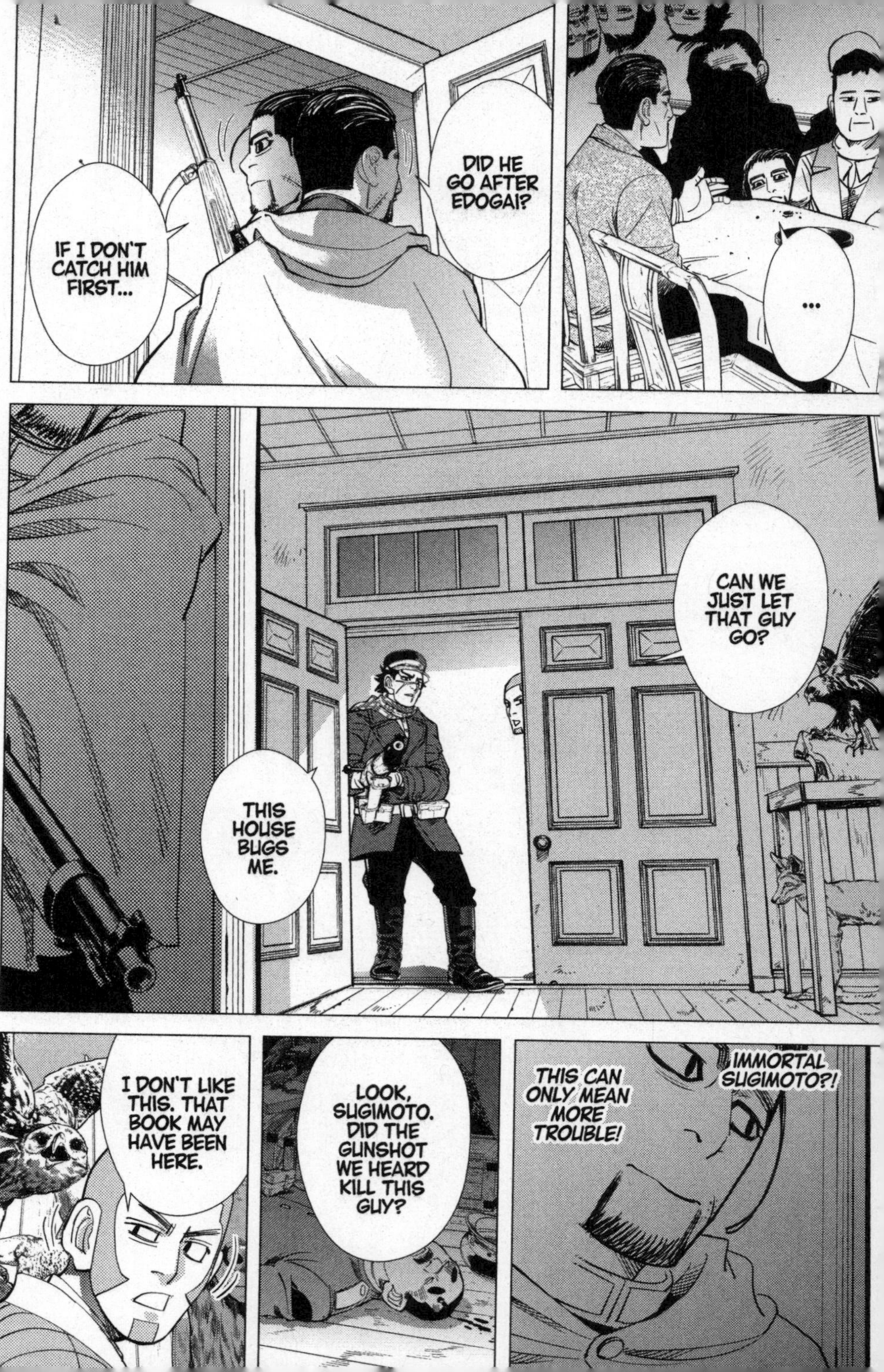
...
DID HE GO AFTER EDOGAI?
IF I DON'T CATCH HIM FIRST...
CAN WE JUST LET THAT GUY GO?
THIS HOUSE BUGS ME.
IMMORTAL SUGIMOTO?!
THIS CAN ONLY MEAN MORE TROUBLE!
LOOK, SUGIMOTO. DID THE GUNSHOT WE HEARD KILL THIS GUY?
I DON'T LIKE THIS. THAT BOOK MAY HAVE BEEN HERE.

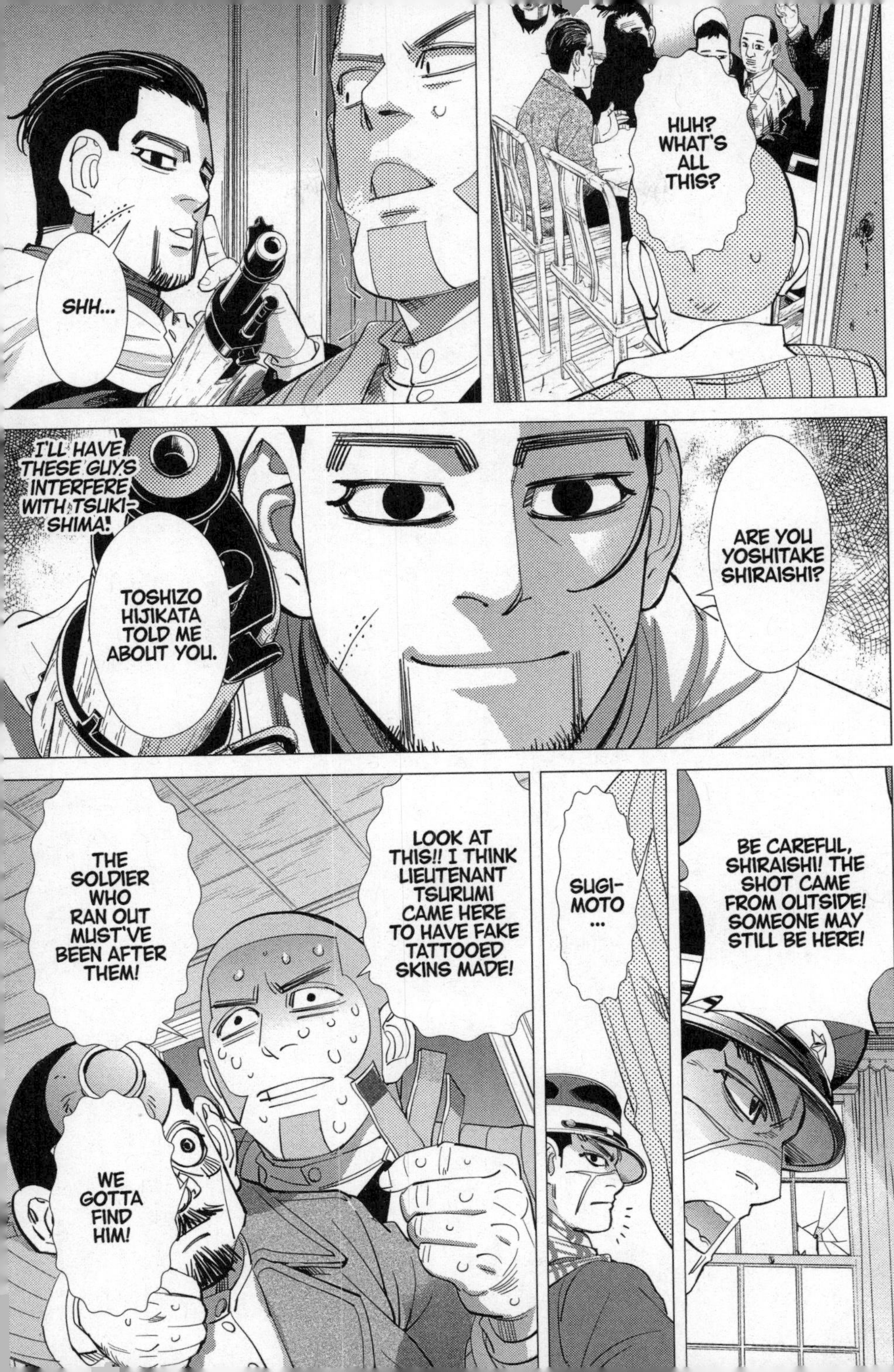
HUH? WHAT'S ALL THIS?
SHH...
ARE YOU YOSHITAKE SHIRAISHI?
TOSHIZO HIJIKATA TOLD ME ABOUT YOU.
I'LL HAVE THESE GUYS INTERFERE WITH TSUKI-SHIMA!
BE CAREFUL, SHIRAISHI! THE SHOT CAME FROM OUTSIDE! SOMEONE MAY STILL BE HERE!
SUGI-MOTO ...
LOOK AT THIS!! I THINK LIEUTENANT TSURUMI CAME HERE TO HAVE FAKE TATTOOED SKINS MADE!
THE SOLDIER WHO RAN OUT MUST'VE BEEN AFTER THEM!
WE GOTTA FIND HIM!

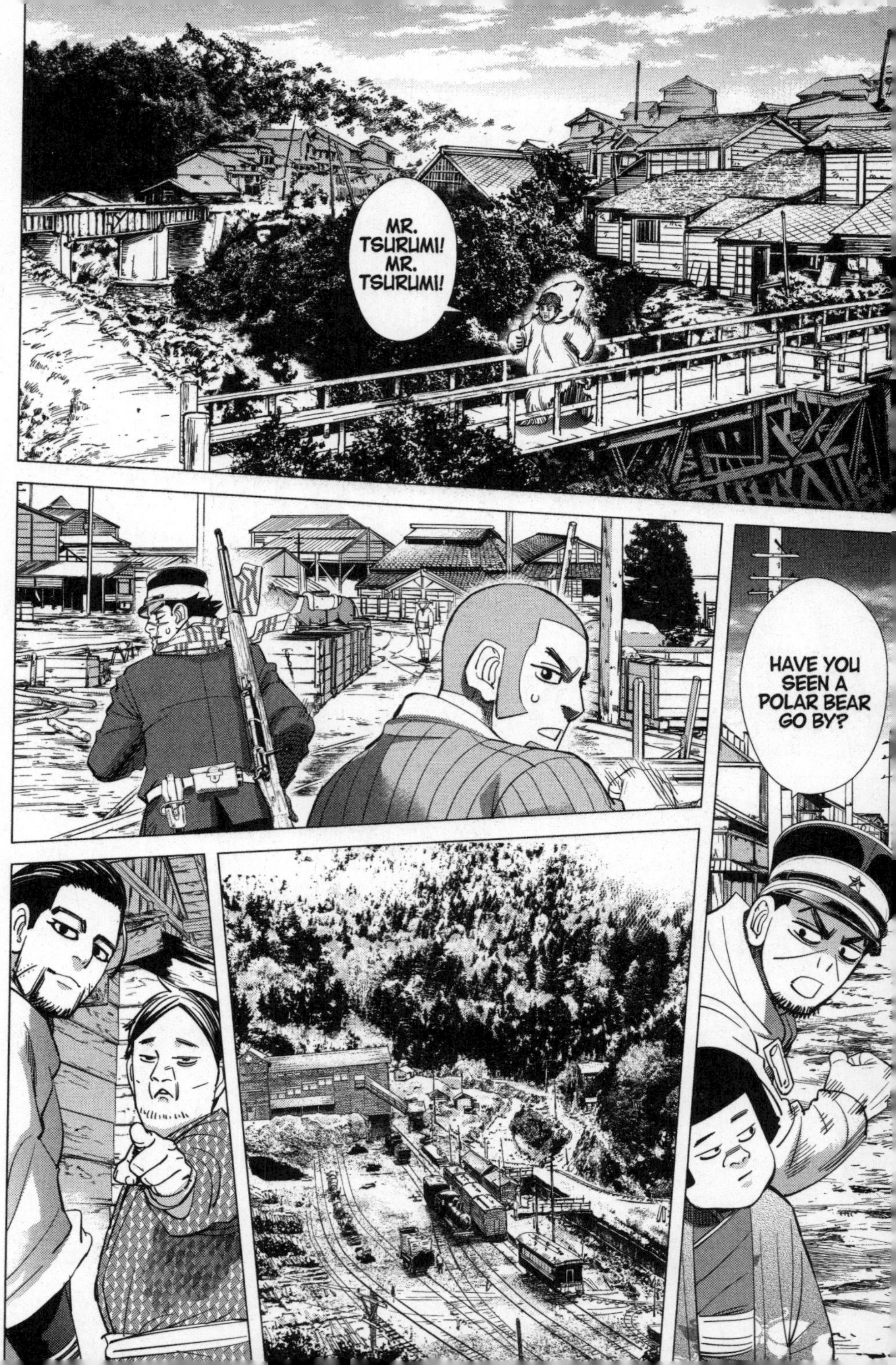
MR. TSURUMI! MR. TSURUMI!
HAVE YOU SEEN A POLAR BEAR GO BY?

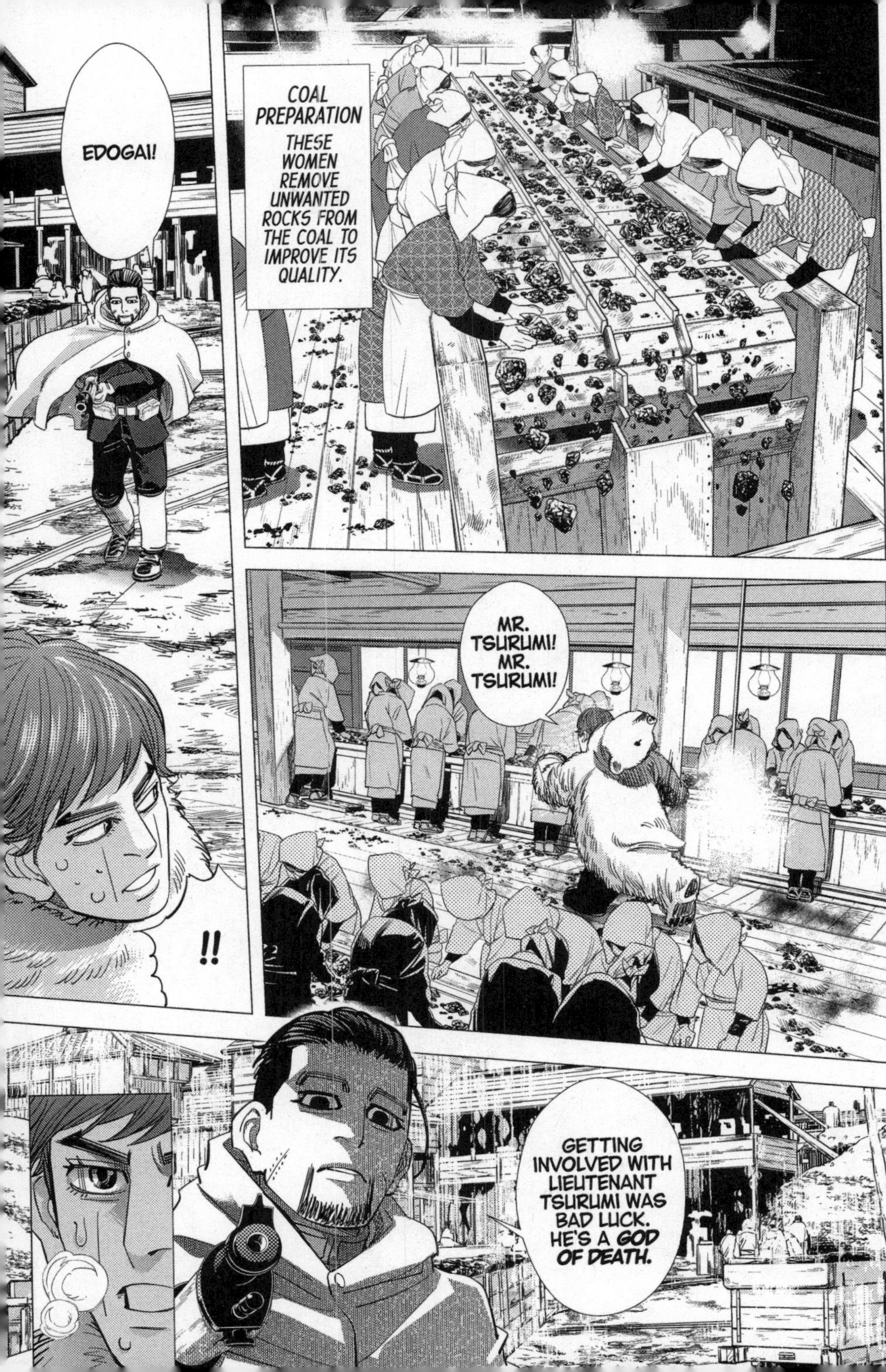
COAL PREPARATION
THESE WOMEN REMOVE UNWANTED ROCKS FROM THE COAL TO IMPROVE ITS QUALITY.
EDOGAI!
MR. TSURUMI! MR. TSURUMI!
!!
GETTING INVOLVED WITH LIEUTENANT TSURUMI WAS BAD LUCK. HE'S A ***GOD OF DEATH.***

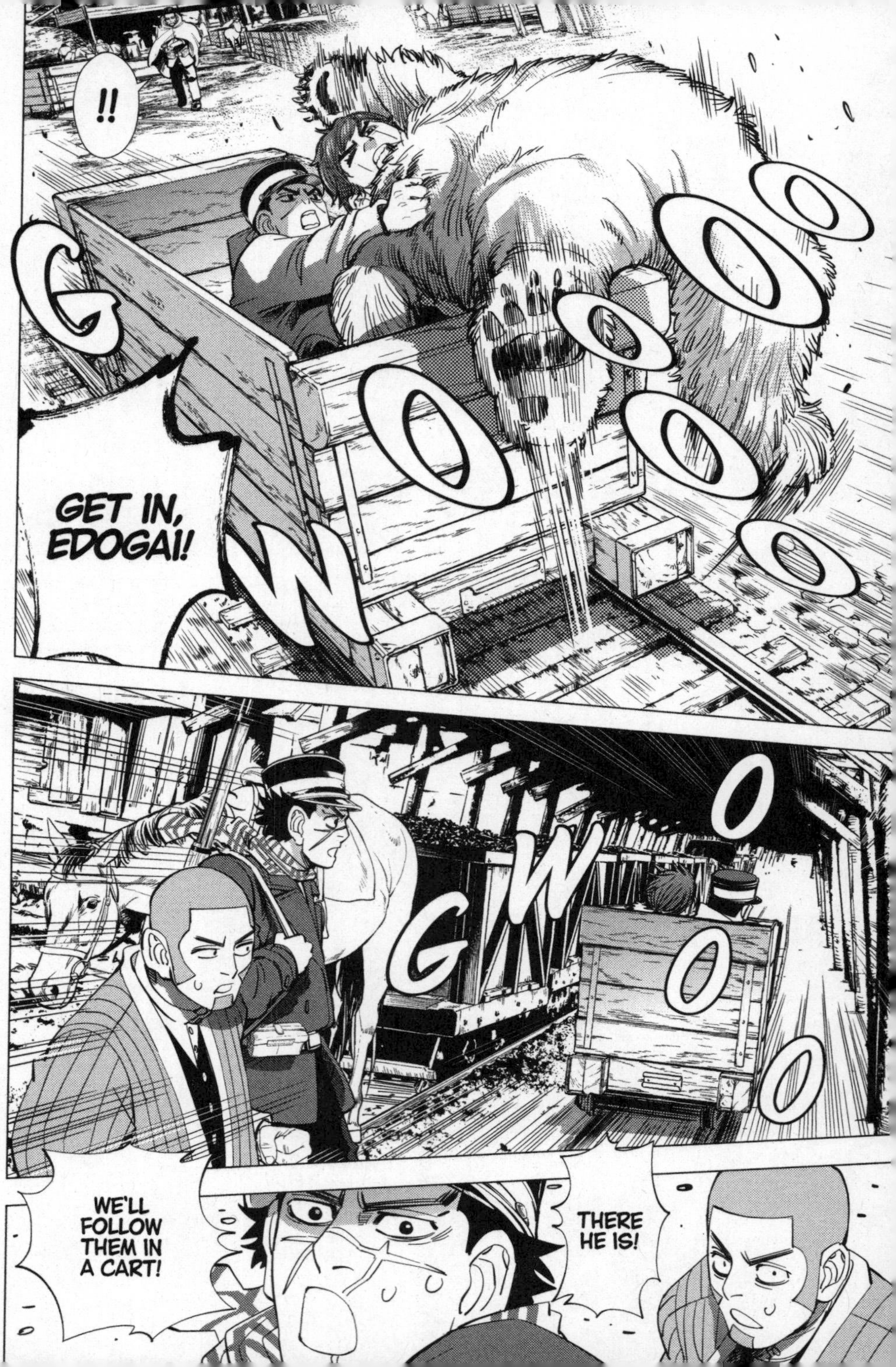
GWOOOOOOOOOOO
!!
GET IN, EDOGAI!
GWOOOO
THERE HE IS!
WE'LL FOLLOW THEM IN A CART!

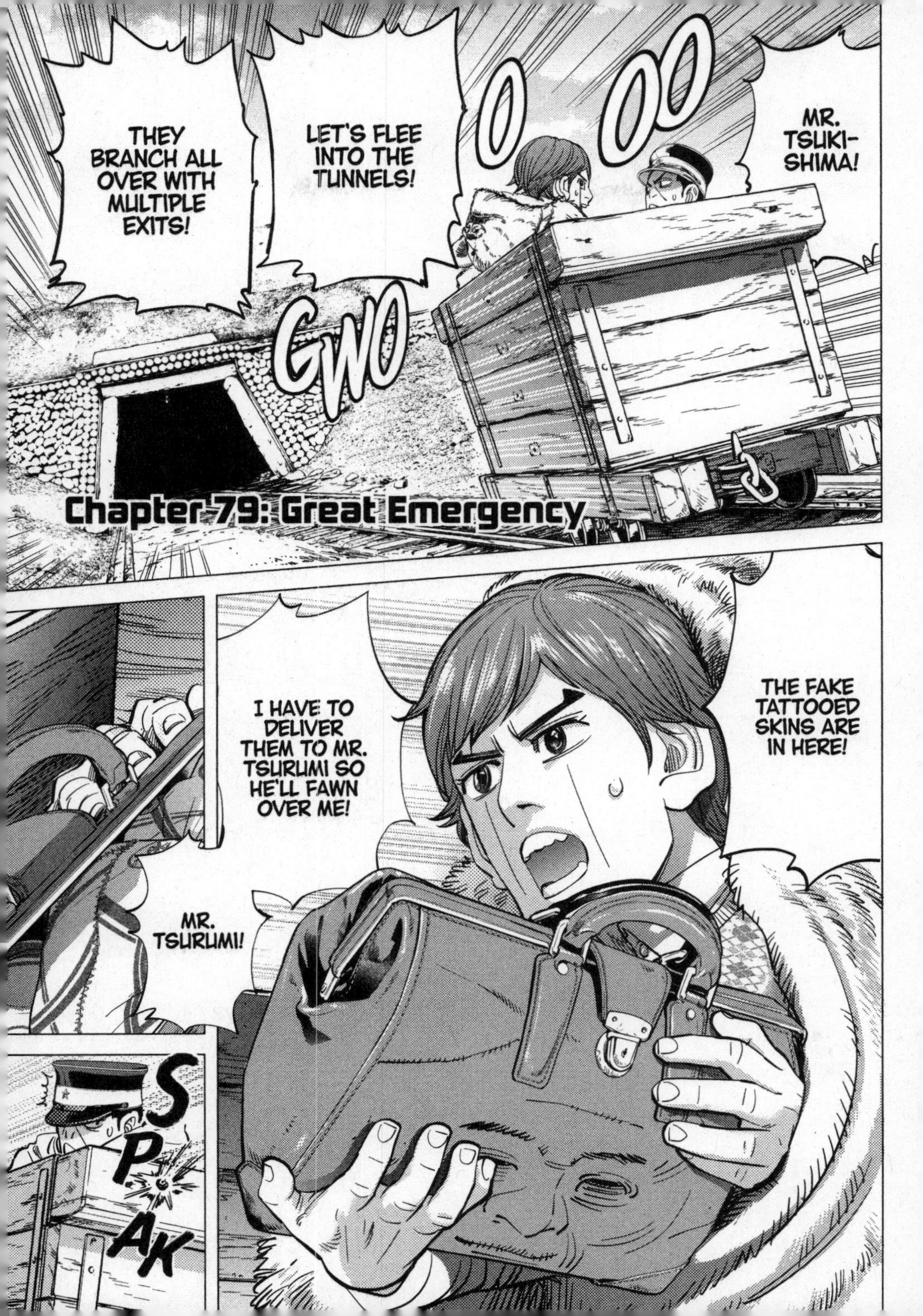
MR. TSUKI-SHIMA!
O OO
LET'S FLEE INTO THE TUNNELS!
THEY BRANCH ALL OVER WITH MULTIPLE EXITS!
GWO
Chapter 79: Great Emergency
THE FAKE TATTOOED SKINS ARE IN HERE!
I HAVE TO DELIVER THEM TO MR. TSURUMI SO HE'LL FAWN OVER ME!
MR. TSURUMI!
SPAK

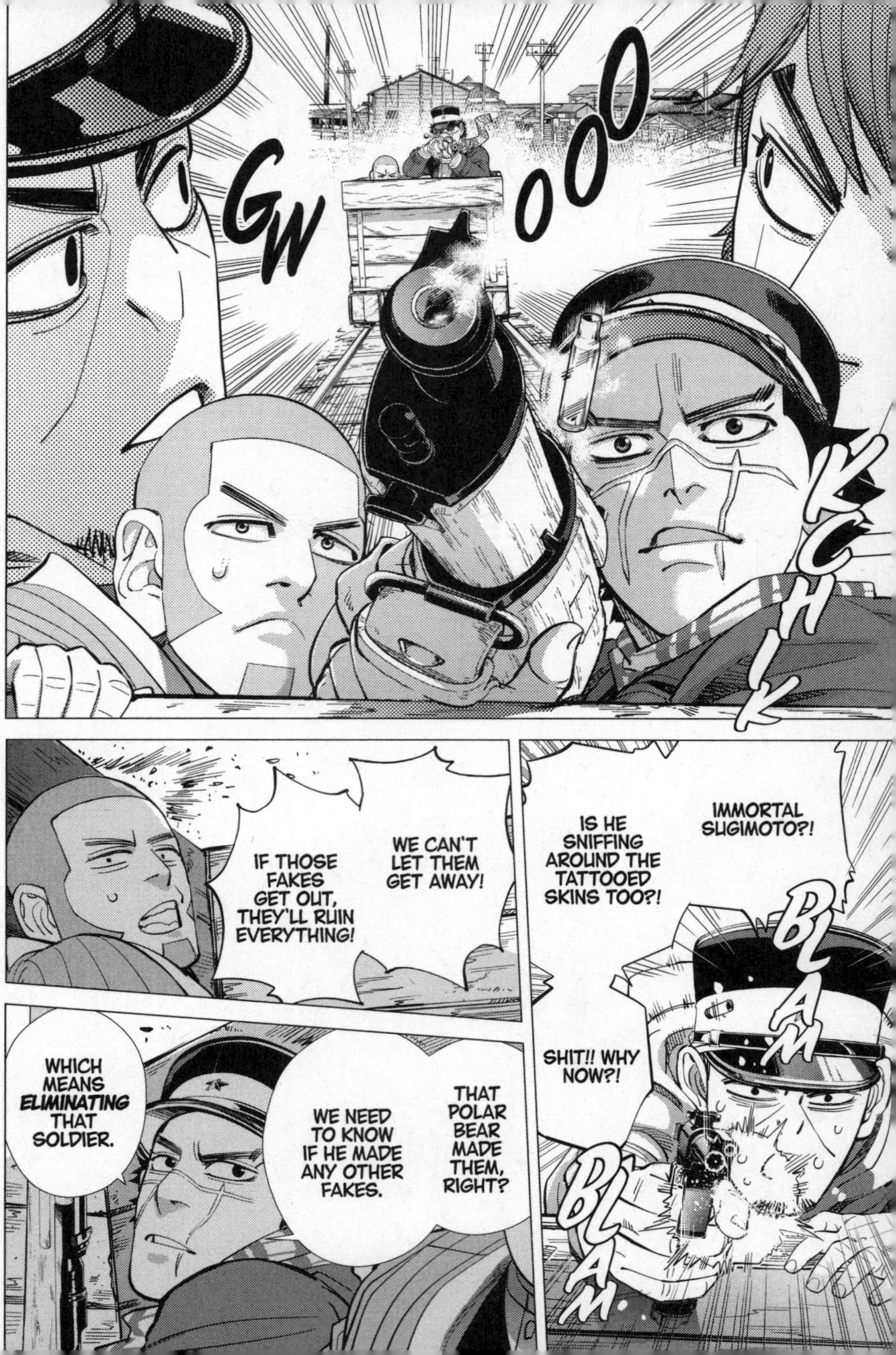
GWOOOOO
KCHIK
IMMORTAL SUGIMOTO?!
IS HE SNIFFING AROUND THE TATTOOED SKINS TOO?!
BLAM
SHIT!! WHY NOW?!
BLAM
WE CAN'T LET THEM GET AWAY!
IF THOSE FAKES GET OUT, THEY'LL RUIN EVERYTHING!
THAT POLAR BEAR MADE THEM, RIGHT?
WE NEED TO KNOW IF HE MADE ANY OTHER FAKES.
WHICH MEANS **ELIMINATING** THAT SOLDIER.

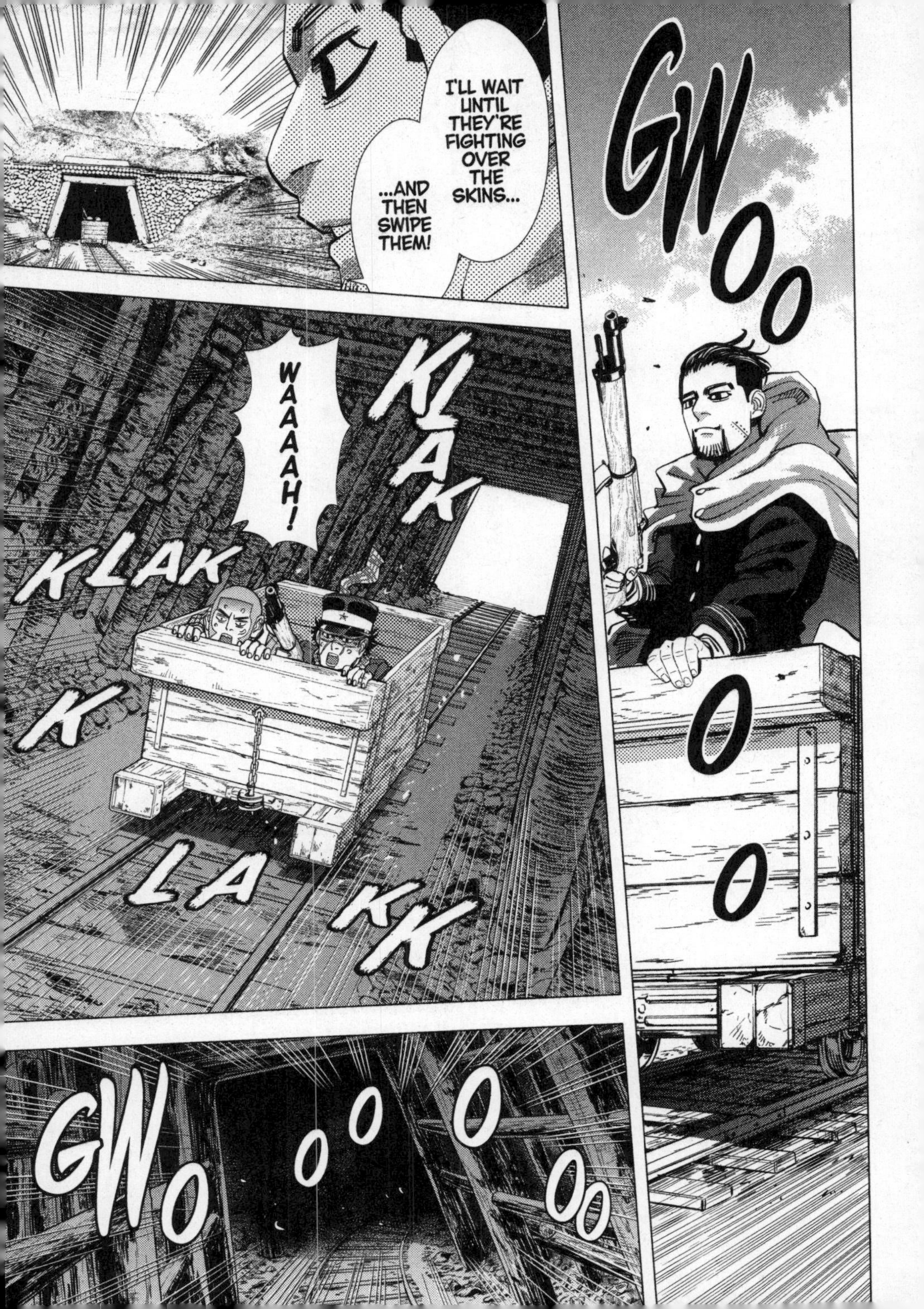
GWOOO
O
O
I'LL WAIT UNTIL THEY'RE FIGHTING OVER THE SKINS...
...AND THEN SWIPE THEM!
KLAK
WAAAAAH!
KLAK
K
LA
KK
GWOOOOOO

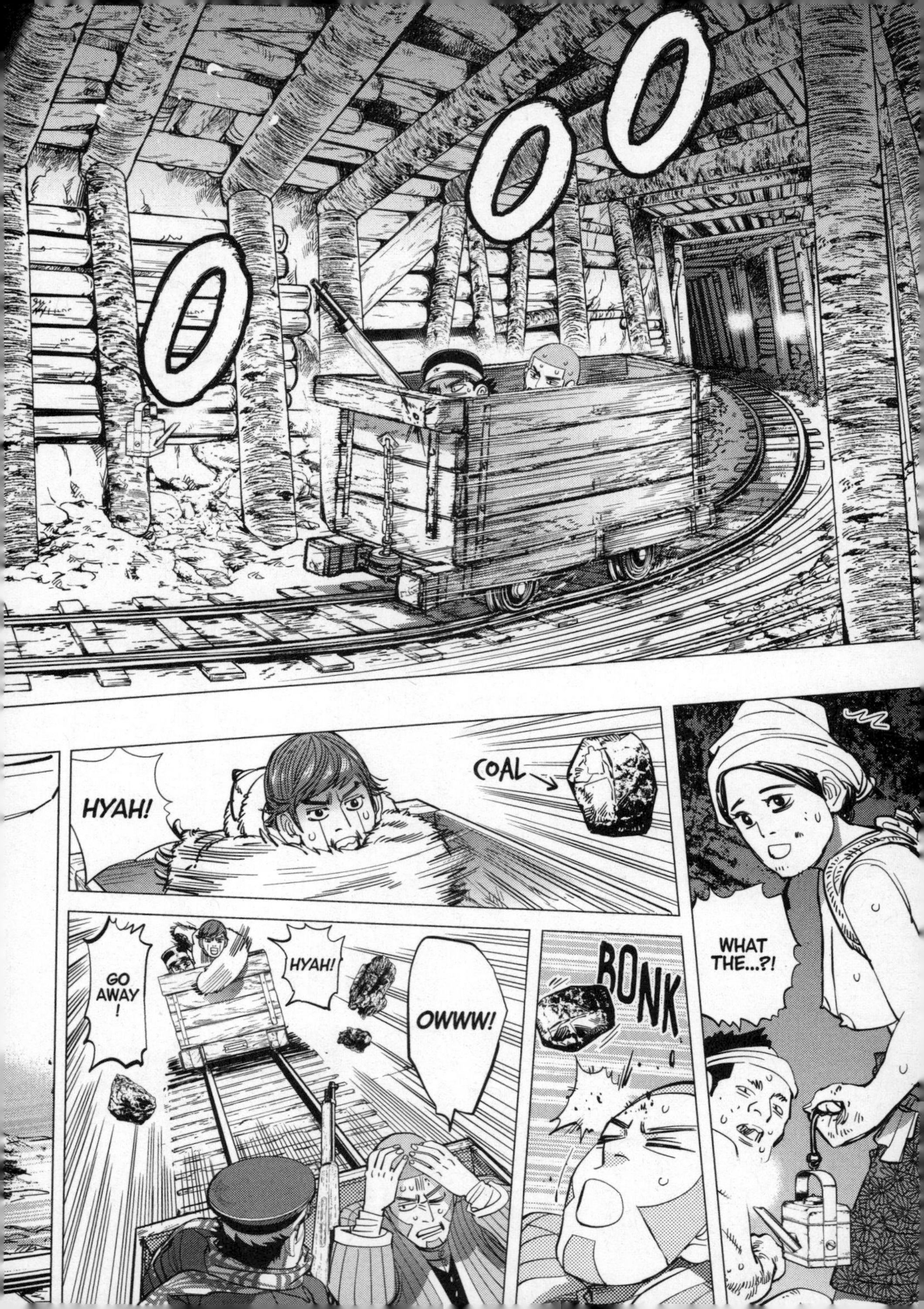
WHAT THE...?!
COAL
HYAH!
BONK
OWWW!
HYAH!
GO AWAY!

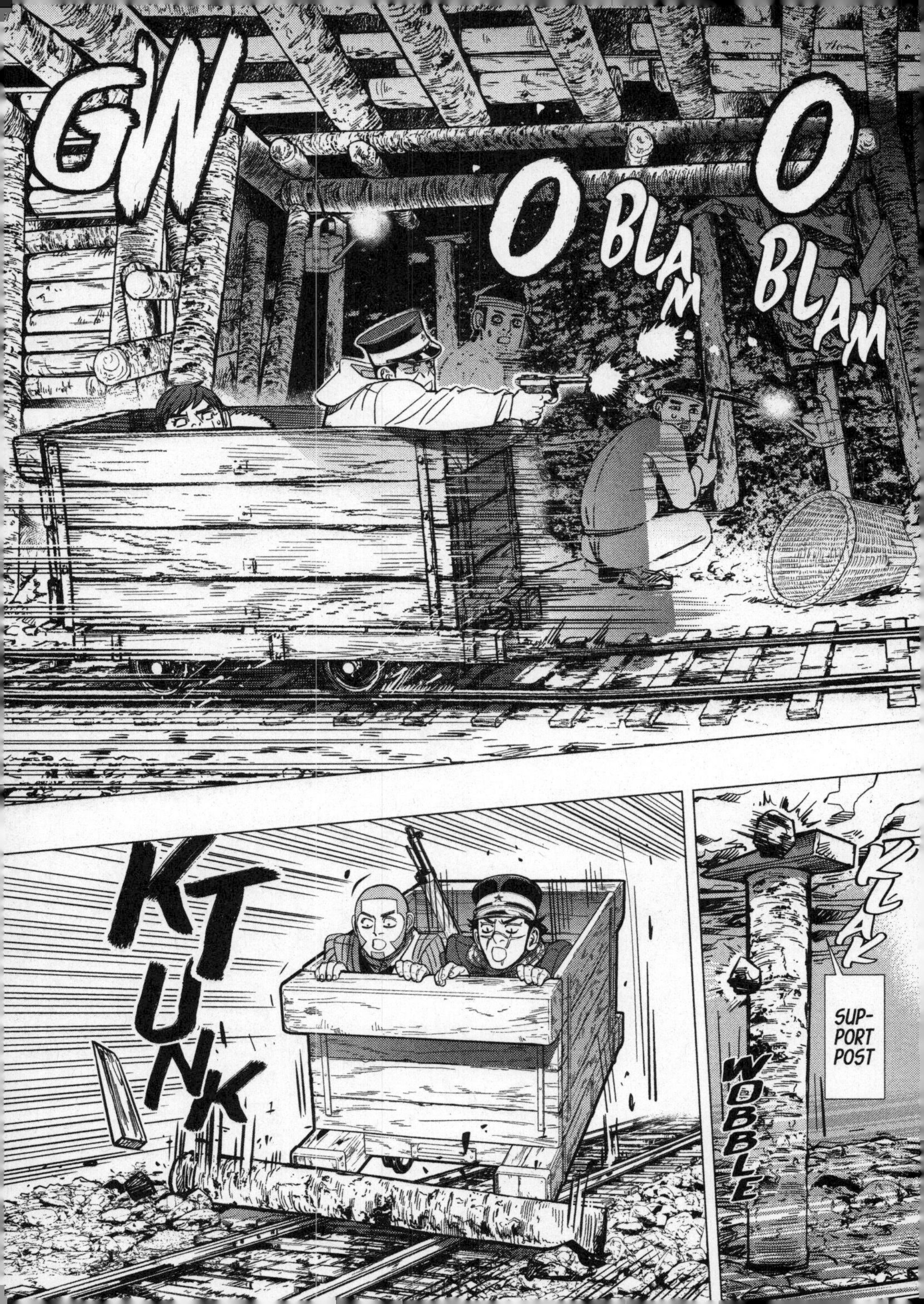
GNOO
BLAM
BLAM
BLAM
KLAK
SUP-PORT POST
WOBBLE
KTUNK

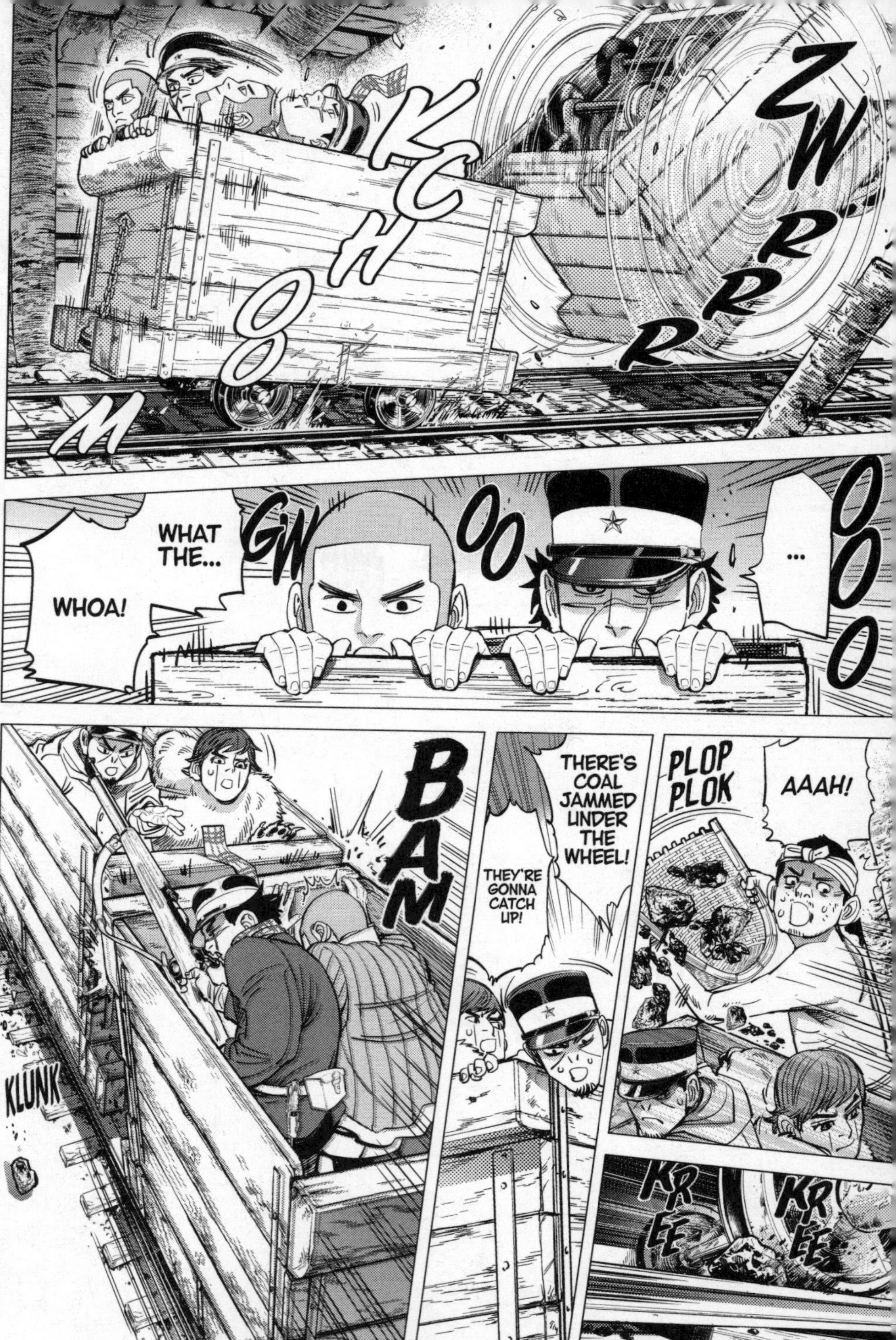
ZWRRRR
KCHOOM
...
GWOOOOOO
WHAT THE...
WHOA!
AAAH!
PLOP PLOK
KREE
KREE
THERE'S COAL JAMMED UNDER THE WHEEL!
THEY'RE GONNA CATCH UP!
BAM
KLUNK

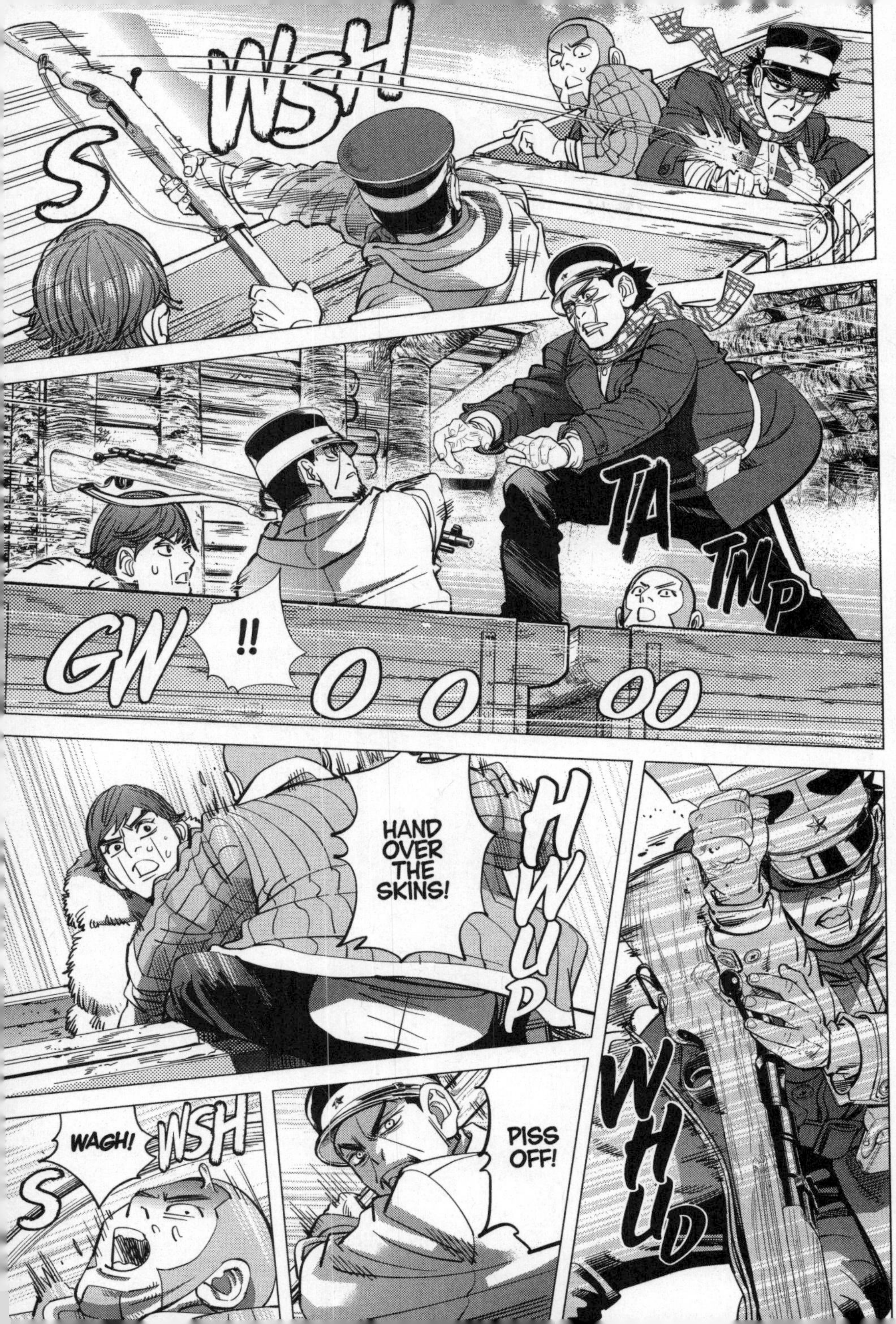
S
WSH
TA
TMP
!!
GW
O O OO
...
WHUD
HAND OVER THE SKINS!
HWUP
PISS OFF!
WAGH!
S
WSH

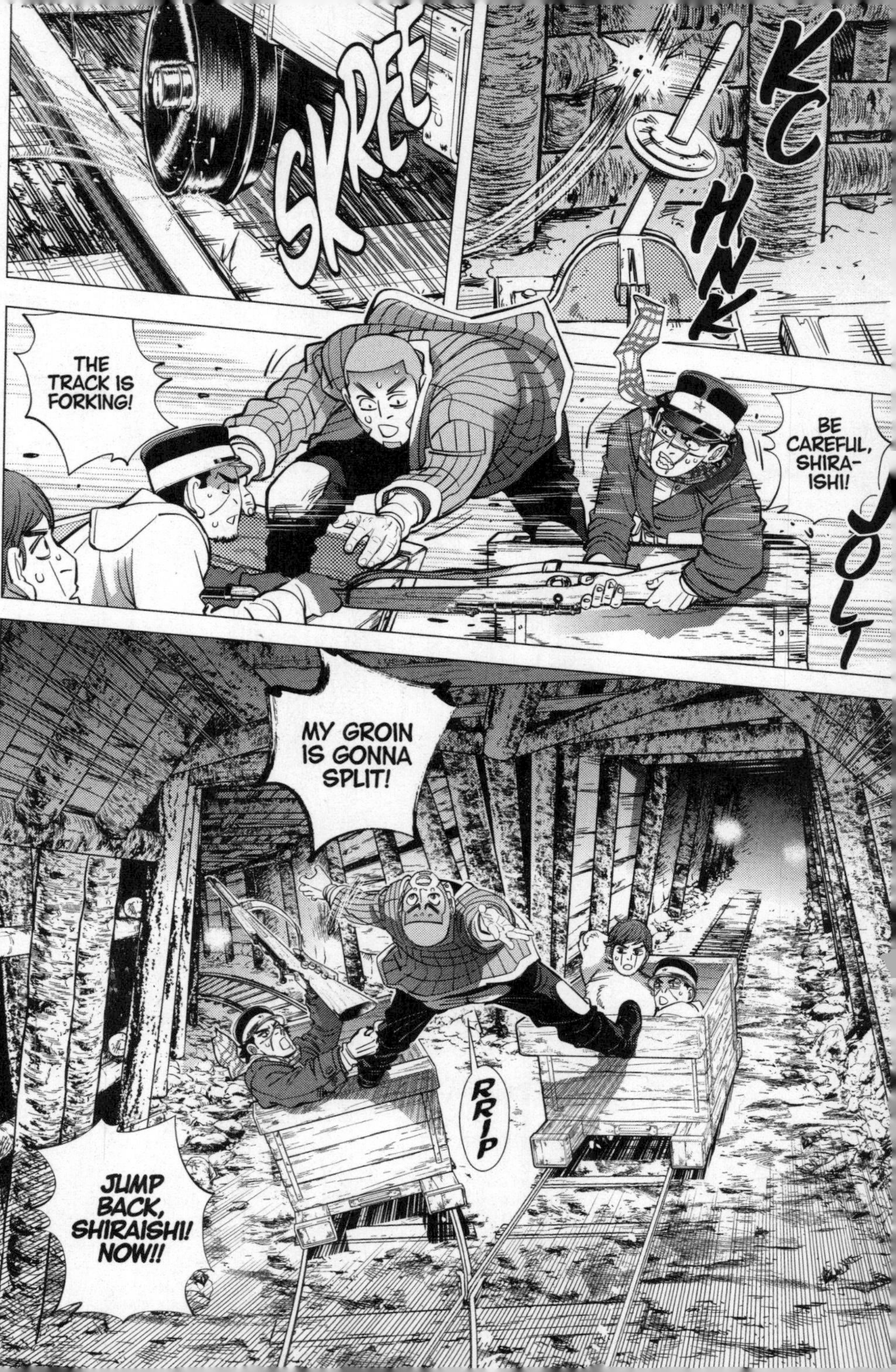
KCHINK
SKREE
BE CAREFUL, SHIRAISHI!
JOLT
THE TRACK IS FORKING!
MY GROIN IS GONNA SPLIT!
RRIP
JUMP BACK, SHIRAISHI! NOW!!

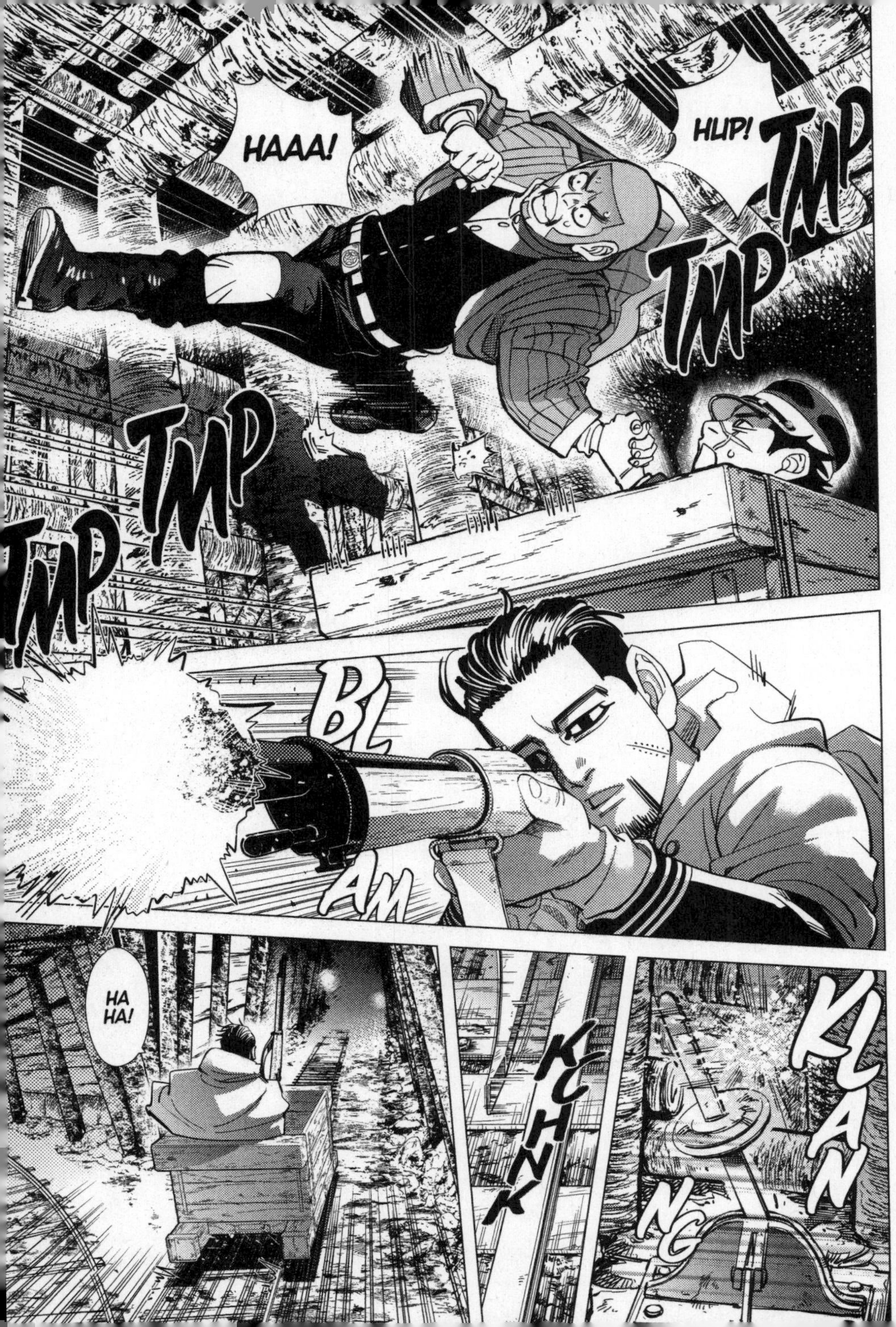
HUP!
TMP
TMP
TMP
HAAA!
TMP
TMP
TMP
BLAM
KLANNG
KCHNK
HA HA!

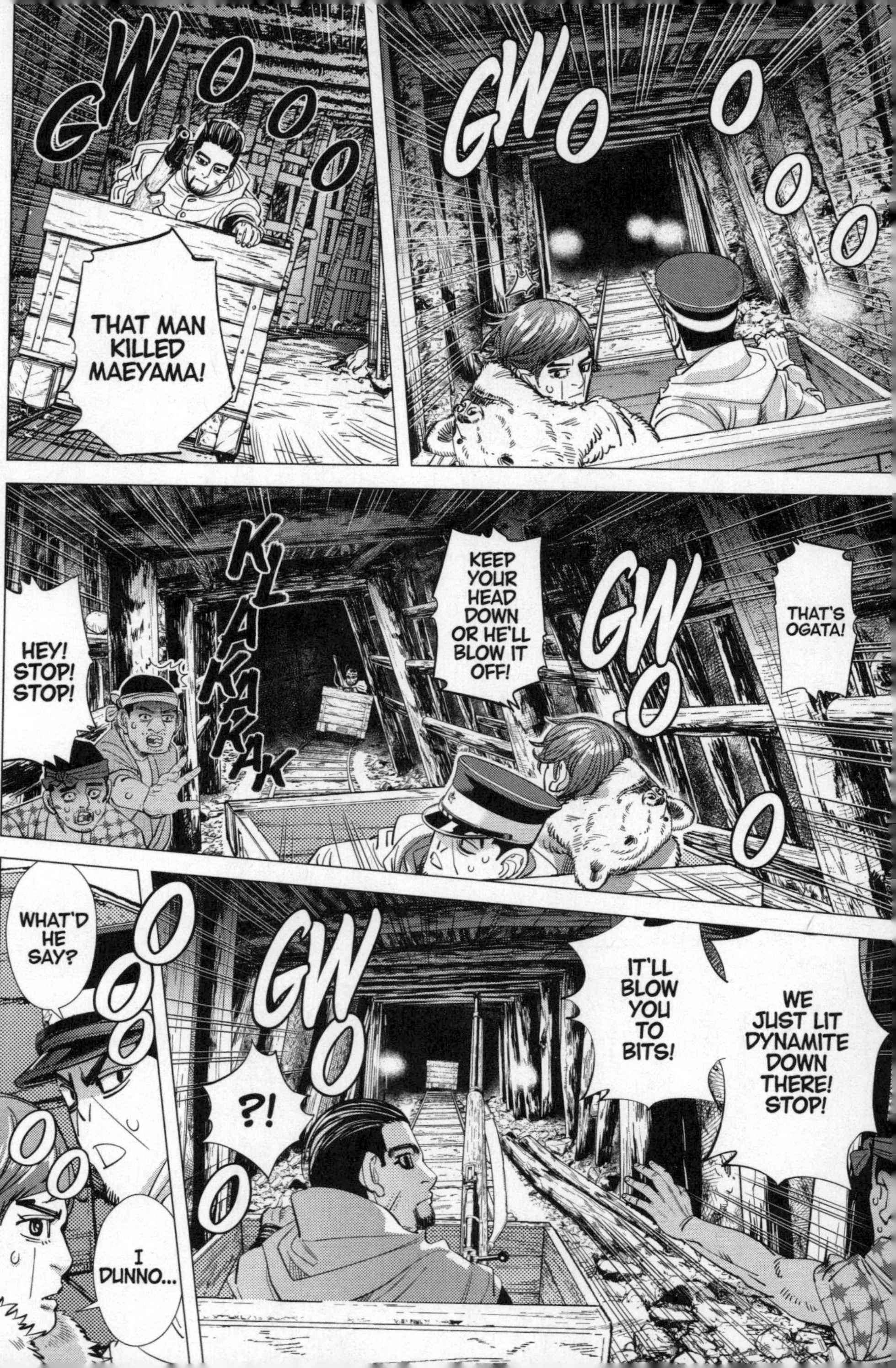
GWOOOOO
GWOOOO
THAT MAN KILLED MAEYAMA!
THAT'S OGATA!
GWOOO
KEEP YOUR HEAD DOWN OR HE'LL BLOW IT OFF!
KLAKAKAK
HEY! STOP! STOP!
WE JUST LIT DYNAMITE DOWN THERE! STOP!
IT'LL BLOW YOU TO BITS!
?!
GWOOOOOOO
WHAT'D HE SAY?
I DUNNO...

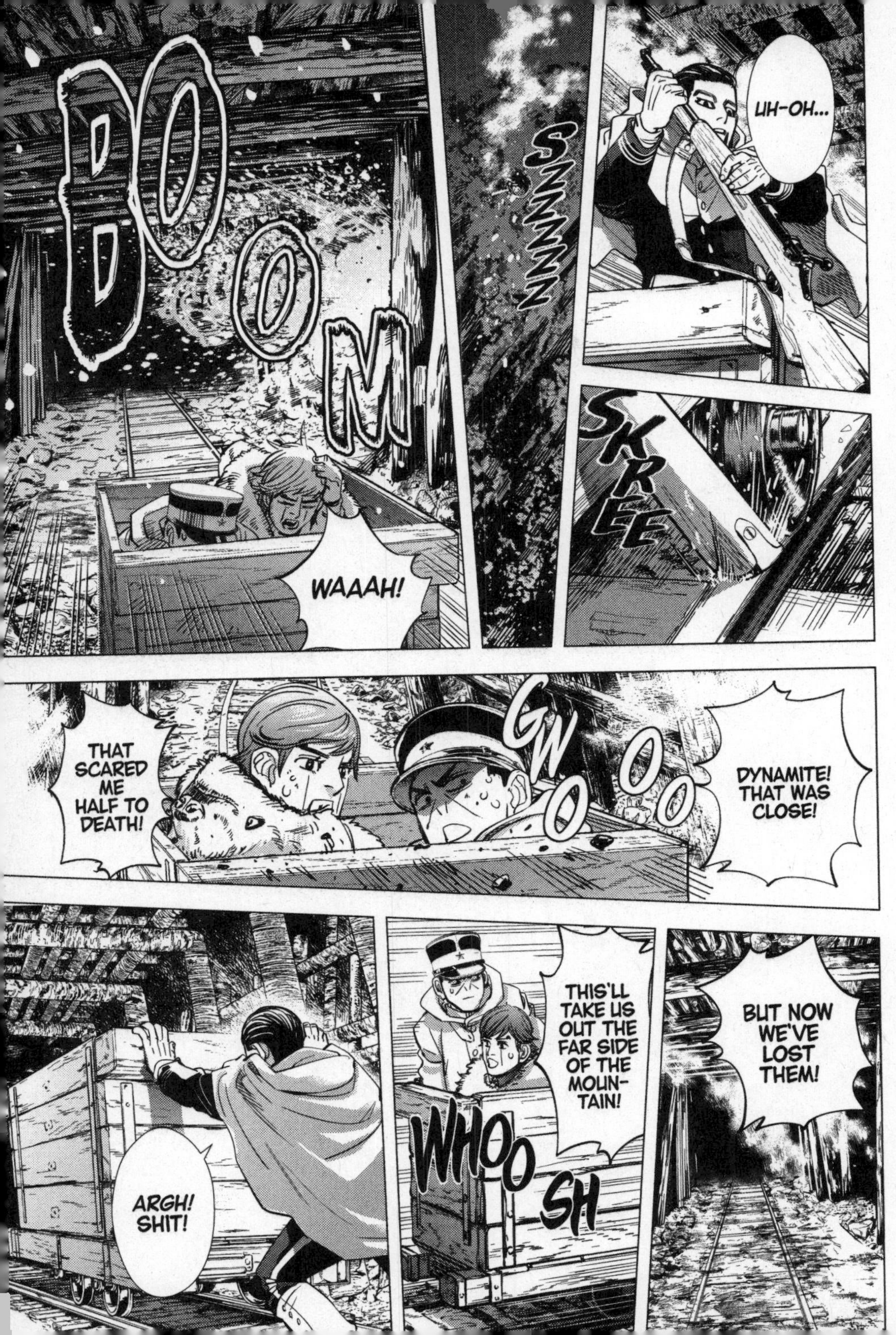
UH-OH...
SKREE
SZZZZZZ
BOOM
WAAAH!
DYNAMITE! THAT WAS CLOSE!
GWOOO
THAT SCARED ME HALF TO DEATH!
BUT NOW WE'VE LOST THEM!
THIS'LL TAKE US OUT THE FAR SIDE OF THE MOUN-TAIN!
WHOOOSH
ARGH! SHIT!

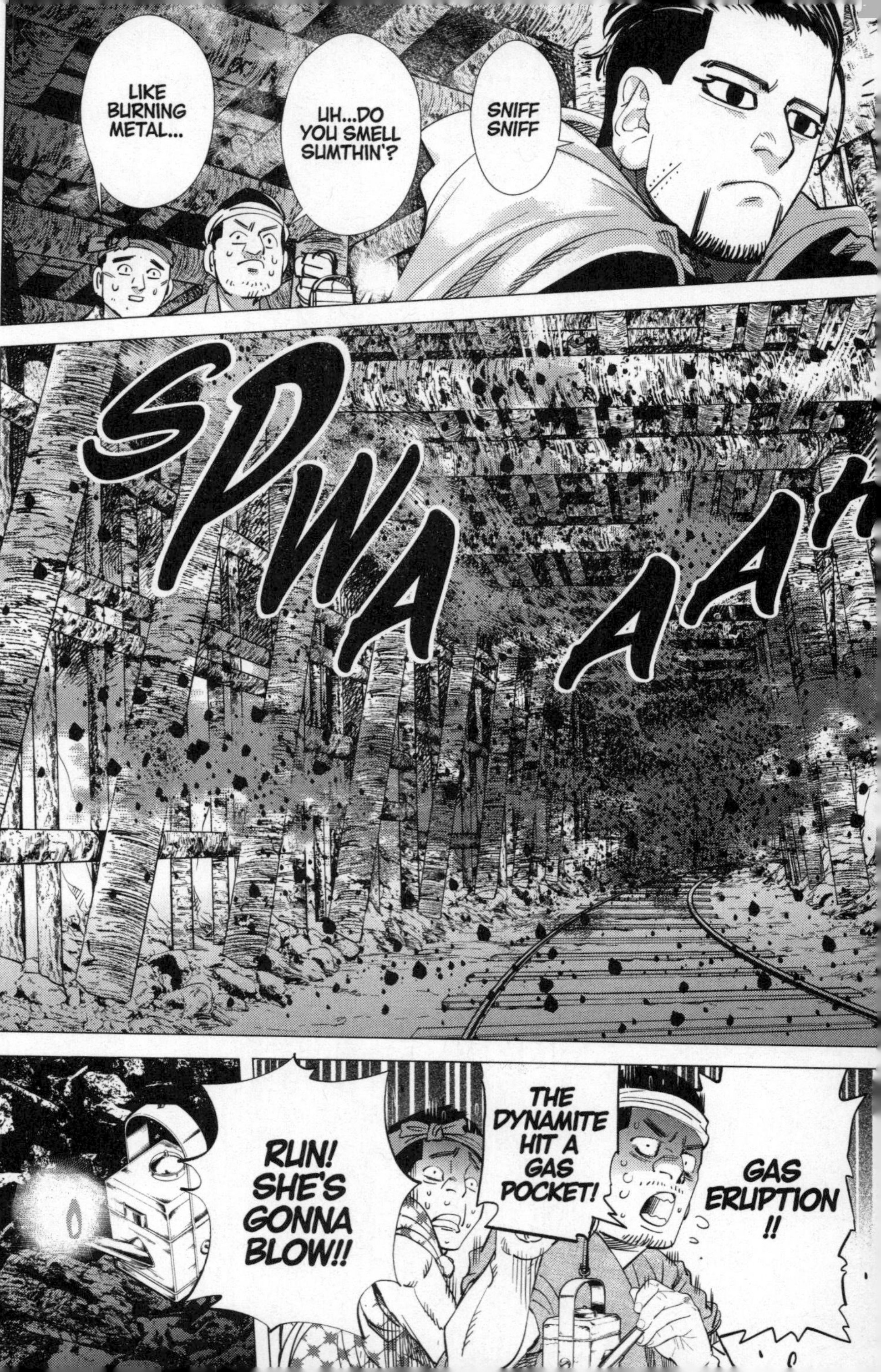
SNIFF SNIFF
UH...DO YOU SMELL SUMTHIN'?
LIKE BURNING METAL...
SDWAAA
GAS ERUPTION !!
THE DYNAMITE HIT A GAS POCKET!
RUN! SHE'S GONNA BLOW!!

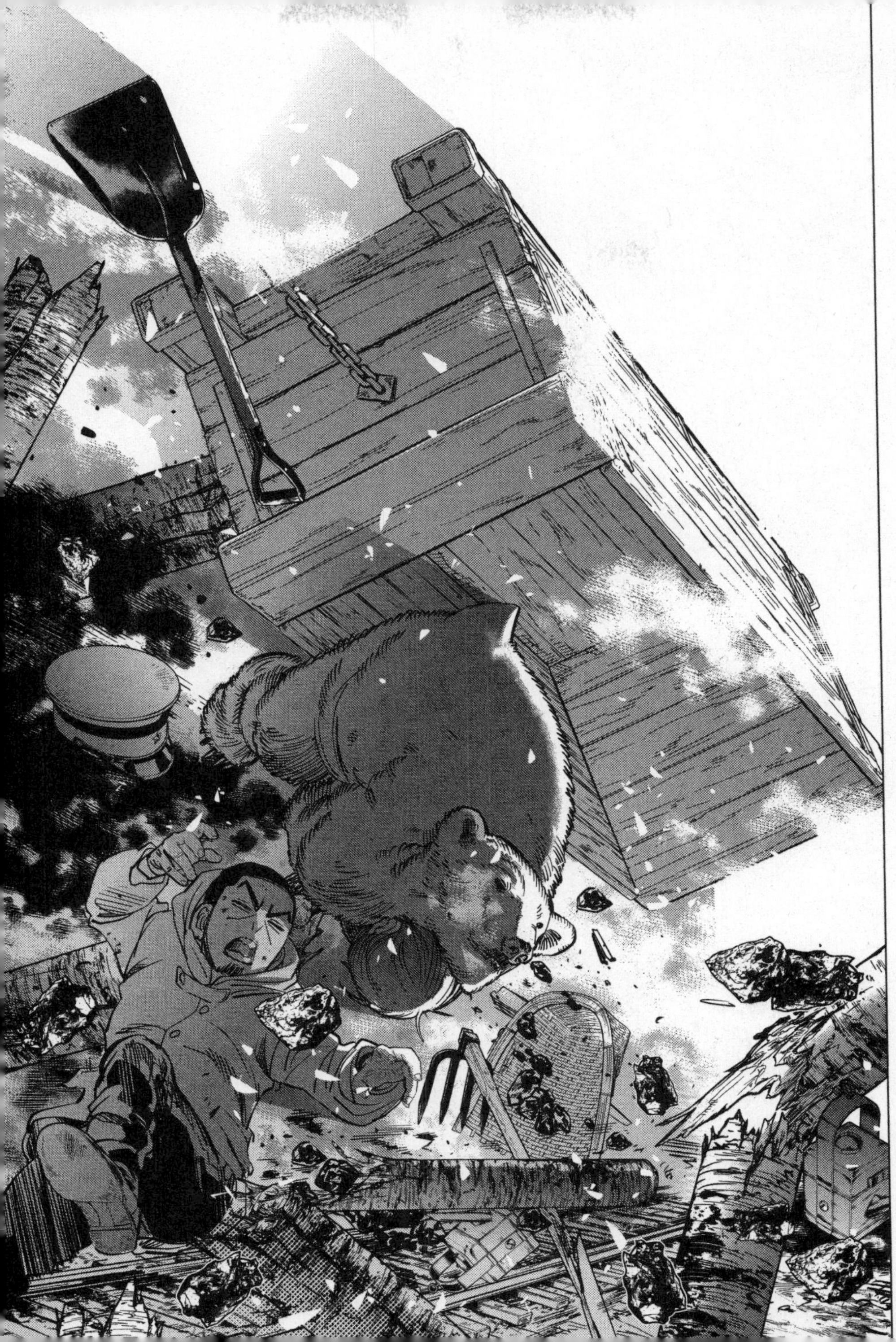

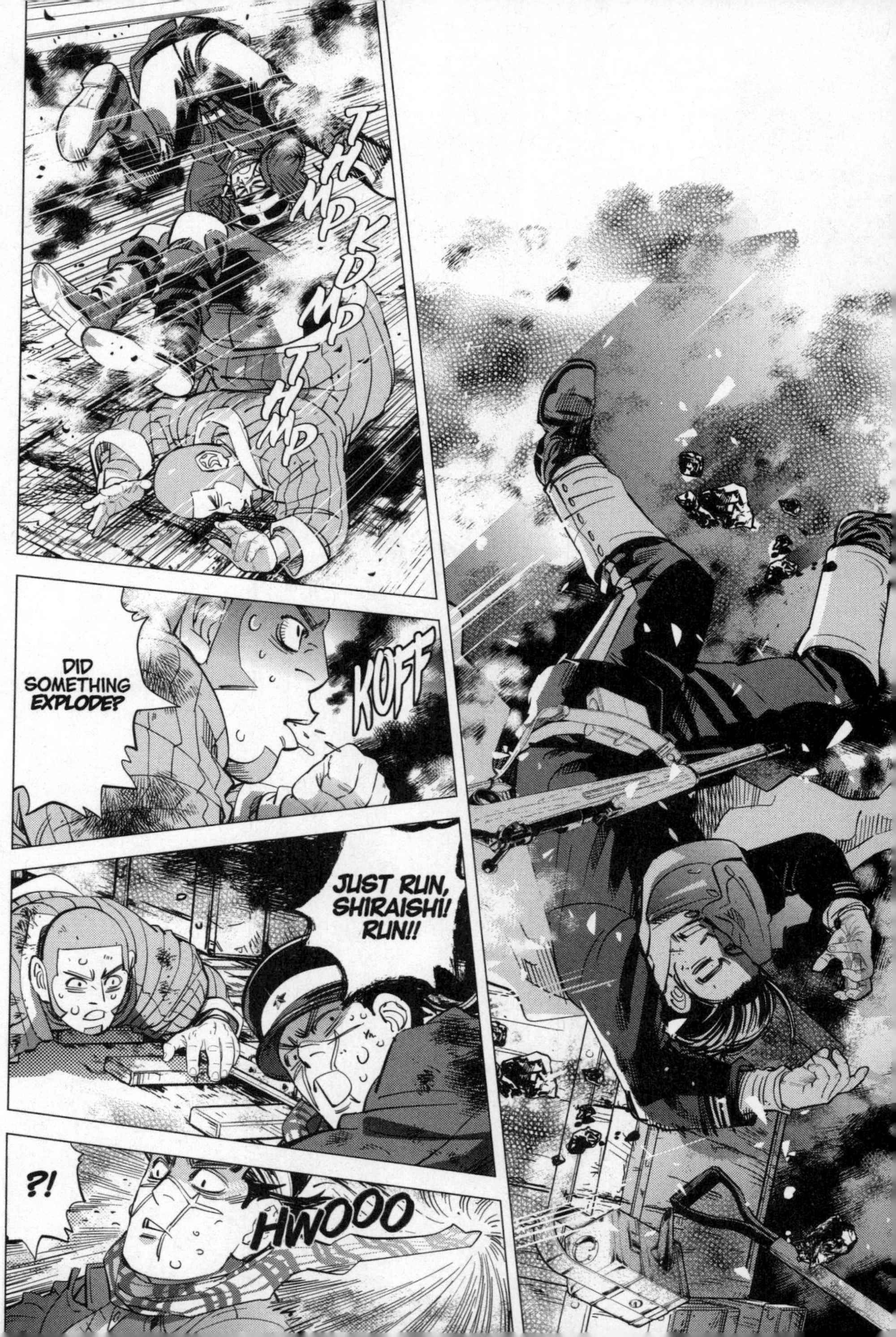
THMP KDMP THMP
DID SOMETHING EXPLODE?
KOFF
JUST RUN, SHIRAISHI! RUN!!
?!
HWOOO

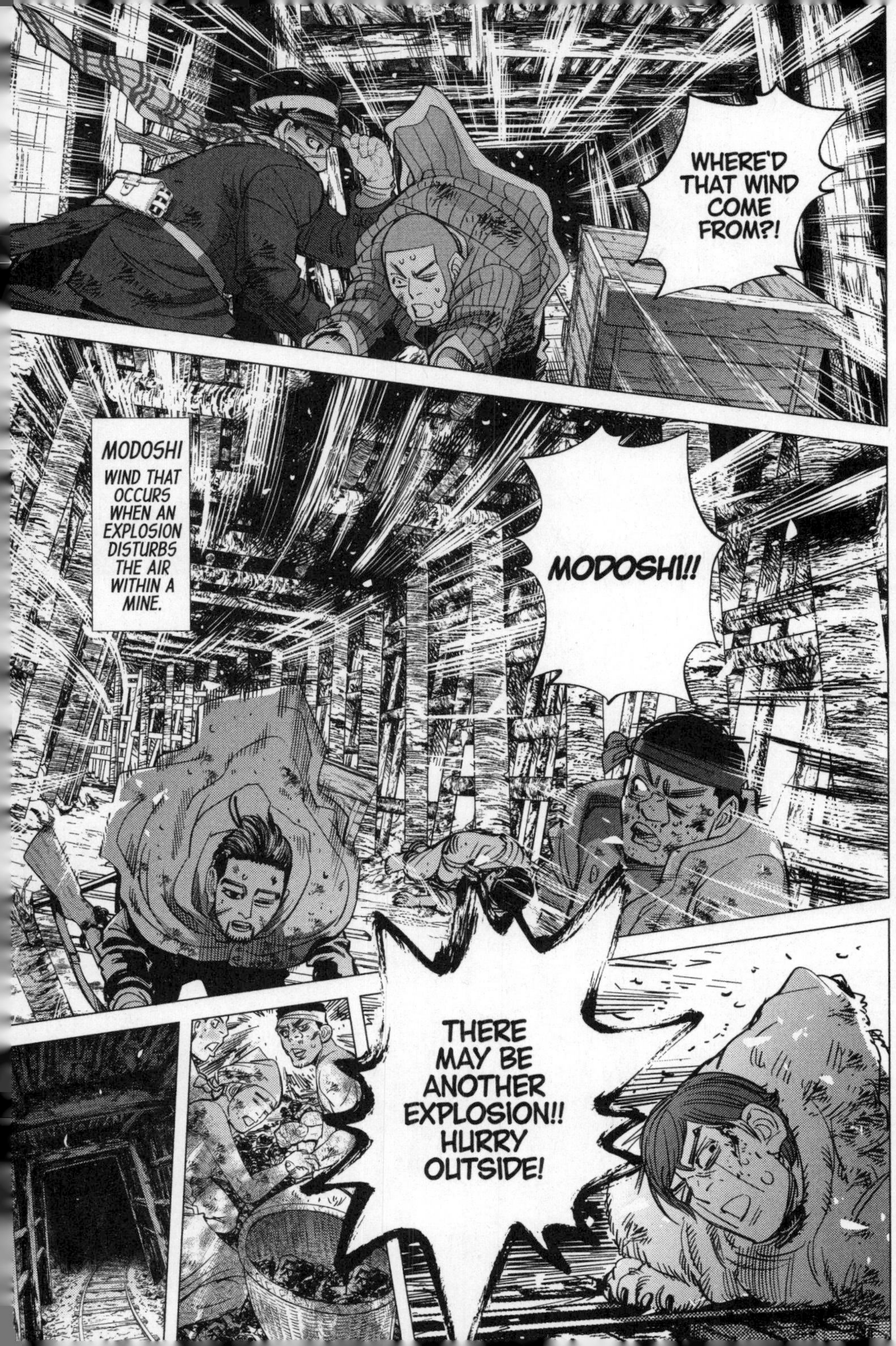
WHERE'D THAT WIND COME FROM?!
MODOSHI!!
MODOSHI WIND THAT OCCURS WHEN AN EXPLOSION DISTURBS THE AIR WITHIN A MINE.
THERE MAY BE ANOTHER EXPLOSION!! HURRY OUTSIDE!

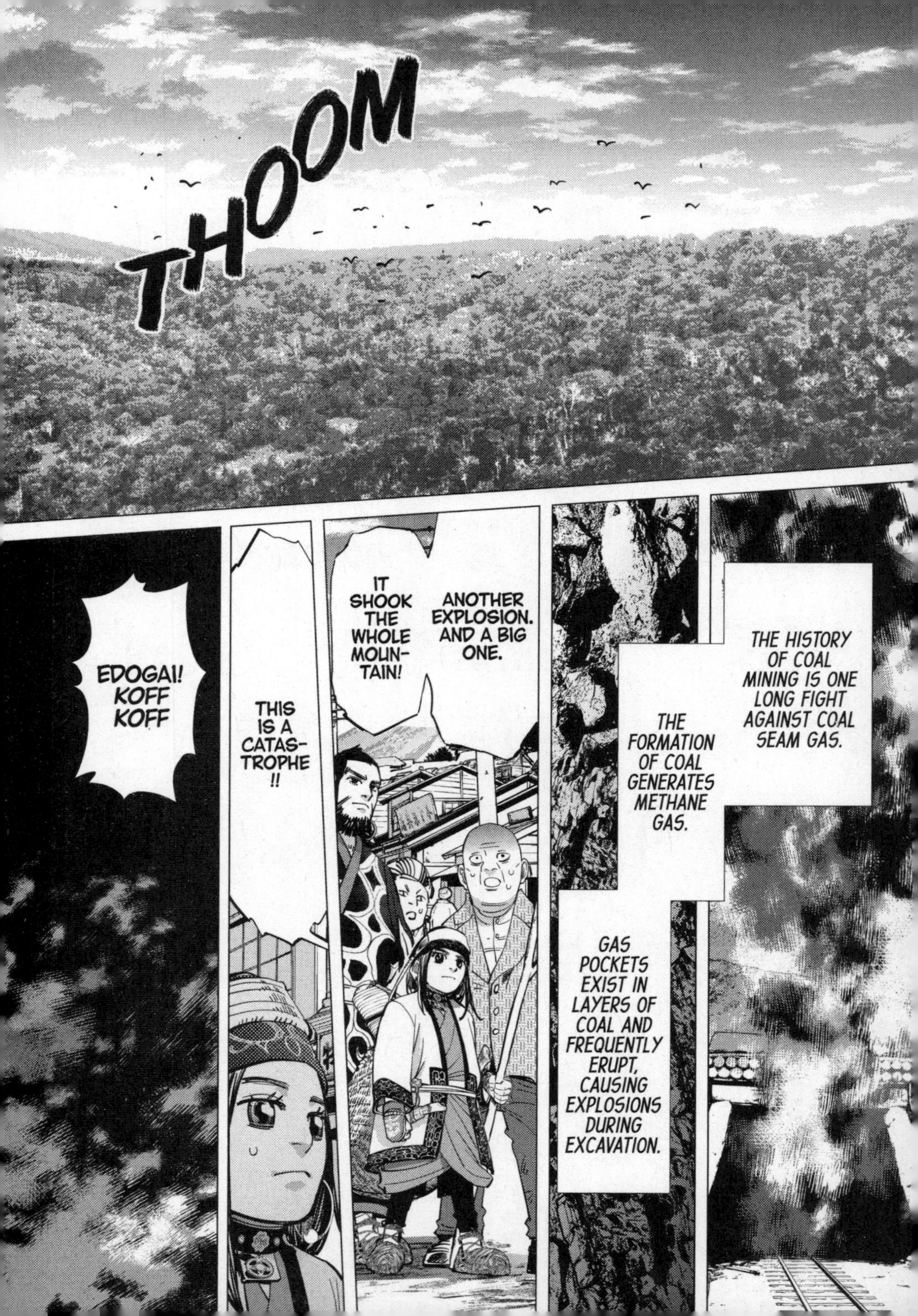
THOOM
THE HISTORY OF COAL MINING IS ONE LONG FIGHT AGAINST COAL SEAM GAS.
THE FORMATION OF COAL GENERATES METHANE GAS.
GAS POCKETS EXIST IN LAYERS OF COAL AND FREQUENTLY ERUPT, CAUSING EXPLOSIONS DURING EXCAVATION.
ANOTHER EXPLOSION. AND A BIG ONE.
IT SHOOK THE WHOLE MOUN-TAIN!
THIS IS A CATAS-TROPHE !!
EDOGAI! KOFF KOFF

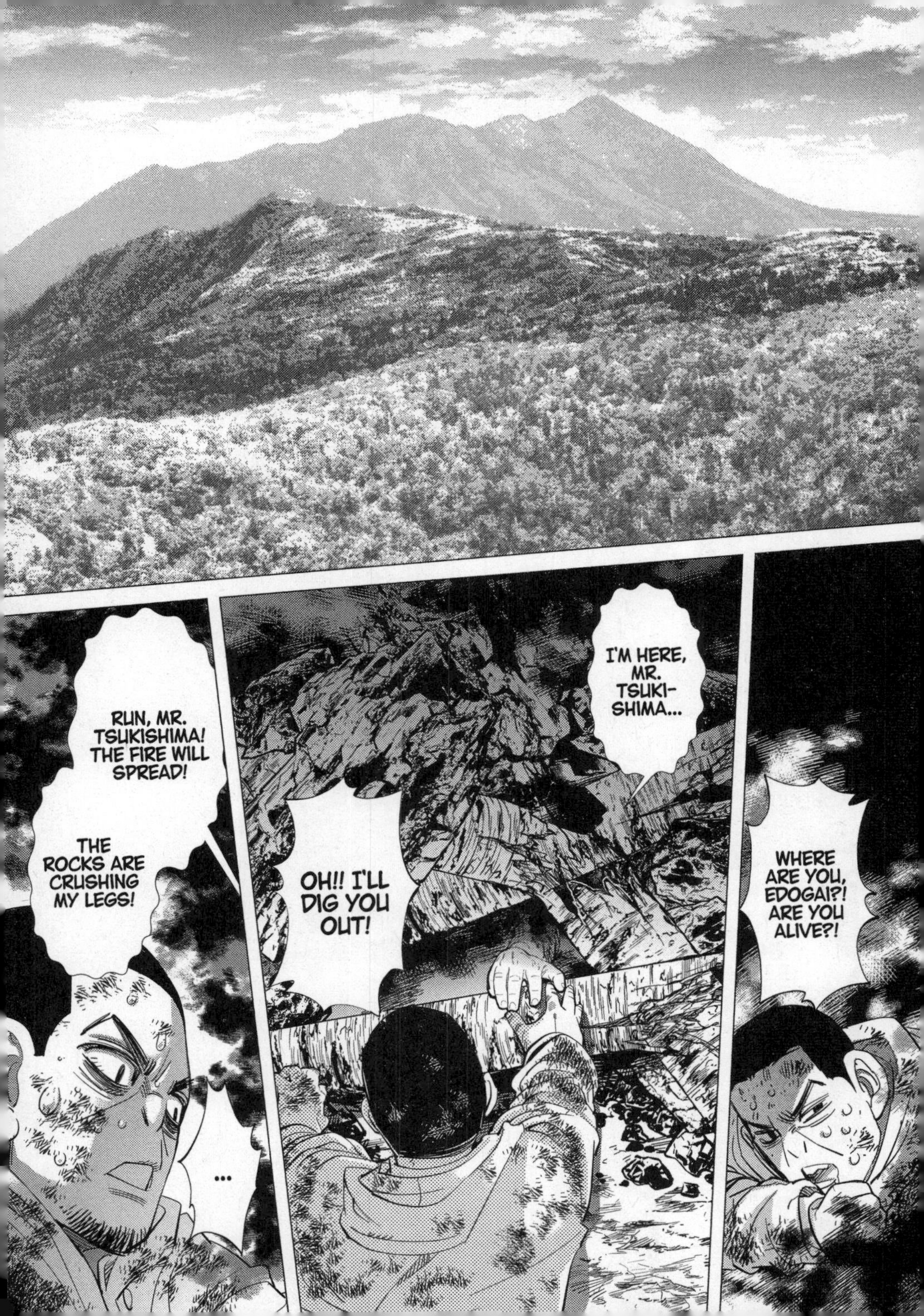
WHERE ARE YOU, EDOGAI?! ARE YOU ALIVE?!
I'M HERE, MR. TSUKISHIMA...
OH!! I'LL DIG YOU OUT!
RUN, MR. TSUKISHIMA! THE FIRE WILL SPREAD!
THE ROCKS ARE CRUSHING MY LEGS!
...

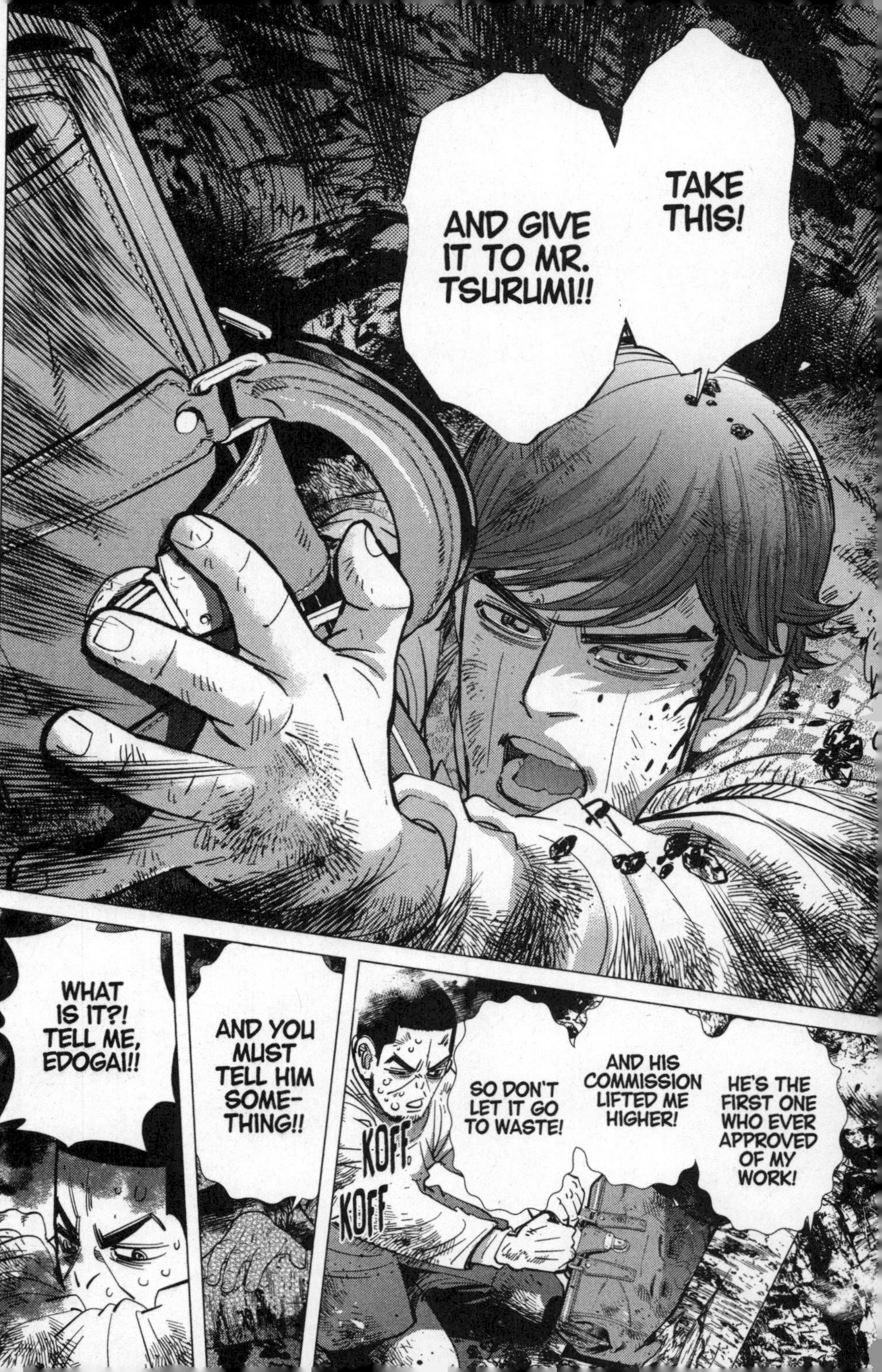
TAKE THIS!
AND GIVE IT TO MR. TSURUMI!!
HE'S THE FIRST ONE WHO EVER APPROVED OF MY WORK!
AND HIS COMMISSION LIFTED ME HIGHER!
SO DON'T LET IT GO TO WASTE!
KOFF KOFF
AND YOU MUST TELL HIM SOME-THING!!
WHAT IS IT?! TELL ME, EDOGAI!!

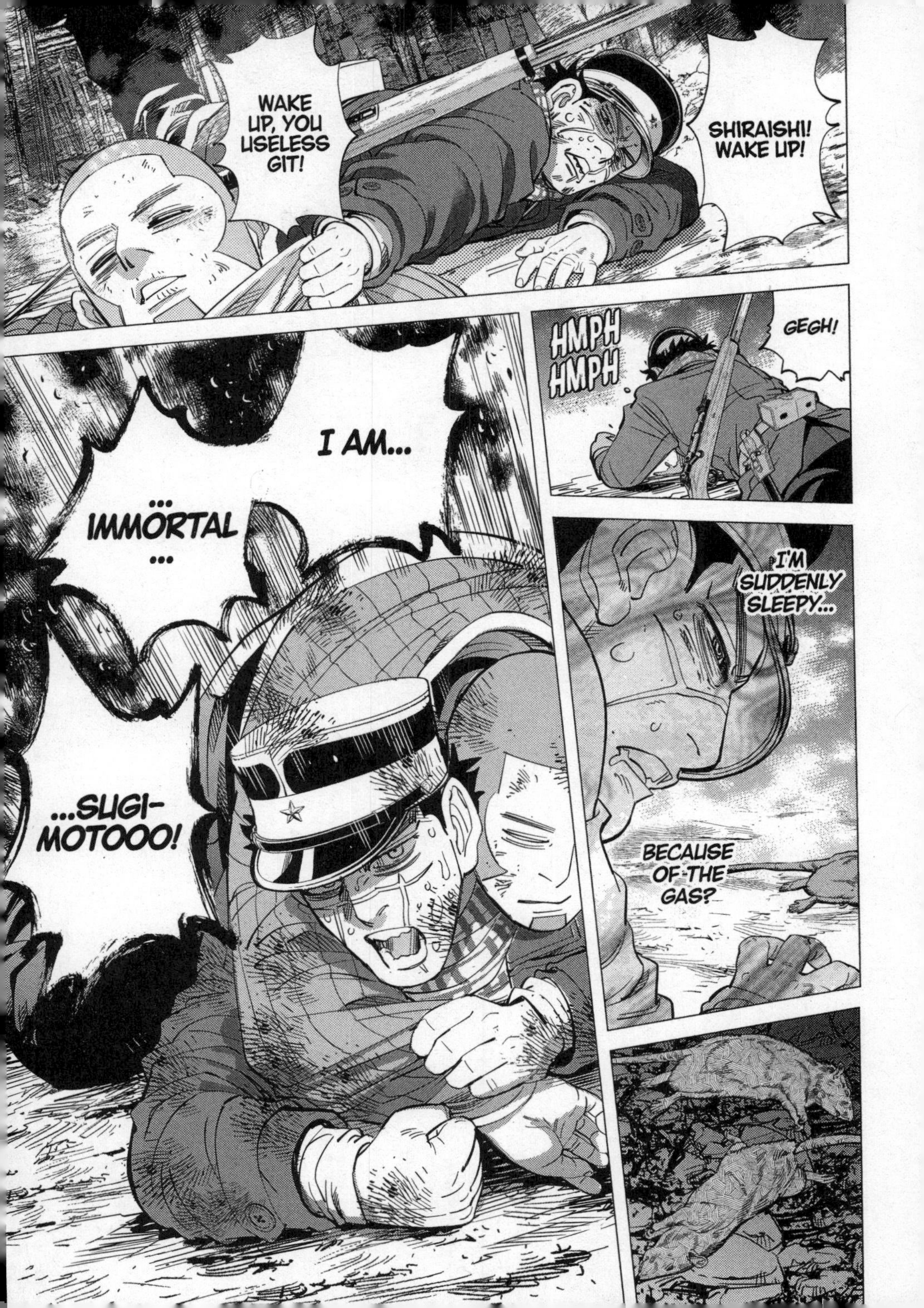
SHIRAISHI! WAKE UP!
WAKE UP, YOU USELESS GIT!
GEGH!
HMPH HMPH
I'M SUDDENLY SLEEPY...
BECAUSE OF THE GAS?
I AM...
... IMMÖRTAL ...
...SUGI-MOTOOO!

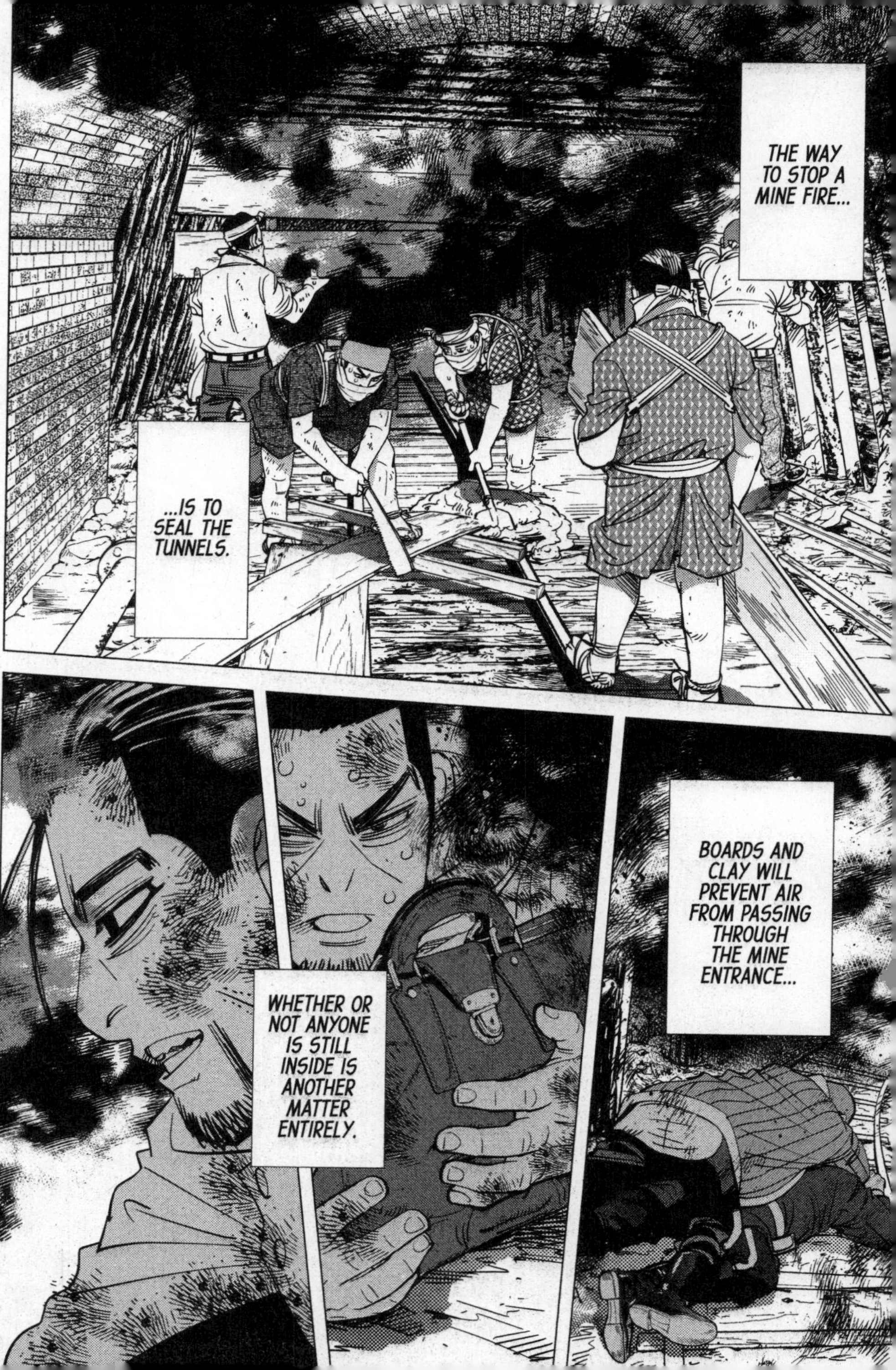
THE WAY TO STOP A MINE FIRE...
...IS TO SEAL THE TUNNELS.
BOARDS AND CLAY WILL PREVENT AIR FROM PASSING THROUGH THE MINE ENTRANCE...
WHETHER OR NOT ANYONE IS STILL INSIDE IS ANOTHER MATTER ENTIRELY.

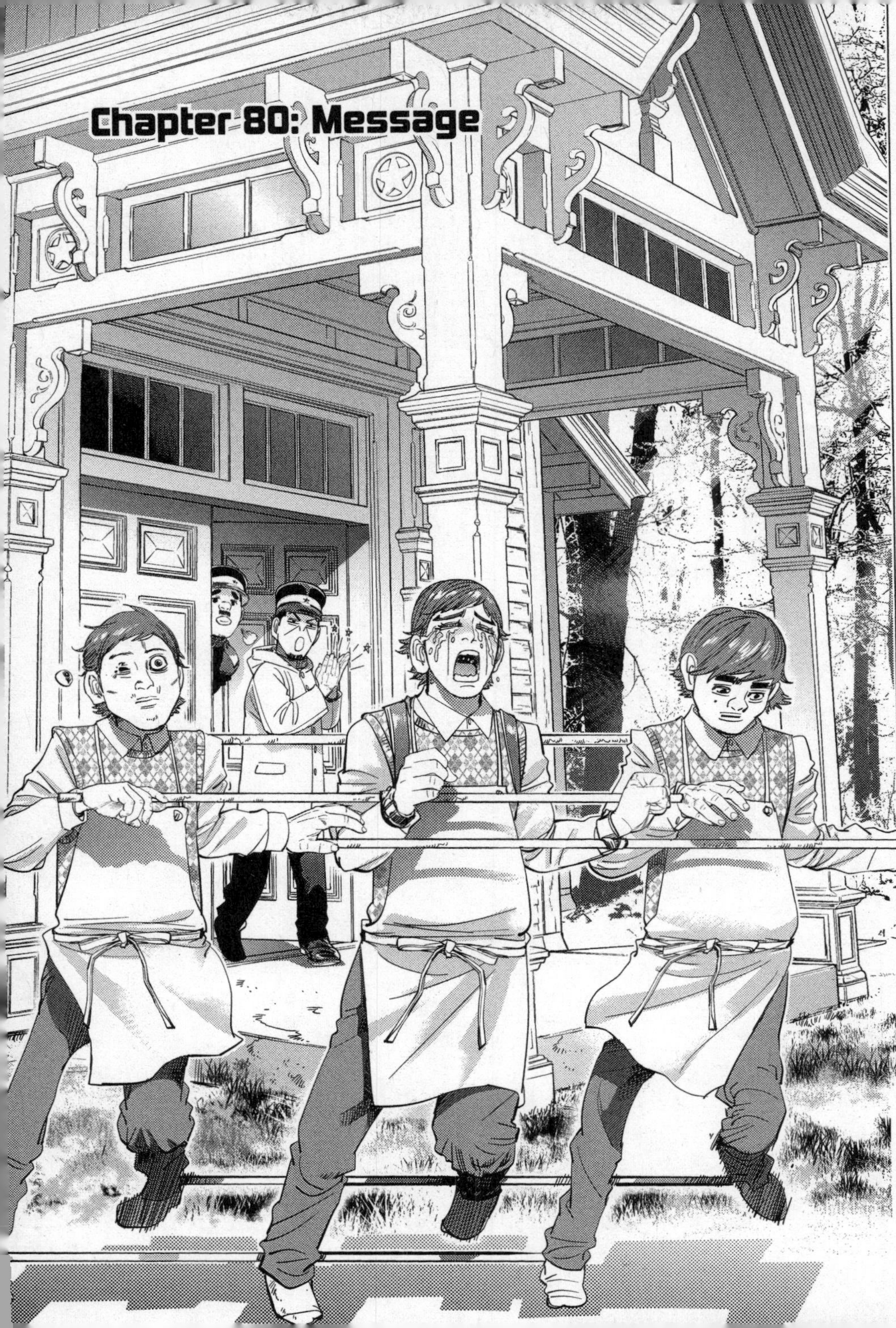
Chapter 80: Message

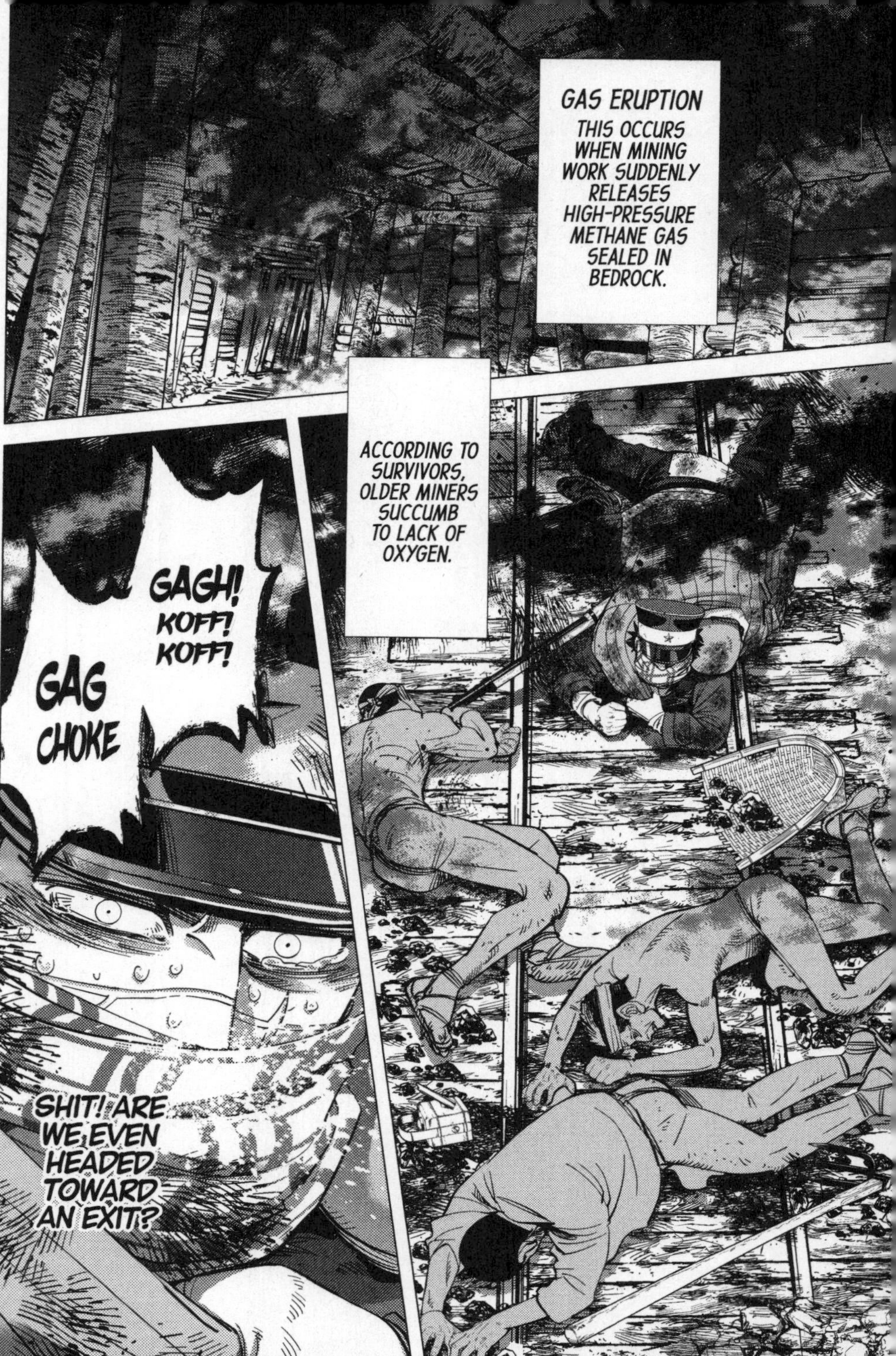
GAS ERUPTION
THIS OCCURS WHEN MINING WORK SUDDENLY RELEASES HIGH-PRESSURE METHANE GAS SEALED IN BEDROCK.
ACCORDING TO SURVIVORS, OLDER MINERS SUCCUMB TO LACK OF OXYGEN.
GAGH! KOFF! KOFF!
GAG CHOKE
SHIT! ARE WE EVEN HEADED TOWARD AN EXIT?

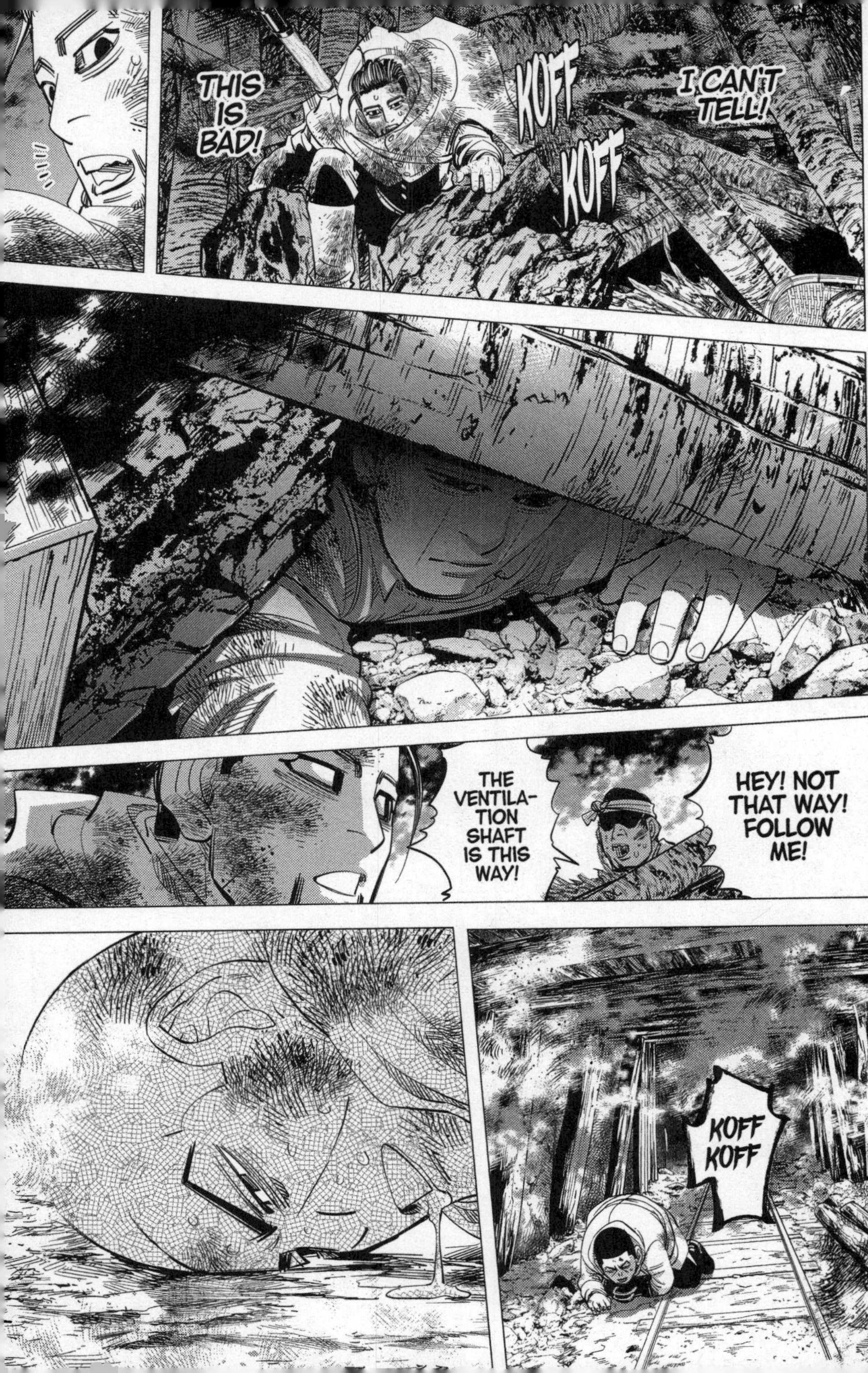
I CAN'T TELL!
KOFF
KOFF
THIS IS BAD!
HEY! NOT THAT WAY! FOLLOW ME!
THE VENTILA-TION SHAFT IS THIS WAY!
KOFF KOFF

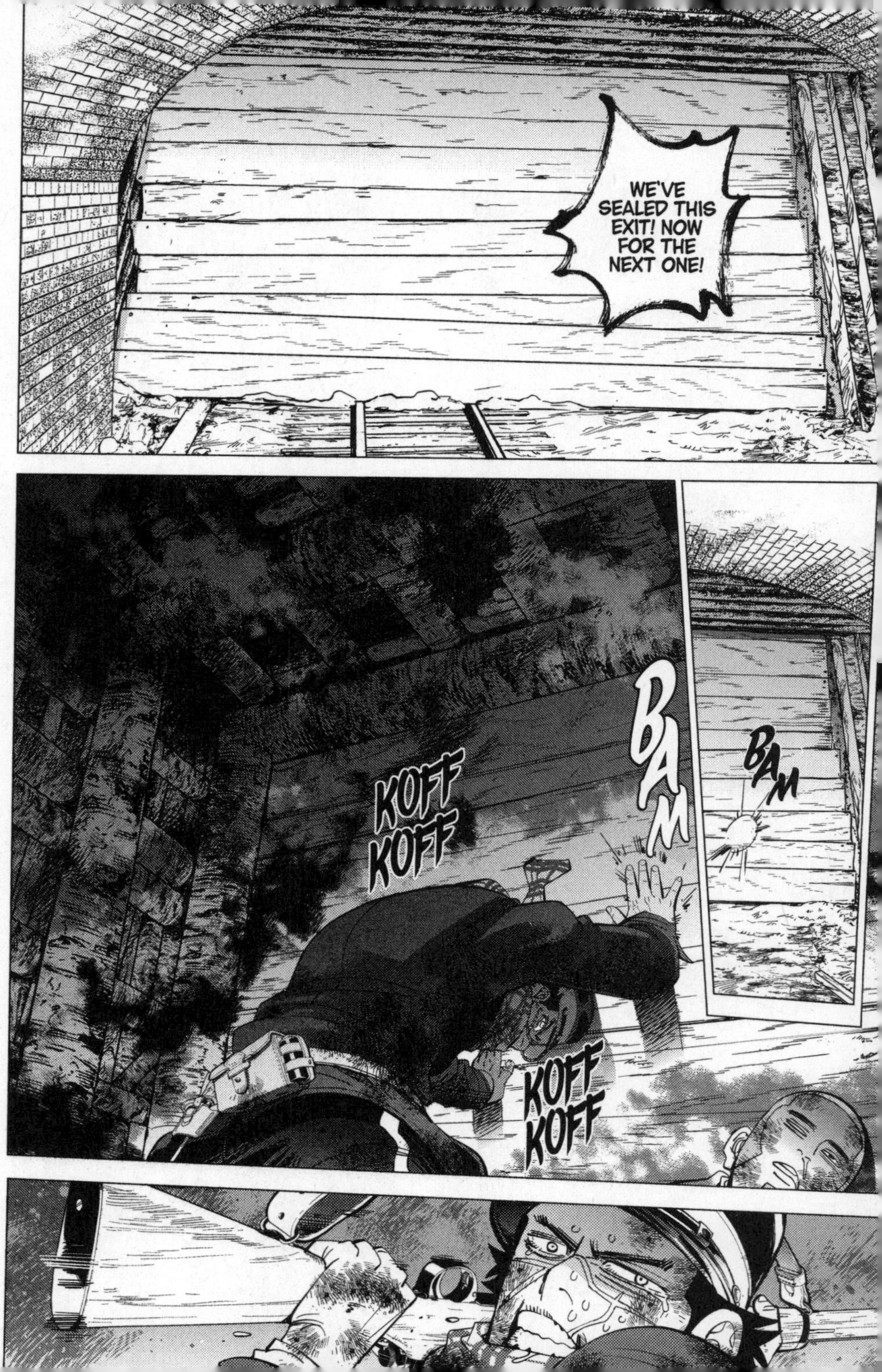
WE'VE SEALED THIS EXIT! NOW FOR THE NEXT ONE!
BAM
BAM
KOFF KOFF
KOFF KOFF

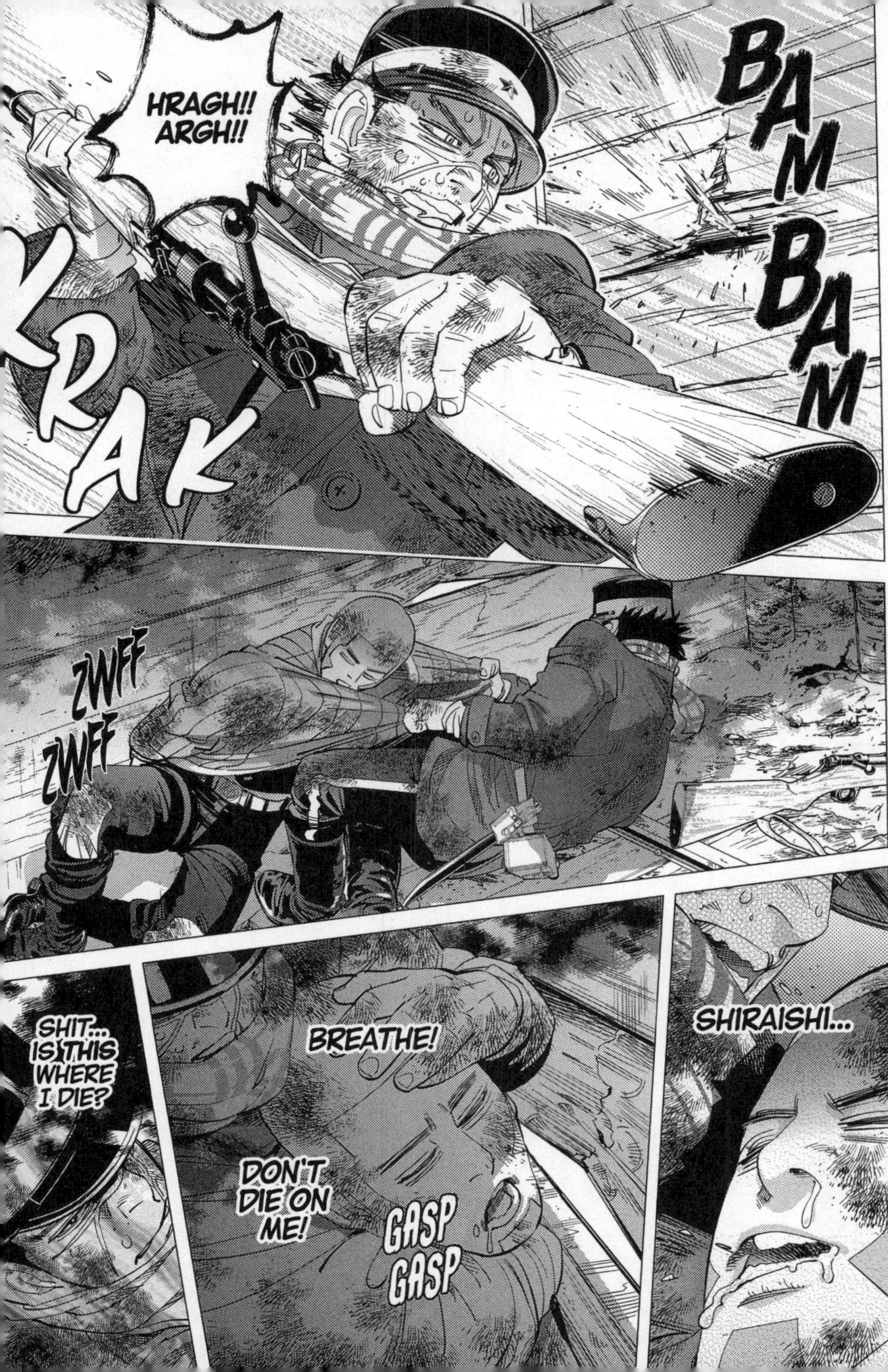
BAM BAM BAM BAM
HRAGH!! ARGH!!
KRAK
ZWFF ZWFF
SHIRAISHI...
BREATHE!
DON'T DIE ON ME!
GASP GASP
SHIT... IS THIS WHERE I DIE?

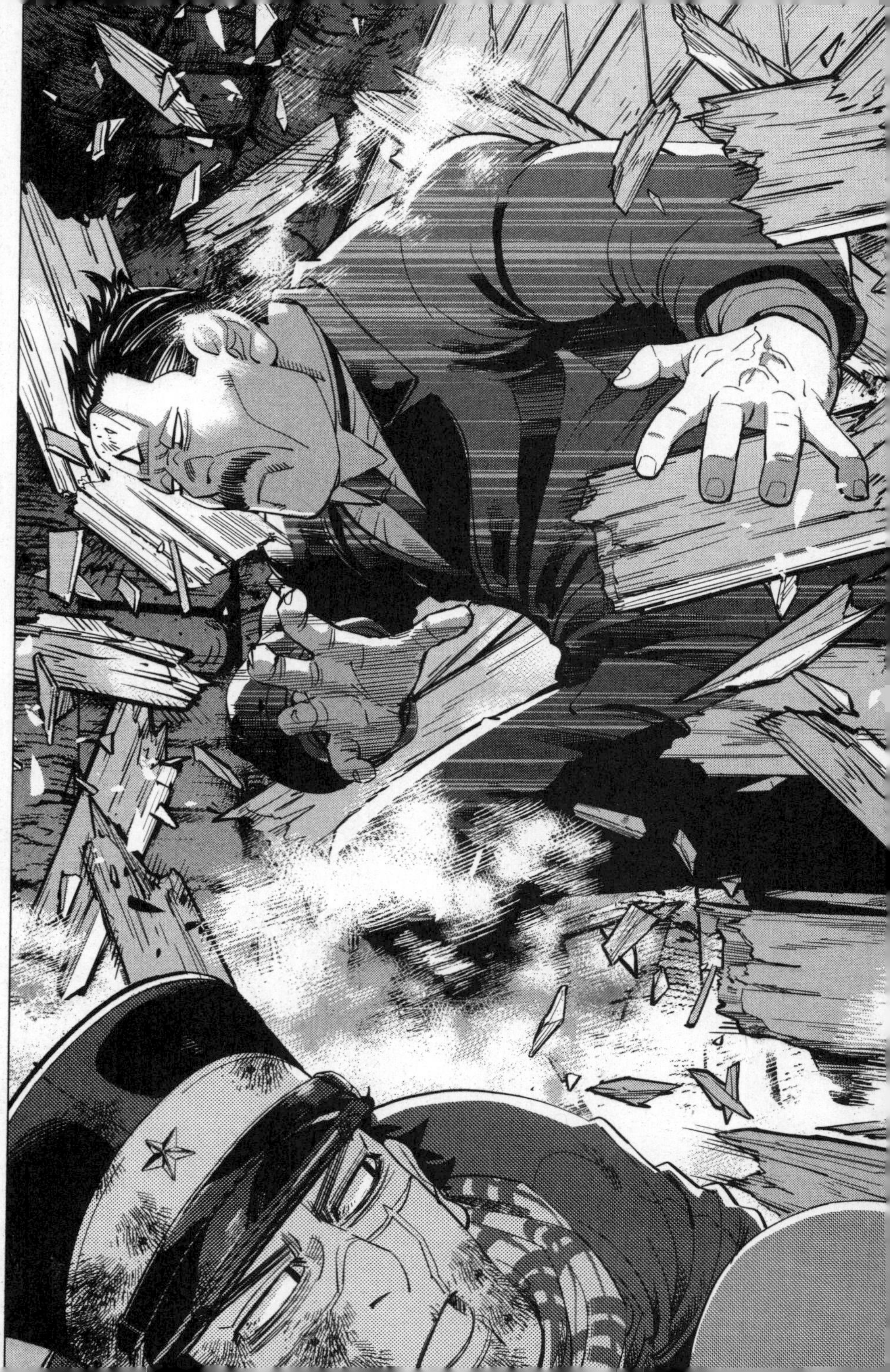

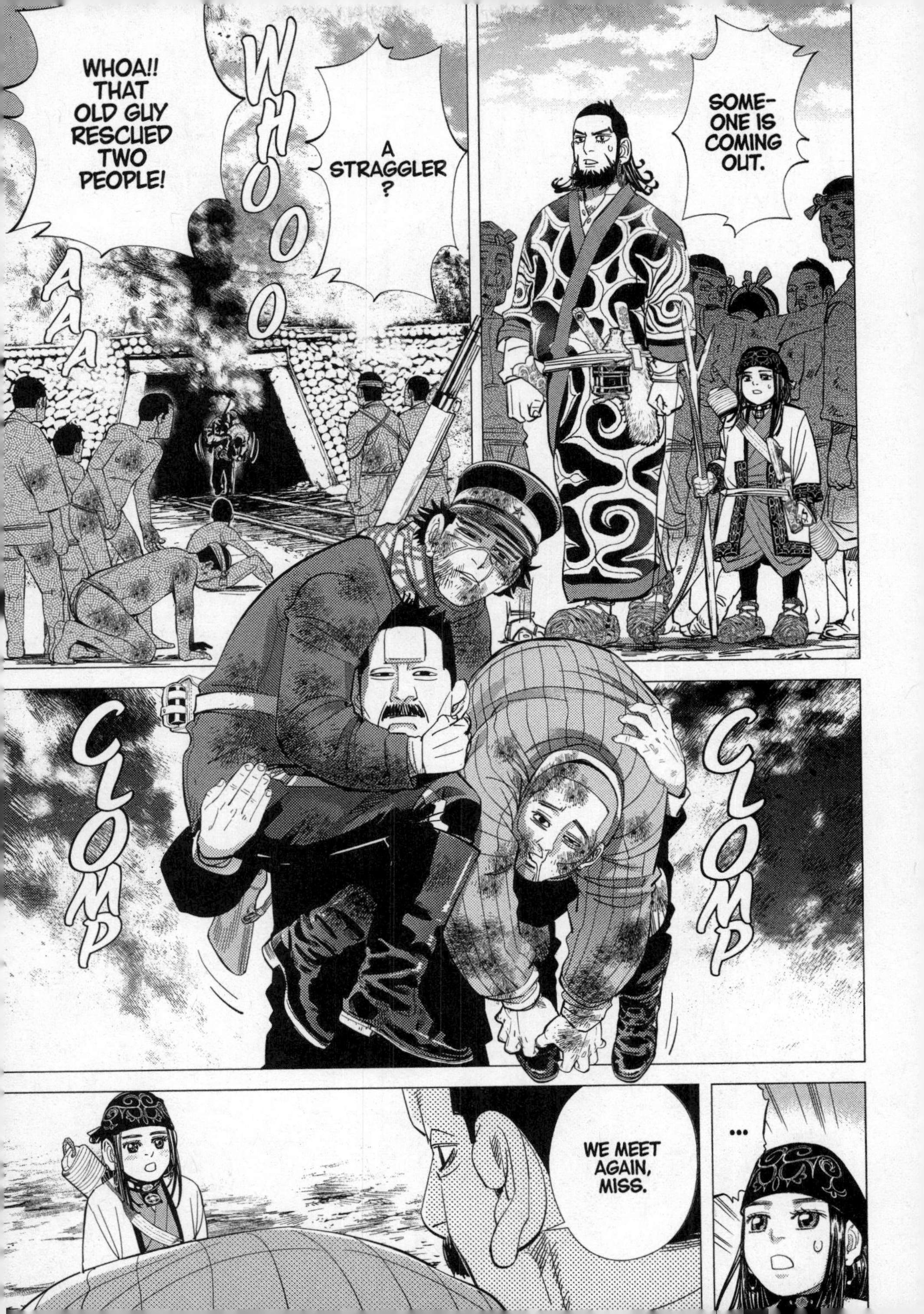
SOME-ONE IS COMING OUT.
A STRAGGLER?
WHOOO
WHOA!! THAT OLD GUY RESCUED TWO PEOPLE!
AAA
CLOMP
CLOMP
...
WE MEET AGAIN, MISS.

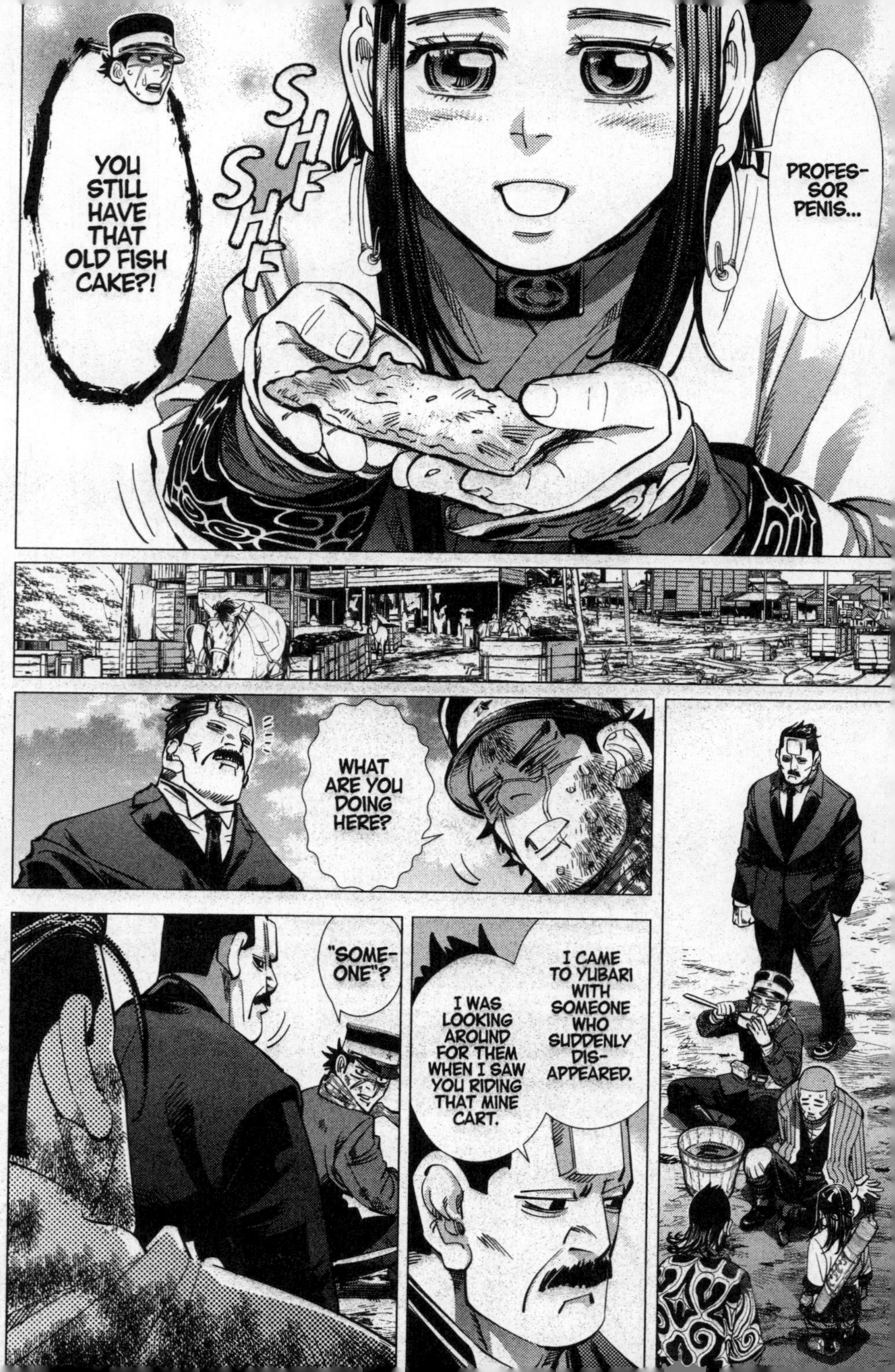
PROFES-SOR PENIS...
SHF SHF
YOU STILL HAVE THAT OLD FISH CAKE?!
WHAT ARE YOU DOING HERE?
I CAME TO YUBARI WITH SOMEONE WHO SUDDENLY DIS-APPEARED.
I WAS LOOKING AROUND FOR THEM WHEN I SAW YOU RIDING THAT MINE CART.
"SOME-ONE"?

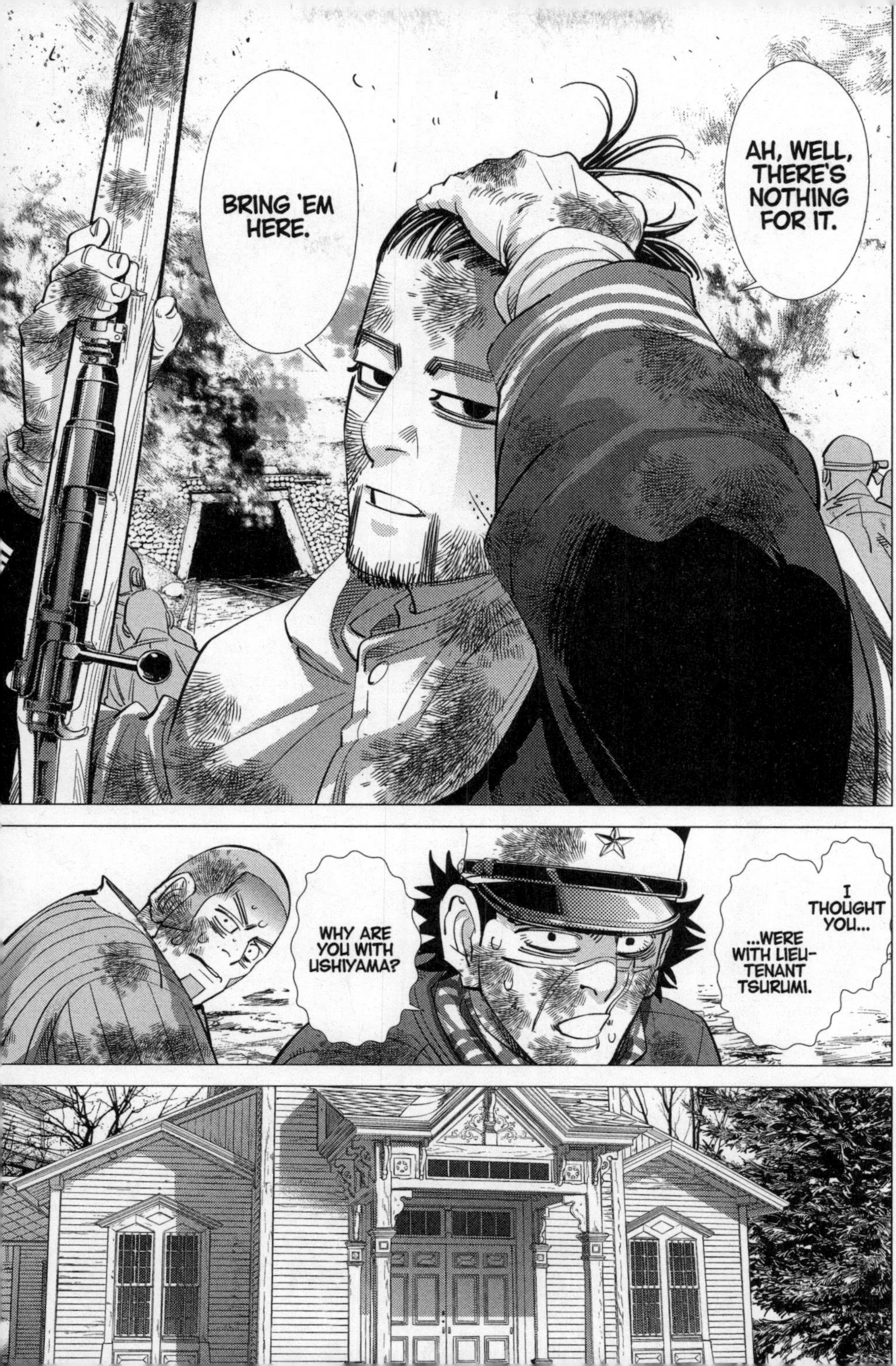
AH, WELL, THERE'S NOTHING FOR IT.
BRING 'EM HERE.
I THOUGHT YOU... ...WERE WITH LIEU-TENANT TSURUMI.
WHY ARE YOU WITH USHIYAMA?

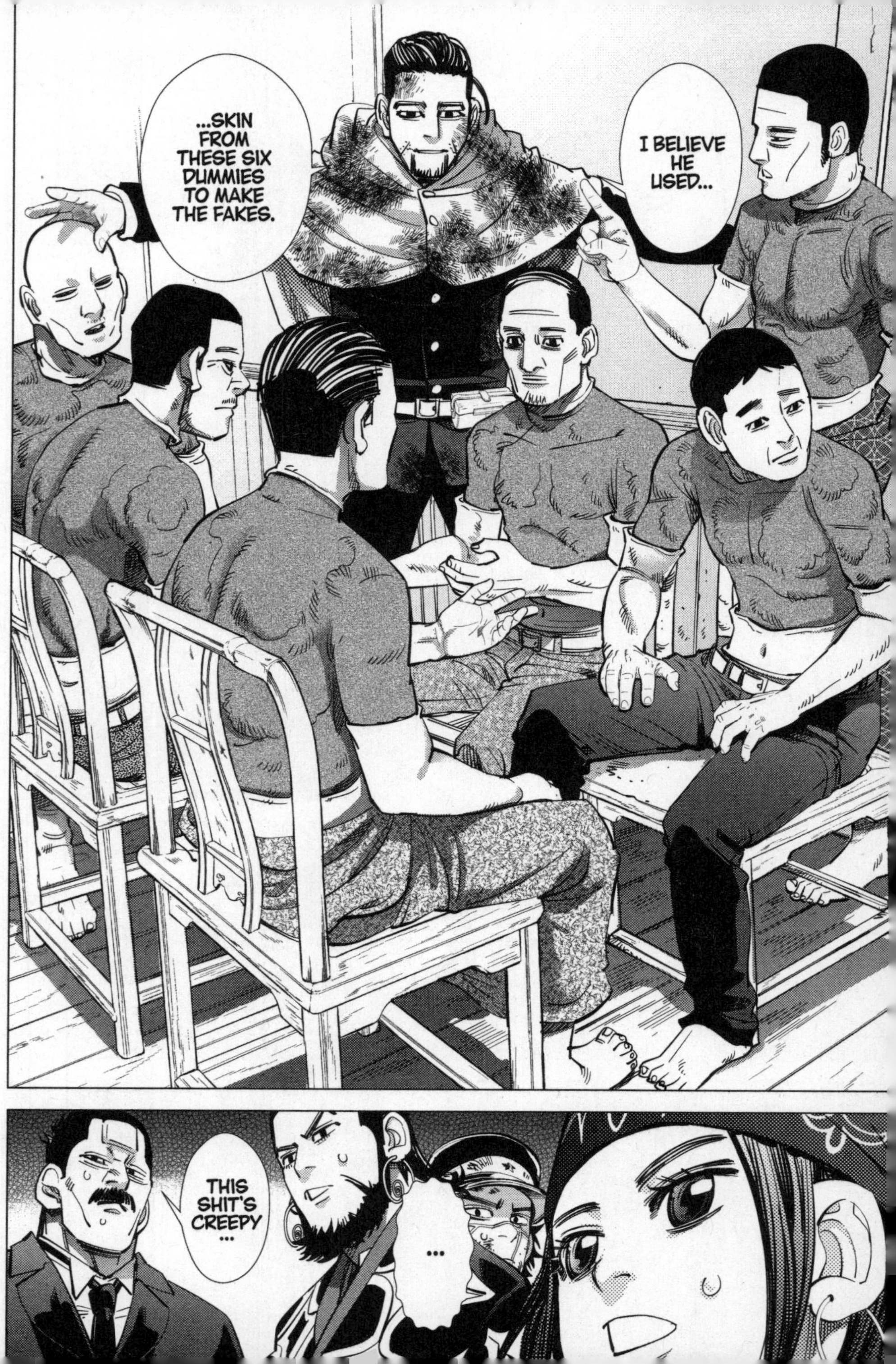
I BELIEVE HE USED...
...SKIN FROM THESE SIX DUMMIES TO MAKE THE FAKES.
...
THIS SHIT'S CREEPY ...

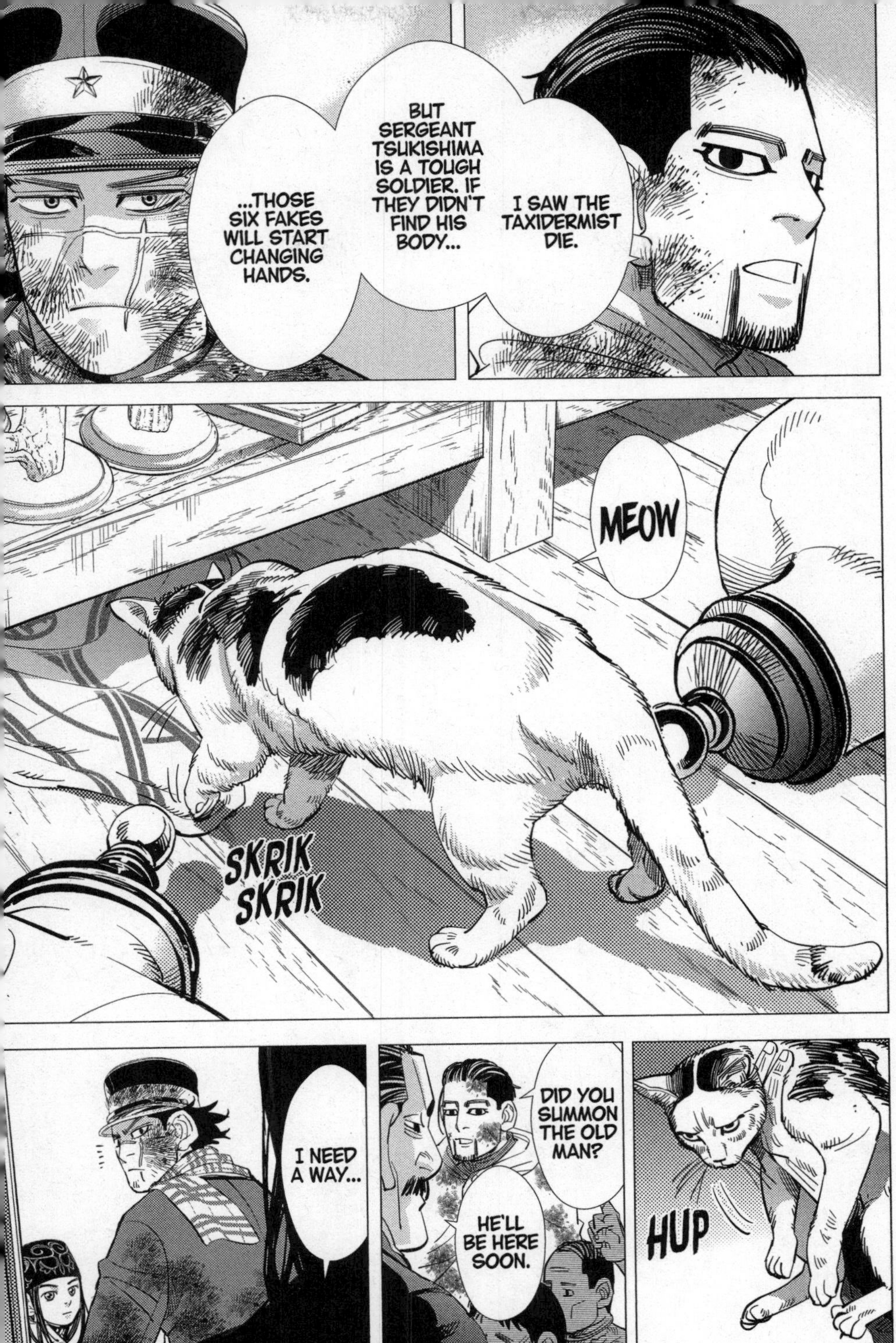
I SAW THE TAXIDERMIST DIE.
BUT SERGEANT TSUKISHIMA IS A TOUGH SOLDIER. IF THEY DIDN'T FIND HIS BODY...
...THOSE SIX FAKES WILL START CHANGING HANDS.
MEOW
SKRIK SKRIK
HUP
DID YOU SUMMON THE OLD MAN?
HE'LL BE HERE SOON.
I NEED A WAY...

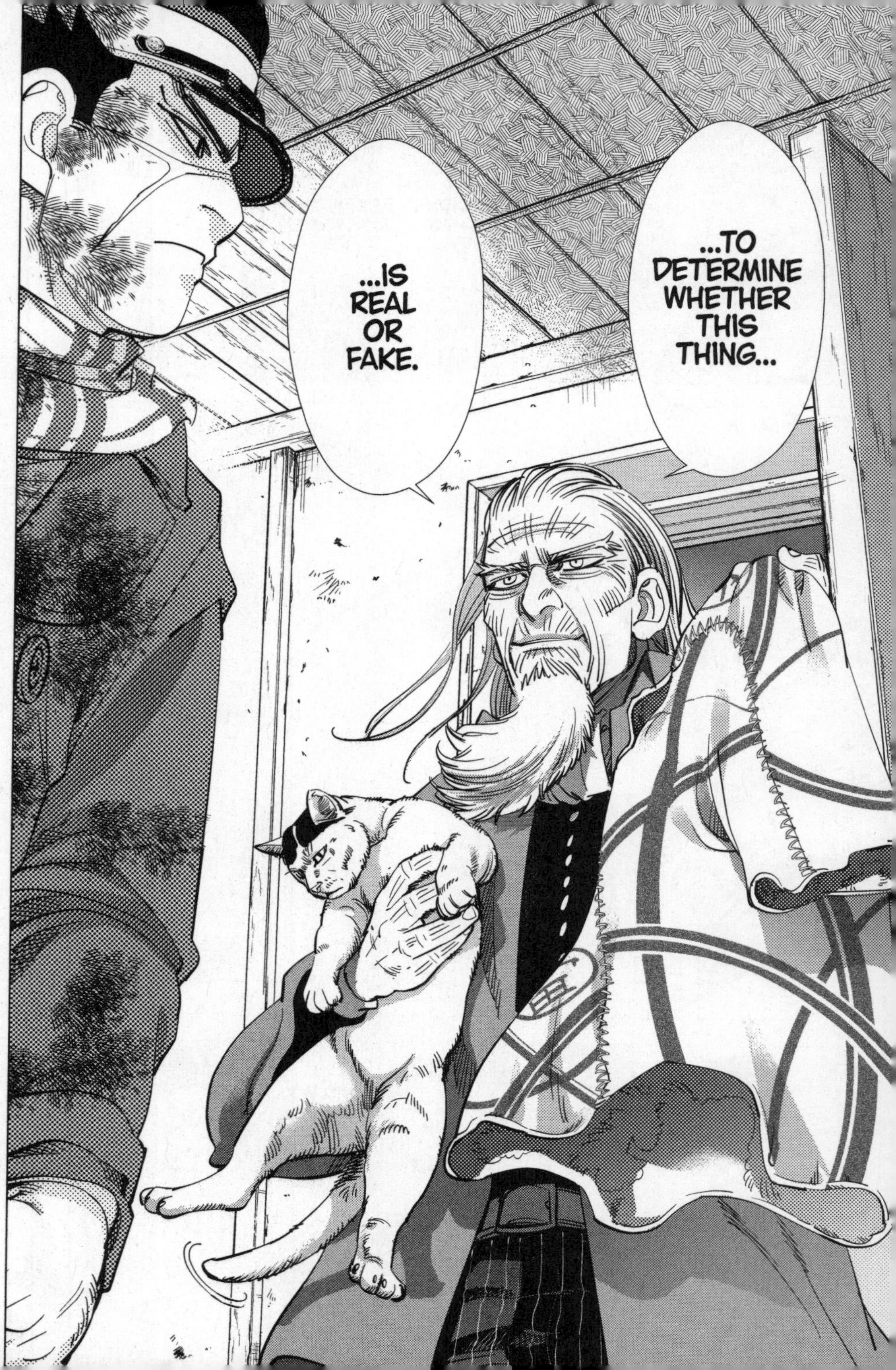
...TO DETERMINE WHETHER THIS THING...
...IS REAL OR FAKE.

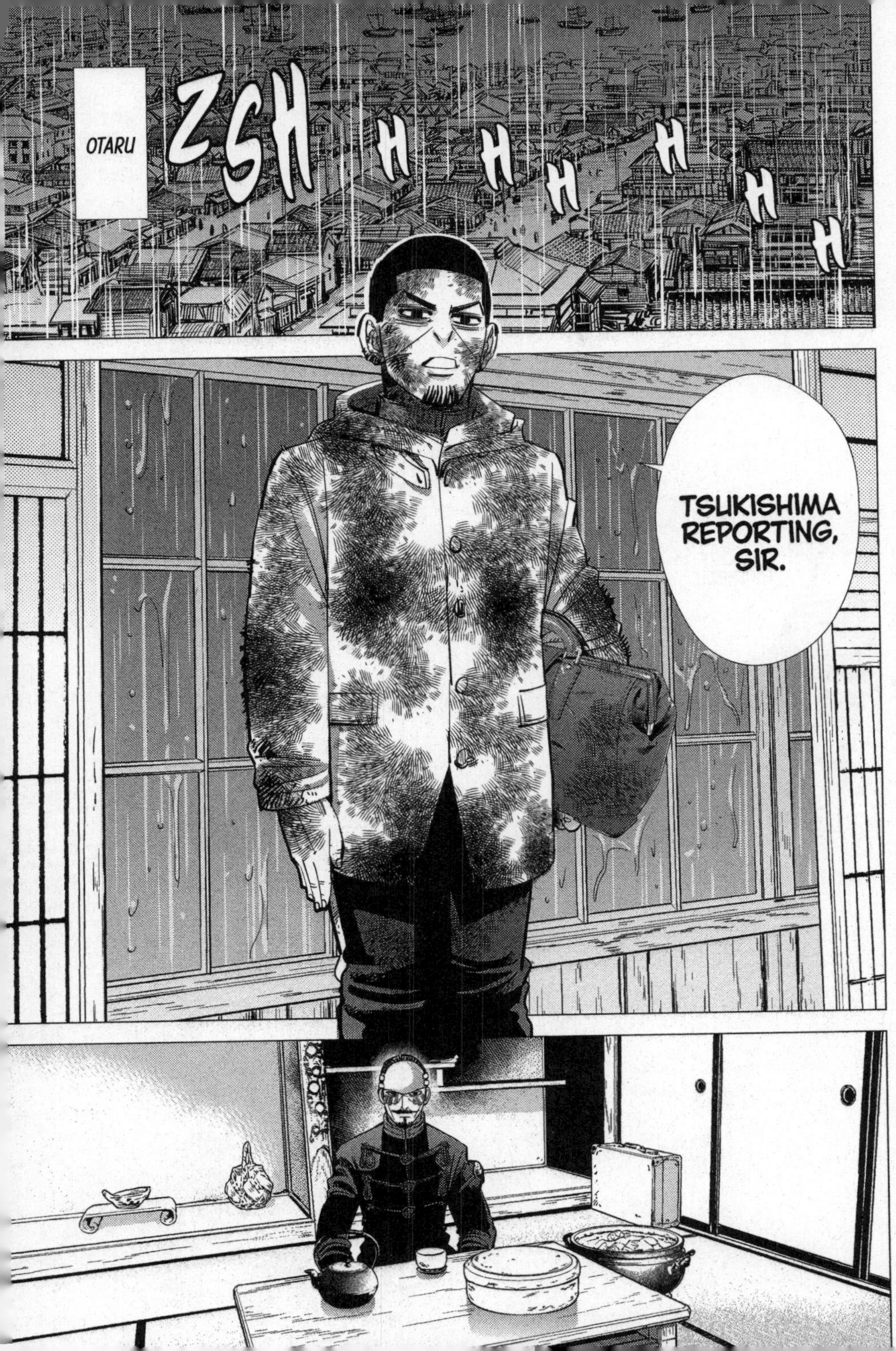

OTARU
ZSHHHHHHHH
TSUKISHIMA REPORTING, SIR.

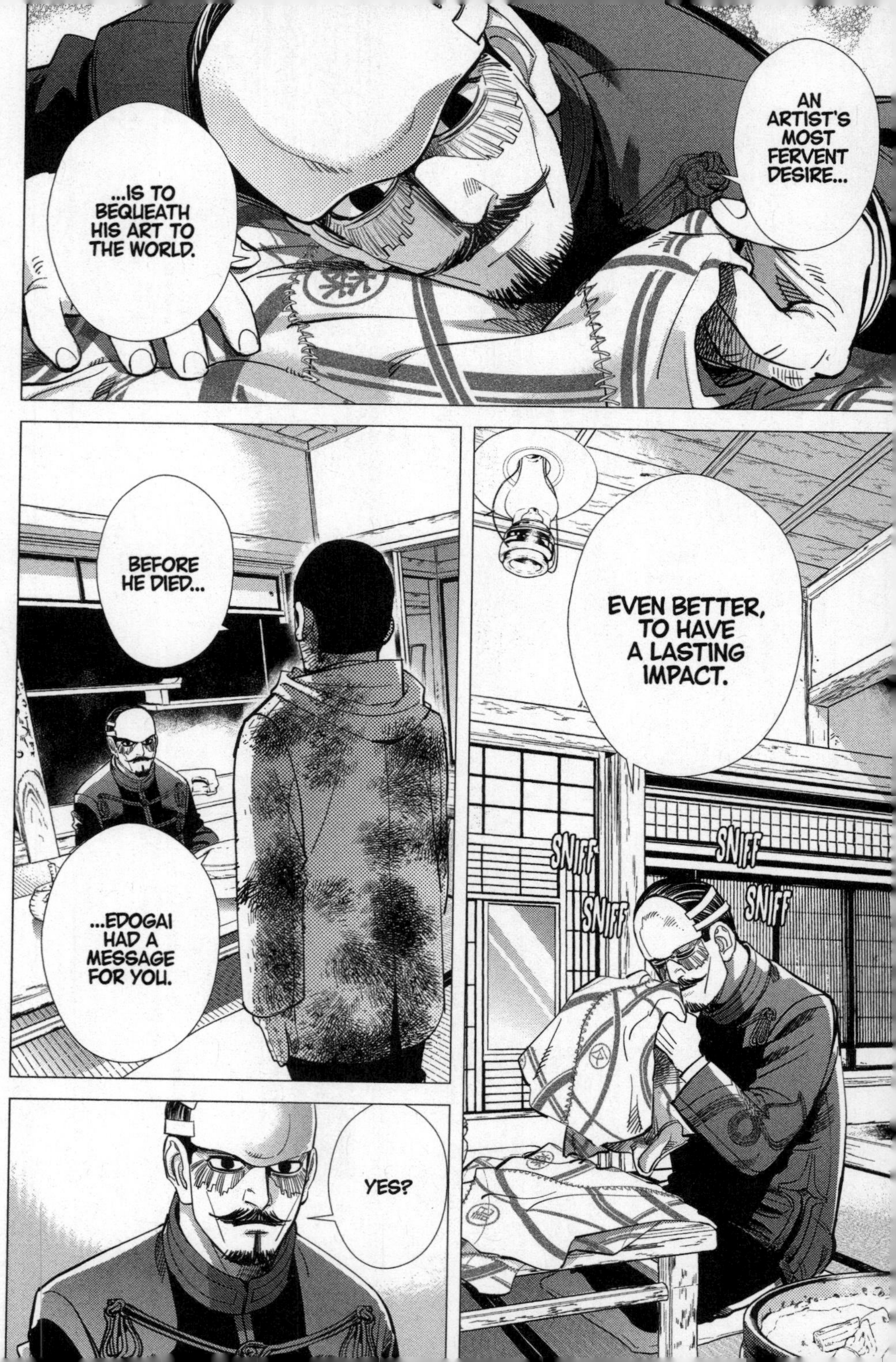
AN ARTIST'S MOST FERVENT DESIRE...
...IS TO BEQUEATH HIS ART TO THE WORLD.
EVEN BETTER, TO HAVE A LASTING IMPACT.
SNIFF
SNIFF
SNIFF
SNIFF
BEFORE HE DIED...
...EDOGAI HAD A MESSAGE FOR YOU.
YES?

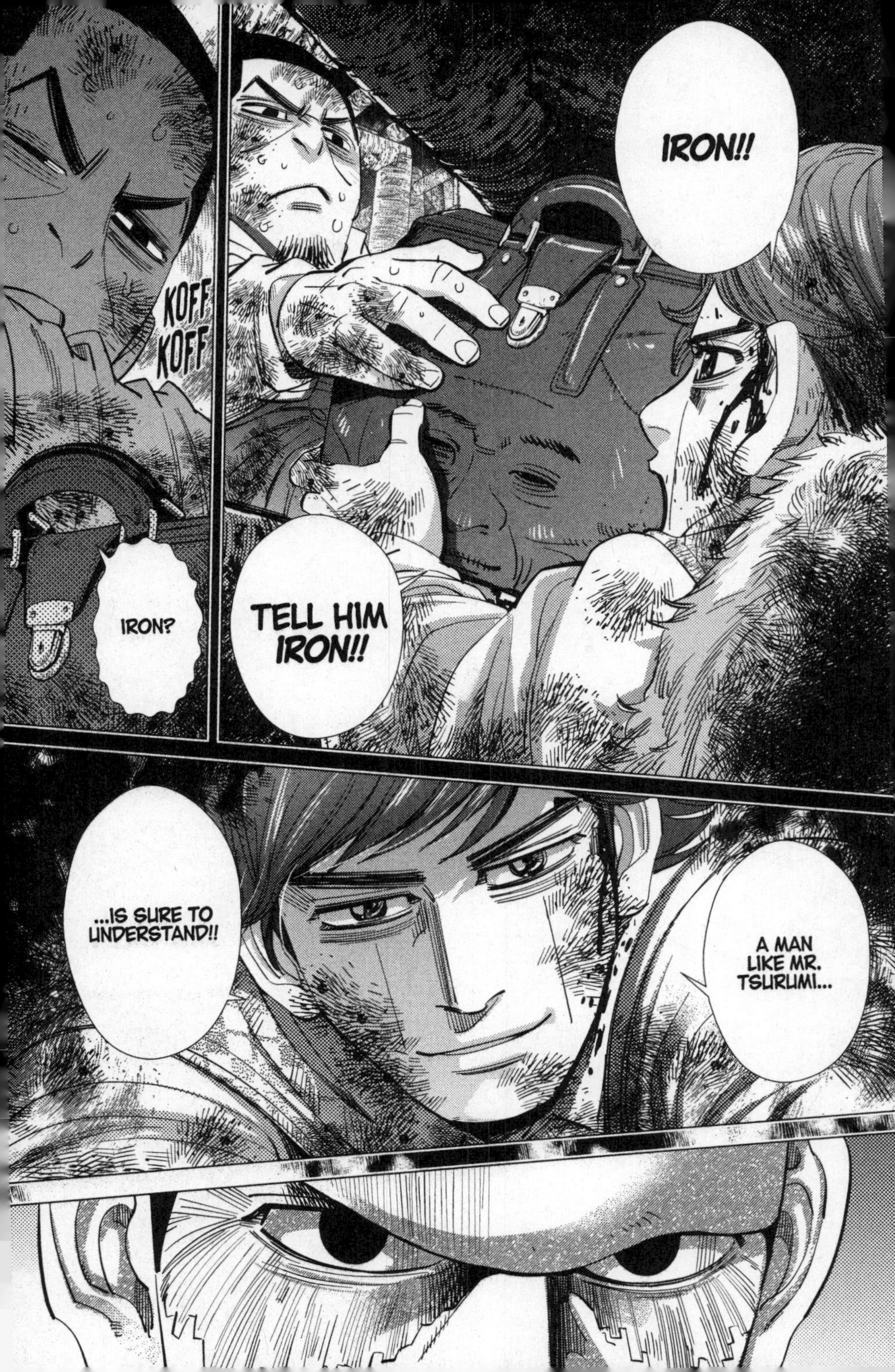
IRON!!
TELL HIM IRON!!
KOFF KOFF
IRON?
A MAN LIKE MR. TSURUMI...
...IS SURE TO UNDERSTAND!!

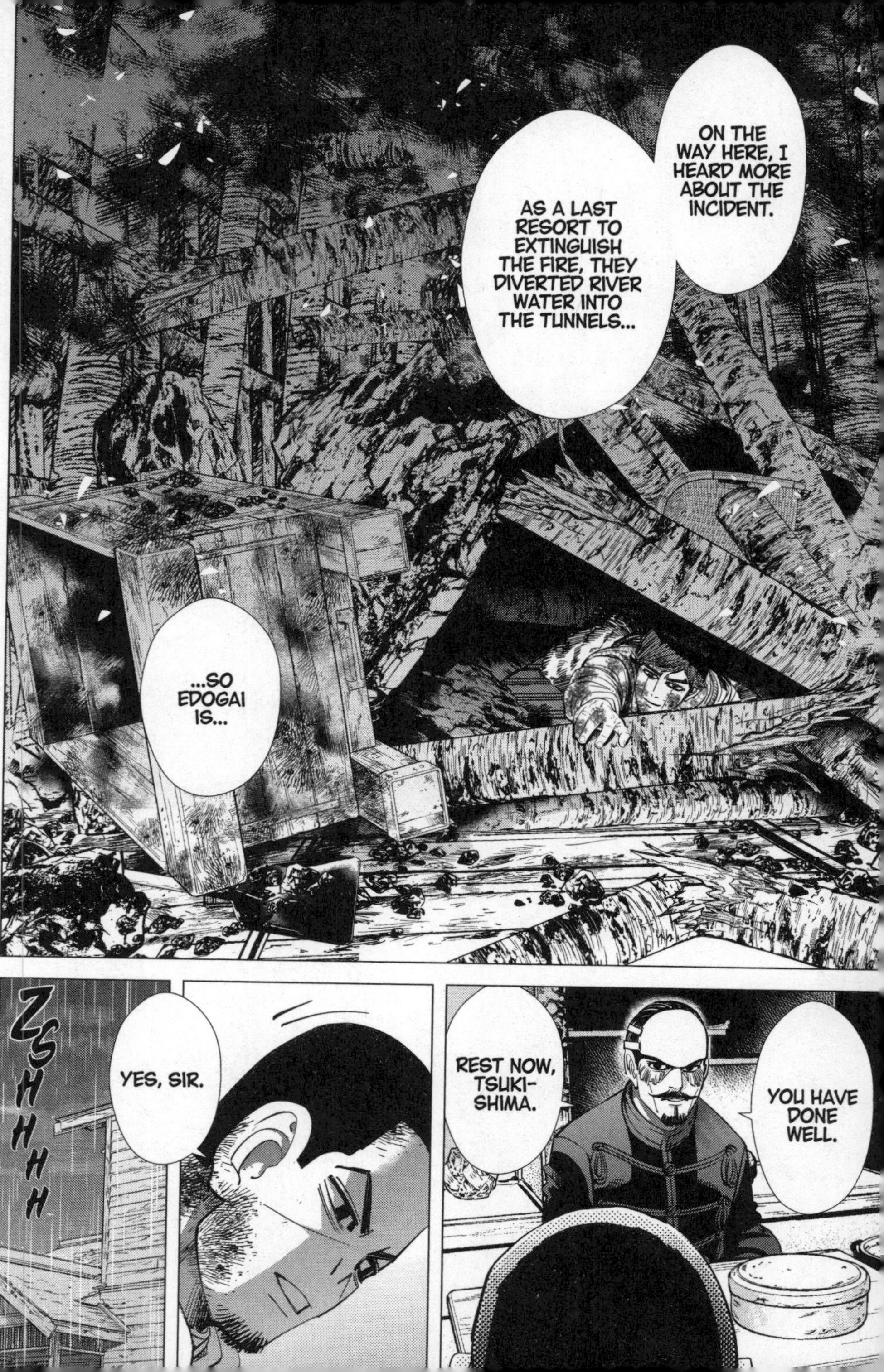
ON THE WAY HERE, I HEARD MORE ABOUT THE INCIDENT.
AS A LAST RESORT TO EXTINGUISH THE FIRE, THEY DIVERTED RIVER WATER INTO THE TUNNELS...
...SO EDOGAI IS...
YOU HAVE DONE WELL.
REST NOW, TSUKI-SHIMA.
YES, SIR.
ZSHHHHH

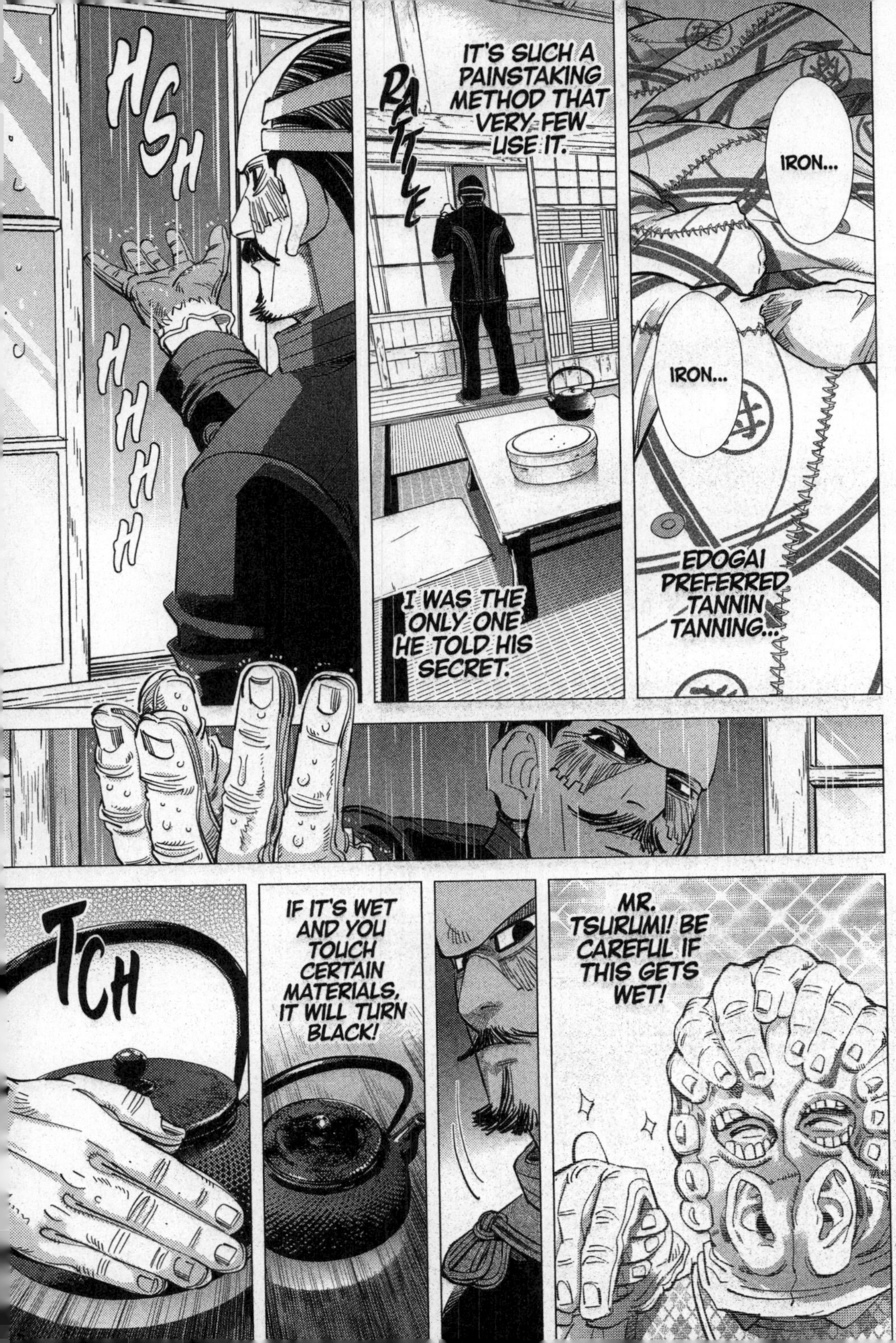
IRON...
IRON...
EDOGAI PREFERRED TANNIN TANNING...
IT'S SUCH A PAINSTAKING METHOD THAT VERY FEW USE IT.
RATTLE
I WAS THE ONLY ONE HE TOLD HIS SECRET.
HSH
HHHHH
MR. TSURUMI! BE CAREFUL IF THIS GETS WET!
IF IT'S WET AND YOU TOUCH CERTAIN MATERIALS, IT WILL TURN BLACK!
TCH

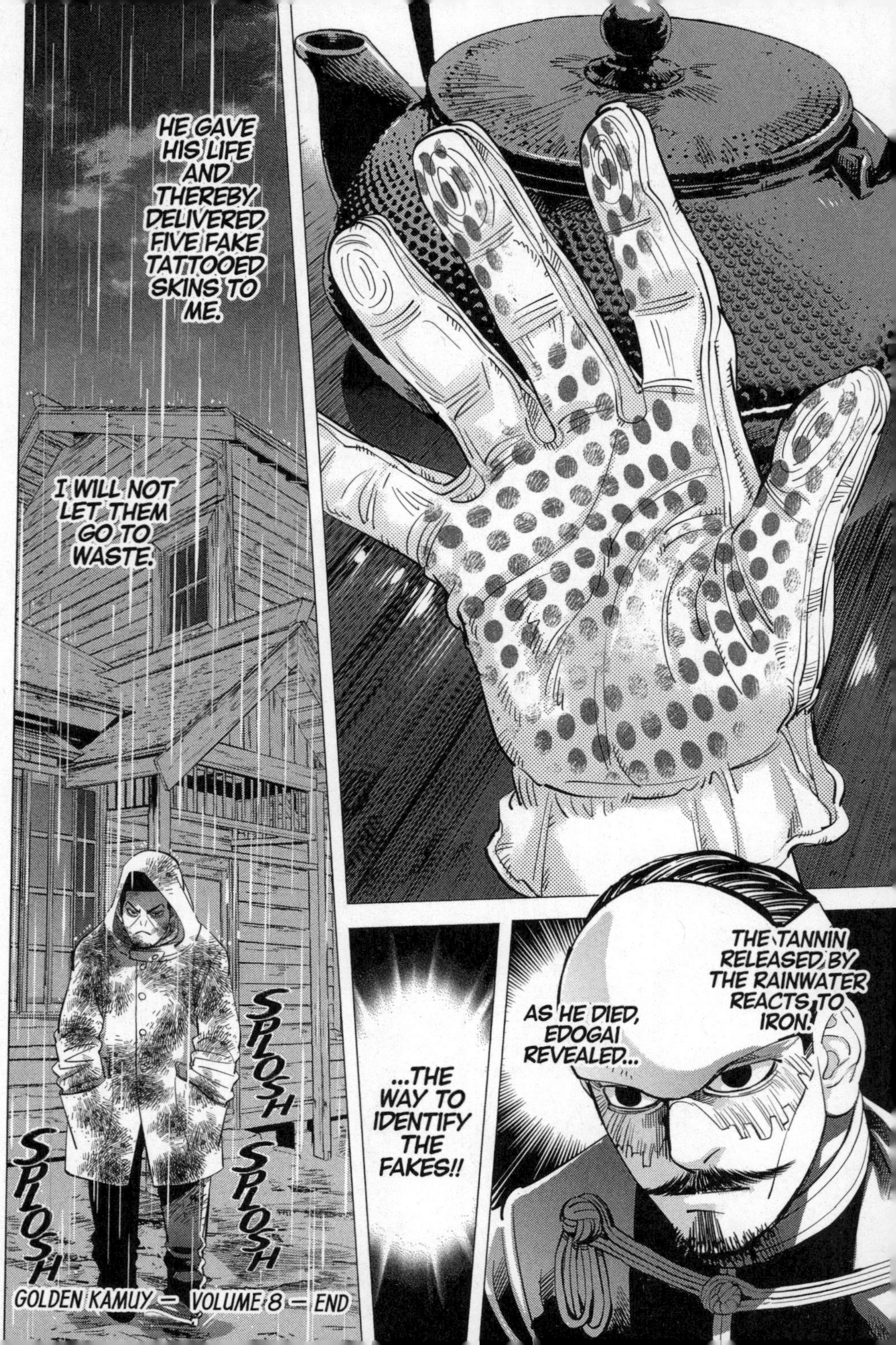
THE TANNIN RELEASED BY THE RAINWATER REACTS TO IRON!
AS HE DIED, EDOGAI REVEALED...
...THE WAY TO IDENTIFY THE FAKES!!
HE GAVE HIS LIFE AND THEREBY DELIVERED FIVE FAKE TATTOOED SKINS TO ME.
I WILL NOT LET THEM GO TO WASTE.
SPLOSH
SPLOSH
SPLOSH
SPLOSH
GOLDEN KAMUY — VOLUME 8 — END

Ainu Language Supervision • Hiroshi Nakagawa

Cooperation from • Hokkaido Ainu Association and the Abashiri Prison Museum
Otaru City General Museum • Waseda University Aizu Museum • Tokyo Riding Club
Kitahara, Jirouta • Goto, Kazunobu • Botanic Garden and Museum, Hokkaido University
Atelier Sugimoto • National Museum of Ethnology
Yubari Regional Historical Materials Research Center

Photo Credits • Takayuki Monma Takanori Matsuda Kozo Ishikawa

Ainu Culture References

Chiri, Takanaka and Yokoyama, Takao. *Ainugo Eiri Jiten* (Ainu Language Illustrated Dictionary).
Tokyo: Kagyusha, 1994

Kayano, Shigeru. *Ainu no Mingu* (Ainu Folkcrafts). Kawagoe: Suzusawa Book Store, 1978

Kayano, Shigeru. *Kayano Shigeru no Ainugo Jiten* (Kayano Shigeru's Ainu Language Dictionary).
Tokyo: Sanseido, 1996

Musashino Art University – The Research Institute for Culture and Cultural History. *Ainu no Mingu Jissoku Zushu*
(Ainu Folkcrafts – Collection of Drawing and Figures). Biratori: Biratori-cho Council for Promoting Ainu Culture, 2014

Satouchi, Ai. *Ainu-shiki ekoroji-seikatsu: Haruzo Ekashi ni manabu shizen no chie* (Ainu Style Ecological Living:
Haruzo Ekashi Teaches the Wisdom of Nature). Tokyo: Kabushiki gaisha Shogakukan, 2008

Chiri, Yukie. *Ainu Shin'yoshu* (Chiri Yukie's Ainu Epic Tales). Tokyo: Iwanami Shoten, 1978

Namikawa, Kenji. *Ainu Minzoku no Kiseki* (The Path of the Ainu People).
Tokyo: Yamakawa Publishing, 2004

Mook. *Senjuumin Ainu Minzoku (Bessatsu Taiyo)* (The Ainu People (Extra Issue Taiyo).Tokyo: Heibonsha, 2004

Kinoshita, Seizo. *Shiraoikotan Kinoshita Seizo Isaku Shashin Shu* (Shiraoikotan: Kinoshita Seizo's Posthumous
Photography Collection). Hokkaido Shiraoi-gun Shiraoi-cho: Shiraoi Heritage Conservation Foundation, 1988

The Ainu Museum. *Ainu no Ifuku Bunka* (The Culture of Ainu Clothing). Hokkaido Shiraoi-gun Shiraoi-cho:
Shiraoi Ainu Museum, 1991.

Keira, Tomoko and Kaji, Sayaka. *Ainu no Shiki* (Ainu's Four Seasons). Tokyo: Akashi Shoten, 1995

Fukuoka, Itoko and Sato, Kazuko. *Ainu Shokubutsushi* (Ainu Botanical Journal). Chiba Urayasu-Shi: Sofukan, 1995

Hayakawa, Noboru. *Ainu no Minzoku* (Ainu Folklore). Iwasaki Bijutsusha, 1983

Sunazawa, Kura. *Ku Sukuppu Orushibe* (The Memories of My Generation). Hokkaido, Sapporo-shi:
Miyama Shobo, 1983

Haginaka, Miki et al., *Kikigaki Ainu no Shokuji* (Oral History of Ainu Diet).
Tokyo: Rural Culture Association Japan, 1992

Nakagawa, Hiroshi. *New Express Ainu Go*. Tokyo: Hakusuisha, 2013

Nakagawa, Hiroshi. *Ainugo Chitose Hogen Jiten* (The Ainu-Japanese dictionary). Chiba Urayasu-Shi: Sofukan, 1995

Nakagawa, Hiroshi and Nakamoto, Mutsuko. *Kamuy Yukara de Ainu Go wo Manabu*
Learning Ainu with Kamuy Yukar). Tokyo: Hakusuisha, 2007

Nakagawa, Hiroshi. *Katari au Kotoba no Chikara – Kamuy tachi to Ikiru Sekai*
(The Power of Spoken Words – Living in a World with Kamuy). Tokyo: Iwanami Shoten, 2010

Sarashina, Genzo and Sarashina, Hikari. *Kotan Seibutsu Ki <1 Juki / Zassou hen>*
(Kotan Wildlife Vol. 1 – Trees and Weeds). Hosei University Publishing, 1992/2007

Sarashina, Genzo and Sarashina, Hikari. *Kotan Seibutsu Ki <2 Yacho / Kaijuu / Gyozoku hen>*
(Kotan Wildlife Vol. 2 – Birds, Sea Creatures, and Fish). Hosei University Publishing, 1992/2007

Sarashina, Genzo and Sarashina, Hikari. *Kotan Seibutsu Ki <3 Yachou / Mizudori / Konchu hen>*
(Kotan Wildlife Vol. 3 – Shorebirds, Seabirds, and Insects). Hosei University Publishing, 1992/2007

Kawakami Yuji. *Sarunkur Ainu Monogatari* (The Tale of Sarunkur Ainu). Kawagoe: Suzusawa Book Store, 2003/2005

Kawakami, Yuji. *Ekashi to Fuchi wo Tazunete* (Visiting Ekashi and Fuchi). Kawagoe: Suzusawa Book Store, 1991

Council for the Conservation of Ainu Culture, Ainu Minzokushi (Ainu People Magazine). Dai-ichi Hoki, 1970

Hokkaido Cultural Property Protection Association. *Ainu Ifuku Chousa Houkokusho <1 Ainu Josei ga Denshou Suru
Ibunka>* (The Ainu Clothing Research Report Vol. 1 – Traditional Clothing Passed Down Through Generations of Ainu
Women). 1986

Okamura, Kichiemon and Clancy, Judith A. *Ainu no Ishou* (The Clothes of the Ainu People). Kyoto Shoin, 1993

Yotsuji, Ichiro. Photos by Mizutani, Morio. *Ainu no Monyo* (Decorative Arts of the Ainu). Kasakura Publishing, 1981

Yoshida, Iwao. *Ainushi Shiryoshu* (Collection of Ainu Historical Documents).
Hokkaido Publication Project Center, 1983

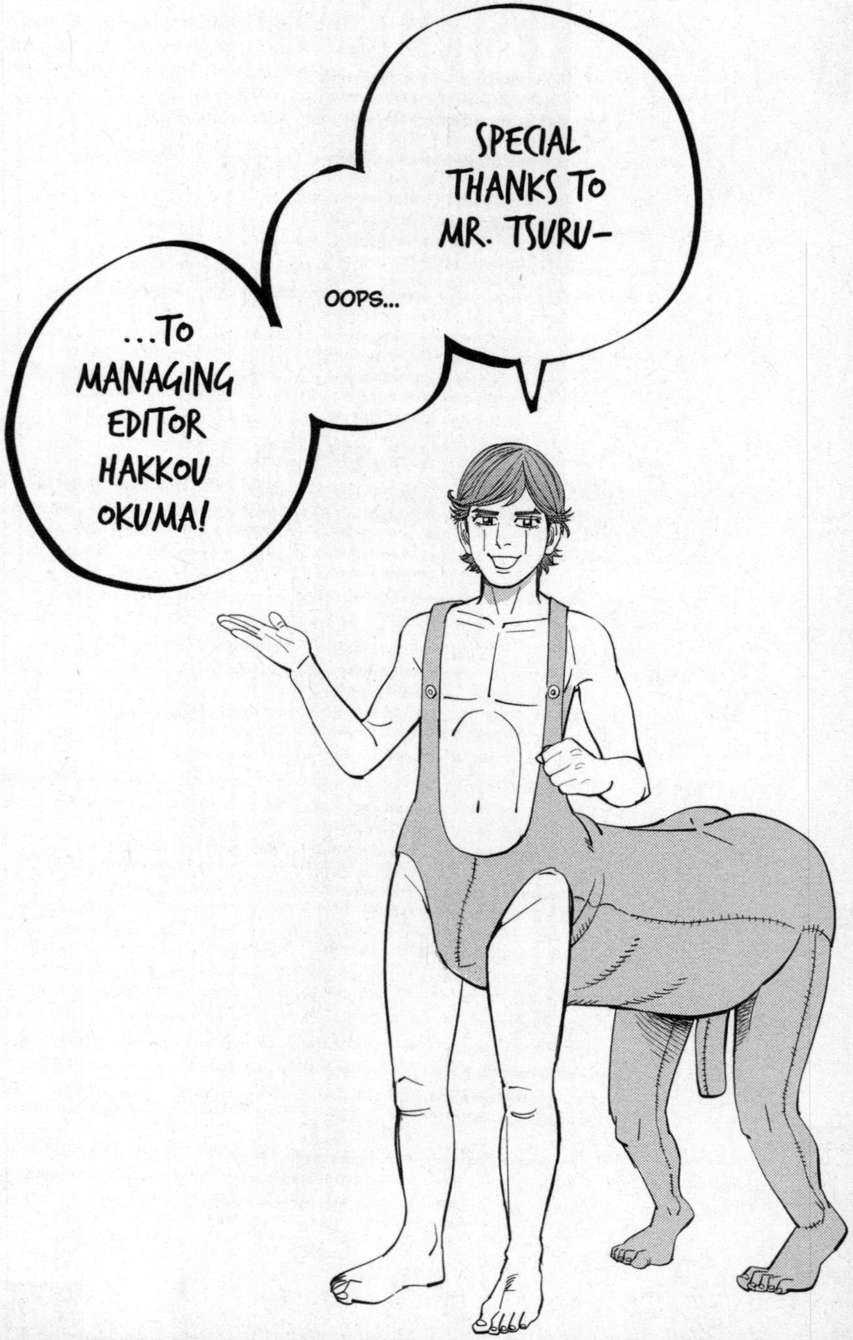
SPECIAL THANKS TO MR. TSURU-
OOPS...
...TO MANAGING EDITOR HAKKOU OKUMA!

Kanto or wa yaku sak no arankep sinep ka isam.

Nothing comes from heaven without purpose. —Ainu proverb

TETRAPE (WEED BARK CLOTHING)

KARAFUTO AINU CLOTHES MADE
FROM FIBERS OF NETTLES

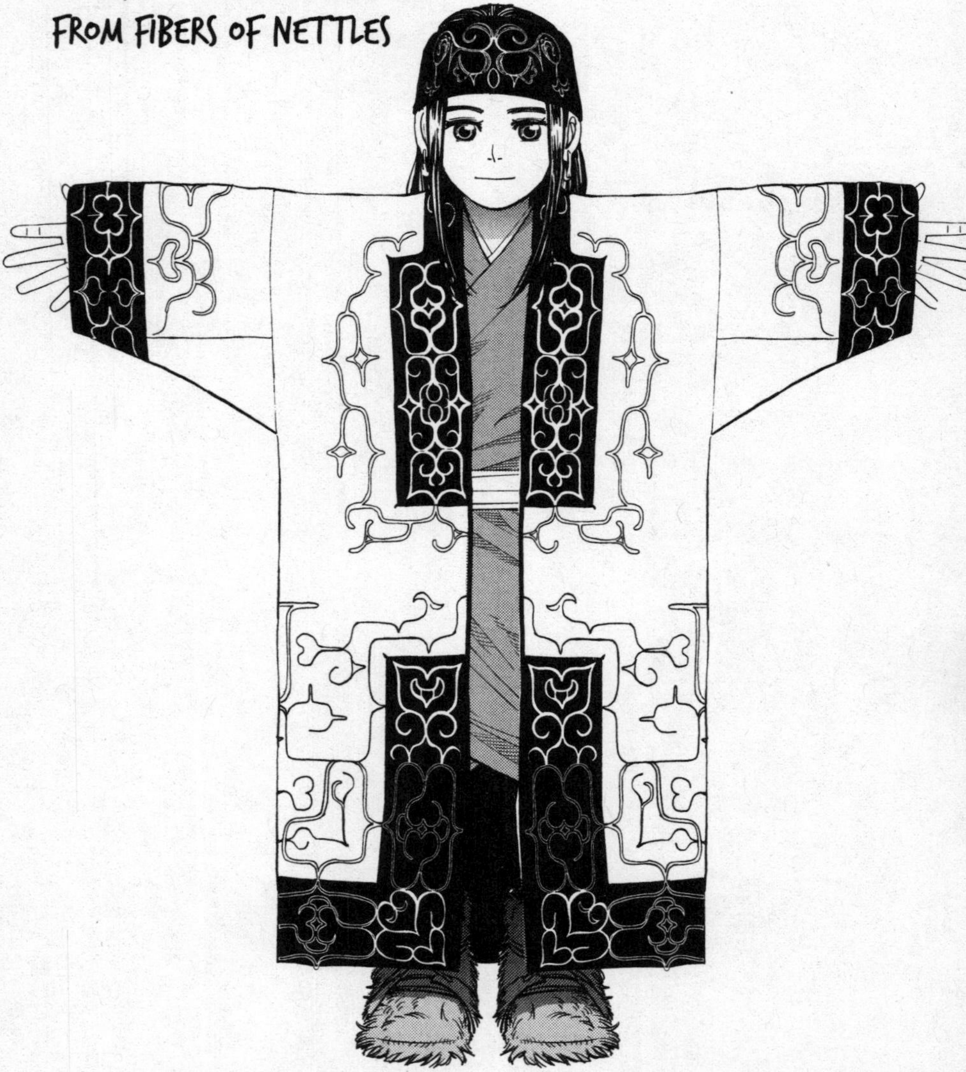

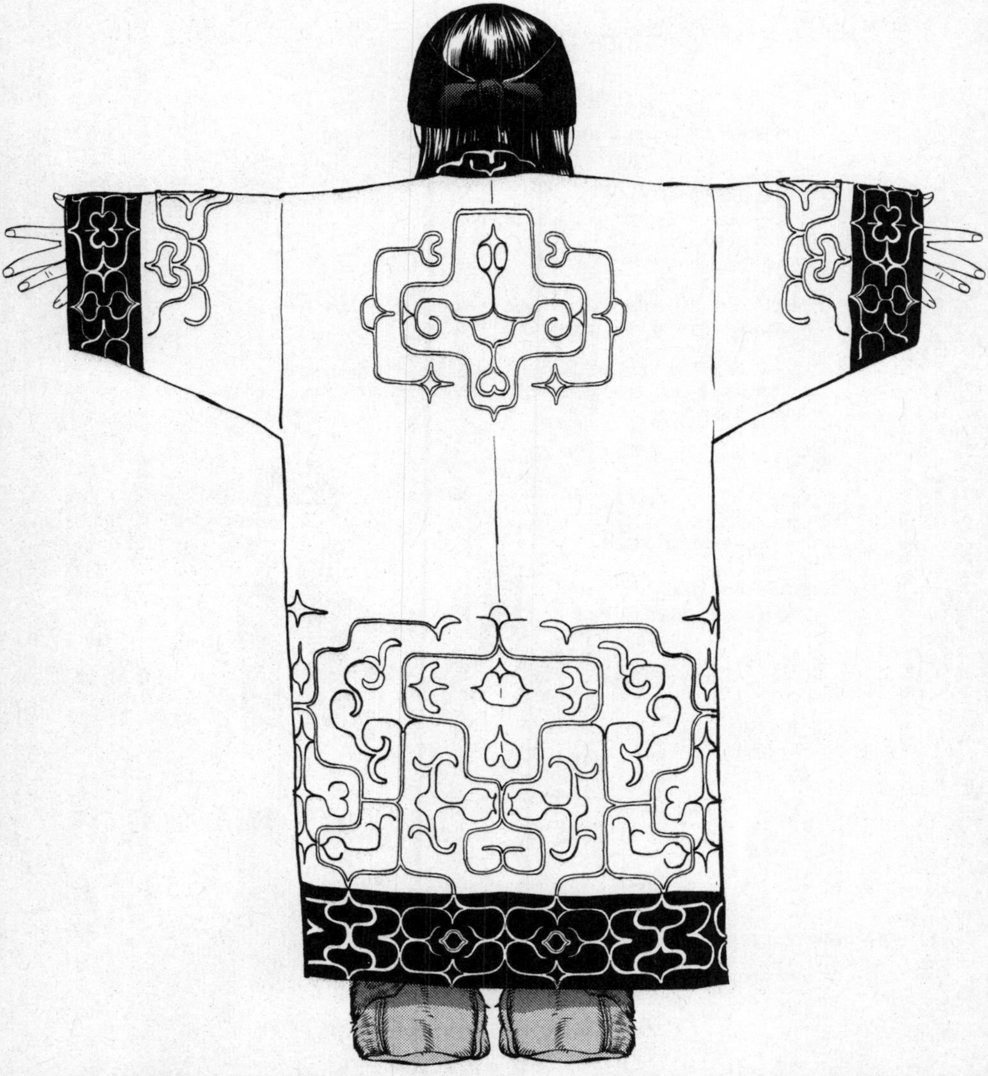

GOLDEN KAMUY

Volume 8
VIZ Signature Edition

Story/Art by Satoru Noda

GOLDEN KAMUY © 2014 by Satoru Noda
All rights reserved.
First published in Japan in 2014 by SHUEISHA Inc., Tokyo.
English translation rights arranged by SHUEISHA Inc.

Translation/John Werry
Touch-Up Art & Lettering/Steve Dutro
Design/John Kim
Editor/Mike Montesa

The stories, characters and incidents mentioned in this
publication are entirely fictional.

No portion of this book may be reproduced or transmitted in
any form or by any means without written permission from the
copyright holders.

Printed in the U.S.A

Published by VIZ Media, LLC
P.O. Box 77010
San Francisco, CA 94107

10 9 8 7 6 5 4 3 2 1
First printing, February 2019

PARENTAL ADVISORY
GOLDEN KAMUY is rated M for Mature and
recommended for mature readers. This
volume contains graphic violence, strong
language and adult themes.